Leading
Psychoeducational Groups
for Children and Adolescents

To my grandparents and great aunts who provided me with support, love,
and guidance as part of my family group.

Leading
Psychoeducational Groups
for Children and Adolescents

Janice L. DeLucia-Waack
University at Buffalo, SUNY

SAGE Publications
Thousand Oaks ▪ London ▪ New Delhi

For information:

Sage Publications, Inc.
2455 Teller Road
Thousand Oaks, California 91320
E-mail: order@sagepub.com

Sage Publications Ltd.
1 Oliver's Yard
55 City Road
London EC1Y 1SP
United Kingdom

Sage Publications India Pvt. Ltd.
B-42, Panchsheel Enclave
Post Box 4109
New Delhi 110 017 India

Printed in the United States of America

Library of Congress Cataloging-in-Publication Data

DeLucia-Waack, Janice L.
Leading psychoeducational groups for children and adolescents /
Janice DeLucia-Waack.
     p. cm.
Includes bibliographical references and index.
ISBN 978-1-4129-1401-7 (pbk.)
   1. Social work with children. 2. Social work with teenagers. 3. Social group work. 4. Group counseling for children. 5. Group counseling for teenagers. 6. Educational counseling. 7. School social work. I. Title.
HV713.D44 2006
371.4'6—dc22

                                        2006002098

This book is printed on acid-free paper.

10   11   12   13   14   8   7   6   5   4   3   2

Acquisitions Editor:	Art T. Pomponio
Editorial Assistant:	Veronica Novak
Production Editor:	Denise Santoyo
Copy Editor:	Liann Lech
Typesetter:	C&M Digitals (P) Ltd.
Indexer:	Nara Wood
Cover Designer:	Janet Foulger

Contents

CHAPTER 1

Introduction

"EVERYBODY NEEDS A FRIEND"*

I don't know why bad things happen to good people like you
But I do know there's a way to work things through
I'm not your boss and I don't want to tell you what to do
But everybody needs a friend
You gotta find somebody to talk to
You're gonna need somebody to talk to
You gotta tell somebody what you've been through
Everybody needs a friend
Now a friend is someone who is there to try and understand
A friend could be a boy or girl, a woman or man
A friend is someone you can trust to lend a helping hand
And everybody needs a friend
You gotta find somebody to talk to
You're gonna need somebody to talk to
You gotta tell somebody what you've been through
Everybody needs a friend
Now some people feel funny 'bout when stuff goes on at home
And they're out there in the school yard feeling all alone
Time goes by and they just feel as lonely as a stone
Until the day they find a friend
You gotta find somebody to talk to
You're gonna need somebody to talk to
You gotta tell somebody what you've been through
Everybody needs a friend. (Conley, 1994)

---

*Reprinted with permission of D. Conley.

This song emphasizes some of the major themes and benefits of psycho-educational groups for children and adolescents. I often use the song as a stimulus to generate discussion in initial sessions about how groups can be useful. Group members quickly identify the themes:

- Everybody needs a friend.
- Friends support you.
- You can talk to a friend.
- Friends can be different.
- Everyone has stuff to talk about, especially related to school and home.
- It is good to talk about your problems.
- It is good to talk about your feelings.
- People get lonely if they do not have friends to talk to.

We then talk about how groups are a safe place for children and adolescents to connect, feel supported, and talk about their feelings and challenges.

Another lead-in to psychoeducational groups that I often use with adolescents is the movie *The Breakfast Club*. I ask group members as part of the introductory activities to reflect on the movie and talk about how each character acted out his or her poor self-esteem in a different way and what all of the characters learned about themselves as a result of being in that Saturday detention group. Typical answers often focus on how each character felt alone despite very different family situations and groups of friends; and how each experienced difficulty in different areas—sometimes personal, sometimes academic.

"Younger clients may benefit more from group treatment" (Fuhriman & Burlingame, 1990, p. 14). The intent, function, and delivery may be substantially different in group work than other therapy, and may benefit a populace with developmentally appropriate needs. As such, "groups can be especially helpful to adolescents in making a successful transition from childhood to adulthood. They can provide support, facilitate new learning, help ease internal and external pressures, and offer hope and models for change" (Gladding, 1995, p. 221). Techniques implemented in group are different from those in individual treatments, which may be particularly helpful in the instances of therapeutic work with a younger population.

> There are many advantages to groups for adolescents: they are a natural way for adolescents to relate to each other, they emphasize the learning of life skills, they focus on generalizing behaviors practiced in the group to real-life situations, and they provide multiple feedback and increase self-esteem that comes about through helping others. (Shechtman, Bar-El, & Hadar, 1997, pp. 203–204)

Much has been written that suggests groups for children and adolescents are just as effective but also differ in style and content from groups for adults.

Psychoeducational counseling and psychotherapy groups are standard counseling practice in a variety of settings. The majority of research on groups with children and adolescents is conducted in schools (Prout & Prout, 1998; Riva & Haub, 2004).

In addition, psychoeducational groups are the most commonly utilized groups in the schools, both for prevention and as a first intervention for students at risk (Vera & Reese, 2000). Psychoeducational interventions assist group members in sharing and developing coping skills and behaviors to deal with new or difficult situations. Such groups also address social competence deficits, adjustment to parent divorce, behavior problems, and learning disabilities (Dagley, Gazda, Eppinger, & Stewart, 1994; Hoag & Burlingame, 1997). Smead (2003) sums up nicely by saying

> the child will participate in the interpersonal experience for the purpose of learning improved ways of functioning. Specifically, that the child will be exposed to new cognitive concepts, ideas, and explorations of her issues. Secondly, that more adaptive behaviors will be explored, discussed, and practiced for transfer to school and home. Third, that improved self-esteem, efficacy, and emotional satisfaction will result from learning from the healing interactions of the group experience. (p. 11)

Current topics for psychoeducational groups include the following:

- Loneliness
- Body image
- Disordered eating
- Career development
- Career exploration
- Job skills
- Interviewing skills
- Conflict resolution
- ADHD/ADD
- Bullying prevention
- Shyness
- Relationship skills
- Communication skills
- Friendship skills
- Middle school transition issues
- Cultural differences
- Family relationships
- Cognitive coping skills
- Self-esteem
- Making friends
- Social skills
- Children of parents who have cancer
- Children of divorce
- Grief
- Teen pregnancy/parenting skills
- Parenting skills
- Anger management
- Aggression
- New students
- Prevention of depression
- Depression management
- Antisocial behavior
- Defiance
- Self-harm/suicide prevention
- Substance abuse

There are more reasons than just cost-effectiveness to use groups as both preventive and remedial strategies for children and adolescents. Depression for many people, and particularly for adolescents, is often related to a lack of social skills or cognitive strategies that result in not having friends or having relationship difficulties, feeling isolated and alone or different, and having unrealistic expectations and beliefs about oneself. Group therapeutic factors, such as universality, altruism, vicarious learning, and interpersonal learning, operate to help group members develop better relationship skills; develop adaptive thought patterns; and normalize feelings, thoughts, and events. If a lack of social skills and/or unrealistic expectations about oneself are the predictors of depression in adolescents, then it makes sense to teach social skills and self-assessment strategies that help students develop a more balanced and realistic self-concept in an effort to prevent depression, poor self-esteem, and relationship difficulties.

Carrell (2000), writing from her work with a more remedial population, has some valid points about why groups are effective with children and adolescents:

1. Groups challenge the myth of uniqueness by emphasizing shared emotions and experiences.

2. Groups provide adult leadership that adolescents want but with avenues to assert power and independence.

3. Groups reduce the discomfort of adult-child dynamics that occur in individual counseling, particularly with adolescents with bad experiences with adults.

4. Groups confront adolescent self-absorption because in groups members need to take turns talking and helping each other.

5. Groups may be the first place that an adolescent truly experiences peer acceptance. (pp. 14–15)

All of Carrell's (2000) points are certainly applicable to psychoeducational groups, emphasizing support, learning of new skills, and how to help and be helped.

Very little has been written in the field of group work specifically about psychoeducational groups for children and adolescents. The topic is much more likely to be covered as a chapter in a group text, rather than in an entire volume. Often, the focus of these chapters is on the content and structure of these groups, rather than on how to design effective groups or what leadership skills are needed to lead such groups effectively. Most of the current literature on psychoeducational groups has been focused on choosing goals and activities with little emphasis on the other areas, such as processing of these activities to apply what has been learned. This book has been written to address that need and provides specific suggestions on how to both structure and lead psychoeducational groups for children and adolescents in both schools and community agencies.

Goals of This Book

My reasons for writing this book are both theoretical and pragmatic. First, theoretically, a great deal of literature suggests that the focus, pace, content, and leadership style must vary by age of the group participants. What little has been written specifically about psychoeducational groups does not differentiate based on age of group members, even though much theory and research has supported a clear differentiation in goals, interventions, and leadership style by age. Groups with children and adolescents need interventions to help group members discuss their feelings, connect with others, and identify potential solutions for their concerns (Smead, 1995).

Children and adolescents often respond better to nonverbal techniques than "talk therapy" exercises because of their limited vocabularies and their disposition to display feelings through play (Gladding, 1998). Creativity in activities and exercises is helpful. Drawing, singing, dancing, using puppets, role-playing, and play writing are all ways to identify and express feelings and to brainstorm and practice new behaviors and coping skills. This book will suggest specific interventions that cultivate interest and participation on the part of children and adolescents, and also meet the goals of teaching new skills and adaptive behaviors. Theoretically, there is some support for the application of therapeutic factors to groups for children and adolescents. According to Fuhriman and Burlingame (1990), common process dimensions in groups are the therapeutic relationship, therapeutic interventions, and therapeutic factors. All three of these topics will be a focus of this book.

The structure and length of groups for children and adolescents is also very different from that for adult groups. Psychoeducational groups tend to be briefer in terms of number of sessions and session length, but also more structured, with activities designed to facilitate discussion of a topic and/or development of new skills and behaviors. Thus, interventions for groups that may meet no more than 6 to 8 sessions and for brief amounts of time, sometimes only 35 minutes, will be suggested.

Pragmatically, counseling, psychology, and social work practitioners typically have received training in adult counseling and therapy groups, which tend to be of longer duration and smaller in size than psychoeducational groups. Thus, information and training are needed to adjust the goals, structure, time frame, and interventions used in a psychoeducational group. Furthermore, the techniques, interventions, and leadership behaviors that are needed for children and adolescent groups need to be differentiated from those needed for adult groups.

I am probably a good example of the incongruence between how I was trained and what seems to work best in psychoeducational groups. My group training taught me to appreciate and use the process and interactions in groups. However, as anyone who has led a group for children and adolescents knows, if you begin the group by asking "What should we talk about today?" the answers could range from the movie they saw Saturday night to Pokémon to the meanest teachers in the school. Thus, I learned the importance of balancing structure with content and the importance of directing, but not controlling, the direction and process of the group. Process is important and needs to be attended to in all groups; however, psychoeducational groups use skill development (cognitive, affective, and behavioral) as the content and focus of the group, whereas interactional patterns develop around the content and can be used when necessary to facilitate group goals. I hope that this book will be helpful to new counselors and psychologists in training as they learn how to lead psychoeducational groups, and also to established practitioners who want to more effectively lead psychoeducational groups for children and adolescents.

The biggest mistake that leaders make is trying to run a psychoeducational group like a counseling or therapy group, or a counseling group like a psychoeducational group. If people expect content and techniques (e.g., how to study more effectively), then they will be frustrated by the lack of structure and the probing of a counseling group style. If they are expecting time to share and discuss and analyze relationships, and they get activities and exercises, they will be frustrated.

The goal of this book is to provide a single resource that provides comprehensive directions about how to organize and lead psychoeducational groups based on the Association for Specialists in Group Work's (1998) *Best Practice Guidelines* for planning, performing, and group processing. Other books have either focused on how to lead counseling groups in general for children, or psychoeducational groups for all ages, but not specifically on psychoeducational groups for children and adolescents. Several books designed for groups with children and adolescents have suggested the content and specific activities to be used for different kinds of groups (e. g., children of divorce, grief, communication skills), but have not addressed specific leadership skills.

The *Best Practice Guidelines* (ASGW, 1998) address planning, performing, and processing groups. Planning focuses on pregroup decision making, and selection and preparation of both members and leaders. Performing focuses on group leadership skills, provision of effective interventions, and assessment of effectiveness. Processing focuses on using interventions to help members learn and evaluate group interventions to assess effectiveness, supervision, and follow-up with group members. This book will address these areas with specific suggestions about how to organize groups as well as suggestions about content using the model of Planning, Performing, and Processing.

How This Book Is Organized

My approach to this book is very applied and pragmatic. Based on a review of current research, theory, and practice on groups, specific strategies to lead psychoeducational groups in general will be outlined, and suggestions will be made about the content for specific topical groups (e.g., children of divorce, grief, anger management, bullying behaviors, etc.). The uniqueness of this book lies in the integration of research and practice to suggest effective leadership strategies.

Some people might ask why the combination of research and practice. My answer would be that research informs practice, and practice informs research. Yes, all counselors and psychologists know that mantra from their graduate training; thus, they conscientiously read every page of every research journal to which they subscribe (and of course, they subscribe to all in their counseling practice area) the day they receive it in the mail. So, let me tell you my story, the one that I tell my students during the first day of class every year. Remember, this comes from the person who has taught at least one group course a year since I began my academic career (sometimes as many as four) and whose major area of research is what makes groups effective.

Our counseling program had decided to add a new practicum and internship site, a family support center working with students and their families at an alternative middle and high school. It was a brand-new facility fully equipped with two-way mirrors, the ability to call into the counseling rooms, and the ability to be fully videotaped. I volunteered to be part of the first team of counselors, both observing behind the two-way mirror and perhaps serving as a co-therapist for a family or two. When the school counselors and a supervisor heard that I would participate, they asked me to lead an anger management group for ninth-grade boys. I agreed, and 2 weeks later, I was standing in the outer room of the principal's office waiting to escort the 8 ninth-grade boys (who had been selected by the school counselor) to the family support center. The principal announced over the loudspeaker, "Would the following boys report to the office to go to their anger management group?" Remarkably, all of them arrived within 5 minutes, but all were muttering that they did not belong in this group. Then, the principal, in front of me, the boys, and everyone else present in the office, went around the room and told each boy what he had done to merit being in this group. Each of the boys had exhibited some violent behavior in the school, ranging from kicking in a door to punching a fellow student.

Luckily, my co-leader, who was a counseling intern in the school and knew most of the boys, arrived to help me escort our newly formed group to our room. Needless to say, the boys spent most of the first two sessions complaining that they had to be in this group. It was difficult for me to even get the boys to tell me their names. In addition, much of their energy was spent on investigating the microphones, cameras, and who was behind the observable mirror.

In the second session, I learned that one boy's father had recently committed suicide, and two others were on medication for depression. During the third session, one of the boys kept repeating that he did not understand why he was in group and why he had been singled out when everybody in the school probably belonged in an anger management group. As co-leaders, we agreed with him about this because it was an alternative school, and I added that my understanding was that this group, and another group, were the pilot groups. If they worked well, then all other students would attend similar groups. The boys did not know this. At the end of that session, one group member asked if they could observe the group that followed them. Before I could answer no, my co-leader said, "Of course." I jumped in and said that there are some conditions: You must get permission from the teacher of the class that would be missed and make up any work before next week, you must introduce yourselves to the group members and ask their permission to observe, you must be willing for those group members to observe your group sessions, and you must participate in the discussion behind the two-way mirror in the same way the counselors do.

Thinking that the group members could not possibly commit to any or all of these things, I began the fourth session by introducing an activity around how they express anger. There was some variation in participation between members (two of them were very quiet, one with a hood over his face), but several of them were able to identify that they did not express anger until they were really angry, and then they exploded. As I began to close the session, one of the group members interrupted me to ask if they were going to be able to observe the next group session. Before I could answer, he informed me that they had permission from their teacher, had decided he would be the spokesperson to talk to the next group, and that they were willing to be observed and also to participate behind the two-way mirror. Astonishingly, the next group agreed to be observed. The boys went behind the two-way mirror, and within 5 minutes of starting the session, one of them called into the counseling room. It was the boy who rarely spoke and who had kept his hood over his face most of the previous group session. He told me to address the boy who was sitting in the corner with his chair pulled out of the circle and ask a question, because he really wanted to participate but needed somebody to draw him in. I did, and the boy responded and began to participate. Several other phone calls were made into the group session; all were on target and suggested very good interventions.

Each week after that, the boys observed the other group's session and provided helpful feedback. During the fifth session, the boy who rarely spoke came in with his hood over his face again. However, I sat next to him and at one point looked at him directly and said, "I want to see your face. Please take your hood down." And he did. During the sixth session, the topic for discussion was strategies to express anger without violence. The boys had a very hard time coming up with strategies, but at one point one of them looked at the two of us co-leaders and asked, "What do you do?" During the eighth and final session, we asked the boys to reflect on what was helpful, what they learned from this group, and what we might have done differently to be more helpful. Surprising were several of the comments: (a) Keep them on topic more, (b) use more activities so they learned new ideas, (c) let them observe more sessions so they understood what happened in group more quickly, and (d) tell them why they were in group earlier so they were not so angry about it.

So how does one make sense of this? First is the question, What lessons did I relearn from this experience? I want to emphasize the word *relearned* because I already knew these basic principles based on other groups I had led or the research that I had conducted on preparing members for group, effective group interventions, and group therapeutic factors. The lessons that follow serve as the basis for much of what follows in this book:

- The importance of clearly identifying the purpose and the scope of the psychoeducational group, which, in turn, suggests selection criteria for group members and useful activities to meet their individual goals.
- The importance of individual screening interviews to begin to connect with the group members, gather important background information, determine whether group members are a good fit for the group, clarify the goals of the group, and help potential members decide how they can best benefit from this group (even if it is an involuntary group).
- The importance of selecting members for group so that there is some similarity in terms of problem severity but also some variety in coping skills so that members can connect with each other but also learn from each other.
- The importance of group members internalizing the norms and ground rules so that the group becomes *their* group.
- The importance of group members helping to choose topics and interventions that they believe match their goals.
- The importance of teaching group process to group members so that they can use it to meet their goals and help direct the group.
- The importance of not labeling group members as resistant but seeing their reluctance as a message to the group about who they are, what their strengths and weaknesses are, and what group feels like for them.
- The importance of using content activities to help group members identify their strengths and on what skills they need to work.

Second, and maybe most important, is the question, Why did I ignore what I know about effective group interventions? The easy answer is that I thought I was such a good group leader that I could make any group effective. The rejoinder to that is that no matter how good a group leader you are, your group members ultimately determine whether they change and grow. It is the group leaders' job to motivate group members to make the most of their group experience, but they can't do the work for them.

But my overconfidence is not the only answer to this question. There are other answers, ones that are also probably more reflective of what happens in schools and counseling agencies every day, and explain more fully why psychoeducational groups for children and adolescents often don't happen or aren't very effective.

The first and probably most compelling reason is lack of time. There is no time to assess the needs of potential group members; screen group members; prepare group members; choose activities that specifically meet group members' needs; wait until a good mixture of group members agrees to participate; or meet with a co-leader to get to know that person and his or her style, and plan for and discuss our groups. Yet the reality is that leading psychoeducational groups effectively takes more time in the planning stage than in the performing or processing stages. Good group design, early connections with group members, and careful selection of group members goes a long way toward ensuring effective psychoeducational groups. The estimate that seems most accurate is that two thirds of the time spent on a psychoeducational group should happen before the first group session. And how should the time be spent? Assessing population needs, choosing group goals from the literature to meet population needs, choosing members carefully using screening interviews and preparation sessions, and selecting and creating group sessions using the literature to meet group goals.

The second major reason is the assumption that others (staff and counselors) understand what happens in psychoeducational groups and how to select group members who will benefit from the experience. There is often a misperception that because psychoeducational groups have a specific focus (e.g., anger management), all members must be similar in their behavioral manifestation of the problem. And yet Yalom's (1995) unyielding premise that there must be heterogeneity in coping skills and behaviors in order for members to learn from each other is certainly applicable to psychoeducational groups. It would be helpful to have group members who displayed different ways of expressing their anger so that the range of responses resulting from problem solving, brainstorming, and suggesting alternative behaviors would be maximized. In addition, school and counseling staff often refer students to group simply because they are not making progress in individual counseling or because "being confronted by a group is what they need." Such referrals imply a lack of understanding about the goals and purpose of psychoeducational groups. Children and adolescents, on some level, must be able to connect to the group leader and at least some of the group members in order to try out new behaviors and be willing to receive feedback from others.

The third major reason is the assumption that group members know what their strengths and weaknesses are and, because of this, are motivated to participate in a group. In contrast, effective leaders need to help students systematically to identify what strengths they bring to group and what skills they need to develop.

The fourth major reason is the assumption that group members know what the goals of the group are and know how to participate effectively. Again, group leaders need to communicate and discuss with potential group members individual and group goals, as well as how to get the most out of a psychoeducational group. Screening interviews are an integral part of this process.

So, you have the long answer to why this book will emphasize interventions based on current counseling practice and research. This book is organized sequentially so that leaders can use it as a guide to developing and planning a psychoeducational group. It follows an outline suggested by the Association for Specialists in Group Work (1998) of Planning, Performing, and Processing. Chapters 2 and 3 focus on the planning aspect, including pregroup decision making, procedural considerations, design of group sessions, and selection of group members using screening interviews and preparation sessions. Chapters 4 to 8 focus on aspects of Performing, and Chapters 9 to 11 focus on Processing. Each chapter includes a plan for implementation, suggested references for content and skills, examples of psychoeducational groups, and suggested training activities. In addition, appendixes include the three relevant Association for Specialists in Group Work documents; samples of materials that can be used in planning and implementing groups; and a table that suggests resources for specific psychoeducational groups, including resources for parents, general information about the topic for counselors, and specific materials (books, games, videos, and session outlines) to be used as part of the group.

What Are Psychoeducational Groups, and How Are They Different From Other Types of Groups?

The Association for Specialists in Group Work (ASGW, 2000) delineated four types of groups based on their goals and interactional processes—task/work, psychoeducational/guidance, counseling, and therapy groups—to aid in the selection of the appropriate type of group for different populations (e.g., age groups) with different goals (e.g., combatting depression, learning social skills, preventing eating disorders). This delineation is important because any type of group work previously, and sometimes still today, is viewed as group therapy. Many people view group therapy, or therapy in general, negatively, and so the understanding that groups can be preventive; focus on learning new skills, cognitive styles, and behaviors; or address developmental issues is useful in defining and promoting group work. It is very helpful in the schools and working with children and adolescents to provide all interested parties (staff, parents, children, and adolescents) with a description of what psychoeducational groups do, focusing on the preventive nature and the skill-building emphasis. People in general are less intimidated with this kind of information, which often addresses their fear that they're going to be "psychoanalyzed," or, more realistically, that their children will be labeled as "problem children."

By definition, counseling groups "address personal and interpersonal problems of living and promote personal and interpersonal growth and development" (ASGW,

2000, p. 331), whereas therapy groups "address personal and interpersonal problems of living, remediate perceptual and cognitive distortions or repetitive patterns of dysfunctional behavior, and promote personal and interpersonal growth and development" (ASGW, 2000, p. 331). Examples of counseling and therapy groups include general interpersonal groups; training groups for students learning to be counselors or therapists; and groups directed at the amelioration of specific problems such as depression, eating disorders, or sexual abuse. By nature, counseling and therapy groups seem more appropriate for persons with severe interpersonal difficulties and for adults.

In contrast, psychoeducational/guidance groups focus on skill development to prevent problems. Psychoeducational/guidance groups use "group-based educational and developmental strategies" (ASGW, 2000, p. 330), particularly role-playing, problem solving, decision making, and communication skills training. Psychoeducational/guidance groups teach specific skills and coping strategies in an effort to prevent problems; such skills and strategies might include anger management, social skills, self-esteem, assertiveness, and making friends.

In schools, the goals of most groups that are psychoeducational in focus are to teach new skills and prevent potential problems (Riva & Haub, 2004). Kulic, Horne, and Dagley (2004) clarified the use of psychoeducational groups in general with children and adolescents:

> The group format is a logical choice . . . given the amount of time children and adolescents spend in groups with their peers, both in and out of the classroom. The group is the primary socializing influence through the early developmental stages of life and it provides the context within which children and adolescents will receive preventative interventions and will practice and utilize them in their "real lives." (p. 139)

Their meta-analysis revealed that 79.8% of all studies of child and adolescent prevention groups occurred in school settings, and most (73.2%) were short term, with interventions lasting less than 6 months.

A recent study (Bridbord, DeLucia-Waack, & Gerrity, 2006) provides some interesting data about the types of groups being led, for what age, and for what length. This study included group co-leaders in psychology, medicine, counseling, and social work. In all, 72.2% of the co-leaders surveyed labeled their groups as therapy groups, 13% labeled their groups as counseling groups, 11.1% labeled their groups as psychoeducational groups, and 14.8% labeled their groups as support groups (the total percentage amounted to more than 100% because some indicated more than one type of group). A total of 70.4% of the co-leaders indicated that their groups were ongoing (more than 30 sessions), 5.6% indicated that their groups would meet for 21 to 30 sessions, 18.5% reported that their groups would meet for 11 to 20 sessions, and 5.6% indicated that their groups would meet for 10 or fewer sessions. Among the co-leader teams surveyed, 75.9% co-led adult groups, 13% co-led adolescent groups, 3.7% co-led children's groups, and the age of group members is unknown for 7.4% of the groups surveyed. Thus, although the focus in the literature has traditionally been on long-term counseling and therapy groups for adults, the data suggest the need for more information on psychoeducational groups, short-term groups, and groups for children and adolescents.

So, how are psychoeducational groups different from counseling and therapy groups? First, goals for psychoeducational groups tend to be behavioral and specific. Often, they focus on the development of skills, cognitive styles, and coping strategies. Typical goals might include the following:

- Identifying and expressing feelings
- Identifying and disputing irrational thoughts that make one feel sad
- Encouraging the understanding of what it means to be a friend and to have friends
- Replacing students' nonconstructive friendship behaviors with more appropriate ones
- Promoting understanding of the stress response and individual stressors
- Teaching three main techniques for managing stress
- Teaching organizational skills

There are also sometimes differences related to the diversity of individual member goals between psychoeducational and counseling and therapy groups. Psychoeducational groups have a common set of group goals or a topic on which to focus, with individual members choosing one or more goals that best apply to them. For example, in an anger management group, the general goal might be to teach more adaptive ways to express anger. For some students, their goals might focus on identifying anger and expressing it verbally. Other students might have goals related to disputing irrational beliefs that make them angry, whereas other students might focus on replacing maladaptive ways of expressing their anger with more constructive behaviors. In counseling and therapy groups, the group goal may be much more general, such as interpersonal relationships. Thus, the range of individual member goals may be much greater, perhaps ranging from depression and anxiety to eating disorders.

Second, the structure of psychoeducational groups is much different from that in counseling and therapy groups. Structure is essential to providing safety and continuity in all groups. However, in psychoeducational groups, structure is necessary to manage time efficiently and to focus on relevant issues (DeLucia-Waack, 1997; Gladding, 1998). Much more structure is also provided in psychoeducational groups with the use of activities to teach and practice skills included as a vital part of each session. Counseling and therapy groups may occasionally use an activity to teach skills or practice new behaviors, but not on a regular basis.

The focus also varies in psychoeducational groups as opposed to counseling and therapy groups. Counseling and therapy groups use process to illuminate maladaptive cognitions and behavior patterns and then intervene using group interventions. Psychoeducational groups focus on the content of a preselected activity designed to meet specific group goals. That is not to say that process is ignored in psychoeducational groups; in actuality, group process is used to teach new skills and behaviors. For example, psychoeducational groups may often close with members answering the questions, What did you learn today? and How did you learn it? Answering these questions helps group members to identify new strategies, but perhaps even more importantly, it helps them to identify how they learned the new strategies. Identification of the learning process may help them to apply the strategies in future group sessions and also outside of group. Another example of group process being used in a psychoeducational group to teach new skills would be when it is evident that group members are having difficulty brainstorming on a specific problem. The group leader may then ask the members to reflect on what makes this task so difficult. The answers may vary: It is hard to identify feelings, it is hard to admit that one doesn't know the answer, it is hard to think about changing, or members may know the answers but are not willing to share them with other group members. Each different answer would illustrate a different group dynamic occurring that would necessitate a different group of focus and group leader intervention.

In addition, psychoeducational groups tend to be much shorter in treatment and session length than counseling and therapy groups. Psychoeducational groups tend to be short, typically ranging from 6 to 20 sessions, whereas the length of counseling and therapy groups may range from 3 months to ongoing. In addition, the standard length of the group session for counseling and therapy groups is usually one-and-a-half hours, whereas psychoeducational groups may be as short as 30 to 45 minutes, particularly if conducted in a school setting.

The role of the leader also is a little different in psychoeducational groups. There is more of a teaching role and a role of content expert in psychoeducational groups. These group leaders need to be knowledgeable about the topic that they are leading and the use of activities to teach related skills. Group leaders of psychoeducational groups also must focus more on getting members involved in activities, brainstorming, problem solving, and giving specific feedback to keep members focused on the group task and skills to be learned. In contrast, although leaders of counseling and therapy groups need to provide structure in order to maintain safety in the group, they may also allow members much more latitude in choosing topics to be discussed in group because of the focus on the process of groups and the group becoming a microcosm of the group members' world.

The therapeutic factors involved in effective psychoeducational groups are different from those in effective counseling and therapy groups (Kivlighan & Holmes, 2004). Yalom's (1995) 12 therapeutic factors are widely discussed in the literature and have received a substantial amount of attention in the research. They are instillation of hope, universality, imparting of information, altruism, corrective recapitulation of primary family group, development of socializing techniques, interpersonal learning–input, interpersonal learning–output, cohesiveness, catharsis, existential factors, and imitative behavior. Kivlighan and Holmes (2004) conducted a cluster analysis of 24 studies to examine the underlying structure of the studies that have examined the roots of importance of therapeutic factors in group. They concluded that there were four different types based on the ranking of importance of therapeutic factors. The four types of groups are Affective Support, Affective Insight, Cognitive Support, and Cognitive Insight. Both the Cognitive Support group cluster and the Cognitive Insight group cluster seem most related to psychoeducational groups. Cognitive Support groups rated vicarious learning, guidance, and self-understanding as the three most important therapeutic factors. In the Cognitive

Insight group cluster, the most important therapeutic factors were interpersonal learning, self-understanding, and vicarious learning. Kivlighan and Holmes (2004) reported that the Affective Support and Affective Insight group clusters, which seem to resemble counseling and therapy groups, rated an entirely different set of therapeutic factors as most important. The Affective Support group cluster emphasized acceptance, catharsis, interpersonal learning, and self-understanding, whereas the Affective Insight group cluster emphasized acceptance, instillation of hope, and universality. Thus, related to psychoeducational groups, it is important for leaders to facilitate role-playing and practice along with teaching new skills to create environments that most closely resemble Cognitive Support and Cognitive Insight groups.

How Are Child and Adolescent Groups Different From Adult Groups?

The answer to this question is parallel in many ways to the differences between psychoeducational and counseling and therapy groups. Part of this is because psychoeducational groups tend to be designed more for children and adolescents, and thus, this overlap occurs.

Goals for child and adolescent groups tend to be much more preventive and skill based. Regardless of the type of group, much of the focus is on teaching and practicing social and interpersonal skills. Common topics in many psychoeducational groups are the identification and expression of feelings, friendship skills, communication skills, conflict-resolution skills, brainstorming, problem solving, and decision making. Even in groups for children and adolescents who have been identified as being at risk or having some kind of difficulty, the focus is going to be on teaching new, more adaptive skills, cognitive strategies, and coping skills. For example, in a children-of-divorce group, one focus would be to help recognize feelings of sadness and anger, and to begin to express them. In counseling and therapy groups, the assumption is often that adults have learned basic interpersonal skills but for some reason choose not to or are unable to use their interpersonal skills. When this occurs, the focus of counseling therapy groups is to help explore the group members' reluctance to use interpersonal skills.

There also is a difference in the degree of structure needed in child and adolescent groups as opposed to groups for adults. Adults typically are much more used to sitting and talking for what seems to be a very long time for most children and adolescents. Verbal interactions are the method of choice in adult groups, whereas with children and adolescents, interventions need to be relatively short (10 to 15 minutes), focused and specific, and multimodal in nature. In conjunction with a high degree of structure needed for child and adolescent groups, there is also a need for directive, specific, involved, and caring leadership. Leaders of groups for children and adolescents need to keep the group members on task and gently correct awkward social interactions. Again, the assumption is not that adolescent group members are being resistant but that they may not have learned the necessary social skills to participate in a group. Correspondingly, group leaders need to focus their behavior on creating interactions within the group so that members can give and receive feedback, problem solve, and brainstorm in order to learn and practice new behaviors.

Summary

Groups for children and adolescents must be designed and implemented differently from groups for adults. In particular, because of their focus on skill building, psychoeducational groups need to be structured and goal focused, and should include specific activities designed to meet the goals of the group and individual group members. This book will describe an outline from planning a group to designing sessions to implementing them and also evaluating their effectiveness.

Suggested Training Activities

1. Identification of Themes, Topics, and Interventions for Specific Psychoeducational Groups From the Literature

Look at current issues of journals that focus on either groups or counseling for children and adolescents. Examples might include the *Journal for Specialists in Group Work; Small Group Research; International Journal of Group Psychotherapy; Group Dynamics: Theory, Research, and Practice; Social Work With Groups: Journal of Counseling and Development; The Professional School Counselor; Journal of Child and Adolescent Group Therapy; Journal of Adolescence; Journal of Group Psychotherapy, Psychodrama, and Sociometry; Journal of School Psychology; Psychology in the Schools; School Psychology Review; School Psychology Quarterly; Small Group Behavior; Special Services in the Schools; Adolescence; Child and Adolescent Social Work Journal; Child Development; Journal of Adolescent Health; Journal of Early Adolescence; Journal of Research on Adolescence; Journal of Youth and Adolescence;* and *New Directions for Child Development.* Identify what kinds of groups are being led for children and adolescents. What are the topics? What are the goals? What kinds of interventions are being used? Is there any research to support the efficacy of these group interventions?

2. Identification of Themes, Topics, and Interventions for Specific Psychoeducational Groups From the Field

Interview a counselor, psychologist, or social worker who works primarily with children and adolescents. Ask him or her to describe the type of groups usually implemented with children and adolescents in his or her agency. What are the topics? What are the goals? What kinds of interventions are being used? What treatment manuals or guides are used for these groups? How successful have they been? What problems has he or she encountered in leading these groups?

CHAPTER 2

Planning for a Psychoeducational Group for Children and Adolescents

T his chapter focuses on the planning aspect of group leadership. As alluded to in the first chapter, planning is essential to effective group leadership. Planning often takes as much time as, sometimes even more time and energy than, the performing or leadership part of the group. Good planning ensures that group members have been carefully selected and prepared for group, group goals match individual goals, group interventions have been selected to meet group goals, and co-leaders have a good working relationship and a plan for the group.

A specific outline will be provided sequentially as a guide through the planning process. Suggestions will be included about how to select, organize, and arrange activities and will include relevant resources. Important topics to be discussed in this chapter are pregroup decision making based on the goals and population of the group, selection of interventions, securing of agency and school support, recruitment strategies, selection criteria, leadership preparation, and supervision.

There are several very good reasons why group leaders often skip one or more of these vital steps in this planning process, some already mentioned in the scenario in the first chapter. Other possible reasons will be highlighted throughout this chapter.

Pregroup Decision Making

Several important decisions need to be made about the structure, content, and interventions to be used long before the group starts. However, these decisions cannot be made in a vacuum; information must be gathered about what has been shown to be effective, the setting, and potential participants' needs and interests.

Needs Assessment

A needs assessment is the first step in gathering essential information to plan a psychoeducational group, and there are several ways to do it. One way is to ask potential group members. In the schools, even in elementary schools, students can be provided with list of potential group topics and asked to indicate in which groups, if any, they would like to participate. Experience in the schools also suggests that it is helpful to ask students not only in which groups they would be interested, but also what groups other students might find useful. Appendix H contains a survey that might be used to assess student needs. Teachers are also a valuable source of information about what kinds of groups students would benefit from. Additionally, counselors in the schools and community agencies who are working with children and adolescents individually on personal and social issues are a good source of information about groups that would be appropriate for these students. Once data have been collected using a student survey and staff and counselor input, group leaders may then decide what groups are most needed at this time.

Group Goals

A group leader decides the general goals for the group prior to selection of group members, then tailors specific content and interventions once individual members of the group are identified. Based on the topics and goals determined from the needs assessment, the counselor decides if the group will be psychoeducational or counseling oriented in its focus. Psychoeducational groups are often appropriate because of their structure and focus on skill building in a school setting.

At this time, group leaders need to look at the current research and practice literature related to the group topics they have identified. Once a group topic is chosen, it is essential to utilize the most up-to-date resources that suggest a current theoretical understanding of the problem or need, specific group goals that are attainable, topics that are typically addressed in this type of group, and group interventions and activities that are focused on the topics and that meet group goals. Current group counseling texts such as Sam Gladding's (2003) *Group Work: A Counseling Specialty* and Corey and Corey's (2002) *Groups: Process and Practice* include chapter(s) focused specifically on groups for children and adolescents. In addition, journals such as the *Journal for Specialists in Group Work; Small Group Research; International Journal of Group Psychotherapy; Group Dynamics: Theory, Research, and Practice; Social Work With Groups; Journal of Counseling and Development; The Professional School Counselor; Journal of School Counseling; Journal of Child and Adolescent Group Therapy; Journal of Adolescence; Group; Journal of Group Psychotherapy, Psychodrama, and Sociometry; Journal of School Psychology; Psychology in the School; School Psychology Review; School Psychology Quarterly; Small Group Behavior; Special Services in the Schools; Adolescence; Child and Adolescent Social Work Journal; Child Development; Journal of Adolescent Health; Journal of Early Adolescence; Journal of Research on Adolescence; Journal of Youth and Adolescence;* and *New Directions for Child Development* provide cutting-edge information about current group research and practice.

For example, an article by Sommers-Flanagan and her colleagues (Sommers-Flanagan, Barrett-Hakanson, Clark, & Sommers-Flanagan, 2000) in the *Journal for Specialists in Group Work* addresses psychoeducational school-based groups for depressed students focusing on coping in social skills. Using a cognitive-behavioral framework, goals for treatment and corresponding group topics, group characteristics, and group interventions are described in a session-by-session format. Most issues of the *Journal for Specialists in Group Work* include these kinds of articles.

Another very helpful source of information about what groups are needed, what groups have typically worked, and what interventions have been most useful are from practitioners in the field. School counselors should attend local school counseling meetings to talk to other school counselors who have led groups in the schools. Mental health counselors should talk to colleagues as well as other professionals in the field. When I was designing interventions using music for children-of-divorce groups, the school counselors who piloted group sessions were very helpful in two ways. One, they were very clear that 8 sessions for a children-of-divorce group was realistic, not the 20 that I was proposing. Second, they were very helpful in figuring out the order of sessions that worked best for students. There was a session titled "Is It My Fault?" that originally was planned for the second session. Several school counselors said that it would not work during the second session because the children were not ready to disclose such a personal fear so early. Moving the session to later in the group made it much more effective because the children were more comfortable and thus willing to disclose their fears.

Once a range of possible group goals has been identified based on the current literature and practice, specific goals then may be chosen based on interviews with potential group members about their concerns, a formal assessment of member concerns, or group discussion and consensus of which issues should be focused on in the group. Interview and assessment procedures will be discussed in detail in the next chapter.

It is helpful to write out the goals as a first step toward planning the group for several reasons. Why? First, all activities should be based on the specific goals. As a general guideline, at least one session should be spent on each goal or area of concern. For example, reasonable goals for a 6-week children-of-divorce group for second and third graders are gaining an accurate picture of the divorce process, normalizing the common experiences and feelings related to divorce, and providing a safe and supportive place to talk about divorce-related concerns. A self-esteem group for eighth graders might include the following goals: gaining an understanding of what self-esteem is and what role it plays in their lives, understanding how the attributions we make affect the way we view ourselves, identifying positive and negative attributions, learning how to dispute negative and irrational self-talk, and assessing actual skills in specific areas to gain a realistic sense of strengths and areas to improve.

As an example, to choose specific goals for a children-of-divorce group, DeLucia-Waack (2001) includes a checklist for potential group members of which situations are difficult for them. The situations correspond to specific group sessions. If a majority of the students indicate "I worry about what's going on with the lawyers or in court," then group sessions related to legal aspects of divorce will be included. The Morganett (1990) and Smead (1995) books both include pretests for different groups to help identify areas of concern. Potential members, their parents, and any administrators who must give their approval should then be informed of the specific goals of the group.

Gender Mix and Group Size

Based on the goals of the group, decisions must be made as to the size and gender mix of the group. Ideal group size varies according to the age of the children beginning with three to six children for younger children, five to seven children for ages 6 to 9, and up to eight children in preteen and teen groups. Projected attendance may also be a factor in how many students are invited to participate in a group. If there is a high rate of absenteeism among the students selected, it may be useful to include one or two more students so that there is always a critical mass for each group session. For therapeutic factors to work, there needs to be enough group members for interaction to occur. It is very hard to lead a group consisting of two co-leaders and two group members, even with younger children or group members who require a lot of attention. The interaction is pretty limited, and it is hard to get members to interact with each other rather than the leaders.

Mixed-gender groups seem to work well up until early middle school, when gender pressures set in. It is ultimately up to the style and experience of the group leader whether to lead mixed- or single-gender groups. Some counselors report that the diversity in emotions and reactions in mixed groups enhances effectiveness (Kalter, 1998). Other counselors lead same-sex groups in middle school to lessen the self-consciousness and decreased self-disclosure that may result from boys and girls being in the same group (Hines & Fields, 2002). Carrell (2000) suggests using mixed-gender groups for older teens because so much of their focus and concern is on relationships.

Length and Number of Sessions

The ideal length of the group sessions also varies according to the age of the group members: 20 to 30 minutes is optimal with children six and under, 30 to 40 minutes with children aged six to nine, and 40 to 75 minutes with those older than nine (Gazda, 1989; Thompson & Rudolph, 1988).

In middle and high schools that typically operate on a period schedule, groups logically last for one period minus the time it takes students to get to their group. Alternating the schedule each week allows students to not miss the same class each week. For example, a group might meet during Period 1 the first week, Period 2 the second week, Period 3 the third week, and so on.

Here is another good example of practitioners informing researchers and, ultimately, the literature. I have suggested previously (DeLucia-Waack, 2001) that the number of sessions for a divorce group in the schools is typically between six and eight. Although it makes sense that a longer group would provide more time to deal with substantive issues, an informal poll of school counselors suggested that because of time constraints, six to eight weekly sessions is all that can be provided within a calendar year. To counter the limited number of sessions, school counselors reported that students may participate in groups during several different grade levels. This format is also useful in that it allows children and adolescents to address the same issues at different developmental stages and as they encounter different issues. It also encourages and supports the ideas that it is normal for students to "repeat" group. This concept of repeating group at different age levels makes a lot of sense because the topics and issues may vary as the students get older, but the skills and the concepts are the same.

Group length for other settings may vary. Mental health agencies, for example, may be able to sustain longer groups. An ideal length for most psychoeducational groups in this setting is 12 to 16 sessions, allowing time to deal with more complex issues and behavior change to occur (the old adage is that it takes 10 weeks to acquire a new habit or behavior).

Court-referred groups, on the other hand, may vary significantly with regard to length. For children and adolescents who are attending court-referred groups because of a parental problem or issue, the group most likely will be shortterm and prevention focused; that is, one 4- or 8-hour session or four 2-hour sessions focused on how to adjust to parents divorcing. For students who are court referred for their own actions (i.e., fighting, drug usage), the number of sessions is generally longer. Even though the population is at risk, these groups are also typically very structured and focused on skill development such as anger management skills, stress management, problem-solving skills, life skills, and cognitive restructuring or criminal thinking errors (Morgan, 2004).

Regardless of the length of the group, the first session or two must be devoted to the establishment of ground rules and goals for the group, the introduction of members, and development. At the end of the group, at least one session, if not two, must be devoted to termination with the goals of helping the children to summarize what they have learned, express their feelings about the group and group members, and discuss how they will use what they have learned outside of group. Thus, a general guideline to determine how many sessions are needed would be to include one to two sessions for introduction, one to two sessions for termination, and one to two sessions for each goal to be addressed.

Session Structure

Structure is essential to providing safety and continuity to the children. Structure is also necessary to manage time efficiently and focus on relevant issues (DeLucia-Waack, 1997; Gladding, 1991). Depending on the type of group and the age of group members, the level of structure may vary. The younger the group members, the more structure is necessary. Psychoeducational groups tend to be more structured, with activities designed to facilitate discussion of a topic and/or development of new skills and behaviors. To make the transition from one group session to the next, it is helpful and creates a sense of trust to have a structure for each group session that is expected and predictable.

Psychoeducational group sessions typically have four parts. The opening reviews material from a previous session, discusses homework efforts, and/or introduces the topic for this session. The working part focuses on the goals of the group, allowing discussion and interaction around a specific topic or skill to identify, learn, and/or practice potentially effective behaviors. The processing activities part typically uses questions to help make sense of the working activities and apply them to life outside of group. The closing activities part helps group members to prepare to leave group.

Opening. At the beginning of a session, structure focuses members on what they will need to discuss that day (Morganett, 1990) based on past sessions or new topics for the session. If group members were asked to complete a task between group sessions, it is important to begin with a review of what they have done. The assignment typically is to practice a new behavior or coping strategy learned in the previous session or some kind of assignment in preparation for a new topic. Asking group members to review what they did with regard to this assignment and what they learned, and then using some focusing statements to direct them toward the topic of the day, are useful strategies.

Possible ways to begin sessions include check-ins or go-rounds that focus members on what they want to talk about and work on that day, review of homework from previous sessions, and the reading of a poem or paragraph that relates to the issues previously discussed in the group or as an introduction to a new topic. For example, in an anger management group, members might have been asked to identify situations where they felt irritated in the past week. The group leader may then comment on some of the similarities expressed by the group members, and then lead into a discussion of how to express irritation and other feelings in a way that will productively change the situation. To reinforce new strategies that have been learned in the previous week, group leaders may ask group members to identify one strategy that each of them tried during the week; and if they did not try a strategy, when they might have tried one. A strategy in a children-of-divorce group to normalize the experience of having parents who are divorced is to play a song that lists many people, real and imaginary, whose parents are divorced. Group members are then asked to add to the list of people that they know whose parents are divorced, including both children and adults. Another technique that is helpful as part of the opening to lead into skills that will be practiced during this session is to ask students to write down on a piece of paper one situation during the past week with which they could use help. The papers are then crumpled, thrown in the middle of the circle, and redistributed so the situations are now anonymous. Situations are then read aloud to emphasize universality and identify potential skills and coping strategies needed, and then later can be used as a basis for role-plays. General questions to open group sessions include the following:

- What did you do this week with what you learned in the previous session?
- Could we have a report on how you did with your homework assignments?
- What would you like to practice this week that you learned from last week?

Working. The working part of the session is focused on a discussion of skill-building based on the goals of the group. Teaching and practicing specific skills such as assertiveness, expression of feelings, and communication skills may be helpful in most psychoeducational groups to both facilitate effective interactions in groups and meet interpersonal group goals. In addition, techniques such as role-playing and Gestalt empty or two-chair techniques may help develop new interpersonal skills and explore issues. Such techniques allow group members to explore and express feelings to others or to experience two sets of conflicting thoughts and feelings.

All groups with children and adolescents need to include interventions to discuss feelings, connect with others, and identify potential solutions for their concerns, regardless of the theme or topic of the group (Smead, 1995). These skills assist group members in identifying potential areas of strength and improvement, practicing new skills, and learning content specific to group goals.

Children and adolescents often respond better to nonverbal techniques than verbal exercises because of their limited vocabularies and disposition to display feelings through play (Gladding, 1998). Creativity in activities, particularly singing, dancing, puppets, role-plays, and music, is a way to identify and express feelings and to brainstorm and practice new behaviors and coping skills (DeLucia-Waack, 2001; Gladding, 1998). Even adolescents who initially remark that puppets or stuffed animals are silly or too young for them will often pick up one or more of these items and hold them in group. Techniques also need to focus on the development of new skills and serve as a reminder of when to implement them. How to choose activities, as well as suggestions for integrating them within sessions and processing them to promote learning, will be the major focus of the rest of the book.

Some structure works well for older adolescents as well. Even for groups with more of a counseling focus for adolescents, beginning each session with a short activity, maybe 10 to 15 minutes at the most, helps them to generate some insight into their personal issues and perhaps introduce a framework within which to work on personal issues. Completing a brief checklist of strengths, or reading and then discussing a poem related to the group topic of the day, helps to focus the group members and to get ready to work on group and individual goals.

Processing. Processing is probably the most overlooked part of any group session, but particularly with regard to child and adolescent groups, and psychoeducational groups. Some people say that children are not capable of processing, whereas others say that processing is unnecessary because in psychoeducational groups, members are learning specific skills so the transfer of skills happens automatically. However, if one looks at the definition of processing, it becomes clear that processing is essential to the effectiveness of all groups, regardless of age, goals, or population. According to Stockton, Morran, and Nitza (2000), processing can be described as

> capitalizing on significant happenings in the here-and-now interactions of the group to help members reflect on the meaning of their experience, better understand their own thoughts, feelings and actions, and generalize what is learned to their life outside of the group. (p. 345)

Processing questions are intended to help members reflect on their reactions to the exercise, learn about themselves, and transfer their learning to their real lives.

Processing can be extremely useful in the teaching and application of specific skills related to the goals of a psychoeducational group. For example, in a test anxiety group, discussing what it is like to speak in group allows group members to identify their source(s) of anxiety, perhaps normalize their anxiety if other members also share it, and begin to generate possible interventions for when anxiety occurs outside of group.

In addition, as part of ending the group session, it is important for group leaders to assess and reinforce what group members have learned from the group today. Simply asking group members to identify what they have learned from this session and how they will use it in the upcoming week helps to ensure that the new information and skills are being integrated and applied. It was always amazing to me how clearly group members, even young children, could state what they learned from group that day. In addition, however, it was also comical, but perplexing to some extent, to hear comments that were tangential or did not seem to relate to the session at all. Thus, the importance of clearly identifying what members have learned is emphasized. Processing is an important piece of each group session, and it takes a relatively small amount of time, maybe 3 to 8 minutes out of a 45- to 60-minute group. Some ways to process at the end of sessions include summaries (by leader, one member, or briefly by all), go-rounds of what each person has learned today and/or thought was most helpful, brief written reactions given to the leader, and/or rating sheets. Go-rounds are often helpful at this time, such as the following:

- What I learned from group today was . . .
- One thing that I will take from group today was . . .
- One new skill I will try out during the week will be . . .
- What, if anything, did you learn in today's session?
- What did you hear yourself or anyone else say that seemed especially significant to you?
- If you were to summarize the key themes that were explored today, what would they be?
- What was it like for you to be here today?

To emphasize altruism, role modeling, and interpersonal learning, it is helpful to ask questions such as the following:

- With whom did you most connect today, and why?
- Each of you finish the sentence: "The thing I liked *best* (or least) about this session was _____."
- Who was most helpful to you today, and why?
- From whom did you learn the most today, and what did you learn?
- Could we have everyone say what he or she is feeling right now?
- I like it when you _____.
- You had some different feelings during this session. What did you learn about yourself from this?

The Critical Incident Questionnaire (Kivlighan & Goldfine, 1991) asks group members to respond in writing to the following questions: "Of the events which occurred in this group session today, which one do you feel was the most important to/for you personally? Describe the event: what actually took place, the group members involved, and their reactions. Why was this important to you? What did you learn from this event?" This is another example of research informing practice, and vice versa. As part of a research study on children-of-divorce groups, group members were asked to complete the Critical Incident Questionnaire after certain sessions to assess therapeutic factors occurring in the groups. Several of the group leaders told me that they found the written information so helpful that they began asking group members to verbalize their answers to the whole group as part of processing at the end of each group session. A version of the Critical Incident Questionnaire appears in Appendix M.

Questions that help identify what group members learned in group and how they helped others in group emphasize therapeutic factors and reinforce communication, problem solving, and social skills. Such questions might include the following:

- How did we work together today as a group?
- What did someone say or do today that was most helpful for you? What did you learn from it?
- What did we do as a group to generate new ideas? Try a new behavior? Learn something?
- What did you do today to help yourself learn something new?
- What did you do differently today in group?
- What did you do today to help someone else learn something?
- Does anyone want to give anyone else any feedback?
- Are there any changes you'd like to make in the group?
- What is each of you willing to say about each other's work?
- How is the group going for you so far?

Closing. At the end of a group session, structure helps to clarify what has been learned (Gladding, 1991). The closing part of the group session should also identify goals to work on between group sessions and also help group members to transition out of group. Recognizing that a group session is a very small part of the members' week, it is essential to help them practice and apply what they have learned in group, outside of group. Group members should leave the session with something to think about or practice before the next group session. Smead (1996) advocates inviting, rather than requiring, members to try out new behaviors if they are ready between group sessions. General assignments to the whole group or a specific assignment to individual group members may be part of the closing. It is most helpful to involve group members in the development of the homework. Several ways to do this include asking group members to identify a specific situation during the week in which they will practice a skill they have learned; asking group members to identify one new behavior they will try out during the week; or asking group members to monitor a certain situation, feeling, or behavior during the week in anticipation of the next group session (e.g., identify situations where you compare self to others unfavorably).

- What would each of you like to do between now and the next session?
- Is there anything anyone wants to work on at the next session?
- I'd like to go around the group and have each of you complete the sentence: "One thing I need to practice outside of group is _____."
- Let's spend the last 10 minutes talking about your plans for the coming week. What is each of you willing to do outside of the group?
- What are you willing to do with the tension (or any other feeling) you feel?
- What will help you to remember what you want to do differently?
- What can you do between now and the next session to practice what you've just learned?
- A homework assignment I'd like you to consider is _____.

It is also important to recognize that many uncomfortable feelings and thoughts may arise as a result of participation in a group session. This in and of itself is not bad as people learn the most when they are a little uncomfortable. However, group members often need to leave group and return to their "real lives." For children and adolescents, this may mean going back to a class or some sport or social event where they have to interact with other students. Thus, it is important to include as part of the closing of a group session some transitional element that helps students leave some of the intense feelings and emotions in the room and transition back to their real lives. Some kind of creative element or ritual is helpful here. Reading an inspirational poem or listening to music that is upbeat or soothing may be useful. Sometimes, playing music to which the group members can dance, to virtually shake off the negative emotions, is useful. Several songs by Dan Conley (1994) are useful to end a session in an upbeat or calming way: "Everybody Needs a Friend," "So Am I," "And I Need a Lot of Love," "Bad Mood," and "I Am a Kid."

Materials

Because of the usefulness of creativity in activities with children and adolescents, it is essential to have a variety of materials on hand. Practical items such as a chalkboard, chalk, paper, crayons, markers, and so on are always needed. In addition, books, videos, and games that focus on teaching or practicing skills related to expression of feelings, communication, and social skills are also useful. Appendix G contains a list of games, books, and videos to be used in specific psychoeducational groups. In addition, puppets are especially helpful when working with children in general. It is essential to have a variety of puppets to act out the situations. Group leaders can be creative in their collection of puppets: bath mats, oven mitts, as well as puppets made by the children as an activity all work well. To encourage the expression of a wide range of thoughts, feelings, and verbalizations, it is important to include some puppets that are scary, fuzzy, and furry, as well as those that have lots of different roles: queens, kings, princesses, firefighters, police officers, and so on. Furthermore, an effort should be made to include toys that appeal to a range of ethnic groups and age levels. A basket of stuffed animals is useful for any age level; even teenagers often walk in and grab a stuffed animal to cuddle during a group session.

Smead (2003) emphasizes the importance of stuffed animals as metaphors. She might say to a group member,

> You can always count on the frog, being so patient and flexible waiting for a dragonfly meal to come along, and living in so many difficult and unpleasant places. If the frog can be flexible, you can be flexible too with your parents' divorce and the times you need to be patient or flexible, or whatever stressful situation that child might be facing. (p. 12)

She suggests the use of props as a metaphor for new skills or behavior for several reasons: The prop as a metaphor helps group members to understand and discuss in the abstract a concept in a more concrete form; props are frequently viewed by children as playing with toys, which lowers the threat and increases the interest in group; and props stimulate the transfer of learning from the group to the outside world because the prop helps group members remember from week to week what they have learned. Smead suggests the following as props: viewing animals such as the monarch butterfly, crow, turtle, giraffe, and crab from the Native American perspective and what each animal means in terms of medicine gifts and how it can help; pacifiers as metaphors of baby behavior that is no longer working to get along with other people; straws as examples of when to be flexible; and candy as an example of differences between people. For ease of assembly when planning each group session, begin with a list of materials that will be needed for the session.

Outline and Content of Group Sessions

Once group leaders have identified typical goals and interventions specific to the type of group they plan to lead and have begun to select potential group members (specifics will be provided about how to do this later in this chapter and in the next chapter), it is time to begin to plan the content and order of the group sessions. Not all groups will focus on and/or accomplish all of the goals that have been previously identified. The decision about which sessions to include must be based on the number of sessions the group will have, the overall goals of the group, and the individual needs of the group members. Psychoeducational groups in the schools, whether small groups or classroom guidance activities, should focus on teaching social skills and self-instructional models of thought and behavior change. This section describes how to choose activities and programmatic activities that address these two foci and also meet specific group goals. Care should be taken to plan interventions based on the goals of, the time allotted for, and the size of the group.

In psychoeducational groups, activities are an essential part of the group structure to teach and practice new behaviors and skills. Group leaders tailor activities to the main task inherent in the current group stage and overall group goals. From the very beginning of the first group session, all group activities, processing of group activities, and group discussions should emphasize group goals and norms such as self-disclosure, self-exploration, and feedback as they relate to the facilitation of group goals. The chapters that follow describe the four stages of group and the main tasks and foci of each stage, and suggest potential interventions and activities.

When designing a psychoeducational group, there are a variety of materials and resources from which to choose. There are fully developed treatment modules for specific types of groups that leaders may follow step by step; resources that include outlines for individual group sessions that address certain goals; and also books, games, videos, and other materials that may be used within a group session. This part of the book will first discuss how to choose and sequence group sessions that will meet the goals of a specific psychoeducational group, taking into consideration age of group members, treatment length, and individual needs of group members. First, an outline will be described that will aid in selecting group sessions. At the end of this section, there will be a brief review of the programmatic treatment modules available for different psychoeducational groups. Throughout the chapters that follow, specific activities and interventions will be suggested for different types of psychoeducational groups.

Matching Sessions to Group Goals

It is important to decide prior to the onset of a group the sequence and content of each group session because so much of what happens in group is interconnected. For instance, in screening interviews, preparation sessions, and the first session, it is useful to describe group goals, typical group topics and themes, and interventions that will be used. Thus, those decisions need to be made ahead of time. In addition, any homework assigned during a session should lead logically into the topic and interventions that will occur in the following sessions. Moreover, it is important for group leaders to plan for the sessions in advance and gather group materials.

A general guideline for planning the group should be at least one session each for both opening and termination sessions, and one to two sessions focused on each goal. Generally, an 8-week psychoeducational group should have two to three goals. It would then be possible to spend 5 to 6 weeks on the content to meet these two or three goals. Conyne (2003) suggested a model for skill acquisition that suggests that most skills need to be addressed in more than one session. The model is as follows:

- Present content to be learned
- Describe relevant skill
- Demonstrate skill
- Practice, perhaps in pairs
- Give performance feedback
- Discuss application to real-world settings
- Retry skill
- Hold general processing discussion with entire group

Goals should generally focus on changing or teaching new skills and behavior in three areas: affect, cognition, and behavior. Affect focuses on the feelings elicited, with the general goals of psychoeducational groups being increasing positive affect and decreasing negative affect. Cognitions include both maladaptive and adaptive thoughts that group members think about themselves, the people with whom they interact, and the situations in which they are involved. General goals of psychoeducational groups related to cognitions include the identification, generation, and reinforcement of positive thoughts that help the group members try out new behaviors and feel good about themselves. Another goal related to cognitions in psychoeducational groups is identification and disputing of irrational beliefs that make group members feel depressed or bad about themselves, or interfere with social skills. Behavioral goals for psychoeducational groups include the teaching of skills related to expression of feelings, communication, conflict management, stress management, and relationships. It is a good idea to include one goal from each of the three categories as general goals for psychoeducational groups. For example, in a social skills group, the affective goal might be identification of negative feelings in social situations, the cognitive goal might be identification of the thoughts that make the student feel bad in social situations, and the behavioral goal might be the teaching and practicing of how to introduce yourself to new people.

Table 2.3 in this chapter is a planner for an eight-session group. The idea is to list for each session the session number, topic, title, interventions to be used, and homework to be assigned, along with space to make notes after each group session. Appendix D includes another, more detailed outline of a planning sheet that helps group leaders to plan each session in advance by organizing around the parts of each session—opening, working, processing, and closing—as well as identifying issues related to group members, goals, previous sessions, and group process. An example of a planning sheet for an eighth session of a children-of-divorce psycho-educational group is also included in Appendix F.

To decide which sessions should be included in a specific psychoeducational group, it is necessary to go back and compare what the literature suggests as important goals, topics, and interventions with the needs of potential group members and the setting in which the group is to be conducted. Table 2.1 in this chapter is a grid that helps systematically organize group goals and interventions suggested in the literature (and by other practitioners) as a backdrop to plan a specific group. Once it is apparent what the common group goals are for a particular group based on the literature and current group practice, group leaders can then choose on which goals this particular group will focus. Table 2.2 in this chapter is an example of a grid that two school psychologists created as part of their planning for a grief group. As you can see, nine general group goals that are typical of grief groups for adolescents were identified. Based on interviews with potential group members, they chose to lead a 10-session group that would have four general goals related to resolving grief.

Matching Interventions and Activities to Session Topics

Once group leaders have identified goals for a specific group, it is important to survey the literature to see which interventions are suggested to meet these goals and also what specific group sessions have already been designed to incorporate these interventions to achieve these goals. It does not make sense to reinvent the wheel every time a group leader leads a new group. This is probably one of the biggest deterrents to leading groups, particularly psychoeducational groups. Psychoeducational groups, as should be evident by now, take a great deal of time to plan and to examine

Table 2.1   Grid for Choosing Sessions

Goals for Group Based on Literature and Counseling Practice (list goal, reference, and date; indicate cognitive, behavioral, or affective)	Interventions Suggested in the Literature to Address This Goal (describe and list reference and date)	Sessions Designed by Others to Address Goal/Intervention (list reference, date, pg. #)

Now examine your grid: What goals have interventions and sessions designed for them? Those that do not have full sessions designed for them are the sessions that you now need to design, complete with goals, activities, and processing questions. The idea is not to reinvent the wheel here but to see what is already out there and then to add to the literature with new sessions for this type of group.

the literature, a luxury most group leaders do not have. Thus, it is important to identify resources such as those by Morganett, Smead, and others that will be described throughout this book, so that interventions that have already been shown to be effective can be used. The first column in the grid in Table 2.1 lists group goals gathered from the literature and counseling practice. The second column lists interventions suggested to meet the goals for this particular type of psychoeducational group. The third column identifies group sessions already designed to meet specific group goals. Now it is time to examine the grid: Which goals have interventions and sessions designed to meet them? Which do not? Any that do not will need interventions and group sessions created for them, including goals, activities, and processing questions. The idea is not to reinvent the wheel but to see what is already out there and then to add to the literature with new group sessions for this type of group.

For example, a group leader may decide to use the second and third sessions of an anger management group by Morganett (1990) because the interventions outlined in the sessions meet the goals of the particular group being led. Or someone may choose to use "The Kids' Grief Kit" (LeGrand, 2002) as part of a grief group to help children identify the different stages of grief. Table 2.2 illustrates the use of the literature and local resources to identify specific interventions and entire group sessions that may be used in a grief group.

Matching Interventions and Sessions to Group Stages

One of the initial tasks inherent in group work is to choose an activity that is appropriate for the stage of the group with which you are working. According to

Table 2.2   Example of Grid to Choose Sessions Based on What Is Already in the Literature for a Grief Group (Scime & Lewis, 2004)

Group Goals Based on the Literature and Counseling Practice	Interventions Suggested in the Literature to Address This Goal	Sessions Described in the Literature to Address This Goal
Improve self-esteem (Huss & Ritchie, 1999; Sandler et al., 2003)	Morganett (1990) provides a thorough, eight-session self-esteem group	Morganett (1990), pp. 87–102
Reduce depression (Huss & Ritchie, 1999; Sandler et al., 2003)	Cognitive reframing (Sandler et al., 2003) Coping with family rituals and holidays (Moore & Herlihy, 1993)	Moore and Herlihy (1993), p. 58
Increase self-efficacy related to ability to cope with loss (Huss & Ritchie, 1999; Sandler et al., 2003)	Discussion (Morganett, 1990)	Morganett (1990), p. 198
Understand and accept death (Morganett, 1990; Pfeffer, Jiang, Kakuma, Hwang, & Metsch, 2002; Samide & Stockton, 2002)	Discussion (Morganett, 1990) Members write questions about death and put them in a box for leader to answer (Samide & Stockton, 2002) Share with the group about grief experience (Huss & Ritchie, 1999)	Morganett (1990), p. 186 Samide and Stockton (2002), p. 200
Discuss feelings about death (Morganett, 1990; Samide & Stockton, 2002)	Educational presentation about Kübler-Ross theory (denial, isolation, anger, bargaining, depression, acceptance) (Morganett, 1990) Sharing the event (Freeman, 1991; Moore & Herlihy, 1993) Art or play therapy (Samide & Stockton, 2002) Create a list of all possible feelings related to death (Huss & Ritchie, 1999)	Morganett (1990), p. 188 Freeman (1991), p. 329 Moore and Herlihy (1993), p. 56
Validate and normalize feelings about grief (Samide & Stockton, 2002)	Create a personal memorial for the deceased (Morganett, 1990)	Morganett (1990), p. 193
Educate about the grief process (Huss & Ritchie, 1999; Samide & Stockton, 2002)	Teach a mini-lesson on Kübler-Ross theory (Moore & Herlihy, 1993) Age-appropriate explanation of the stages of grief (Samide & Stockton, 2002) Presentation of Parkes's and Worden's tasks of grief (Freeman, 1991)	Moore and Herlihy (1993), p. 56 Samide and Stockton (2002), p. 201 Freeman (1991), p. 329

Group Goals Based on the Literature and Counseling Practice	Interventions Suggested in the Literature to Address This Goal	Sessions Described in the Literature to Address This Goal
Recognize importance of rituals to memorialize the deceased (Morganett, 1990; Samide & Stockton, 2002)	Discussion (Moore & Herlihy, 1993; Morganett, 1990) Create a montage of memories related to the deceased (Samide & Stockton, 2002) Have group members describe their funeral experiences (Freeman, 1991)	Moore and Herlihy (1993), p. 57 Morganett (1990), p. 191 Samide and Stockton (2002), p. 200 Freeman (1991), p. 330
Acknowledge and cope with changes following death (Moore & Herlihy, 1993; Samide & Stockton, 2002)	Draw pictures of before and after the death (Samide & Stockton, 2002)	Samide and Stockton (2002), p. 201

Yalom (1995), structured activities, when chosen appropriately, can serve to accelerate the group past a particularly slow or stuck phase of the group. Following the framework postulated by K. Jones and Robinson (2000), activities should be chosen based on the following three stages: initial, working, and ending. Group leaders should tailor activities to the main task or issue inherent in the stage through which the group is currently working. They also suggest that intensity should be a key determinant in the choice of an activity by stage. They define intensity as

> the extent to which the group topic, structured exercises, and group techniques do the following: (a) evoke anxiety among the group participants, (b) challenge group participants to self-disclose, (c) increase awareness, (d) focus on feelings, (e) concentrate on the here and now, and (f) focus on threatening issues. (p. 358)

Initial-stage activities should focus on building trust and introducing members to the group and to each other. Working-stage activities should focus on assisting members to self-disclose, become involved in the process of group, and learn new behavioral and thought patterns to meet group goals. Ending activities focus on assisting the members in termination and bringing what they have learned to use once the group has ended. Thus, the chosen activity should focus on overcoming obstacles that are inherent in each respective stage.

Initial Stage. Activities used during the initial stage of the group should focus on helping the members introduce themselves to the group, meet their fellow members, and overcome their anxiety (K. Jones & Robinson, 2000). This stage is characterized by encouraging interactions that are of low intensity and focus on orienting

Table 2.3   Eight-Session Group Planner

Session #	Topic	Session Title
Session 1:		
Interventions:		
Notes:		
Homework:		
Session 2:		
Interventions:		
Notes:		
Homework:		
Session 3:		
Interventions:		
Notes:		
Homework:		
Session 4: *Note to Leader: Remind members that there are four sessions left.*		
Interventions:		
Notes:		
Homework:		
Session 5:		
Interventions:		
Notes:		
Homework:		
Session 6:		
Interventions:		
Notes:		
Homework:		

Session #	Topic	Session Title
Session 7: *Remind members that there is one session left. Assign homework to integrate what has been learned.*		
Interventions:		
Notes:		
Homework:		
Session 8: *Ending*		
Interventions:		
Notes:		

members to the norms, processes, and interactions of the group. These activities should involve minimal affective components and should be nonthreatening. The focus should be on decreasing, rather than increasing, the members' anxiety. Because members tend to feel anxious and relatively unwilling to disclose, activities should parallel this constraint on interaction. Choosing an activity that focuses on high levels of disclosure and affect would be too intense and threatening for members at this stage. Typical activities focus on introductions, trust building, and modeling of appropriate behavior. Examples of activities for the initial stage include "Autobiography" (Bridbord, 2002), "Guess Who?" (Doughty, 2002), and "Looking at Process" (B. Brown, 2002).

Middle Stage. The middle stage of group is characterized by intense affect, increased self-disclosure, and an accelerated willingness to work on one's own issues. As the group moves past the initial conflicts of safety and trust, a higher sense of cohesion develops, allowing for increased self-exploration and expression. Thus, members are more willing to take risks with the activities presented. Subsequently, activities chosen for this stage of group should be of high intensity. That is, these activities should encourage members to increase their self-awareness; increase affective involvement; take risks and try out new behaviors, skills, and attitudes; and work through personal issues that may interfere with trying out new behaviors and skill sets. Activities for this stage of group should be challenging for the members as well as anxiety provoking. Through this, members will be assisted in contributing the appropriate amount of disclosure within the group. More intense activities will match the group members' increased willingness and eagerness to explore new ways of thinking and behaving. Activities at this stage might also assist members in working with conflict, recognizing a wider range of emotions and expressions, and focusing on the here and now. Activities that can be used during the working stage of group include "A Group Image" (N. Brown, 2002), "Our Two Faces" (Gerrity, 2002), and "Fiddler on the Roof" (Horne, 2002).

Ending Stage. Activities that are chosen for the ending stage of group should focus on issues surrounding termination. In light of impending termination, members should move away from the high-intensity encounters and focus on the integration and application of new skills and attitudes. Thus, activities selected for this stage should focus on exploring what the members have gained from the group and how it will affect their lives in the future. Activities could also focus on helping the members say goodbye to each other and expressing what they have learned and gained from each other. Activities should be less intense than in the working stage and should focus on assisting members to achieve closure from the group. Examples of activities that are appropriate for the termination stage of group include "Closing: Thanking Others" (DeLucia-Waack, 2002a), "Closing: What Have We Learned About Ourselves" (DeLucia-Waack, 2002b), "My Core Self: The Center of the Quilt" (Thomas, 2002), and "Feedback as Poetry" (Wilson, 2002).

Summary. In summary, the selection of an appropriate activity for group centers around the stage of group. Each activity should match the needs and struggles inherent in each stage. One final consideration for selecting an activity that is appropriate for the group centers around the demographic characteristics of the group. It is important to choose an activity that is appropriately matched to the age level of the group (Yalom, 1995). If this care is not taken, young group members may be faced with an activity that is too advanced for their understanding, whereas older group members may perceive the activity as not sophisticated enough for their maturity level.

Programmatic Interventions

There are several programmatic interventions designed specifically for adolescents in the schools, for use in small groups and also in classroom guidance. Martin E. P. Seligman has developed a program titled "Positive Psychology for Youth" that was financed by a $2.8 million federal grant. The goal is "to prevent depression by giving children the tools to deal with challenges faced in high school and life" (Simon, 2004, p. 14). His idea is to bring techniques to children and adolescents not identified as at risk for depression or mental illness. Students in language arts class receive interventions that focus on identifying signature strengths; identifying their top five character traits (available at authentichappiness.com); and then using the strengths with family, friends, and community to bolster well-being and buffer against depression. The 23 lessons are delivered once a week for 90 minutes based on Dr. Seligman's theory that there are three routes to happiness: the Pleasant Life (the pleasures of touch, taste, and smell, and sensations such as euphoria and excitement) and building positive emotion; the Good Life (gratification from using signature strengths in relationships, work, and academics) and building signature strengths, emphasizing the link between negative thoughts and feelings, and how to dispute negative beliefs; and a Meaningful Life, with lessons on philanthropy, teamwork, and the meaning of life.

Other programs have been investigated extensively and show positive results. Shure's (1992) *I Can Problem Solve* (ICPS) uses a social skills training and social problem-solving approach with children in kindergarten through sixth grade, typically 6 to 10 children learning up to 59 lessons over a period of approximately 3 months. ICPS has been shown to reduce impulsivity, increase participation, and improve problem-solving skills. Goldstein and McGinnis's (1997) *Skillstreaming* curriculum includes several versions for different age groups and populations that use modeling, role-play, performance feedback, and generalization as techniques to improve prosocial skills and reduce aggression. *Skillstreaming* is based on a social skills deficit model in which 50 skills are available to be taught depending on group goals. It is recommended that groups consist of six to eight members, which are co-led for 45 to 50 minutes weekly. The *Life Skills Training* program (Gazda, Ginter, & Horne, 2001) also has been shown to develop skills for living, such as self-identity, problem solving, decision making, social skills, and physical health. The *Classroom Climate* program (Shechtman, 1997) has been effective in enhancing social relationships in the classroom, improving the social status of special needs students in junior high classes, and reducing adjustment problems among elementary school students. The *Problem-Solving for Life* intervention (Spence, Sheffield, & Donovan, 2003) integrates two components, cognitive restructuring and problem-solving skills training, into regular education for students in high school and was shown to be effective in reducing depression and increasing problem-solving abilities. A universal school-based prevention program called *LIST-A* (Possel, Horn, Groen, & Hautzinger, 2004), based on cognitive therapy, includes modules of assertiveness; social competence training; and the relationship between cognition, emotion, and behavior. They reported that for high school students, *LIST-A,* implemented in five sessions, was effective in reducing depressive symptoms, increasing social support, and changing irrational beliefs.

The *Skills for Living* books provide specific group outlines for different types of children and adolescents (Morganett, 1990, 1994; Smead, 2000b). All include interventions related to expressing feelings, problem solving, decision making, and self-esteem, but applied to specific problem areas (e.g., grief, children of divorce, anger management, self-esteem, school success). Brigman and Earley's (1991) *Group Counseling for School Counselors: A Practical Guide* describes eight-session groups for a number of topics: understanding yourself and others; friendship; self-concept; celebrating self; refusal skills; handling conflict; standing up to bullies; family groups, such as divorce, loss, at-risk, and the buddy system; academically at risk; pregnancy education/support group; and new student programs. They also have a book on *Peer Helping: A Training Manual* (Brigman & Earley, 1990). My book on using music in children-of-divorce groups (DeLucia-Waack, 2001) provides suggestions on how to select goals and also suggests specific group sessions to meet different goals. The Association for Specialists in Group Work published a book several years ago that includes specific activities to be used in group sessions, and the activities are organized by stage of group, goals for the invention, type of group, and group population (DeLucia-Waack, Bridbord, & Kleiner, 2002). Later in this chapter, there is a table in the section on Resource Gathering that identifies resources, including relevant group activities.

Agency and School Support

Formal and informal support is essential throughout the school or agency in which groups are being led. Administrative support is needed so that resources are allotted (time, money, space, personnel) and appropriate procedures are followed. In addition, colleagues must understand and support the use of psychoeducational groups in order to refer group members appropriately and ensure the success of a group program.

Administration

Leaders of a group must decide what channels to take to obtain approval to lead this group in their school or agency. Does a proposal need to be submitted? To whom should the proposal be submitted? What should the proposal include? In general, a thorough proposal should have (a) a rationale for the group based on current counseling literature and research, and a needs assessment of the population to be served; (b) goals, format, and duration of the group; (c) recruitment, screening, selection, and consent procedures; (d) specific interventions and activities; and (e) evaluation procedures. In a school setting, permission may be needed from any or all of the following people: the head of counseling or guidance services, the principal, the director of pupil services, the superintendent, and/or the school board. In an agency, permission may be needed from the director of clinical services, the director of the agency, and/or the board of directors. When proposing a psychoeducational group, it is important to clarify the purpose, the goals, and the population to be served. The common misperception that all groups are group therapy and thus are long term and directed at persons with severe problems often needs to be disputed.

Co-Workers

Co-workers also need to understand the goals, targeted population, and typical interventions to be used in a psychoeducational group. In agencies, counseling practitioners need to believe in the efficacy of psychoeducational groups in order to convey with a sense of enthusiasm how groups work for potential members, because how groups as a treatment modality are presented to potential group members greatly influences their willingness to participate. In addition, counselors need to understand how psychoeducational groups work and what the selection (and deselection) criteria are in order to make appropriate referrals. Appendix I includes an informational sheet as an example of information to give about possible referrals to group.

Similarly, in a school setting, teachers need to believe in the efficacy of psychoeducational groups in order to be willing to allow students to be taken out of their classrooms. It is especially important to help teachers understand how participating in a psychoeducational group will help the student function better in the classroom both academically and socially. The dilemma for teachers is often that with increasing academic standards, those students who struggle the most personally also struggle academically, and missing class time means falling even further behind academically. Group leaders need to help teachers understand the value of psychoeducational groups and also work with the teachers to maximize the value of participating in a psychoeducational group while minimizing the value of missed class time. Such techniques as rotating the time of the group each week so that students would miss a class only once every 7 or 8 weeks, notifying a teacher ahead of time so missed work may be done in advance or at home, allowing students to come late to group after taking a quiz, and so on, all are helpful.

As suggested earlier, the more information provided to teachers about what happens in psychoeducational groups, the better. Regardless of the theme of a psychoeducational group, the focus is on teaching social skills that are relevant to classroom behavior. If teachers can reinforce these newly learned behaviors to group members (and other students in the classroom), the whole school community benefits. Teachers are also not trained extensively in psychosocial and developmental issues of children, and the more counseling professionals can provide information to teachers about these issues, the more they will understand and be helpful to children. Group work specialists who provide changing family groups throughout central Ohio suggested that "acquainting teachers with the effects of family transition on children, information about the group, and the benefits children receive by participating, are important" (Beech Acres Airing Institute, 1993, p. 9).

Recruitment Strategies

Recruitment efforts should focus on children and adolescents who would like to participate in a specific kind of group and those who are identified by professionals and/or family members as having difficulty related to the area. Referrals may come from a variety of sources. In schools, teachers, parents, students, and administrators may all suggest to the counselor that a child or adolescent may benefit from participation in a particular type of group. Self-referral is also possible. In agencies, referrals may come from counselors who are working with a child or adolescent in individual counseling as well as from parents and school personnel.

It is important to get specific information from whoever is making the referral about the needs of the potential group member and how this person might benefit from a group. Sometimes, people may make a referral when individual counseling is not working, when a student is disruptive in class, or because they think somehow the group may change the maladaptive behavior. While getting specific information from the referral source, it is also essential to make it clear that there will be an assessment process to make sure that this particular group is the best intervention for the person being referred.

Group leaders should also keep in mind that although teachers and administrators may be a valuable resource when asking for referrals for a group, there is also a potential risk of breach of confidentiality. For example, it is helpful to ask teachers to recommend students who may benefit from a changing families group because they often know the current family situations of the students and their resulting level of stress. A teacher may recommend that a child participate in such a group, but it is important that he or she understand that the school counselor cannot report back to the teacher about a student's progress in the group and/or disclose what happens in the group. Once a group meeting time has been scheduled, it is important that confidentiality is not violated by a general announcement that the children-of-divorce group is meeting now in the library (Ritchie & Huss, 2000). The teacher should be informed that the student is leaving his or her class to meet with the school counselor, but no specifics need be (or should be) given. For the most part, teachers are concerned about the welfare of their students and genuinely want to help their students. Typically, they are not asking for information to gossip but to understand the situation. It is then helpful to give teachers general information about what happens in group such as typical activities, topics that will be discussed, and new behaviors that will be learned so the teachers can reinforce these changes as well. In addition, information about topical issues is often welcomed by teachers. A group leader may not be able to give specific details about a group member in a body image group to prevent eating disorders, but he or she can provide some general guidelines about how to encourage positive body image and healthy eating habits that teachers can use when interacting with all students.

Hines and Fields (2002) suggested that in the schools, one way to recruit and screen potential group members is to first conduct a classroom guidance unit in a classroom for all students. This is to be a purely preventive strategy focused on teaching skills but also allows the group leader to interact with students and assess whether a psychoeducational group would be helpful to certain students. In addition, the students become acquainted with the group leader, which begins the connection process.

If a child or adolescent is participating in a psychoeducational group and also seeing an individual counselor, social worker, or psychologist, it is useful for the parent and group member to sign a consent form so that the group leader and counselor can communicate. One way to keep the practitioner who is providing individual counseling up to date on what happens in each group session is to send him or her a copy of the planning session with a few sentences added commenting on the specific group member's participation during that session. Again, this keeps everyone working with a child or adolescent on the same page.

Group Leader Preparation

Co-Leadership

Co-leadership for psychoeducational groups for children and adolescents is preferable, specifically a male-female co-leadership team. The benefits of co-leadership are helpful in any group: two role models, two leaders who cooperate and work together, and two sets of eyes and ears to observe the content and process of the group. It is suggested that co-leadership is better for a variety of reasons, such as efficiency (e.g., the group can still continue if one leader is sick or unavailable), effectiveness (e.g., two leaders can track group members more easily), supervision and training of new group therapists, or as a way to model healthy communication patterns (e.g., male/female interactions) between co-leaders in front of the group members (Dies, 1994; Shapiro, 1999). It is also theorized that co-leaders who model appropriate interactions between themselves, such as resolving disagreements or compromising, will have group members who demonstrate better skills in these areas. In addition, a male-female co-leadership team can model collaboration between male and female adults, and provide contact with supportive and caring adults of both sexes. A male presence in the group is particularly important because many children may not have much contact with an adult male, especially if they are in an elementary school setting (Kalter, 1998). Although such a model of co-leadership may be time intensive and difficult to arrange, it is highly valuable and worth the effort. The co-leader does not necessarily need to be a counselor. If the group is psychoeducational in nature and thus pretty structured in its content, only one leader needs to be a counselor. The other leader could be a teacher if the groups are led in school. However, it is important that the second co-leader is empathic and supportive and able to provide some structure to the group. In agencies, it may be possible to recruit a youth worker or a caseworker who works with children but who has not been trained as a counselor.

Regardless of their skills and experience, co-leaders must commit to weekly planning and supervision sessions to prepare for their group and to process what has happened. A dedicated hour each week is essential to working cooperatively with a co-leader. The time is spent planning individual goals and strategies for each child, reviewing session events and group process, and planning for future sessions. When co-leadership is not possible, a solo group leader should still set aside an hour a week to plan and process for the group.

In order to prepare for the group, leaders need to think about it from several different perspectives. How will they as counselors prepare for the group personally and professionally? How will they prepare others for the group, specifically their school or agency (including administrators), parents, and group members? What are their beliefs about the nature of the problem, the symptoms, possible causes, and interventions, and how a group can best help these group members? To do this, personal values and experiences with the particular problem area must be explored. In addition, the current counseling literature about what is most effective with this population and problem area in terms of themes, interventions, structure, and so on must be examined as previously described in this chapter. To begin to establish trust and cooperation, co-leaders should meet regularly before the group starts to discuss theoretical orientation, leadership style, and goals and interventions for the group. Each co-leader should assess his or her strengths and weaknesses as a leader of the particular group that he or she is planning. Assessment of the group leadership skills needed should include the type of group (psychoeducational or counseling), the age of group members, and the focus and goals of the group. The Co-Facilitator Inventory (Pfeiffer & Jones, 1975) as well as Group Leadership Questionnaire (Wile, 1972) provide specific situations that may occur in group as a stimulus for discussion. Several self-assessment instruments are also available related to group leadership style and behaviors that can be completed individually and then discussed as co-leaders. *Critical Incidents in Group Counseling* (Tyson, Perusse, & Whitledge, 2004) also provides very specific incidents with group leaders' suggestions on how to work with them as they occur in groups.

While previous models of group leadership development vary in the number and emphasis of stages, Dugo and Beck (1997), drawing from earlier models in the literature, suggested a co-leadership model of development that consists of nine phases: Phase 1, "Creating a Contract"; Phase 2, "Forming an Identity"; Phase 3, "Building a Cooperative Team"; Phase 4, "Developing Closeness"; Phase 5, "Defining Strengths and Limitations"; Phase 6, "Exploring Possibilities"; Phase 7, "Supporting Self-Confrontation"; Phase 8, "Integrating and Implementing Changes"; and Phase 9, "Closing." Dugo and Beck emphasize Phase 1, "Creating a Contract," as essential to becoming an effective cotherapy team and insist that cotherapists should not lead a group together unless they have at least reached Phase 3, "Building a Cooperative Team." Bridbord, DeLucia-Waack, and Gerrity (2006), based on a study of 54 co-leadership pairs, concluded that co-leaders' perceived theoretical compatibility and differences in co-leader confrontation leadership style best predicted co-leadership relationship satisfaction, emphasizing the importance of co-leaders working together to develop a joint leadership style.

Resource Gathering

Different categories of essential resources are needed when planning for psychoeducational groups. They include general resources related to best practices in group work, how to lead psychoeducational groups for children and adolescents, and also references specific to the type of psychoeducational group to be led. Figure 2.1 contains essential references for group leaders in the first two categories. Appendix G contains references and resources organized by specific type of psychoeducational group.

In the first category, general references related to best practices in group work, the Association for Specialists in Group Work has created three important documents with major implications for group leadership that should be included as resources for all psychoeducational groups. The *Professional Standards for the Training of Group Workers* (ASGW, 2000) delineates and defines four types of groups, and presents core and specialty training guidelines. The knowledge, skills, and experiences for each type of group are identified in this document. Specifically, core training requires coursework in group work, a minimum of 10 clock hours in group membership or leadership, and specific knowledge such as theories of group development, assessment of group functioning, and group process and observational skills. Knowledge and leadership skills specific to each type of group also are identified.

The *Principles for Diversity-Competent Group Workers* (ASGW, 1999) provide guidance about the complicated issues inherent in conducting groups with diverse populations. Counselor self-knowledge, knowledge of other cultural worldviews, and diversity-appropriate group interventions are delineated. A section in the *Handbook of Group Counseling and Psychotherapy* (DeLucia-Waack, Gerrity, Kalodner, & Riva, 2004) also provides guidelines for leading in a variety of diverse groups. Specifically, group leaders need to be aware of their own biases, racism, and assumptions about mental health and counseling as well as possess specific knowledge and skills to be effective with different cultures and lifestyles.

*Anderson, A. (1994). Stories I'd tell my patients: Pulling weeds and planting flowers. *Eating Disorders: The Journal of Treatment And Prevention, 2,* 184–185.

Barlow, C. A., Blythe, J. A., & Edmonds, M. (1999). *A handbook of interactive exercises for groups.* Needham Heights, MA: Allyn & Bacon.

Begun, R. W. (1995a). *Ready-to-use social skills lessons & activities for grades PreK–K.* Champaign, IL: Research Press.

Begun, R. W. (1995b). *Ready-to-use social skills lessons & activities for grades 1–3.* Champaign, IL: Research Press.

Begun, R. W. (1996a). *Ready-to-use social skills lessons & activities for grades 4–6.* Champaign, IL: Research Press.

Begun, R. W. (1996b). *Ready-to-use social skills lessons & activities for grades 7–12.* Champaign, IL: Research Press.

Brigman, G., & Earley, B. (1991). *Group counseling for school counselors: A practical guide.* Portland, ME: J. Weston Walch.

Carrell, S. (2000). *Group exercises for adolescents: A manual for therapists* (2nd ed.). Thousand Oaks, CA: Sage.

Coon, C. (2004). *Books to grow with: A guide to using the best children's fiction for everyday issues and tough challenges.* Portland, OR: Lutra.

Cowne, E. L., Hightower, A. D., Pedro-Carroll, J. L., & Work, W. C. (1990). School-based models for primary prevention programs with children. In R. P. Lorion (Ed.), *Protecting the children: Strategies for optimizing emotional and behavioral development* (pp. 133–160). New York: Haworth.

DeLucia-Waack, J. L. (2001). *Using music in children of divorce groups: A session-by-session manual for counselors.* Alexandria, VA: American Counseling Association.

DeLucia-Waack, J. L., Bridbord, K. H., & Kleiner, J. S. (Eds.). (2002). *Group work experts share their favorite activities: A guide to choosing, planning, conducting, and processing.* Alexandria, VA: Association for Specialists in Group Work.

DeLucia-Waack, J. L., & Donigian, J. (2004). *The practice of multicultural group work: Visions and perspectives from the field.* Pacific Grove, CA: Wadsworth.

DeLucia-Waack, J. L., Gerrity, D., Kalodner, C., & Riva, M. (Eds.). (2004). *Handbook of group counseling and psychotherapy.* Thousand Oaks, CA: Sage.

Dossick, J., & Shea, E. (1988). *Creative therapy: 52 exercises for groups.* Sarasota, FL: Professional Resource Press.

Dossick, J., & Shea, E. (1990). *Creative therapy II: 52 more exercises for groups.* Sarasota, FL: Professional Resource Exchange.

Dossick, J., & Shea, E. (1995). *Creative therapy III: 52 more exercises for groups.* Sarasota, FL: Professional Resource Press.

Fleming, M. (1993). *101 support group activities for teenagers at risk for chemical dependence or related problems.* Center City, MO: Johnson Institute/Hazelden.

Foster, E. S. (1989). *Energizers and icebreakers for all ages and stages.* Minneapolis, MN: Educational Media Corporation.

---

*This column appears in most issues and has some really good stories to use as metaphors in groups.

(Continued)

Figure 2.1   General References for Leading Psychoeducational Groups

Figure 2.1 (Continued)

Freeman, S. M. (1993). *From peer pressure to peer support: Alcohol and other drug prevention through group process: A curriculum for grades 9–10* (rev. ed.). Center City, MO: Johnson Institute/ Hazelden.

Goldstein, A. P., & McGinnis, E. (1997). *Skillstreaming the adolescent: New strategies and perspectives for teaching prosocial skills.* Champaign, IL: Research Press.

Gregson, B. (1982). *The incredible indoor games book: One hundred and sixty group projects, games, and activities.* Redding, CA: Fearon Teacher Aids.

Grothe, R. (2002). *More building assets together: 130 group activities for helping youth succeed.* Champaign, IL: Research Press.

Harris, F. W. (1989). *Great games to play with groups: A leader's guide.* Redding, CA: Fearon Teacher Aids.

Jones, K. D., & Robinson, E. H. (2000). Psychoeducational groups: A model for choosing topics and exercises appropriate to group stage. *Journal for Specialists in Group Work, 25,* 356–365.

Karp, C. L., Butler, T. L., & Bergstrom, S. C. (1998). *Activity manual for adolescents.* Thousand Oaks, CA: Sage.

Liebmann, M. (2004). *Art therapy for groups: A handbook of themes and exercises* (2nd ed.). New York: Brunner-Routledge.

McGinnis, E., & Goldstein, A. P. (1997). *Skillstreaming the elementary child: New strategies and perspectives for teaching prosocial skills.* Champaign, IL: Research Press.

McTavish, S. (2004). *Life skills: 225 ready-to-use health activities for success and well-being.* Champaign, IL: Research Press.

Moe, J., & Ways, P. (1991). *Conducting support groups for elementary children K–6: A guide for educators and other professionals.* Center City, MO: Johnson Institute/Hazelden.

Morganett, R. S. (1990). *Skills for living: Group counseling activities for young adolescents.* Champaign, IL: Research Press.

Morganett, R. S. (1994). *Skills for living: Group counseling activities for elementary students.* Champaign, IL: Research Press.

Richardson, R. C. (1996). *Connecting with others: Lessons for teaching social and emotional competence.* Champaign, IL: Research Press.

Roehlkepartain, J. L. (1997). *Building assets together: 135 group activities for helping youth succeed.* Champaign, IL: Research Press.

Schaefer, C. E., & O'Connor, K. J. (1983). *Handbook of play therapy.* New York: Wiley.

Search Institute. (2004). *Building assets is elementary: Group activities for helping kids (ages 8–12) succeed.* Champaign, IL: Research Press.

Smead, R. (2000). *Skills for living: Group counseling activities for young adolescents.* Champaign, IL: Research Press.

Stoiber, K. C., & Kratochwill, T. R. (Eds.). (1998). *The handbook of group intervention for children and families.* Needham Heights, MA: Allyn & Bacon.

Tyson, L., Perusse, R., & Whitledge, J. (Eds.). (2004). *Critical incidents in group counseling.* Alexandria, VA: American Counseling Association.

Wolfe, D. A., Werkerle, C., Gough, R., Reitzel-Jaffe, D., Grasley, C., Pittman, A., Lefebvre, L., & Stumpf, J. (1996). *The youth relationships manual: A group approach with adolescents for the prevention of woman abuse and the promotion of healthy relationships.* Thousand Oaks, CA: Sage.

The *Best Practice Guidelines* (ASGW, 1998) address planning, performing, and processing groups. Planning focuses on pregroup decision making and selection and the preparation of both members and leaders. Performing focuses on group leadership skills, provision of effective interventions, and assessment of effectiveness. Processing focuses on using interventions to help members learn and evaluate group interventions to assess effectiveness, supervision, and follow-up with group members.

The *Handbook of Group Counseling and Psychotherapy* (DeLucia-Waack et al., 2004) also includes several chapters that review current research, theory, and practice related to therapeutic factors (Kivlighan & Holmes, 2004), effective leadership (Riva, Wachtel, & Lasky, 2004), training for group leaders (Stockton, Morran, & Krieger, 2004), choice and use of activities (Trotzer, 2004), processing in groups (Ward & Litchy, 2004), and measures of group process and outcome (DeLucia-Waack & Bridbord, 2004). In addition, Shechtman's (2004) chapter on group counseling and psychotherapy with children and adolescents, and Riva and Haub's (2004) chapter on group counseling in the schools, are also very relevant. The *Handbook of Group Research and Practice* (Wheelan, 2005) summarizes research and practice on major topics related to groups.

In the second category of specific resources about how to lead psychoeducational groups for children and adolescents, there are several classic articles that are very helpful in planning and organizing psychoeducational groups for children and adolescents. They are Furr (2000) on designing psychoeducational groups, K. Jones and Robinson (2000) on choosing activities in psychoeducational groups, and Ritchie and Huss (2000) on selecting group members for psychoeducational groups. There are also several articles that are very helpful that discuss how to process activities; they are included in Figure 2.1 and also will be discussed in more detail in Chapter 8.

Figure 2.1 in this chapter also identifies books that include outlines for complete psychoeducational groups as well as books that include different activities that can be used to meet different goals in psychoeducational groups. Appendix G is organized by the topic of psychoeducational group, and includes information for parents; information for group leaders; and books, videos, games, and activities to be used.

Supervision

The ASGW *Professional Standards for the Training of Group Workers* (2000) suggest a minimum of 1 hour a week planning time for group leaders, either individually or with a co-leader. The ASGW Best Practice Guidelines (1999) consistently emphasize the importance of supervision and/or consultation with other group workers as an integral part of effective and ethical group work. Specifically, group leaders must

> process the workings of the group with themselves, group members, supervisors, or other colleagues, as appropriate. This may include assessing progress on group and member goals, leader behaviors and techniques, group dynamics and interventions, and developing understanding and acceptance of meaning. Processing may occur both within sessions and before and after each session, at time of termination, and later at follow up, as appropriate. (ASGW, 1999, p. 4)

Consistent with these standards, research studies have supported the premise that supervision leads to improved competency of counseling skills. Yalom (1985) reported that without supervision, group therapists were not able to identify mistakes and generate new plans of action; instead, they became stuck in a cycle of repeated ineffective interventions. Supervision by an experienced group leader of psychoeducational groups is recommended for group leaders who do not have much experience. It has been suggested that, whenever possible, psychoeducational groups be co-led. The term *supervision* will be used to describe the activity of an experienced group leader providing supervision to an inexperienced leader or co-leader as well as the activity of two co-leaders meeting to plan and process group sessions. The guidelines and steps suggested may also be useful for a solo group leader to think about and plan his or her psychoeducational group.

It is useful to think of the focus of supervision as having three parts—conceptualizing the case, planning and evaluating the effectiveness of techniques and interventions, and exploring personal reactions to group events and members—with the goal of each being effective group leadership behavior. Case conceptualization for group work includes a theoretical perspective of both the group as a whole in terms of group stages, and specific members, in terms of personal growth and development. Where is the group in its development? Are individual members making progress toward their goals? What is happening in group that facilitates progress toward individual member goals? What is happening in group that hinders progress toward individual member goals? The focus on techniques and interventions includes the selection and practice of specific interventions, techniques, and leader behaviors for future sessions as well as the evaluation of those from previous sessions.

Discussion of personal reactions to clients and group incidents is also helpful in understanding how clients and group events affect the other members, the group as a whole, each co-leader, the co-leader relationship, and the supervisory relationship. Personal reactions to clients often may interfere with the planning and execution of specific interventions. At other times, personal reactions to a group member or an incident in a group session may be similar to what others in group experienced, thus providing important information about what is happening in group. As an example, DeLucia-Waack (1999) described specific countertransference that group leaders may experience when leading an eating disorders group and provided suggestions about how to use supervision to address the countertransference.

DeLucia-Waack (2002c) provides a format for each supervision session that allows time for discussion, planning, and processing, as follows:

- **Reporting** of what specifically happened in the most recent group session in terms of events, member behavior, and leader behavior and reactions. What happened? Who sat where? Who did what? Who said what? How did members react, verbally and nonverbally?
- **Reflection** on what happened in the most recent group session. What worked? What didn't work? What felt productive? When did it feel like the group was working or making progress? When didn't it? What made you uncomfortable? When did you feel comfortable? How well are you working together?

- **Integration** of what has been happening in group sessions and theoretical perspectives on group stages, therapeutic factors, and leader interventions. In what stage is the group? What behaviors exemplify the stages? What issues need to be addressed based on the stage? How do members' goals compare to typical goals for this stage? How are members working on their goals? What do they need to continue to do? How can you help them work on their goals?
- **Planning** for what needs to happen in the next session based on the previous levels of discussion. What are the goals for the group as a whole and each member individually? What content issues need to be addressed? What process issues need to be addressed? What needs to happen to help the group work together more productively? What needs to happen for individual members to work more productively? Specifically who will do what and when?
- **Evaluation** of what was helpful during the supervision session. What was helpful today? What did you learn? How did you learn it? What will you do differently next group session?

Appendixes D and E contain outlines of group planning sheets and progress notes that can be used to facilitate the evaluation of group interventions and planning for future sessions. Appendix F contains examples of group planning and progress notes for a psychoeducational group for children of divorce.

The group planning sheet is completed by the group leader(s) prior to a group session by identifying themes, issues, and interventions that were unfinished from the previous session, as well as identifying new topics and interventions. The group processing sheet is completed after a group session as preparation for the supervision session. The goal of the group processing sheet is to help group leaders examine what happened in the session by first identifying specific events, and then reflecting on the effectiveness of the leader interventions and the group member interactions within two theoretical frameworks (Yalom's categories of effective leader behavior and critical incidents related to Yalom's therapeutic factors). The group processing sheet helps group leaders to focus on reactions, both realistic and countertransference, to specific group members and group incidents. Specific questions and issues to discuss in supervision can then be identified. More experienced group leaders may not need to write out their answers but may use the processing sheet as a cognitive organizer for discussion in supervision to prompt them to cover all the major issues.

Conyne (1999) suggested a similar model, Deep Processing, which consists of the following steps: Transpose, Reflect, Discover, Apply, and Evolve. This model also may be useful as a framework for discussing, evaluating, and planning group interventions and sessions. Greenberg (2002), in his book on group counseling in the schools, also provides a comprehensive checklist to evaluate the effectiveness of the group session and specific group leader interventions. It asks questions that assess group leaders' ability to stay on task, learn the group members' names, keep students focused, and so on. Group leaders might use such a checklist as a basis for discussion in their supervision sessions. Greenberg also includes a similar checklist for classroom guidance activities.

Several issues will arise as co-leaders begin to work together and the group members move into the transition and then the working stage. Co-leaders must negotiate their differences in styles. At each supervision session, some time should be spent on how the relationship is progressing, differences in style, feedback for each other in terms of what works and does not work in the group, and their level of trust with each other. It is important to do this for several reasons. One, it sets the precedent that time and attention will be given to the relationship. Second, co-leaders begin to have these discussions when conflict is low or nonexistent so that when conflict does arise, they have had some experience in talking about the relationship and giving feedback. In facilitating these discussions, the supervisor must focus on specific behavioral feedback that is both positive and negative, and facilitate risk taking in both supervision discussions and group sessions.

Summary

Planning as defined by ASGW (1998) focuses on pregroup decision making and planning. It is essential to begin with an assessment of "community needs, agency or organization resources, sponsoring organization mission, staff competency, attitudes regarding group work, professional training levels of potential group leaders regarding group work, client attitudes regarding group work, and multicultural and diversity considerations" (ASGW, 1998, p. 238). Group leaders can then decide the purpose, population, and goals of the group, which determines whether the group will be psychoeducational, counseling, or therapy focused. To make this decision, group facilitators should ask organizing questions: Who will be members? What is the reason for forming this group? Is this a prevention or treatment intervention? What is the intended outcome? How long are the group interventions? Are the goals realistic for the length of the group? The answers to these questions will allow leaders to choose group content and format that appropriately address these needs.

Once group goals, content, format, and interventions have been decided based on an integration of group member needs and current literature, community support can be secured and recruitment strategies begun. Group leaders must begin to prepare for the group by gathering resources and making decisions about leadership style, potential co-leadership, and supervision. This chapter provided specific strategies to be used during planning. The following chapter will focus on aspects of planning related to potential group member screening, selection, and preparation.

Suggested Training Activities

1. Write a Group Paper to Develop a Psychoeducational Group

- Choose a class member to be your group co-leader and choose a type of psychoeducational group on which to focus. You must decide the focus of your group and the age of the members. Together, you will be leading a 10-session (45 minutes each) psychoeducational group. You will be designing and implementing a psychoeducational group. Your paper should *serve as a guide* for others leading this kind of group. It will contain the following topics based on a review of the literature (including theory, practice, and research):

- Statistics and theory to support the need for this type of group—why is this group needed and why would group work be useful with this population and/or problem? What therapeutic factors would operate to make this group helpful to members? Use what literature is written to support this section and then speculate where there is none.
- A grid that identifies (a) goals for this group based on the theoretical and research literature, (b) typical interventions and activities that address these themes and topics from the literature, (c) actual sessions already available in the literature that meet the goals, and (d) sessions that need to be designed to meet goals identified in the literature. The grid was discussed earlier in this chapter.
- Specific goals for your group based on the current literature and your population
- Procedural decisions (time, length of group, place, etc.)
- Co-leadership planning and processing: What do co-leaders need to discuss, plan, do before they lead together and this kind of group in particular?
- Leadership gathering of materials and resources: What do they absolutely have to read and know before they lead this group?
- Recruitment procedures (flyers, letters, etc.)
- Selection criteria
- Screening interview outline
- Preparation outline and model
- Outline of 10 group sessions. Include goals, themes, and topics for each session (should include cognition, behavior, and affect). When appropriate, you may use sessions that have already been outlined in the literature. (Make sure that you give proper credit to the authors.) Use the grid constructed earlier in this assignment to decide which sessions you should outline in detail by identifying which goals have not had specific sessions developed for them and available in the literature.
- Evaluation of process and outcome (include measures, evaluation questionnaires, etc.). Be specific about which measures will be used to assess which goals, and group environment and therapeutic factors.
- Resource materials: List videos, games, books, and resources for parents.
- References

2. Develop a Co-Leadership Relationship

- Choose a co-leader.
- Complete some or all of the following individually to assess your group leadership skills and typical interventions:
  - Co-Facilitating Inventory (Pfeiffer & Jones, 1975)
  - Therapist Self-Description Questionnaire (Bernard, Drob, & Lifshutz, 1987)
  - Leadership Characteristics Inventory (Makuch, 1997)
  - Group Leadership Questionnaire (Wile, 1972)

- Group Counseling Survey (Carter, Mitchell, & Krautheim, 2001; Slocum, 1987)
- Skilled Group Counseling Scale (Smaby, Maddux, Torres-Rivera, & Zimmick, 1999)
- Trainer Behavior Scale (Bolman, 1971)
- Corrective Feedback Self-Efficacy Instrument (Page & Hulse-Killacky, 1999)
- Self-Assessment of Group Leadership Skills (Corey & Corey, 2002)
- Group Leader Behavior Rating Form (Corey & Corey, 1987; DeLucia & Bowman, 1991)
- Group Leadership Self-Efficacy Instrument (Page, Pietrzak, & Lewis, 2001)
- Attitudes Towards Group Leadership (Corey & Corey, 2002)

- Discuss your answers with your co-leader. Process with questions such as, What did you learn about each other? How are your styles similar? How are your styles different? What decisions have you made about how to handle potential situations in group? What decisions still need to be made? What potential areas of conflict were identified? If they were resolved, how did you resolve them? If they weren't resolved, what needs to be discussed in supervision?
- Begin to plan your co-leadership style with regard to a theoretical conceptualization of how this group should work, and how to handle differences in theory, style, and opinion. Begin to discuss how to open and close sessions, how responsibility will be shared equally for both content and process, and how to plan and process group sessions.

3. Create a Flier

Create a flier to advertise a specific group to potential group members. Decide how and where to distribute the flyers.

4. Create an Informational Sheet for Schools

Write an informational sheet that could be distributed to teachers in schools about a specific psychoeducational group that provides general information about the goals and interventions to be used in the group, as well as suggestions about who to refer as potential group members.

5. Create an Informational Sheet for Agencies

Write an informational sheet that could be distributed to counseling professionals in an agency about a specific psychoeducational group that provides general information about the goals and interventions to be used in the group, as well as suggestions about who to refer as potential group members.

6. Develop a Proposal for a Psychoeducational Group

Write a proposal to be given to the administration in a school setting or agency setting that provides a rationale for a specific psychoeducational group using the outline detailed under the Administration section of the Agency and School Support heading.

CHAPTER 3

Pregroup Interviews and Group Sessions

Once procedural decisions have been made about the type, goals, length, and time frame of a psychoeducational group, it is time to begin the selection process for potential group members. Two key aspects are important to group member selection: (a) providing information to potential group members (and their parents when necessary) about details of the group (goals, topics, typical interventions) so that they are truly giving informed consent when they agree to participate; and (b) gathering information to decide whether potential group members would benefit from participation in this particular group based on their goals, willingness to participate, and interpersonal skills. In this chapter, the focus will be on using pregroup screening interviews and preparation sessions to select potential group members who are most likely to benefit from participation in a psychoeducational group.

Informed Consent for Group Members (and Parents)

To make an informed decision about participation in a group, children and adolescents (and parents) must be given information about the type of group; its goals, format, structure, and typical interventions; and the leadership style and credentials of the group leader(s). It is helpful to provide parents with both verbal information and written materials. A one-page handout that summarizes goals, topics, and interventions; discusses confidentiality; and provides contact information is helpful. The American Counseling Association's (1997) *Ethical Standards* are very specific about information to be disclosed in order to obtain informed consent: purposes, goals, techniques, procedures, limitations, potential risks, limits of confidentiality, and benefits of services. The ASGW's (1998) *Best Practice Standards* also suggests discussion of group leader credentials and the roles and responsibilities of group members and leaders. Appendix I contains an example of an informational form for parents about psychoeducational groups.

An issue that is often raised when leading groups has to do with information and consent needed for a child to participate. It is important to establish with an administrator(s) whose consent is necessary. Is the consent of the custodial parent alone valid and/or even acceptable when parents have joint custody? Should the noncustodial parent be informed of the group as it may affect his or her relationship with the child (hopefully positively)? How is consent handled when the child or adolescent lives with another family member but one or both parents have legal custody? What about high school students who are almost but not quite of legal age? Some schools take the stance that if a student wants to participate in a group, his or her consent is enough. Other schools assume consent unless a parent indicates otherwise. Typically, the student handbook provides information about the types of group and individual counseling services available through the school, and that parents should contact the school if they do not want their son or daughter to participate in any of these activities.

Ritchie and Huss (2000) provide a valuable reference with regard to how to make decisions related to selection, screening, and recruiting of minors in a way that protects confidentiality and addresses issues of informed consent. They make several valuable suggestions about how to secure parental consent without violating confidentiality. Wilcoxon and Magnuson (1999) also provide specific suggestions about how to balance the needs and demands of custodial and noncustodial parents, and most importantly, the student, while taking into consideration each individual situation and ethical and legal issues.

For children and adolescents as potential group members, make sure that they are informed about the group at a level they can understand. Leaders should choose words that are appropriate to the grade level, and use examples whenever possible. It is helpful to explain goals, typical activities, and ground rules before the students enter the group to ensure that they understand and are ready to participate. Such information must be included at several points: verbally explained during a pregroup screen interview, in writing to either or both the student and the parents, and during the first group session.

Before beginning the process of recruiting and informing potential group members, group leaders must clarify with their administration the order of how information will be presented. For example, some schools first send a letter to the parents informing them about a particular type of group and asking parents to consent, which is then followed by pregroup screening interviews conducted with potential group members. Other schools may interview students first to assess whether they would benefit from this particular group, and then if they are interested in participating, notes are sent home to parents for further consent.

Selection Criteria

Regardless of the order in which potential group member and parental consents are obtained, it is important to develop clear selection criteria. When Yalom

(1995) writes about the selection of members for psychotherapy groups, he actually emphasizes "deselection criteria" more than selection criteria. This holds true for psychoeducational groups as well, to some extent. The goal is to create a group where children and adolescents feel accepted and cared about so that they are willing to try out new behaviors and ways of thinking. If students do not feel a part of the group or feel judged, they will not participate fully or sometimes at all. Selection criteria will be discussed on three levels: (a) general rules and guidelines that apply to most psychoeducational groups, (b) specific criteria developed around the goals for the psychoeducational group, and (c) potential group members' willingness to participate in a psychoeducational group.

General Selection Criteria

The following general selection criteria are suggested for psychoeducational groups for children and adolescents:

- All group members must be within 2 years of each other so that they are similar in emotional development (Smead, 1995). This is crucial for younger children but is still important even for teenagers. Group members must be close to each other in maturity level in order to work together and learn from each other.
- Siblings should not be in the same group due to conflict of loyalty and the difficulty of the group in acknowledging two perspectives in the same family.
- Ideally, there should be a mixture of family situations or problems among the children with variation in living situation, communication skills, level of distress, and strengths and weaknesses. These differences will serve to promote peer role models, generate alternative solutions to problems, and instill hope.
- Any one group member should not be so different that he or she feels isolated or scapegoated by the group. Although it is impossible to prevent scapegoating, a conscious effort to select and link members based on their similarities (e.g., feelings, experiences) may help group members to make connections and increase cohesiveness among members. It is important that group members connect with each other around the topic of the group. Gender, race, socioeconomic status, and ethnicity of group members should be taken into consideration when trying to prevent scapegoating (Hines & Fields, 2002).
- In schools, it is particularly important that no two group members have a history of significant conflict with each other. Because these groups are so short, there is no time to repair damaged relationships. Trust must be established, and it is easier to do so when there is no history of past conflict. Riva, Lippert, and Tackett (2000) described this as compatibility, suggesting that if two students have a relationship that might negatively affect the group process or put confidentiality at risk, then these students are not compatible.
- Each group member must have at least one person in the group with whom he or she can initially connect and one person who will be able to serve as a role model for him or her.

Deselection criteria include the following:

- Students whose goals do not match group goals
- Students who are overly hostile, angry, or aggressive
- Students who are extremely hyperactive and who cannot focus on a group activity for even a short length of time
- Students who cannot empathize with others
- Students who are extremely sensitive to criticism
- Students who are in crisis or suicidal

There are some exceptions to these criteria based on the group. In an anger management group, some members, by definition, would be angry or aggressive. The key is not to create a group of all angry or aggressive members, but to try to also include group members who hold in their anger so that members can learn from each other and serve as potential role models for each other. The best suggestion regarding including group members who are angry or hyperactive, or who cannot empathize with others, would be to include one or two members with these characteristics, but do not have it be a common characteristic of all group members. Remember that group members must be able to serve as role models for each other as well as present different strengths and approaches to increase the range of problem-solving options.

Specific Criteria to Assess Fit With Group Goals

The range of behavior that will be addressed within a specific psychoeducational group needs to be identified clearly. From there, goals (behavioral, cognitive, and affective) will be determined. Based on these goals, specific criteria can be generated to decide which group members will benefit most from participation in this group. For example, students exhibiting restricting or binge-eating behavior may not be good candidates for a positive body image group. However, those students may be a good fit for bulimia prevention that focuses on the identification and modification of feelings to prevent disordered eating behaviors (Weiss, Katzman, & Wolchick, 1985).

Homogeneity with regard to problem type and severity in psychoeducational groups for children and adolescents is essential. Group members must be able to initially connect with each other around the group goal (e.g., improving self-esteem or learning ways to make friends) to promote universality, hope, and cohesion. Although there can be some range in terms of the severity of concern, group members need to be on the same general level of needing help. For example, it would not be wise to put a student who is potentially suicidal in an improving self-esteem group. This person would end up either feeling isolated and scapegoated or taking up much of the group's time and attention because he or she is perceived as needing the most help.

However, heterogeneity is also needed with regard to group members. One might ask, how can you achieve heterogeneity when you have already selected a homogeneous group? Smead (2000b) sums it up by saying "a coping model is what we are looking for in a group—youths who have the same [homogeneous] major issue but who are different in terms of experience and personality" (p. 7). Key differences related to this coping skills model are as follows:

- Different coping skills to deal with different situations (e.g., internalizing vs. externalizing anger)
- Different stages of dealing with the problem (e.g., students whose parents have been divorced for several years and students whose parents are newly separated)
- Different attitudes about the problem situation
- Different values regarding the situation
- Different disclosure levels
- Different emotional response levels
- Different emotional responses to the situation
- Different cultural heritage
- Different socioeconomic levels
- Different levels of resiliency
- Mixed gender
- Different family situations
- Different birth order

The criteria must be somewhat wide ranging in order to get a good number of students and a good mix. Smead (1995) calls this concept "role balance." She emphasizes that

> excluding all members who have hit someone or thrown something from an anger management group might make it very difficult to find any members at all. The ultimate goal in the selection of members for an anger management group would be to have members who display the wide range of ways to express anger, balancing those members who hold their anger in with those members who act it out physically. (p. 5)

Potential Group Members' Willingness to Participate in a Psychoeducational Group

There are some clear indicators of who is most likely to benefit from groups. Riva et al. (2004), based on a review of the literature, suggested two areas of attention in selecting group members for counseling groups: interpersonal and intrapersonal characteristics. Piper and McCallum (1994) emphasized, as inclusion criteria, a moderate amount of social ability and frustration tolerance, and a commitment to changing interpersonal behaviors. For psychoeducational groups, this means choosing potential group members who can interact somewhat cooperatively within a group (e g., can disagree without hitting someone) and who express some willingness to learn and try out new behaviors.

Selection/Inclusion Grid

To ensure that all the information necessary to make a decision about the appropriateness of a potential group member for a group is included, I suggest creating a grid with four columns. Once the grid is created, questions to assess each area can be inserted into the screening interview so that all important areas are covered. Each goal, selection, and deselection criterion should have at least one question that assesses its content as well as some general questions about how the potential group member participates in groups. Table 3.1 in this chapter includes the grid.

The first column in the grid is Group Goals. They should be specific, including behavior, cognition, and affect. For an 8- to 10-session psychoeducational group, a total of three to five goals is realistic. For example, in an anger management group in the schools, typical goals might be (a) identify situations that make group members angry, (b) teach new ways of thinking in situations that make group members angry, and (c) practice new behaviors in situations that make group members angry.

The second column in the grid is Selection and Deselection Criteria Based on Group Goals. This column should include both criteria that you want group members to possess, and criteria that would indicate exclusion from the group. The American Counseling Association *Code of Ethics and Standards of Practice* (1997) states that group leaders "select group members whose needs and goals are compatible with the goals of the group, who will not impede the group process, and whose well-being will not be jeopardized by the group experience" (p. 2). Thus, it is important to select members who fit well within a group as well as deselect members who do not fit with the group, may be harmed by the group, or may harm others. It is important to think about the range of group members that can be accommodated in the group based on the goals, focus, interventions, and length. If the group is psychoeducational in nature, then those with more severe problems may not benefit or may interfere with other group members' learning.

Consequently, first, how well the group member's goals fit with the group goals must be assessed. Second, other criteria related to the specific group topic must be assessed. For example, in an anger management group, a selection criterion might be the ability to identify situations that make group members angry, and a deselection criterion might be using violence on a regular basis to express anger. To assess, you might ask in the interview, "How often do you get angry, and what do you typically do to express your anger?"

In an effort to assess how likely the group member will be to experiment with new behaviors, it is important to assess willingness to reflect on his or her interpersonal style and to make changes. Useful questions are as follows: "What have you tried to do that has worked?" "What hasn't worked?" "How have your family and relationships influenced your goal(s) and problem(s)?" To assess intrapersonal and interpersonal variables, group leaders may ask about potential members' relationships with others (e.g., "Describe how you typically act in a group of people"), their expectations that the group will help them (e.g., "How much do you expect this group to help you?"), and the ability to be self-reflective or psychologically minded (e.g., "Describe some things you would like to change about yourself but find it hard to").

Table 3.1   Outline for Screening Criteria Grid

Group Goals	Selection and Deselection Criteria Based on Group Goals	Questions to Ask During Screening Interview That Assess Specific Screening Criteria	How Well Does This Member Fit in This Group
(1a) Behavioral (1b) Cognitive (1c) Affective	(1) How well do their goals fit with group goals?	(1a) What would you like to get out of this group? (1b) What would you like to learn from this group? (1c) How would you like to be different at the end of this group? (1d) Related to the theme of our group, "___," what do you need to learn? (1e) What have you tried to do that has worked? What hasn't worked? (1f) How has your family and relationship history influenced your goal(s) and problem(s)?	(1a) Is goal(s) realistic? (1b) Does goal(s) fit with group goal?
	(2) Can this goal be worked on in this group?	(2a) How do you see yourself working on this goal in group? (2b) How would the group help you with this goal? (2c) What things could you do in this group to help you with this goal? (2d) What activities and interventions that we just discussed do you think might be helpful?	(2a) Do they have insight into the development of the problem and what the issues are?
	(3) Specific selection and deselection criteria related to the topic and theme of the group	(3) These questions relate to the severity of the problem and help define whether this group member's goal(s) can be met during this group.	(3a) Do they perceive the problem as something they can change, or over which they can have control?
	(4) General selection criteria for groups	(4a) How do you typically participate in groups? (4b) Have you ever been in a psychoeducational or counseling group before? Was it helpful? Why or why not? (4c) How comfortable are you talking about your feelings? (4d) How comfortable are you talking about this problem or issue?	(4a) Are they willing to participate? (4b) Do they typically participate in groups? (4c) Are they willing to try and help others and also to be helped by others?

(Continued)

Table 3.1 (Continued)

		(4e) What strengths would you bring to this group? (4f) What unique contribution would you make to this group? (4g) How could you help others with similar concerns? (4h) Where do you see yourself having the most trouble as we begin to talk about some of these issues?	(4d) Do their concerns seem like typical ones expressed by most group members? (4e) With whom could they connect? (4f) For whom could they serve as a role model?
	(5) Willingness to agree to the ground rules and procedures of this group	(5a) Are you willing to attend all group sessions on time? (5b) Are you willing to keep things confidential? (5c) Are you willing to self-disclose? (5d) Are you willing to try new behaviors?	

The third column in the grid is Questions to Ask During the Screening Interview That Assess Specific Selection Criteria. For each selection criterion, there should be least one question that assesses fit of group goals, selection or deselection criteria, commitment to ground rules, and general group participation criteria. For example, the group leader should describe the group goals and then ask members what their specific goal would be. How would they like to be different at the end of the group? What changes would they like to make?

The fourth column in the grid is called How Well Does the Member Fit in This Group? Group leaders must now take the information that they have learned and assess how well the group member might function in group. Questions in this column related to goals might include the following: Does the group member have a goal for the group? Is the goal realistic based on the goals of the group and the length of the group? Does the goal fit with group goals? Does the group member have insight into the development of the problem and what the issues are? Does he or she perceive the problem as something that can be changed—something over which he or she can have control? Has the group member been in counseling before, or is he or she currently? Is he or she willing to sign a consent form for you to speak with his or her current counselor?

In addition, other questions about potential group member fit include the following: Is he or she willing to participate? How willing is the group member to disclose information related to the topics to be discussed in this group? How does

- Conduct your lit review to identify specific goals, themes and topics, interventions, and selection and deselection criteria.
- Identify the needs of the population.
- Select goals based on the needs of the population and the type of group (psychoeducational or counseling).
- Decide on selection criteria related to the activities, focus, and structure of your group. Include inclusion and exclusion criteria.
- Outline your screening session in terms of what information you will provide, what questions you will ask to assess for appropriateness for group based on questions 4 and 5 (Table 3.1). Include questions that relate to the problem/issue focus of the group and behaviors that are needed to participate in the group.

Figure 3.1   Directions for Identifying Screening Interview Questions

he or she typically participate in groups? Is he or she willing to try and help others and also to be helped by others? Do his or her concerns seem like typical ones expressed by most group members?

It is also helpful at this time to think about how well each group member would fit with other group members. Smead (1995) suggested that group members should not be so different in terms of their situation or problem that they feel isolated or scapegoated by the group. Although it is impossible to prevent scapegoating, a conscious effort to select and link members based on their similarities (e.g., feelings, experiences) may help group members to make connections and increase cohesiveness among members. Each group member should have at least one other person in the group with whom he or she can initially connect on some similarity of experience, situation, or problem. In addition, it is helpful to consciously plan for each group member to be able to serve as a role model for someone else in the group to facilitation altruism and hope. Consequently, two questions should be included related to fit: (a) To which other group member(s) would this person be able to relate? and (b) For whom could this person serve as a role model in the group? Figure 3.1 in this chapter suggests an outline for organizing questions to be used in the screening interview.

Screening Interviews

As I conduct workshops about how to lead effective groups in schools, one of the comments I hear most often from practicing school counselors is, "So you really use a screening interview to select who will be in the group; I always thought it was just a formality." And then they go on to describe how hard it is to get students to participate in a group, so they accept everyone into the group who shows interest.

When I ask about the success rate of their groups, I often hear that their groups fall apart before the last session. In addition, my own experiences with leading groups suggest that although it may take a little longer to get groups started, effective screening is much more likely to ensure a successful and productive group.

I have led many eating disorders counseling groups, and screening was essential to choosing group members who would benefit from group. Often, when potential group members heard the list of topics, issues, and interventions that typically occurred in an eating disorders group, they decided that individual counseling would be a better option for them at this point in time. It was certainly better for them (and other group members) not to begin this group at all than to drop out and feel badly for themselves while also possibly creating feelings of guilt for the members who stayed in the group (who then wondered if they did something to make the person leave the group). Screening interviews also often helped decide whether a psychoeducational group or counseling group was most appropriate for a potential group member. It became apparent that if potential group members' goals were related to losing weight (when they were not overweight) rather than understanding the connection between their disordered eating behavior, their feelings, and their relationships, a psychoeducational group was more appropriate. Psychoeducational groups are focused on identifying potentially problematic thoughts and behaviors and replacing them with more appropriate thoughts and behaviors. Group members in psychoeducational groups for eating disorders (e.g., Weiss et al., 1985) begin to learn new ways of thinking and behaving but often struggle to implement these new strategies consistently. Counseling groups help group members to examine what gets in the way of implementing these strategies and improving self-esteem, depression, and relationships. For eating disorders groups with a counseling focus that I led, one clear criterion was that the group members needed to understand that what they were thinking and feeling and how they related to people influenced their eating-disordered behavior; thus, in order to change their eating-disordered behavior, they needed to examine and possibly adapt how they thought about, felt about, and related to people.

What follows is a list of suggestions on how to create an effective screening interview for psychoeducational groups and a tentative outline for screening interviews.

Goals of the Screening Interview

All students should be interviewed by the leader(s) of the group to assess their ability to participate in and benefit from group. An interview lasting 30 to 45 minutes should be sufficient. There are several goals for an effective screening interview. The first is to provide information to the potential group member. It is essential to give information about the goals of the group; general guidelines and ground rules (e.g., attendance, respect for others, confidentiality); and procedural information, such as length and time of sessions, group topics, activities, and typical interventions. The second goal is to assess how well a potential group member's needs, issues, and goals match group goals. The third goal is to assess a potential group member's interpersonal style and potential to succeed in this group. The interview allows the group leader(s) the chance to observe the potential group member's behavior to see if he or she can talk about the presenting problem and, to some extent, to see if he or she can follow directions and stay on task. The screening interview also gives the leader an opportunity to observe the potential group member's verbal and nonverbal behaviors, specifically level of comfort, eye contact, willingness to self-disclose, posture, tone of voice, and ease of communicating. The fourth goal is to address any questions or concerns that the potential group member might have about participation in this group. In addition, it is important to begin to establish a relationship with the potential group member to develop trust and the willingness to reflect on current behaviors and try out new behaviors. Meeting with potential group members individually also helps group leaders to begin to think about which members will be able to serve as role models for each other. Appendix J includes a sample screening interview that can be adapted for most psychoeducational groups.

Sequence and Format of the Screening Interview

The screening interview should be an interactive process where both parties have a chance to ask questions, gain information, and decide whether this particular group is a good fit for the potential group member. If the sequencing of topics is not attended to, a potential group member may be first bombarded with a great deal of information and then asked an overwhelming series of questions all in a row. It is also important to think about putting the potential group member at ease by beginning with the information that is the least anxiety provoking and gradually increasing the depth of the topics and questions as the interview progresses. To avoid a stilted interaction and encourage a collaborative discussion, the following sequence for the screening interview is suggested:

1. *Introduction of Group Leaders, Purpose of the Screening Interview, Procedural Details of the Group, and the Goals of the Group.* It is important to discuss briefly who the leaders are, their credentials, and the purpose of the screening interview. Procedural details such as when the group meets, where, and for how long are important to disclose at the beginning. There is no sense conducting a whole interview only to find out the person has a commitment at the time the group meets. Related to goals, it is useful to discuss what the group can and cannot do, what are appropriate individual goals, and when a potential member needs to decide on a goal.

2. *Potential Group Members' Goals for the Group.* Following from a general overview of group goals and typical individual goals, it is useful to discuss with potential group members what their goal(s) would be for this group. Background information should also be gathered in terms of how they perceive their problem, issue, or concern; what they think has influenced the development of the problem (e.g., family, work, situational factors); and what has worked and what has not worked related to the problem area or the theme of the group.

3. *Information About Procedures and Ground Rules for This Group.* Ground rules specific to the group should be discussed at this time, such as commitment to the group for a period of time, how and when new members join the group,

confidentiality, fees, no socializing outside of group, attendance, punctuality, respect for others, and willingness to self-disclose and take risks. It is important to frame group norms as necessary to keep group members safe and to learn from group, rather than merely as rules to be followed. If group members, particularly adolescents, hear "rules," it sometimes encourages rebellion.

4. *Commitment to Ground Rules.* It is important to ask if the potential group member can commit to these ground rules, particularly attendance, confidentiality, and willingness to participate. Depending on the group, leaders may ask group members to sign an informed consent as well.

5. *Information About How Groups Work and Specific Interventions and Activities to Be Used in This Group.* At this time, group leaders should provide information in terms of how groups work, roles of leaders and members, and specific interventions and activities that typically occur in this kind of group. Some discussion of group process is helpful, such as problem-solving, role-playing, and giving feedback.

6. *How Will This Potential Group Member Be Able to Work on His or Her Goals in This Group?* Based on the earlier discussion of typical themes, topics, activities, and interventions to be used in the group, potential group members should be asked how they will work on their goal. What activities and topics seem relevant? The emphasis during this discussion is on helping the group member connect to the group and develop an investment in participating in the sessions and trying out new behaviors.

7. *Questions Related to Specific Selection and Deselection Criteria for This Group.* At this time, it is important to ask for specific information that will help decide whether the potential group member is a good fit for this type of group. For example, in a grief group, it is important to not include people with a very recent death, so one criterion might be at least 3 months from the significant person's death. In a psychoeducational anger management group, one deselection criterion might be use of violence on a regular basis.

8. *Questions Related to How This Potential Group Member Would Act/Contribute as a Group Member.* This category of questions relates to potential group members' interpersonal style. It is important to assess how comfortable they feel discussing the topic of the group, how they deal with disagreements or feedback that is difficult to hear, and how they typically act in groups. Asking questions about what potential group members are thinking and feeling as they go through the interview also gives information about how they might act in group. Such questions include, How was this interview for them? How did they feel about disclosing to strangers? How did they feel about talking about their problems? Verbal responses to interview questions as well as nonverbal reactions will be important sources of information throughout the interview.

9. *Any Questions or Concerns the Potential Group Member Has About Being in This Group.* Potential group members often have misperceptions about how groups operate or what happens in group. It is helpful to ask if they have any questions or concerns and to address them directly, because misperceptions may negatively influence their participation in group.

10. *Closing of Screening Interview.* As the screening interview ends, it is helpful to clearly describe to the potential group member the process of what will happen. If he or she is a good candidate for this group, the group leader might inform the member of this now. If other things need to happen first (further assessment, another interview, co-leaders must meet, parental consent), the potential group member should be informed of what needs to happen and the time line of when this will occur. Referrals should be made for other counseling interventions if the group is not a viable option.

Measures to Assess Group Member Fit

Several measures have been developed that may be useful in selecting group members who will be successful in psychoeducational groups. They fall into two categories: attitudes toward group and group leadership, and group member fit for group. A brief description of relevant measures follow.

Group Therapy Survey (GTS) (Slocum, 1987). The GTS is the only measure that assesses misperceptions about group therapy with some empirical support. The GTS has 25 items rated on a 4-point scale from *strongly agree* to *strongly disagree.* Slocum (1987) suggested that the items were based on three categories of unfavorable expectations: It Is Unpredictable, It Is Not as Effective as Individual Therapy, and It Can Be Detrimental. Internal consistency of the GTS was reported as .59 using a sample of 96 students with a mean age of 20.2 years (range 16 to 50 years). Later, Broday, Gieda, Mullison, and Sedlacek (1989) conducted a factor analysis using a sample of 147 students with an mean age of 18 and suggested three slightly different factors. They used only 15 items that together predicted 41% of the variance with a Cronbach's alpha of .59 (individual variances predicted are indicated in the parentheses): Positive Attitudes (7 items, 20%); Self-Disclosure Fears (4 items, 13%); and Misconceptions (4 items, 8%).

Recently, Carter et al. (2001) revised the GTS by replacing the words "group therapy" with "group counseling," modifying the wording of a few items, and using a 5-point scale from *strongly agree* to *strongly disagree,* with high scores indicating more positive attitudes toward counseling. A factor analysis of the Group Therapy Survey-Revised (GTS-R) with a sample of 212 students with a mean age of 20 years (range from 17 to 50 years) indicated three subscales using 20 of the 25 items that together predicted 41% of the total variance (individual variance predicted in parentheses): Efficacy (27%), Myths (8%), and Vulnerability (6%). The internal consistency of the overall GTS-R as measured by Cronbach's alpha was .88, and for the individual subscales, .78 for Efficacy, .77 for Myths, and .75 for Vulnerability. The 2-week test-retest reliability coefficient for the overall GTS-R was .79 for a different sample of 93 college students with a mean age of 23 years. Reported means were 3.66 for Efficacy, 3.69 for Myths, and 3.43 for Vulnerability, suggesting neutral or positive attitudes toward group counseling from college students who presented for counseling.

The GTS is one of the few group measures that has been examined with regard to cultural influences. Leong, Wagner, and Kim (1995) found that attitudes toward group counseling were predicted by level of acculturation for Asian American students. Using a sample of 134 Asian American college students (95% between 21 and 24 years old), a hierarchial multiple regression analysis indicated that the integration subscale of the Acculturation Attitudes Scale (Kim, 1988) positively and significantly correlated with Positive Attitudes subscale ($r = .35$, $p < .01$).

The revised version of the GTS may be useful with adolescents, particularly those who might have a negative perception of groups and/or counseling. Information from this measure may help identify areas of misperception that need to be clarified with potential group members.

Expectations About Counseling (EAC) (Tinsley, Workman, & Kass, 1980). The Expectations About Counseling measure "was developed for use in assessments of expectancies for specific, theoretically relevant dimensions of counseling behavior" (Subich, 1983, p. 422). The short form consists of 60 items rated on a 7-point scale from *definitely do not expect this to be true* to *definitely expect this to be true*. The scale measures five categories: client attitudes and behavior (responsibility, openness, motivation); counselor attitudes and behavior (acceptance, confrontation, genuineness, directiveness, empathy, self-disclosure, nurturance); counselor characteristics (attractiveness, expertise, trustworthiness, tolerance); characteristics of process (immediacy, concreteness); and quality of outcome (outcome). The EAC may also be useful in identifying negative attitudes toward counseling and/or groups in adolescents.

The Group Assessment Form (GAF) (Lynn, 1994). The GAF was designed specifically for children and adolescents to measure social competence based on information collected from the adolescent and parent. It assesses motivation for group, appropriateness for group, and an outline of recommended treatment goals and techniques for group.

Readiness for Group (RFG) (DeLucia-Waack, 2006). Based on current literature that suggests that several factors predict which group members are most likely to benefit from group, a short measure designed to be completed after a screening interview was developed to assess whether potential group members have the motivation and skills to participate in a counseling or psychoeducational group. The model for this measure is the Group Psychotherapy Evaluation Scale (Kew, 1975), which used cut-offs to predict which group members were better suited for group therapy. The RFG is completed by the group leader(s) after a screening interview and assesses the following categories: amount and quality of communication; capacity for change; willingness to discuss problem; commitment to change; identification, fit, and specificity of goals; ability to serve as a role model for others; potential for connection with others; level of anxiety; amount of interviewer activity; and interviewer connection with potential group member. After an initial interview, potential group members are rated on a 5-point scale ranging from 0 = *low emphasis* to 4 = *high emphasis*. These items are based on the literature that predicts dropouts from group in adult groups.

Preparation Sessions

...ion

...nt expectations, defines group rules, ...les and skills needed for effective group ...lingame, Fuhriman, & Johnson, 2001, ...own to be related to the development of ...ction, decreased risk of dropping out, ...nar & Kaul, 1994).

...bout what other members will be like, ...em, and how they will benefit from ...unrealistic expectations of the groups ..., Crandall, 1985; Yalom, 1995). Research has suggested that preparing potential group members, using a preparation session, helps acclimate members to how groups work and allows both group leaders and members an opportunity to assess members' fit for a particular group. Preparation sessions typically include information about how groups work, roles of group leaders and members, topics and typical activities, and a chance to practice typical behaviors. Group members have a chance to experience what it is like to interact with other group members around the themes and topics of the group. Group leaders also are able to assess the following for each group member: willingness to participate, willingness and ability to disclose thoughts and feelings, willingness and ability to follow directions and answer questions, potential conflicts between group members, and who can serve as role models and connections for each group member. During a preparation session, the potential group member's ability to fit in with others can be assessed. Members may sometimes act very differently with one or both group leaders than they do with several potential group members. It is important that group members be selected so that the group is diverse, yet members should be connected with one another. Group members should also be selected based upon their willingness to work with others and what they can bring to group. In addition to specific procedural information about the group, it is important to provide potential group members with information about how groups work in terms of the process.

From a practical standpoint, leaders can use preparation techniques to convey procedural information and help group members gain some understanding about how groups function. There is no standard method of preparation, yet Couch (1995) suggested a four-step model: identify the clients' needs, expectations, and commitment; challenge any myths and misconceptions; convey information; and screen the person for group fit.

The importance of using preparation sessions as an instrument for both the group leaders and the potential group member to decide whether the group member is ready to be in group became clear to me when supervising a college eating disorders group. The leaders of the group came to me saying they were having trouble keeping members in the group, and the dropout rate was affecting the morale of those members who chose to stay. A student of mine was conducting a dissertation on the effectiveness of different types of preparation sessions for training groups, and so we decided to use a variation of it with potential members of the eating disorders group in an effort to orient them to the themes, topics, and typical interventions used in this type of group. The anecdotal results were pretty impressive. Based on the preparation sessions, the group leaders did not deselect any members. However, about half of the potential group members that participated in a preparation session then decided that they were not ready to join the group; most elected to begin or continue in individual counseling. Even more astounding was the fact that none of the group members who chose to participate in the eating disorders group after completing a preparation session then dropped out of the group. The preparation session seems to have had the effect of helping group members decide whether they were ready to be in a group or not before they began the group, thus greatly eliminating the number of dropouts.

Sequence and Format of the Preparation Session

The preparation session occurs after potential group members have had a pre-group screening interview and have met the initial criteria to participate in the group, but prior to the first session. It allows them to gain a better understanding of how the group will work, as well as gives them an opportunity to practice some of the typical group behaviors. In addition, the preparation session allows group leaders to see how group members interact with each other. It also serves the serendipitous purpose of allowing leaders to maintain contact with group members but not actually begin group. This is especially important when selection of members is taking awhile and group leaders want to continue interaction with group members in order to maintain their interest without starting the group with a small number of members.

There is general consensus about the format and content of the preparation session. A format that includes cognitive, vicarious, and experiential methods in an effort to address the different learning styles of group members is recommended. The content should include group member and group leader roles, how groups typically function, and skill training. Bowman (Bowman & DeLucia, 1993; Bowman & DeLucia-Waack, 1996) developed a preparation session for groups that has been modified for use with specific psychoeducational groups. An example of the outline for the session, handouts, and experiential activities can be found in Appendix K. Cummins (1996) provides an example of how to adapt Bowman's preparation session for a specific type of group, an eating disorders group.

The format is flexible and can be used with a small group of potential group members, two potential group members, or one potential group member. Ideally, before a group begins and when a substantial number of potential group members have been identified, group leaders can conduct a preparation session that allows them to observe individual group member behavior and interactions between potential group members. If the group has already begun or a group preparation session has already taken place, two potential group members could participate in the preparation session together. Preparing two members at the same time would allow them to interact with the group leaders and also with each other, hopefully promoting connections and cohesiveness. One potential group member could also be prepared by one group leader. This would allow the potential group member to meet and interact with both group leaders if only one of the group leaders had conducted the screening interview.

The preparation session is designed to take approximately an hour and consists of cognitive, vicarious, and experiential components. The cognitive component is a written handout that describes what a psychoeducational group is, the roles of group leaders and members, goals for psychoeducational groups, specific skills to be used in psychoeducational groups, and typical topics and interventions for this type of psychoeducational group. The vicarious component consists of viewing 10 to 15 minutes of a videotape of a typical psychoeducational group. Potential group members are then asked to identify instances of the specific skills that they had read about earlier in the handout, and how other group members responded to the use of these skills. The Smead (1996) videotape is a good example of an anger management group for elementary school students. Bowman and DeLucia-Waack (1996) suggested using a segment from popular films such as *The Breakfast Club, Twelve Angry Men,* or *Lord of the Flies.* Finally, in the experiential component, potential group members are asked to participate in a series of short role-plays to practice skills identified in the handout and viewed on the videotape. In the handout, videotape, and experiential activities, behaviors that are typically focused on for psychoeducational groups for children and adolescents are self-disclosure, feedback, challenging, and role-plays.

If conducting the preparation session with multiple potential group members, they should pair up with each other to practice the skills. This allows them to practice new behaviors and also to begin to make connections with other group members, and it allows group leaders a chance to observe between-member interactions. If two potential group members are participating in the preparation session together, they would also pair up to role-play the skills. If the preparation session is being conducted with one group leader and one potential group member, then they would role-play the skills together.

Summary

Once decisions have been made about the goals and activities in a psychoeducational group, the process of selecting and preparing potential group members can begin. Goals and focus of the group determine selection (and deselection) criteria. This chapter suggested outlines for pregroup screening interviews and preparation sessions in an effort to choose group members who will be successful in psychoeducational groups.

Suggested Training Activities

1. Devise Selection Criteria and a Screening Interview

- Create a grid that includes
  - Goals for your group
  - Selection criteria related to who would benefit and not benefit from the group

> – Questions to be asked in the interview to assess for selection (and deselection) criteria
>
> – Any instruments you might use to assess selection criteria

- Outline a screening interview for your psychoeducational group.
- Complete a planning sheet for your screening interview identifying what each co-leader will do.
- Practice the screening interview with at least two potential group members. Videotape your interviews.
- Complete the Readiness for Group measure on each potential group member to assess his or her readiness to participate in this particular psychoeducational group.
- Using the CLINICKING section of the Co-Facilitating Inventory (Pfeiffer & Jones, 1975) and the outline for supervision suggested in the previous chapter (Reporting, Reflection, Integration, Planning, Evaluation), view the videotapes of the screening sessions and assess the effectiveness of the outline for the screening interview.
- Rewrite guidelines for the pregroup interview based on the evaluation to increase effectiveness.

2. Develop a Preparation Session

Adapt the preparation session in Appendix K to the type of psychoeducational group you plan to lead. Include a description of goals, themes and topics, and specific interventions. Adapt the experiential activities to your specific group.

- Complete a planning sheet for the preparation session interview identifying what each co-leader will do.
- Practice the preparation session with at least four potential group members. Videotape the session.
- Complete the Readiness for Group measure on each potential group member to assess his or her readiness to participate in this particular psychoeducational group.
- Using the CLINICKING section of the Co-Facilitating Inventory (Pfeiffer & Jones, 1975), the processing sheet, and the outline for supervision suggested in the previous chapter (Reporting, Reflection, Integration, Planning, Evaluation), view the videotapes of the screening sessions and assess the effectiveness of the outline for the screening interview.

CHAPTER 4

Group Leadership Skills for Psychoeducational Groups

When group leaders employ a given intervention during the course of a group session, there is the implicit assumption that their behavior will have a positive impact on individual members and/or on the group processes and outcomes. There is a significant amount of research on the development of therapeutic factors in groups and their relationship to group effectiveness. Following from the theoretical question of what combination of therapeutic factors facilitates effective group work is the logical extension, What leadership behaviors facilitate the creation of therapeutic factors that in turn facilitate client change and growth? Riva et al. (2004) suggested that "an essential component related to the effectiveness of therapeutic groups is the leadership. The leader plays a vital role both in the dynamics of the group and the outcomes of its members" (p. 37). Group dynamics and outcomes are influenced by such factors as the leader's interaction style, personal characteristics, and attitudes. For example, researchers have found that leaders who are less controlling, who exhibit warmth/caring, and who set and reinforce clear norms are more likely to have cohesive groups (Antonuccio, Davis, Lewinson, & Breckenridge, 1987; MacKenzie, Dies, Coche, Rutan, & Stone, 1987; Phillips & Zastowny, 1988). Increased cohesiveness, in turn, has been found to be positively related to a variety of group treatment outcomes (Kivlighan & Lilly, 1997; Marziali, Munroe-Blum, & McCleary, 1997).

The term *group leader,* in contrast to *group counselor,* seems to be much more appropriate for psychoeducational groups. The role and focus of interventions are more directed at facilitating communication and interaction between members to promote learning, rather than providing individual counseling to one group member at a time. Moreover, there are differences in focus between counseling and psychoeducational groups, and differences between groups for adults and groups for children and adolescents. Psychoeducational groups present the unique challenge of balancing teaching skills with processing and facilitation skills. Psychoeducational group leaders present new information and direct activities to teach and practice skills, but at the same time must be continually helping group members to make sense of what they are doing and how to apply it in their outside lives. There is much more organization needed in terms of content and structure in psychoeducational groups than counseling groups, but there is also a large demand for in-group processing of events and activities.

This chapter will first present a framework for conceptualizing the application of group leadership skills followed by a discussion of specific skills. Therapeutic factors and specific leadership behaviors will be discussed with regard to psychoeducational groups for children and adolescents. Overarching leadership behaviors will be discussed, and in later chapters, specific leadership interventions will be identified as they relate to the tasks of a particular stage. The training needed to lead effective psychoeducational groups will be discussed as well as specific measures that can be used to assess group leadership behaviors.

Specific Skills

In a classic study of group leadership, Lieberman, Yalom, and Miles (1973) identified four categories of effective group leadership behaviors—Emotional Stimulation, Caring, Meaning Attribution, and Executive Function—and their relationship to successful group outcome.

> Caring and meaning attribution had a linear relationship to positive outcome: the higher the caring and the higher the meaning attribution, the higher the positive outcome. Emotional stimulation and executive function had a curvilinear relationship to outcome—the rule of the golden mean: too much of or too little of this leader behavior resulted in lower positive outcome. (Yalom, 1995, p. 498)

What does Yalom mean by these terms specifically? Caring is conveyed by leader warmth, empathy, support, positive regard, acceptance, genuineness, concern, affection, and support. It is also important to remember that group members receive care from other members as well, and this, too, may influence outcome. Meaning attributions are those interventions that help group members make sense of what happens in group and learn from it. Processing of events and activities that happen in groups are a key part of meaning attribution because they ask group members to identify and apply what they have learned. "Processing can provide members with additional learning about themselves and other members of the group. Through processing, members may also develop a plan of action for transferring this learning to their lives outside of group" (Kees & Jacobs, 1990, p. 23). Executive functions are those behaviors that provide structure to the group, such as creating norms and roles, focusing on goals, setting limits, managing time, pacing, and suggesting procedures. Emotional stimulation behaviors are those that help group members make a personal connection to what is happening in the group, usually by connecting feelings and behavior, which then usually results in meaning attribution. Such behaviors in this category might include challenging, confronting, discussing here-and-now events, role-playing, and self-disclosing.

Logically, these leadership behaviors make sense and are particularly relevant to psychoeducational groups. Group members feel safest when there is a moderate amount of structure and they feel cared about. In addition, they are going to learn the most if there is a connection between thoughts, feelings, and behavior, and they generalize what they have learned in group to their outside lives. For example, in an effort to display all four of these types of behaviors within a first session, a group leader may ask students to identify out loud the animal they most resemble today in group. To convey structure, the group leader then informs the members that they will be invited to talk about this animal later on but that participation will be voluntary. The leader may then ask some questions to promote emotional stimulation: What does this animal do in new situations? How does this animal explore new situations? How does what the animal does resemble how you might be feeling today during this first session of group? How do you typically explore and feel in new situations? As a follow-up to these questions and to help generate meaning attribution, the group leader may ask additional questions: What did you learn from how your animal explores new situations? What would you like to do differently in group today? Is there another animal that someone mentioned that you would like to be more like? What behavior from this animal could you try out today in group? Which animal do you admire? How would you like to be more like that animal? Can you tell another group member what you like about his or her animal? Based on other people's animals, who might you ask for help at some point during this group?

Each set of leadership behaviors will be discussed in relation to psychoeducational groups with children and adolescents. In addition, Morran, Stockton, and Whittingham (2004) conducted a review of the literature on group leadership behaviors and concluded that there were 10 sets of effective leadership behaviors. These will be included in the following discussion. Table 4.1 in this chapter includes a comprehensive list of group leadership skills identified in the literature.

Caring

The focus of the interventions in the Caring category is on helping group members to feel safe, cared about, and accepted so that they can make the most of their group experience by participating, helping others, taking risks, giving feedback, and trying out new behaviors. If caring is genuine, then there can never be enough caring in a group. Members should feel free to be themselves, to share both positive and negative feelings, and to make mistakes. The goal is to help members feel that they are a valued part of the group, and that sharing of their experiences and perceptions is valued and desired by the group to promote learning and growth.

One common misperception in groups is that if people care, they will not say anything that would hurt a group member's feelings or make him or her uncomfortable. The dilemma inherent in this misperception is that sometimes people don't know when they have made a mistake, and group feedback is vital to learning new ways of interacting. Thus, a goal for all psychoeducational groups is to learn to give constructive feedback, both positive and negative, in a way that the person can hear and respond to.

Table 4.1   Specific Group Leadership Skills

Caring	Executive Functioning	Emotional Stimulation	Meaning Attribution
Active Listening	Blocking	Drawing Out	Assessing Strength and Weakness
Clarifying Thoughts	Cutting Off	Facilitating Expression of Feeling	Clarifying Goals
Clarifying Feelings	Focusing	Facilitating Communication Between Members	Clarifying Meaning
Communicate Respect	Protecting	Facilitating Expression of Thoughts	Confronting
Communicate Caring		Feedback	Discussion of Here-and-Now Events
Linking Members		Making Process Comments	Explaining Behavior Patterns With a Theoretical Framework
Supporting		Questioning	Interpreting
		Reflecting Content	Out of Group
		Reflecting Feelings	Modeling
		Reflecting Process	Processing
		Self-Disclosing Feelings	Role-Playing
		Self-Disclosing Thoughts	Self-Disclosing Behavior Change
		Self-Disclosing Behavior	Strategies
		Change Strategies	Suggesting New Behaviors or Ways of Thinking
		Suggesting New Behaviors or Ways of Thinking	Summarizing

Several types of group leadership behaviors have been identified consistently as correlated with client progress and change. Dies (1994) concluded, based on a review of 135 studies, that group members benefited from positive leader behavior such as warmth, support, and genuine interest. In addition, he suggested that "as leaders become more actively negative, they increase the possibility that participants will not only be dissatisfied, but potentially harmed by the group experience" (p. 139). In addition, researchers have found that leaders who are less controlling, who exhibit warmth/caring, and who set and reinforce clear norms are more likely to have cohesive groups. Increased cohesiveness, in turn, has been found to be positively related to a variety of group treatment outcomes. It is particularly important in psychoeducational groups for children and adolescents to make sure that group members feel cared about and supported by the adults in the group, as well as connected to the other group members. Because psychoeducational groups by nature are designed to teach skills and prevent problems, rather than ameliorate them, group members may be less motivated by their interpersonal pain to participate. Thus, it is important to establish group connection and cohesiveness in order for members to attend and participate in psychoeducational groups.

Executive Function

Group leadership behaviors in the Executive Function category create structure within the group so that group members feel safe to share, take risks, and participate fully in the group. A certain level of structure is necessary, particularly in early group sessions, to encourage self-disclosure and self-exploration (Burlingame & Fuhriman, 1994; Dies, 1994; Gazda et al., 2001; Stockton, Rohde, & Haughey, 1992). A high level of structure as groups begin and end, particularly in psychoeducational groups, is needed. Group leaders provide more structure in the initial sessions to establish group norms such as confidentiality, attendance, and participation, and to clarify both group and individual goals. Most of the first session of the psychoeducational group, and sometimes part of the second session, needs to focus specifically on introductions, establishment of ground rules, and group and individual goals. As group members learn how groups work and how to participate effectively, less structure from the leader(s) is needed. More structure is also needed as the group ends to ensure that group members have applied what they have learned in group to their real lives, and also have some insight into what they have learned and how they will apply it, how they have learned it, and how other group members have helped them.

Creating Group Norms. The establishment of group norms to create safety and structure within the group begins with pregroup screening and preparation and continues in the first group session. It is important to frame the creation of ground rules as necessary for group members to feel safe, try out new behaviors, and give feedback within the group. It probably makes the most sense to describe these guidelines as group norms, rather than as rules. Rules have a negative connotation, one that children and adolescents sometimes may want to break out of rebellion. Using some creativity as a framework within which to define the group guidelines, such as the analogy to swimming pool rules, helps to emphasize the safety aspect. Group leaders must develop a clear sense of what guidelines are necessary for the group (e.g, confidentiality, attendance, participation) and have clear examples of how this works for the group. However, in order to help the group members feel ownership and internalize the group norms, it makes sense to begin a discussion about group norms the open-ended way by asking questions such as, What do we need to do to keep this group safe? What do we need to do as members to help each other learn new behaviors? What needs to happen in order for you to feel safe?

Protecting. Protecting can sometimes be indirect and might include member selection/exclusion procedures, the establishment of appropriate group norms, or the modeling of caring for group members. More direct protecting interventions might take the form of intervening to stop a member who is self-disclosing too much or at a level that is significantly more intimate than the rest of the members.

Blocking. Morran et al. (2004) highlighted 10 specific group interventions with research and clinical support. The first category of interventions they identified was protecting group members and promoting safety, which includes protecting, blocking, and supporting. These interventions are typically most useful in the leader's efforts to provide a group climate that is conducive to trust, openness, and cohesion. Research has indicated that members who are dissatisfied with their group experience often implicate the group leader for negligence in providing adequate protection.

Blocking is a specific type of protection that is used to stop a member from storytelling; rambling; or inappropriately probing, gossiping, or invading the privacy of others. Children and adolescents often begin to tell stories that, although interesting, are not directly related to the group, and so because of time constraints, it is necessary to stop further discussion. For example, when asked in the beginning to go around and identify a situation with which each student had difficulty coping over the weekend, a student may begin to identify an incident that happened in the movies and then delve into a detailed discussion of the movie's plot. At that point, the group leader may gently ask the group member to hold the details of the movie until the end of group, and if there is time, the group member may share about the movie at that point, or suggest that because that discussion is not something that needs to stay confidential, the group members may talk about it as they return to their class.

Research suggests that group members frequently attribute their damaging experiences to undue confrontation, criticism, and pressure to self-disclose by other members. Thus, it is essential that group leaders use blocking to protect group members from hostile or angry attacks, or feedback that is not useful. Blocking often occurs and then leads into other interventions, such as conflict resolution. Because group members in the schools often know each other from other situations, they may sometimes bring this information into group. For example, a group member may say to another group member, "I don't like you, so I'm not going to talk to you." At this point, the group leader may intervene by saying, "I'm not sure that that feedback is very helpful. Could you be more specific about why you don't want to talk to this person?" The group member may then respond, "I'm not going to listen to you because you are always making fun of me in the lunchroom." The group leader may focus on the positive by asking about the times in this group that the group member has listened to the other group member. Once some positive interactions between the two group members have been identified, then a discussion can occur about whether the group member feels like he or she has been made fun of by the other group member during the group. If so, a discussion can occur about how they can interact differently. If the incidents have only occurred outside the group, a discussion can occur focusing on how they might change those interactions.

Focusing. Focusing interventions are those interventions that direct, or redirect, the group to the topic or the activity for that particular group session. Focusing interventions are often used as part of the opening of the group to introduce the topic of the group for that session. Group leaders often also gently remind group members of the task or the topic when they begin to get off on tangents or provide details that are not relevant to the activity. Focusing interventions are also used as part of the processing of the group as a reminder of what has happened in group that session, and as a lead-in to asking group members what they have learned and how they will apply it.

Emotional Stimulation

The Emotional Stimulation category of group leadership behaviors emphasizes the identification and exploration of feelings to help group members learn and try out new behaviors. The second category of interventions (Morran et al., 2004), energizing and involving group members, includes drawing out, modeling, linking, processing, interpreting, self-disclosing, and feedback. These interventions are most often used to stimulate emotions, increase member participation, and enhance interpersonal learning.

Drawing Out. Interventions to draw members out include leaders directly asking members to participate or to provide more information about a specific comment, event, or reaction. Drawing out occurs when the leader directly invites comments or involvement to encourage participation from members who find it hard to share with others or with those who share on a surface level but avoid deeper issues. Leaders should encourage participation while still allowing members to choose their own level of sharing.

Drawing out is particularly important in the early stages of group to establish the norm that all members are encouraged to participate. When encouraging participation in general, it is helpful to begin by asking the whole group to comment, "What are people's reactions to this?" followed by an invitation to those people who have yet to speak: "We haven't heard from several people yet. Is there anyone who would like to comment?" If there is one group member who is silent and it is important to hear from that member, or if he or she seems to be having a nonverbal reaction to what is happening, the group leader may want to invite that person specifically to comment. Both the process and the content are important when inviting members to comment. It is helpful to observe who speaks first and who needs an invitation to speak, and also sometimes to ask members what prevented them from sharing their reactions initially.

Modeling. Modeling occurs when leaders demonstrate skills, attitudes, and other characteristics they hope to engender within group members, such as respect and caring for others, appropriate self-disclosure, giving and receiving of feedback, and openness. Many group theorists suggest that modeling is a common factor of nearly all interventions because members naturally observe group leaders and other members, and tend to imitate what they see demonstrated. Research has found that behaviors displayed by the therapist, including interpersonal behaviors, feedback delivery and acceptance, and here-and-now communications, lead to increases in those same behaviors by group members (Dies, 1994). Campbell and Brigman (2005) emphasized the importance of modeling as a key component of the working part of each group session in their psychoeducational groups to improve student achievement and success. They suggest using real situations for group members to practice new strategies in role-plays so that both group leaders and group members can serve as models. Theory suggests that group co-leaders should model appropriate interaction between themselves, particularly resolving disagreements or compromising, so that group members have positive role models for the skills (Riva et al., 2004).

Linking. Linking connects what one group member is saying or doing with the concerns of one or more other members. Linking has been shown to be particularly useful in promoting member interaction, cohesion, trust, and universality among group members. During the selection process and initial stages of group, leaders should think purposefully about how and what they will use to link group members together.

Self-Disclosure. Leader self-disclosure is an intervention whereby therapists reveal their personal feelings, experiences, or here-and-now reactions to group members. As a general rule, leaders should self-disclose only when the information or reaction is directly related to what is happening in the group, when doing so models a behavior for members, or where a direct benefit to the group is anticipated. For example, a leader may comment that he or she feels particularly close to a group member after the member just shared something that was very personal.

Encouraging Feedback. The goal of feedback that occurs between members of the group is to allow members to better understand themselves and what is necessary for personal growth and behavior change, specifically as it relates to positive social interactions. Feedback occurs when both members and leaders share their personal reactions and insights about each other and critical events in the group.

Morran, Stockton, Cline, and Teed (1998) found that corrective feedback from leaders and other group members may be extremely important in that it provides a different perspective, but is also generally hard for group members to hear. During later sessions, a balance of positive and corrective feedback is more useful. In addition, both group member and leader feedback is useful (Flowers, 1979; Morran et al., 1998; Morran, Robison, & Stockton, 1985). Feedback is most effective if negative feedback is followed by, or sandwiched between, positive comments. For example, "Thank you so much for sharing your comments. It took a risk to do so. You chose your words carefully and were very specific. Next time, could you please use eye contact to make your message even stronger?"

Feedback is also most effective when it is specific and behavioral rather than global and emotional (Morran, Stockton, & Harris, 1991). For example, "I don't like you" is not as constructive and useful as, "When I was talking, you were carrying on a conversation with someone else. That hurt my feelings. Please be considerate and listen when I talk. Thank you."

Stage of group appears to influence what kind of feedback is needed and the probability of it being well-received (Morran et al., 1998). In initial sessions, positive feedback should be emphasized, whereas in later stages, there should be a balance of both positive and constructive feedback. In the early stages, leaders should model giving both positive and constructive feedback. In later stages, leaders should encourage both positive and constructive feedback from members, because feedback from other group members is generally more accepted than feedback from leaders (Morran et al., 1985).

Meaning Attribution

The focus of group leadership behaviors in the Meaning Attribution category of group leadership behaviors is on the explanation, clarification, interpretation, and provision of concepts to help members understand thoughts, feelings, and behaviors.

Interpreting. Interpreting involves offering possible explanations for events, behaviors, thoughts, and feelings at a deeper level to be considered as part of the change process. Members typically experience interactions that provide the opportunity to learn more about themselves. Such insight, however, may be difficult for the member to acquire without some cognitive framework being provided by the leader. In such situations, the leader can assist group members by providing a tentative interpretation that can be discussed and considered in the group. Research suggests that leader interpretations help members to integrate complex personal and group-related events, thus encouraging their investment in the group experience, and facilitate generalization from group experiences to personal experiences outside the group. Interpretations about the client's impact on the environment and his or her patterns of behavior were most associated with client change.

Processing of Critical Events and Activities. Processing as an intervention occurs when the group leader and members capitalize on significant happenings to help members reflect on the meaning of their experience; better understand their own thoughts, feelings, and actions; and generalize what is learned to situations outside of the group. Simply experiencing events in group is not sufficient for growth but must be augmented by processing that provides a framework for retaining, integrating, and generalizing the experience. Research findings have identified a positive relationship between higher levels of group processing and greater outcome gains related to both group productivity and individual member achievement, suggesting that processing should go beyond emotional insight and also focus on cognitive dynamics or meaning attributions to help members frame and understand their emotional experiences. Effective processing of critical incidents requires that members engage in a process of sharing and exploring among themselves to make sense of what happened, establish what they have learned from the incident, and begin to plan and practice new behaviors to be used outside of group sessions.

One of the most common mistakes group leaders make is to not process an activity. Indeed, most descriptions of group exercises and activities do not include the direction or guidance necessary for effective processing of activities (Kees & Jacobs, 1990). Processing can be described as

> capitalizing on significant happenings in the here-and-now interactions of the group to help members reflect on the meaning of their experience; better understand their own thoughts, feelings and actions; and generalize what is learned to their life outside of the group. (Stockton et al., 2000, p. 345)

Effective processing requires that members engage in a process of sharing and exploring among themselves to make sense of what happened, establish what they have learned from the incident, and begin to plan and practice new behaviors to be used outside of group sessions. Because of the importance of this skill, specific guidelines for processing key events and activities are detailed in Chapter 8.

Therapeutic Factors

Yalom (1995) suggested that 12 therapeutic factors form the basis for what makes groups effective. The 12 factors are altruism, catharsis, cohesiveness, existentiality, family re-enactment, guidance, hope, identification, interpersonal learning input (feedback), interpersonal learning output (new behavior), self-understanding, and universality. These inconsistencies may be due to differences in the types of groups, populations, and/or methods used to assess therapeutic factors. In an effort to make sense of the inconsistent results, Kivlighan and Holmes (2004) used a cluster analysis of studies that rated the importance of therapeutic factors. Four clusters emerged from the analysis based on the therapeutic factors that were highest and lowest in each cluster. Cluster 1, affective insight groups, rated acceptance, catharsis, interpersonal learning, and self-understanding as the most valued factors. These groups also rated both guidance and vicarious learning as relatively unimportant. Cluster 2, affective support groups, rated acceptance, installation of hope, and universality as the most important group factors. Similar to Cluster 1, members of the groups in Cluster 2 rated guidance and vicarious learning as relatively unimportant. Cluster 3, cognitive support groups, rated vicarious learning and guidance as highly valued, whereas self-understanding was rated much lower. Cluster 4, cognitive insight groups, rated interpersonal learning, self-understanding, and vicarious learning as the most valued therapeutic factors. Two clusters, cognitive support groups and cognitive insight groups, tended to most closely resemble psychoeducational groups, emphasizing the importance of vicarious learning, guidance, interpersonal learning, and self-understanding. Shechtman et al. (1997) examined therapeutic factors reported for adolescents in counseling and psychoeducational groups, and found significant differences based on a type of group. For the psychoeducational group, interpersonal learning, catharsis, and socializing techniques were most valued. Table 4.2 in this chapter includes a model for conceptualizing therapeutic factors, Yalom's four categories of group leadership behavior, and group stages.

Table 4.2   Therapeutic Factors by Group Stage and Yalom's Leadership Behaviors

Leadership Category	Therapeutic Factors (Yalom, 1975)	Definition	Group Stage
Caring	Instillation of Hope	Member recognizes other members' improvement and that group can be helpful; Member develops optimism	Initial
Caring	Universality	Member perceives that other members share similar feelings or problems	Initial
Caring	Cohesiveness	Feeling of togetherness provided and experienced by the group	Initial
Caring	Altruism	Member gains a positive view of himself or herself through extending help to others in group	Middle
Meaning Attribution	Imparting Information	Advice giving by therapist or fellow members	Middle
Meaning Attribution	Interpersonal Learning-Input	Member gains personal insight through other members sharing their perceptions of the member	Middle
Meaning Attribution	Interpersonal Learning-Input	Group provides members with an environment that allows the members to interact in a more adaptive manner	Middle
Meaning Attribution	Existential Factors	Member ultimately accepts that he or she has to take responsibility for his or her own life	Middle
Emotional Stimulation	Corrective Recapitulation of Primary Family Group	Member experiences the opportunity to reenact some critical familial incident with members of the group in a corrective manner	Middle
Emotional Stimulation	Development of Socializing Techniques	Group provides members with an environment that allows the members to interact in a more adaptive manner	Middle
Emotional Stimulation	Catharsis	Member releases feelings about past or here-and-now experiences; this release leads to member feeling better	Middle
Emotional Stimulation	Imitative	Member learns through the observation of others' learning experiences	Middle

Training

Research suggests that there are several differences between novice and expert group leaders and how they think about and approach groups. The differences are as follows:

- Expert group leaders interpreted group process more often (e.g., the group keeps answering questions related to feelings with thoughts) (Hines, Stockton, & Morran, 1995)
- Expert group leaders asked more internal questions about members (e.g., have the group members tried to express themselves in this group?) (Hines et al., 1995)
- Expert group leaders interpreted member behavior more often (e.g, the group member is saying that he is OK with it, but his nonverbals convey his anxiety) (Hines et al., 1995)
- Novice group leaders had more thoughts about whether a group transaction was therapeutic (e.g., did what I say help him to talk about his feelings?) (Hines et al., 1995)
- Experienced group leaders viewed group members and their interactions on three dimensions: dominant/submissive, friendly/unfriendly, and supporting therapeutic work/hindering therapeutic work (Kivlighan & Quigley, 1991)
- Novice group leaders viewed group members and their interactions on two dimensions: dominant/submissive and rate of participation (Kivlighan & Quigley, 1991)
- Increased levels of negative self-talk by group leaders, increased anxiety, and decreased effectiveness (Hiebert, Uhlemann, Marshall, & Lee, 1998)
- A positive correlation between negative self-talk by group leaders and perceptions of group members as being critical of their performance (Nutt-Williams & Hill, 1996)

Thus, it makes sense for training experiences for group leaders, particular for psychoeducational groups, to focus on group leadership skills, conceptualizations of group process and dynamics, and group leader self-efficacy.

Stockton and Toth (1996) suggest that leaders in training need

- Grounding in theory through the accumulation of didactic material
- Opportunities to observe groups in action and to learn and practice group skills before they actually lead a group
- Participation in a personal growth group experience to observe group development from a member's perspective and to develop as people
- Practice in leading or co-leading a group under careful supervision (p. 275)

Each of these areas will be discussed briefly in the following section.

Grounding in Group Dynamics and Leadership Theory

Most graduate programs in counseling, psychology, and social work require at least one course on group leadership. Figure 2.1 in Chapter 2 suggests essential reading in general and also specifically for psychoeducational groups. The Association for Specialists in Group Work's (2000) *Professional Standards for the Training of Group Workers* suggest that graduate coursework on groups be required and include types of group work, group development, group process and dynamics, group leadership, and standards of training and practice (p. 331).

Observation and Practice of Group Leadership Skills

The Association for Specialists in Group Work's (2000) *Professional Standards for the Training of Group Workers* clearly delineate that all group leaders have 10 hours (20 hours recommended) observation of and participation in a group experience as a group member and/or group leader. There are several professional videotapes of group leadership available for training purposes: *Group Work: Leading in the Here and Now* (Carroll, 1985), *Evolution of a Group: Student Video* (Corey, Corey, & Haynes, 1999), *Developmental Aspects of Group Counseling* (Stockton, 1992), and *Understanding Group Psychotherapy* (Yalom, 1990). All four of these tapes are examples of counseling groups with adults and can be used to illustrate group process and dynamics and specific group leadership behaviors. Rosemarie Smead (2000a) has the only videotape that illustrates a group for children and adolescents, *Skills and Techniques for Group Counseling With Youth*. Additionally, the Association for Specialists in Group Work has a series of videotapes on different topics that include didactic information as well as some role-play examples to illustrate group leadership behaviors and interventions for specific groups. The titles are *Group Work With Adolescent Children of Alcoholics* (Slayton, 1995), *Encouraging Risk Taking in Groups* (Kottler, 1995), *Group Work for Eating Disorders and Food Issues* (Kalodner, 1995), and *Reality Therapy Group Work* (Wubbolding, 1995).

Several models have been proposed for teaching group leadership skills. Stockton and Toth (1996) suggested focusing on three areas of skill development for beginning group leaders. First is Perceiving, with the group leader developing a framework for understanding how groups work and the goals of group interventions. Specifically, they suggest the identification of the key interpersonal and intrapersonal events that define group dynamics at each stage of group development. The second is Selecting, where the group leader, based on what he or she understands is happening in the group, must then select an appropriate intervention. This task includes exposing students to an array of interventions and helping them to choose a specific intervention based on the goal. The third is Risking, where group leaders are urged to take risks and try out new interventions in a group session. The focus here is on helping students develop confidence in their interventions.

Downing, Smaby, and Maddux (2001) suggest a model for teaching group leadership skills—the Skilled Group Counseling Training Model—that has 18 skills organized into three stages of counseling: Exploring, Understanding, and Acting. The purpose of the Exploring stage is to develop awareness of a problem and consists of attending (appropriate eye contact, body language, and verbal tracking skills) and questioning/reflecting (accurate, open-ended questioning, paraphrasing, and summarizing of skills). The purpose of the Understanding stage is to develop congruence, and it consists of interchangeable empathy (succinct statement of the feeling and contents of the problem, self-disclosing of a related experience, and asking for specific and concrete expression) and additive empathy (recognizing immediate feelings, identifying the general problem situation and feelings about self, and confronting caringly). The purpose of the Acting stage is to change behavior, and it consists of decision making (deciding to change or not to change, choosing a course of action, and delineating long-term consequences of the decision) and contracting for change (choosing actions to solve the problem, setting action deadlines, and reviewing goals). The model suggests didactic discussion of the skill, observation of videotaped simulation of the skills, and then practice of each skill.

Participation in Group Experiences and Activities

The two major goals for participation in group experiences and activities are for beginning group leaders to experience the process and dynamics of groups, and to also examine their typical behavior in groups, both in an effort to be more effective group leaders. Groups are powerful and can exert considerable influence, both positive and negative. Although an activity may appear relatively nonthreatening when group leaders are planning it, the reality may be that group members have much difficulty conceptualizing or participating in the activity. Psychoeducational group leaders must also believe in the utility of groups and their power through trying out new behaviors and getting feedback to help change behavior. Although traditionally, participation in counseling or therapy groups has been recommended in order to understand group process and dynamics, beginning group leaders may also learn a great deal about group process, dynamics, and leadership from observation of and participation in task and work groups, classroom activities, and group role-plays. Hulse-Killacky (1996) suggested using a group process observer (someone who is experienced in leading groups) to facilitate discussion at the end of each class about the group leadership behaviors of the instructor as they relate to the content process of the class. Corey and Corey (2002) suggested asking students at the end of each class to focus on what they were thinking and feeling, and how they were behaving, throughout the class discussion.

Using structured group experiences rather than role-plays, Toth, Stockton, and Erwin (1998) proposed a six-stage skill-based model for learning specific group leadership techniques that resulted in a significant increase in here-and-now interventions (Toth & Stockton, 1996). The stages included an experiential pretest, didactic presentation of the skills, further observation, and then an experiential posttest. Applicable to both role-play and actual group experiences, Hulse-Killacky (1996) also suggests the use of the Observer Feedback Form and Group Member Reflection Form to help beginning group leaders focus on group process and dynamics and effective leadership behaviors. Each chapter in this book includes a section titled Suggested Training Activities based on the above recommendations.

Group Leadership With Supervision

Specifically for psychoeducational groups, it is recommended that group leaders gain experience of at least a minimum of 30 hours (45 hours recommended) of supervised practice conducting a psychoeducational group. An earlier section in Chapter 2 clearly outlines the tasks and provides guidelines for supervision. In addition, it is suggested that beginning group leaders co-lead with a more experienced leader, often referred to as dyadic supervision in the literature. Leszcz and Murphy (1994) stated that the

> benefits of such a model include the trainee's opportunity to observe directly how an experienced leader conducts group psychotherapy. Similarly, the junior leader may be able to receive direct feedback from the supervising leader about his or her therapeutic style and use of therapeutic interventions. (p. 110)

Triadic supervision consists of a co-leadership team being supervised by an experienced group leader. The advantages of triadic supervision include the provision of comprehensive reporting about the group in supervision, as each co-therapist serves to correct the others' blind spots (Leszcz & Murphy, 1994). Their ability to give one another feedback and together examine the group process, transference, and countertransferential developments within the group and the interpersonal processes can provide significant amounts of support and information.

> However, the co-therapy team is subject to its own process and dynamics, and supervision needs to address issues that invariably arise, including issues of competence, dependency, and rivalry. How the co-therapy relationship develops influences dramatically how the group will function. (Leszcz & Murphy, 1994, p. 112)

Nakkula and Watts (1997) suggested that a uniqueness of supervising group co-leaders is the focus on the co-leaders' relationship, the "friendship-in-the-making" (p. 145) as they refer to it, which requires an interpersonal focus for supervision.

Hulse-Killacky (1996) suggests a Group Leader Reflection Form to help beginning group leaders reflect on a particular group session, what skills they used, what the goal was, what the reaction of the group was, and what they might do differently. Greenberg (2002) suggested a checklist for reviewing leadership behavior and interventions within a group session.

Assessment Measures

Measures have been developed to assess and rate group leadership behaviors in order to give feedback to leaders as part of training experiences and to understand the relationship between group leadership behaviors and the effectiveness of groups. Specific leadership behaviors and self-efficacy related to group leadership behaviors have been included. Several promising measures are also described briefly. Most measures are created so that multiple sources of data can be used: the group leader, the co-leader, the supervisor, group members, and group observers.

Skilled Group Counseling Scale

The Skilled Group Counseling Scale (SGCS) (Smaby et al., 1999) is used to assess group counseling skills and consists of 18 skills, 6 for each of three stages (Exploring, Understanding, Acting) based on the Skilled Group Counseling Training Model. The Exploring stage focuses on appropriate eye contact, body language, verbal tracking skills, accurate open-ended questioning, paraphrasing, and summarizing of skills. The Understanding stage consists of stating succinctly the feeling and content of a problem; self-disclosing a related experience; asking for specific and concrete expression; recognizing immediate feelings expressed when discussing the problem; identifying the general problem situation, actions taken when facing the problem, and feelings about self after taking action; and confronting caringly. The Acting stage focuses on deciding to change or not to change, choosing a course of action and recognizing the immediate implications of taking a course of action, delineating long-term consequences of the decision, reaching agreements about actions to take for solving the problem, setting action deadlines, and reviewing goals and the results of actions taken for resolving the problem. Each item is scored on a 5-point scale from 1 = *not at all* to 5 = *always*, with high scores indicating a greater level of that skill.

Internal consistency using three raters for 78 group counseling sessions was greater than .99 (Smaby et al., 1999). Smaby et al. found significant differences on all three subscales as a result of intensive group skills training using 78 graduate students in counseling. For students who had not received intensive group training, their means ranged from 20.87 to 29.93 on the three subscales; for those who received intensive group training, their means ranged from 88.25 to 89.67. Downing et al. (2001) further examined the application of group counseling skills training to actual group leadership using 13 students completing their master's-level internship. For most of the 18 skills, students maintained the levels of leadership behavior attained at the end of the intensive skills training. Only those skills related to action tended to decline, suggesting that further training, experience, and supervision are necessary to develop such advanced skills.

Trainer Behavior Scale

The Trainer Behavior Scale (TBS) (Bolman, 1971) measures group leader behavior and is composed of 28 items rated on a 5-point scale ranging from *strongly agree* to *strongly disagree*. The items are intended to measure seven dimensions based on a factor analysis: Affection (e.g., she or he shows considerable affection for most members of the group), Conditionality (e.g., she or he gives the impression that she or he likes some kinds of behaviors better than others), Congruence-Empathy (e.g., she or he seems to be in close touch with how members of the group are feeling), Openness (e.g., she or he seems to hold back from expressing her or his own reactions to what is happening in the group), Perceptiveness (e.g., she or he misinterprets what people say), Dominance (e.g., she or he exerts considerable influence over the direction the group takes), and Conceptual Input (e.g., when she or he calls attention to something, she or he gives a theoretical explanation of why it occurred). The higher the score, the more of that specific leadership behavior displayed. Validity for the TBS was assessed by correlating the group leader dimensions with ratings of group climate. Kivlighan and Shaughnessey's (1993) factor analysis suggested two general dimensions, Control and Affiliativeness, that together accounted for 72% of the predicted variance. Congruence-Empathy, Openness, and Affection loaded on the Affiliativeness dimension, whereas Conditionality, Perception, Dominance, and Conceptual Input loaded on the Control dimension. Coefficient alphas for all subscales ranged from .87 to .94 (Kivlighan, Jauquet, Hardie, Francis, & Hershberger, 1993).

Other Promising Measures

Corrective Feedback Self-Efficacy Instrument (CFSI) (Page & Hulse-Killacky, 1999). The CFSI is a 16-item instrument designed to measure group leaders' self-efficacy for giving corrective feedback within counseling groups. The instrument is based on the premise that although group leaders may acknowledge that "by giving corrective feedback in groups, the giver learns to communicate honestly and openly with others as well as to provide opportunities for receivers to learn about themselves" (Page & Hulse-Killacky, 1999, p. 38), they may also have significant anxiety about giving feedback in group, and this hesitancy varies by the type of feedback to be given. Each item is rated on a 6-point scale. A factor analysis indicated two subscales, Therapeutic Efficacy (9 items) and Fears Efficacy (7 items), that together accounted for 47.8% of the variance (Page & Hulse-Killacky, 1999). Convergent validity was demonstrated by significant correlations with the Counselor Self-Estimate Inventory subscales (Larson et al., 1992), whereas discriminant validity was demonstrated by nonsignificant correlations with the NEO subscales (Costa & McCrae, 1992). Internal consistency was calculated with a Cronbach's alpha coefficient of .84. Test-retest reliability over a 2-week period was .74 (Page & Hulse-Killacky, 1999).

Group Leader Behavior Rating Form (GLBRF) (Corey & Corey, 1987). The GLBRF is a 28-item, 7-point Likert-type scale designed to assess group leadership skills. Each item is rated from 1 = *an extremely low degree* to 7 = *an extremely high degree,* with higher scores indicating greater levels of a specific skill. The Guttman split-half reliability coefficient and the equal length Spearman-Brown reliability coefficient were both .97 (DeLucia & Bowman, 1991). DeLucia and Bowman's factor analysis revealed four factors that predicted 58.9% of the variance (individual variance accounted for is indicated in the parentheses): Interventions (44.8%), Facilitative Conditions (5.8%), Application of Theory (4.3%), and Professionalism (4%). "Group leaders can use it as a self-evaluation device, supervisors can use it to evaluate group leaders' training, group leaders can evaluate their co-leaders with it, and group members can use it to evaluate their leader" (Corey & Corey, 1987, p. 65).

Group Leadership Self-Efficacy Instrument (GLSI) (Page et al., 2001). The GLSI is a 36-item scale measuring self-efficacy of group leadership skills. Each item is rated on a 6-point Likert scale from 1 = *strongly disagree* to 6 = *strongly agree,* with higher scores indicating higher self-efficacy for the skill described in the item. Cronbach's alpha for the entire scale was calculated at .95 (Page et al., 2001), with 2-week test-retest reliability of $r = .72$. Two factor analyses indicated support for a one-factor solution for the GLSI that accounted for 38.7% and 37.7% of the total variance. Discriminant validity was demonstrated with nonsignificant correlations between the NEO (Costa & McCrae, 1992) and the S scale of the STAI (Spielberger, 1983). Page et al. (2001) reported a mean of 171.8 ($SD = 19.6$) for group trainees within a range of 36 to 216 and suggested that a total score of less than 152 (less than one standard deviation below the mean) indicates low self-efficacy for group leadership skills.

Leadership Characteristics Inventory (LCI) (Makuch, 1997). The LCI measures group leadership characteristics to assess compatibility of style between co-leaders, link leadership style with efficacy, and enable leaders to adjust their leadership styles according to the group's feedback (Makuch, 1997). This 56-item measure is composed of 10 subscales: Direction Focus, Content Focus, Expression Focus, Immediacy Preference, Structure Preference, Directiveness, Confrontation, Transparency, Verbal Activity, and Empathy. The higher a score on a given subscale, the greater the extent that that specific group leadership behavior is exhibited by a leader. Findings supported the creation of separate norms for ratings by leaders, supervisors, and members. Scale means on members' ratings of leaders are as follows: Group Directed Style (18.96), Individual Directed Style (12.96), Group Process Focus (16.69), Group Topic Focus (13.17), Cognitive Focus (13.41), Affect Focus (19.82), Immediacy Preference (17.43), Structure Preference (14.09), Directiveness (10.70), Transparency (16.09), Verbal Activity (19.04), Confrontation (16.89), and Empathy (21.43) (Makuch, 1997).

Summary

Leading psychoeducational groups for children and adolescents requires leadership skills that provide structure, help group members feel safe, and learn and practice new behaviors. Different parts of the group session and different group stages require different leadership skills. Training to become a group leader must include content about group process and dynamics, therapeutic factors group, and leadership skills. In addition, comprehensive training includes observation of skilled group leadership, opportunities to practice group leadership skills in simulated settings, and supervision of beginning group leadership experiences.

Suggested Training Activities

1. Group Leadership Skill Assessment

- Complete one or more of the assessment measures identified in this chapter.
- Write a one-page summary of your strengths, areas to improve upon, and three group leadership skill goals for yourself as you practice group leadership skills in role-plays or as you lead a group.

2. Observation of Group Leadership Skills in Videotapes

- View one of the videotape examples of group leadership.
- Using Yalom's four categories of leadership—Executive Function, Meaning Attribution, Emotional Stimulation, and Caring—note specific examples for each category. Evaluate whether the intervention was effective.
- Choose one of the assessment measures identified in this chapter and note specific instances of each of these behaviors. Evaluate whether the intervention was effective.
- Using the Group Processing Sheet in Appendix E, write process notes. Then identify leadership behaviors and therapeutic factors.

3. Observation of Actual Group Leadership Skills in Psychoeducational Groups

- Observe an actual psychoeducational group session.
- Take notes on what occurs. Perhaps use one of the assessment forms to identify specific leadership behaviors.
- Using the Group Processing Sheet in Appendix E, write process notes. Then identify leadership behaviors and therapeutic factors.
- Discuss with the group leader(s) what the goals of their specific interventions were and their effectiveness. Ask them what their plans are for the next group session.

4. Observation of Actual Group Leadership Skills in Task or Work Groups

- Observe an actual task or work group session. Classes can be conceptualized as a task group.
- Take notes on what occurs. Perhaps use one of the assessment forms to identify specific leadership behaviors.
- Using the Group Processing Sheet in Appendix E, write process notes. Then identify leadership behaviors and therapeutic factors.
- Discuss with the group leader(s) what the goals of their specific interventions were and their effectiveness. Ask them what their plans are for the next group session.

5. Role-Play Group Leadership Skills

- Create a vignette of a psychoeducational group. Use one from the literature (e.g., Donigian & Hulse-Killacky, 1999; Donigian & Malnuti, 1997; and DeLucia-Waack & Donigian, 2004, all include vignettes of psychoeducational groups as well as counseling groups).
- Plan for the group. Use the Group Planning Sheet in Appendix D.
- Discusss with the co-leader possible interventions and procedures (who will start, end, etc.)
- Role-play for 20 minutes.

- Have a process observer take notes. Have him or her give feedback based on the Process Observer Rating Form (Hulse-Killacky, 1996).
- Complete one or more of the assessment measures identified in this chapter, the Group Leadership Reflection Form (Hulse-Killacky, 1996), or the Checklist by Greenberg (2002).
- Give each other feedback on the effectiveness of interventions.
- Ask members to comment on the effectiveness of interventions and the presence of therapeutic interventions. Ask them to use the Member Reflection Form (Hulse-Killacky, 1996) or the Critical Incident Questionnaire in Appendix M.
- Complete the Group Processing Sheet in Appendix E.
- Conduct a supervision session as outlined in Chapter 2, planning for the next session.

CHAPTER 5

Initial Sessions

Children and adolescents typically (like most of us) come to the first session of a psychoeducational group with conflicting emotions: some excitement and enthusiasm mixed with apprehension and anxiety. It is critical at this point for group leaders to use behaviors in the categories of Executive Functions and Caring to help students acclimate to what is expected of them in groups and identify specific behaviors to help them get the most out of the group experience. A little bit of anxiety is not a bad thing.

The analogy of test anxiety is useful in describing the power of groups and can be shared with beginning group members as a metaphor. If students are not anxious at all about a test, they may not study for the test and they might fail. On the other hand, students may study for a test but get so anxious when it is time to take the test because of the negative things that they tell themselves (e.g., I am dumb, stupid, I don't know the material) that their anxiety may interfere with recall of the material and they may also fail. In the case of student test-taking behavior, a moderate level of anxiety seems most helpful. There is enough anxiety to motivate the student to study but not enough anxiety to interfere with remembering what was studied. Effective group work is similar in that students need to have a little anxiety in order for them to be motivated to try out new behaviors and learn different skills, but the anxiety should not be so overwhelming that it prevents them from attending the group and/or participating.

In this chapter, activities will be described to help group members connect with each other, and to provide information to lessen the anxiety. It is helpful to note the parallels between group stages and relationship development. When people first meet, they are a little hesitant to share and tend to be polite. As the friendship develops, people begin to act a little more naturally, perhaps sharing more of their positive and negative emotions, behaviors, and reactions. Strong friendships develop when friends are able to be who they are, expressing both positive and negative emotions, making mistakes, and giving honest feedback. For group leaders, it is important to observe where group members have trouble with the tasks inherent in each group stage. This may predict where they may struggle in relationships as well.

Identification of these difficulties and interventions to teach specific skills is a major responsibility of the group leaders. Some children and adolescents easily connect to each other (a task of the initial stage) but have a harder time expressing negative emotions and giving honest feedback (the tasks in the middle stages). For others, the tasks of terminating, saying goodbye, and acknowledging how other group members have helped them are more difficult.

Regardless of the length of the group, the first session must be devoted to the establishment of ground rules and goals for the group, introduction of members to each other, and explanation of the purpose of the group. It is also helpful to include some review of important topics discussed in the first session as part of the opening and review in the second session. This chapter will discuss the initial stage of group, focusing on major tasks, therapeutic factors, and leadership behaviors. Possible pitfalls of initial sessions and examples of activities that may be used are also included.

Goals and Tasks

The first sessions are organized around getting group members to know each other and identifying of the focus of the group. It is recommended that at least two sessions be introductory sessions, although with a shorter group (fewer than 8 sessions), one session may be all that can be allotted. The major goals of initial sessions are described, followed by a general outline for a first group session.

Introduce Group Members to Each Other

Even though in a school setting potential group members may often know each other, it is still important to spend some time having them introduce themselves and self-disclose something that casual contact in school would not indicate. In addition, it is important to recognize that some students may have already developed interactional patterns with each other that are not positive or will not contribute to a safe and caring group environment. Thus, one of the goals in an initial session is to help students interact both positively, and potentially differently, from how they have typically acted toward each other outside of group. One way to do this is to emphasize unique aspects that each child or adolescent brings to group and how each will contribute in the group. From the very beginning, it should be emphasized that the rules of interaction within this group may be different from those in other places in which they normally interact, such as in the classroom (e.g., group members are not expected to raise their hand when they wish to talk) or on the playground (e.g., bullying and name calling are not allowed in this group).

An initial icebreaker should include each group member's name to make sure that everyone knows names (and how to pronounce them correctly). A number of activities ask group members to state their name and make some kind of self-disclosure. The self-disclosure may be rather superficial (e.g., something that makes me happy . . .), but it establishes the norm that in this group, self-disclosure is expected. For example, each student introduces himself or herself, and then repeats the names of those who have already introduced themselves (to reinforce their names) and their disclosure. Such a system encourages students to disclose sooner rather than later simply so that they don't have to repeat as many names. It is often helpful for the group leader to go first to set the tone for the activity and model the kind of self-disclosure desired. In one icebreaker, group members are asked to state their name along with a feeling that begins with the same letter as their first name. I would say, "My name is Janice and I am a little jittery today about starting this group." Associating the feeling with the student may help to remember the name. Such an activity also reinforces the group norm of self-disclosure, particularly of feelings, and allows the group leader to link members together, emphasize universality, and also to address initial anxiety directly within the group. If I began this activity, I would disclose my first name, and because group leaders typically wouldn't do this in a group in the schools, I would acknowledge this discrepancy as part of how we may sometimes act differently in group than at other times and places in school. For adolescent groups particularly, if there is a strong need to connect with them, I might tell them it was OK for them to call me by my first name in the group, again emphasizing how we would interact differently within the group, and also the collegiality and importance of working together.

Introduce Group Members to the Purpose and Structure of the Group

Once group members have introduced themselves, it is important to talk about how the group works and what will make this group safe. The major topics include how groups work, ground rules, the role of the group leader, procedural information, and typical interventions and activities. Much of what group leaders discuss will have already been introduced to group members in previous contacts (screening or preparation sessions) verbally and sometimes in writing. The examples of handouts for the preparation sessions in Appendix K have been worded so that most children and adolescents should be able to understand what is being said and include a general explanation of how groups work and the role of the leader

Group members should be informed in the first session, as well as in screening interviews and preparation sessions, when the group will meet, for how long, and where. Specifics such as how they will get to the group (e.g., a pass will be sent, a teacher will bring them, the school counselor will pick them up, whether they should enter the counseling room or wait in a waiting area, etc.) should also be reiterated.

A brief summary of how group will work should focus on problem solving, role-playing, and giving feedback to each other as ways to learn and practice new behaviors, along with a description of specific activities related to group goals that will be used. The role of the group leader is best described as a facilitator of the group with the job of keeping members on task, introducing relevant topics and activities, and helping members to work together. Leaders should also emphasize that group members will be the experts on themselves and the ones who need to evaluate which interventions and skills work best for them. It is also sometimes useful to explain the structure of the group session—opening, working, processing, and closing—so that the group members are aware of and anticipate the transition between topics and activities. My favorite example of elementary students internalizing and anticipating the structure of the group session is the second grader who said to me, "I think we need to move on to processing now. We only have 7 minutes left." Providing the structure of a group session for students serves as a cognitive organizer; in some ways, you have given them the questions that will be asked on the test (during processing). They just need to find the answers in the working part of the session, so as part of that, group members may be consciously asking themselves, "What am I learning?" "What skills seem to work best for me?" "How am I feeling as I'm doing this new behavior?" All of these questions are good for students to consider.

There is a poem titled "Remember" that emphasizes how group members can listen to each other, not give advice, and help members to find the answers and their own solutions.

> "**Remember** . . .
> We are here to **listen** . . .
> not to work miracles.
> We are here to **help** people discover what they are **feeling** . . .
> not to make feelings go away.
> We are here to **help** a person **identify** their **options** . . .
> not to decide for them what they should do.
> We are here to **discuss steps** with a person . . .
> not to take the steps for them.
> We are here to **help** a person **discover** their own strength . . .
> not to rescue them and leave them still vulnerable.
> We are here to **help** a person **discover they can help themselves** . . .
> not to take responsibility for them.
> We are here to **help people learn to choose** . . .
> not to make it unnecessary for them to make difficult choices.
> **We are here to provide support for change!!!**"
>
> —Anonymous

The initial session should also include a discussion of ground rules to ensure safety of the group members and help make the group productive. Discussion, rather than lecture, is to be emphasized. The goal here is for group members to create the guidelines for a successful group so that they take ownership of rules and so that the ground rules are stated in their own words. The analogy of the swimming pool and how pool rules are necessary for everyone to be safe often works well. Students could even begin by stating the rules posted for swimming pools and then translate them into the rules for their group. For example, one person at a time on the diving board could be translated into one person speaks at a time, and no roughhousing could be translated into everyone should be respectful. It is often helpful to write (or have group members write) the guidelines on a blackboard or notepad. The list of ground rules can be displayed each time the group meets as a concrete reminder. The group leaders can add or clarify any ground rules that are necessary that group members do not mention.

As a follow-up to the initial discussion of ground rules and to reinforce them, an activity that could be used in a later session is to have the group members create a banner with the name that they want to call their group on the top, the group guidelines written by the members as the center, and each of the group members' names or symbols around the edges. The banner can then be displayed prominently during each group session and referred to as needed. Making decisions about the group name, how the rules should be worded, and how the banner should be created helps group members to begin to work together, communicate with each other, and decide how to handle disagreements.

Nonnegotiable ground rules such as confidentiality and how interactions will occur (only respectful comments, only one person talks at a time) should be discussed in the screening interviews and presented in writing to children, adolescents, and their parents whenever possible, and then emphasized again in the first session. Typically, students will bring up the topic of confidentiality, and the group leaders can add more details related to limits of confidentiality. These are typical group guidelines:

- Be on time
- Attendance
  - Everyone is expected to be here each session. Let the leaders know beforehand if you will miss or be late
  - Frame this as the group will miss you and worry about you if they don't know where you are. Sometimes, other group members worry that they might have offended a member in the previous session by something they said if that person doesn't show up for the next group session
- Confidentiality
  - What is said in group, stays in group
  - You can talk about what you learned but not how you learned it (e.g., "I realized that I do get angry but don't tell people," not "I realized I don't tell people how angry I am when Alisha told me in group that I wasn't talking to her that day")
  - Limits of confidentiality for the leader include when someone is going to be harmed (self or other) or as required by a court of law
- Be respectful of others
  - One person talks at a time
  - No name calling
  - It is OK to disagree and for others to express different opinions
  - Share reactions to what is happening to each other
  - Use "I" statements
- Take risks
  - Participate
  - Share your reactions and feelings
  - Try new behaviors in group
  - Try new behaviors outside of group

Another important issue that often comes up, and is related to confidentiality, is how group members will greet each other outside of group. This is an important topic to discuss because each member needs to decide what he or she wants to say and whether he or she wants to be acknowledged by others. Sometimes, adolescents will say, "Don't say 'hi.' My friends will ask how I know you and I don't want to tell anyone I am in this group." It is important for them to say what they want to happen as an expression of their assertiveness; also, for group development, this is another task that requires communication, negotiation, and decision making. It is also important to discuss what Yalom calls "out of group socializing." Group members should be up front about whether they are friends with others in the group or socialize with them to some extent. People take risks in groups, and if one member suddenly sees two other group members eating lunch together, that member may wonder if they are talking about him or her. If group members are clear in the beginning about their relationships (e.g., we ride the bus together, swim together, eat lunch together), there may be less suspicion that confidentiality is being broken if everyone knows about the relationships. It is still wise for group leaders to remind members at critical times about the importance of confidentiality and even say to two friends, "It may be hard not to talk about what happened this week. If you have thoughts or feelings, bring them to group next week. Breaking confidentiality would be very harmful to the trust of this group."

There are two other ground rules that are optional but may be useful at different times. One is an invitation for group members to "try out the group," usually for at least three sessions. The first session is often not a good example of how groups work; group members' anxiety is high, and there is a very high level of structure because of the information that needs to be provided, so there is less group member interaction than in other sessions. Group members are asked to attend the first three sessions to get a sense of how groups operate and how they might participate.

Related to the first option is the second ground rule that asks group members to say goodbye to the group if they are going to leave for any reason before the group ends. This allows the group some closure but also sometimes allows the group leaders an opportunity to resolve a conflict in group. For instance, if a group member says to a group leader outside of group, "I'm not coming back anymore because Sue is always mean to me," the group leader now has the opportunity to help that group member bring the issue to the group and resolve it. If the group member is unwilling, he or she still has to come to group and say goodbye. Group members will ask about the reason, and again, this may provide a chance to resolve the conflict.

Identify Individual and Group Goals

Initial sessions should include a discussion of the goals of the group followed by a discussion of individual goals for each group member. Even young children can understand and participate in such discussions. They need to know that they will be focusing on identifying and discussing certain topics and themes. They can also identify specific issues for them (either on their own or through pregroup screening, assessment, and interviews) that they would like to work on or change during the course of the group. Typical goals for a children-of-divorce group might be, "I don't want to feel so caught in the middle between my Mom and Dad," "I don't want to feel guilty when I am with one parent," or "I want to feel less sad when I think about my parents splitting up." Typical goals for an adolescent self-esteem group might be,

"I want to be more realistic about my strengths and weaknesses," "I want to feel better about my body," or "I want to express my feelings more clearly to people."

Goal setting in both individual and group work for children and adolescents is an area that has often been ignored or underutilized. Goal setting is a process of identifying goals based on the assumption that the more specific the goals, the more likely their attainment. It is most likely to improve task performance when the goals are specific and appropriately challenging, feedback is provided to indicate progress in relation to the goal, rewards are given for goal attainment, the manager or experimenter is supportive, and goals assigned are accepted by the individual. Locke and Latham's (1990) qualitative meta-analysis and O'Leary-Kelly, Martocchio, and Frink's (1994) quantitative meta-analysis both strongly supported the use of individual goal setting with task/performance groups. Goal setting was associated with enhanced performance because it mobilized effort, directed attention, motivated strategy development, and prolonged effort over time.

"Writing it [goals] down is about clearing your head, identifying what you want, and setting your intent. Writing things down helps people understand what they want and become proactive in achieving one's goals" (Klauser, 1997, p. 1). The Elaboration Likelihood Model (ELM) of attitude change (Petty & Cacioppo, 1986) has been applied extensively to counseling interventions (Heesacker, Conner, & Prichard, 1995). "Elaboration" is defined as the ability to think about an issue and is theorized to increase the chances of attitude change occurring. In turn, attitude change is assumed to influence behavior directly. Writing down goals facilitates thoughtful action, because the person must contemplate what he or she wants to achieve, thereby increasing the chances of realizing those goals. Attitude change is an important determinant of behavior change in and of itself; attitude also affects other variables that contribute to behavior such as motivation, perceptions of others' attitudes, feelings of self-efficacy, and actual competence. Findings from ELM research indicated that attitudes formed or changed as a result of effortful thinking are more predictive of both behavioral intentions and actions than are attitudes formed or changed with little thinking (Petty, Heesacker, & Hughes, 1997). Researchers have evaluated the use of ELM in the context of training assertive attitudes and behavior (Ernst & Heesacker, 1993), changing sexual aggression (Gilbert, Heesacker, & Gannon, 1991), changing men's traditional male gender role attitudes and enhancing attitudes toward seeking psychological help (Brooks-Harris, Heesacker, & Mejia-Millan, 1996), substance abuse prevention (Scott, 1996), and student achievement motivation (Kivlighan, Schuetz, & Kardash, 1998).

Flowers and Schwartz (1980) reported anecdotally that when group members write on a card two problems that they would like to work on, their participation in the group increases, thereby increasing the chances of making the session productive. Yalom (1985) suggested that these goals be realistic (an important area of personal concern that the client can work on in session), interpersonal (problem is described in relational terms), and here-and-now (relationship problem described in relation to other members of the group). Yalom contends that such agenda setting would help members ask explicitly for what they need and thus help them recognize their own responsibility within the therapeutic process. Dye's (2002) chapter on previewing suggests a way to invite each group member to make a statement, but not a commitment, regarding what he or she might want to work on during a particular group session. In psychoeducational groups, previewing might occur as part of the opening of the group, where the group leaders introduce a topic and then ask group members how this relates to their group goals and what they might want to discuss during that session.

Thus, it seems essential to ask group members to identify their goals verbally and, if possible, in writing. There is something about stating a goal to a group of people that makes it more real and holds the person more accountable. Maybe even more important is the group commitment to help a group member change and achieve his or her goal. In contrast to just having a rather stagnant discussion where each member in a row states his or her goal with no group discussion, it is useful to frame the identification of goals as a discussion involving all members to identify several important points:

- Altruism and group commitment to help members work on each of their goals
- Universality among group members who have similar goals
- Modeling by group members who have strengths and can help certain members work on their goals
- Problem solving and brainstorming of specific ways that the group can help group members work on their goals inside and outside of group

Four questions are useful to help group members identify and clarify their goals:

- What is your goal?
- How will you know when you have achieved your goal?
- How will you work on your goal in group?
- What can the group do to help you work on your goal?

Additional questions are then asked of the other group members:

- What strengths, experience, or skills do you have that might help this group member attain his or her goal?
- How might this person work on his or her goal in group?
- What might the group do to help him or her?
- What can you do as an individual group member to help him or her?

After such a discussion of group and individual goals, it is important for the group leaders to connect members by emphasizing similarities in goals; instill hope and altruism by noting the strengths that group members have identified; and emphasize the importance of differences in perspectives that will be useful when solving problems, making decisions, and brainstorming. Hopefully, through the screening interviews and preparation sessions, group members have begun to identify individual goals related to the group goals. But in an effort to clearly connect individual and group goals and also to shape group members who may have goals that are somewhat inconsistent with the group goals, it is helpful to ask each group member to clearly identify with which group goal his or her individual goal most closely aligns.

Goal setting as an activity is not limited to only the initial session. It is helpful to review goals at the midpoint of group to discuss what progress members have made, what they have learned and how they have learned it, and what they will continue to work on until the end of the group. As part of termination, it is again useful to review progress toward goals and specifically emphasize what members have learned and how they have learned it in order to generalize that learning to outside the group. An activity that is also helpful in the early stages of the group is to ask members to put their goal on a scale from 0 to 10, with 0 being no progress at all toward the goal and 10 being they have achieved their goal. Next, ask the group members to mark where they are on the scale now in terms of their progress toward their goal. To help identify steps to achieve the goal, group members then label each number after their marked number with a behavioral descriptor so that they will know when they have made progress toward the goal. For example, a student in a shyness group may indicate that he or she is currently a 3 on the scale with the goal of being able to socialize in a group. He or she then might label 4 as talk to one person at lunch, 5 as talk to two people at lunch, 6 as go to a party and stay for 15 minutes, 7 as talk to one person at a party, 8 as go to a party and stay for an hour, 9 as talk to two people at a party, and 10 as join a group of people who are already talking at a party. Figure 5.1 contains a sample form that students may use to write down their goals. Leaders may want to keep the goals in order to review them periodically.

Using the metaphor of tending to a garden is another helpful way to introduce the topic of goal setting. Arnold Anderson, in his column "Stories I Tell My Patients," which appears in each issue of *Eating Disorders: The Journal of Treatment and Prevention*, describes brief stories that can be used as metaphors and analogies with clients. "Pulling Weeds and Planting Flowers" (Anderson, 1994) focuses on how, when you want to start a garden, you need to plant things that you want to grow and also weed out other plants. The story emphasizes both the elimination of behaviors that are not helpful and the cultivation of new, more positive behaviors: "It means planting flowers, not just pulling up weeds. The whole purpose of removing your self-defeating patterns of behavior, recognizing what hasn't worked well, is to start cultivating thoughts and behaviors that produce 'flowers'" (p. 184). A discussion of goals focusing on what new behaviors need to be learned and what self-defeating behaviors need to be unlearned could begin with the reading of the story about pulling weeds and planting flowers.

Reduce Initial Anxiety

Providing specific information about what will happen in the group sessions and the role of the leader will help to reduce group members' anxiety. Their anxiety will also be reduced by participating in the screening interviews and the first session. Disclosing about their situation and finding that others have similar situations and/or reasons for being in the group is particularly helpful in alleviating initial anxiety related to group participation. Instillation of hope occurs through connections, identification of how groups work, and the discussion of specific activities to

Name: _____   Date: _____

These are the general group goals. Please circle all that you would like to work on.

1.

2.

3.

(Note to group leaders: Add the specific group goals here.)

What are your individual goals for this group? Be specific. What do you want to learn to do differently after these group sessions? Please list.

1.

2.

3.

How will you know when you have reached your goal? How will you be different? Think differently? Feel differently? Behave differently?

1.

2.

3.

Figure 5.1   Sample of Form to Identify and Evaluate Goals

develop new skills. Linking, connecting, and emphasizing strengths of group members who can help other members is also important in reducing anxiety.

Outline of a Typical Initial Session

What follows is an outline for a typical initial session of a psychoeducational group, assuming that such a session would last between 45 minutes and an hour. If you have the luxury of more time (1 hour to 1½ hours), more time can be spent on each topic. Sometimes, it is helpful to use more than one activity to address a major goal of this stage. How each intervention addresses the tasks and strives to create therapeutic factors is described briefly. An approximate amount of time for each intervention is also included. Note that much of the information has been provided to some extent during earlier interactions, but it is important to remind the group as a whole to help emphasize group norms.

Opening (8 to 10 minutes)

Welcome (1 to 2 minutes). Welcome the students to the group, reminding them of the topic of the group and who the leaders are. If the leaders are not people with whom the students would typically interact, it is helpful to explain their role in the school or agency, where their office is, when they are available, and how to contact them. This provides safety and structure for the group members.

Icebreaker Activity (7 to 9 minutes). Select an icebreaker activity that includes names and focuses on self-disclosure, cohesiveness, and universality. Include one or two processing questions to link group members and emphasize similarities. Thank the first person who shares for taking a risk. Comment on good communication and self-disclosure skills: "I" statements, feeling words, and acknowledging anxiety or uncertainty.

Working (25 to 35 minutes)

Discussion of Ground Rules (10 to 12 minutes). Begin by suggesting that each group needs some guidelines (norms, as they are sometimes called) to help group members feel safe and to guide how members work together to learn and practice new skills and behaviors. Ask members to suggest some guidelines to make the group safe and productive. Record (or have a group member record) the list of guidelines on a blackboard or notepad. Clarify or add any ground rules that you as leaders decided previously were essential for this group (e.g., confidentiality, attendance, respect, one person talks at a time). Perhaps use the analogy of swimming pool rules.

Brief Discussion of Goals of Group (3 to 5 minutes). Leaders should remind group members at this time of the two or three goals for the group that were discussed previously during the screening interview and possibly the preparation session.

Some group members may have received information about the goals of the group in writing. Talking about goals in terms of the major themes for the group is helpful, as well as indicating that each group member will have time to identify his or her specific goals of what he or she wants to learn from the group. It is often useful to begin by asking the group members what the goals are for the group, rather than assuming that they don't know or don't remember and telling them again. This helps to further reinforce and internalize group goals. It also gives group leaders insight into motivation and participation level of specific group members.

Brief Discussion of How Groups Work (5 to 8 minutes). It is helpful to emphasize that the goals of groups like this are preventive in nature. All people can learn new ways of interacting and improve their relationships with people. Communication skills, problem-solving skills, conflict-resolution skills, and decision-making skills are often part of psychoeducational groups. Typically, in each group, some new way of thinking or behaving will be taught, and then there will be a chance to practice the new skills. This is a good time to remind group members of how many sessions there will be, how often they will meet, where they will meet, and so on. It is also sometimes useful to explain the structure of the group session: opening, working, processing, and closing; the role of the group leaders; and some typical activities that may be used in this type of group. Much of this information can be taken from the handout given out for preparation sessions in Appendix K.

Goal-Setting Activity (10 to 15 minutes). This activity should help group members to connect their goals to the goals of this specific psychoeducational group, as well as emphasize similarities and make connections between the group members who may be able to help and support each other. It is helpful to not only identify the goals for each individual group member but also to discuss briefly how the group can help each group member to work on his or her goal.

Processing (6 to 8 minutes)

Two or three processing questions that focus on group members' connections to each other and make them feel more comfortable are appropriate. Focus on the positive and make connections and links at this time. Possible questions include the following:

- What helped you feel more comfortable in group today?
- With which group member(s) did you connect?
- What did you learn about how groups work today?
- What did you learn about yourself today?

Group leaders may comment on positive communication skills such as self-disclosure, risk taking, and modeling; connections and similarities between members; how members helped each other or may help each other based on self-disclosed strengths; and what group members did to help the group work effectively (stayed on task, took turns, talked about feelings and thoughts that are bothering them, disclosed goals, offered to help other members, etc.).

It is important for group leaders to set the precedent that they will compliment members, point out specific behaviors that were effective, and ask group members to comment on the process and effectiveness of the group. The norm must be established early that part of the process of groups is learning new skills, but another key component is evaluating for each individual group member what processes, activities, interventions, and skills work for him or her. This sets the stage so that when negative interactions occur between members or interventions don't work, group members are prepared to discuss what happens as a normal part of the group.

Closing (6 to 8 minutes)

Even in the first session, it is important to ask group members to at least think about group goals, if not specifically try to do something related to them. For a friendship group, the group leader might ask the group members to notice how others start a conversation. For a self-esteem group, the members might be asked to notice when they feel good about themselves. The group leader might describe briefly the topic and activities for the next group session so that group members understand why they are being asked to observe or try out behaviors. The goal is to ask group members to preview and begin, in a sense, to collect data about a topic in anticipation of future group sessions.

Group Leadership Skills

The goals of group leadership behavior in the initial stage are focused on the creation of cohesiveness and connection with the leader and trust in the leader, illumination of how the process of groups works, and the development of goals. Group leaders intervene in a variety of ways to make this happen. Much of their interventions (and preplanning time) should be focused on

- Linking: linking group members to each other in terms of similarities, strengths, how they can work together; linking individual group member goals and problems to the goals of the group to increase hope; and linking what group members will learn in the group to change and improve their life situations outside of group. Specifically, leader comments might include statements and questions such as
    - I've noticed that you two have similar goals. Do you think that you might be able to work together and coach each other when this issue comes up?
    - I've noticed that your goal is similar to a strength another member has mentioned. Do you think that you might be able to ask that member for help when you need it? (To the other member) Do you think that you would be able to suggest ideas when this person needs help?
    - I'm noticing that the group members are describing goals that are very clearly linked to the group goals. And there are several specific interventions throughout the group that will teach skills to help meet those goals.
    - We have talked about some of the skills that we're going to learn in this group. How do you think you can use them outside of group in your real life? When? With whom?

- Supporting: helping members look at their strengths and how they can help themselves and others in group, and encouraging them to take risks and try out new behaviors.
  - What strengths do you bring to group?
  - What do you do well in relating to people?
  - What do your friends like about you?
  - If a friend of yours were to introduce you to this group, what might he or she say about you?
  - How are you a good friend? What do you do specifically that makes you a good friend?
  - What is one unique aspect of yourself that you're going to bring to group?
  - How are you going to help others in this group?
  - What do you need to take risks and try out new behaviors?
  - How are you going to help others to take risks and try out new behaviors in this group?
  - What can others do to help you to learn and change and grow in this group?
  - What are three things you want us to know about you?
  - If you were to introduce yourself as the person you'd like to be, what would you tell us about you?

- Identifying Goals: helping group members to state in very clear behavioral, cognitive, and/or affective terms how they want to be different when the group ends.
  - How do you want to be different at the end of this group?
  - We have talked about the group goals. Now what do you want to work on specifically related to the group goals?
  - What would you most like to say you've learned or decided when you leave the group?

- Clarifying: group members' individual and group goals, strengths, how they want to think, feel, and behave differently (and what they need to learn to accomplish this), how groups work, and how to participate effectively.
  - How would you know when you have achieved your goal?
  - What will your goal look like in terms of different behaviors, feelings, and thoughts?
  - What do you already do well related to your goal?
  - What behaviors, thoughts, and feelings do you want to keep on doing?
  - What changes do you need to make? What new skills do you need to learn?
  - Are you here because you want to be? If not, what can you still get out of it?
  - What do you want to get from this group?
  - What are you willing to do to get what you say you want?
  - Are you willing to try out new things in here?
  - What do you know about groups?
  - With what expectations are you coming to this group?
  - What is it like for you to be here now?
  - What fears or doubts do you have about this group, if any?

- What do you imagine would happen if you were to say the most difficult thing?
- What do you fear most? What do you hope for most?

• Suggesting How Group Works: explaining and modeling positive and effective interventions, and instructing and coaching group members on how to participate, problem solve, brainstorm, communicate, and make decisions.
- When we talk to each other, let's look directly at each other, use "I" statements, use feeling words when necessary, and try to be as specific as possible about behaviors.
- I am feeling a little less anxious about the group now that everyone has introduced himself or herself and talked a little bit about what he or she wants out of group. How about others?
- You have done a really nice job of stating the problem you would like to solve. Let's begin by talking about things that other people might have done about that problem. Then let's generate other ideas about what might work. Once we do that, then you need to identify one or two solutions that you think you want to try and we'll talk about them.
- Realize that you'll take from this group what you are willing to put into it.
- If you are feeling something in here persistently, express it.

• Identifying When Group Works: pointing out group process and asking questions to help group members identify when group is effective and helpful, what the specific things are that each group member contributed, and clearly stating what group members can do in the future to continue to have effective interactions.
- We did a really nice job today of staying on task and following directions. Did anyone notice how we did that? Let's talk about it so we can make sure that we do it again next time.
- Now that you have identified two possible solutions to your situation, let's talk about how that happened. What did we do as a group to help identify and evaluate solutions? What things did group members say that were particularly helpful? What ideas were particularly helpful? And why?

Possible Pitfalls

It is important at this stage to engage children and adolescents in groups. As mentioned previously for psychoeducational groups, the goal is more preventive, and so group members are not in such intense pain that they seek out interventions themselves. Thus, it is important from the beginning to interest adolescents in groups, to "hook" them so that they want to attend and participate. Part of this comes from their connection to the group leader, through initial interviews and supportive comments in the initial sessions, and part of this comes from the feelings of universality, altruism, cohesiveness, and instillation of hope derived from being in a group with other children or adolescents.

The delicate balance comes in providing enough entertainment and fun that students want to come to group and also enough structure that they feel safe and know how to participate in a way that they get something out of the group sessions. For many students, getting out of class is motivation enough to come to group. The group leaders then need to provide further motivation to engage effectively in group so that it truly is a psychoeducational group and not just a "rap" session.

Part of the structure comes in the form of making sure that the group members do not self-disclose too much or inappropriately in the initial sessions. Group leaders must be quick to cut off group members if they have begun to reveal details of explicit sexual behavior, family dysfunction, or acting-out behaviors. Intervening by asking the group member to talk to a group leader further about this one-on-one acknowledges the self-disclosure (both to the group member and the other group members) but keeps the group focused on the task at hand. If the self-disclosure is too deep for the group during the beginning stage, group members may ignore it entirely and make the group member feel unheard. Or, group members may initially support the group member who self-disclosed but distance themselves after they have begun to think about the disclosure. Or, they may then decide that this group member is particularly needy and focus the group on that particular group member, basically saying this person needs help more than we do so we must use the group to help him or her.

Examples of Activities

Initial-stage activities focus on building trust, introducing members to the group and to each other, and developing goals related to the group theme. Icebreaker activities in psychoeducational groups need to be focused on two areas: (a) identification of the individual group members' goals within the context of the overall group goals, and (b) introduction of the norms of self-disclosure, self-exploration, and giving and receiving of feedback. From the beginning of the first group session, all group activities, processing of group activities, and group discussions should emphasize group goals and group norms. There should not be any activities that are done "just for fun." This is not to say that activities shouldn't be fun or that group members shouldn't laugh in group, but that there should always be a purpose for an activity. Children and adolescents are very good at observing discrepancies and pointing them out. If a group leader allows the group to digress or focus on tangential topics for very long, it is harder to get them back on task and focused. There is a fine line between allowing students to chat and get to know each other, and allowing them to digress. With psychoeducational groups, time is of the essence, so an activity may allow members to get to know each other better but also should, in some way, be directed at group goals and norms.

For introductory activities, the purposes should be orienting to the group, building cohesiveness and connection among group members, and promoting the norms of self-disclosure and self-exploration. Group members need structure and guidance in the beginning stage to help figure out how to get the most out of their group experience. Beginning the process of self-disclosure and self-awareness, key elements in all groups, also needs to occur in the introductory group sessions. Any activity that asks members to tell a little about themselves includes self-disclosure.

Thus, if an activity is followed up with processing questions that focus on what it is like to self-disclose, the impact of self-disclosure on other members, and similarities and differences between members, then the process of self-awareness (and connections) has begun.

Common activities include those that get group members up and moving around by asking them to line up according to where they were born (from east to west) or based on how many siblings they have, all encourage some self-disclosure and connections. Other activities use movement to have group members define themselves, such as all the roses on the right side and all the tulips on the left side. Structured go-rounds where group members share relatively nonthreatening but important information that can be processed later are also useful, such as favorite movie and why, how would you spend a million dollars, or favorite holiday.

The "Autobiography" (Bridbord, 2002) and "Getting to Know You—Now and Then" activities (Conroy, 2002) encourage members to self-disclose and get to know other members while emphasizing safety. Another is the "Four Corners Card" (Rice, 1995), which asks group members to list one word in each corner that describes who they are as a person, when they are happy, when they are sad, and what they hope to gain from participation in the group. The "Coat of Arms" activity is also commonly used, with members drawing a symbol in the center to represent who they are (their crest), and then answering questions in each of the four corners to describe and tell about themselves.

Carrell (2000) suggests an activity called "Breaking the Ice" that uses a go-round technique where each group member answers a series of questions. She includes a list of 20 possible questions, such as

- What is the best movie you have ever seen?
- Who is the most important person to live during your lifetime?
- If you could be an animal other than a human, what would you be, and why?
- What was the best day of your life?

She begins with questions that ask members to self-disclose about who they are and what is important to them, and then moves on to what they want learn from this group and their connections with members as they have spoken about these different questions.

It is also sometimes useful to have group members begin by self-disclosing to one another in pairs or dyads. Then one person in the dyad introduces the other person to the rest of the group. This encourages self-disclosure and connections but lessens anxiety by limiting the interaction to one other person. Group leaders can also emphasize good listening skills, questions that were asked to clarify and gain more information, and what it was like to interview (and be interviewed by) another group member.

Using M&M candy is another way to invite self-disclosure in a structured and nonthreatening way. For each different color, choose a question that the student has to answer if they eat that color M&M. It is a fun activity for children and adolescents because they can eat the M&Ms as they do the activity, but they can also choose what they want to self-disclose to the group. Questions might be similar to those suggested earlier in the "Breaking the Ice" activity (Carrell, 2000). The "Trust Walk" (Carrell, 2000) introduces some movement as an icebreaker activity that is done in dyads and asks group members to talk about what it is like to trust somebody, how you know when you trust somebody, and then how trust can be conveyed within the group. "Getting to Know One Another" (Guth, 2002) is another activity that encourages movement and at the same time emphasizes connections between group members, as well as identifies potential strengths and positive group member behaviors. Four concentric circles are taped to the floor, and group members move to the circle that best resembles their level of a particular characteristic (e.g., extrovert, introvert, planner, feelings oriented, thought oriented, calm, etc.).

Karp, Butler, and Bergstrom (1998) emphasize creativity by suggesting an activity called the "Self-Collage," where group members create a collage using pictures, words, and phrases from magazines, newspapers, and other materials. Another variation of this is to have group members decorate the outside of a paper bag to illustrate what others typically know about them. The inside of the paper bag is then decorated to represent characteristics of themselves that group members do not typically share with other people. In a group session, members are asked to talk about the outside of the bag and how it represents them, and then are invited, but not required, to talk about one thing from the inside of the bag. If they do, group leaders then ask members to reflect on what it was like to share this information in the group. If group members do not share something from inside the bag, it is important for them to talk about what needs to happen in group in order for them to be able to share some of that inner part of themselves.

Goal setting may be introduced by the activity "Turning Over a New Leaf" (Dossick & Shea, 1990), which uses the metaphor of a new leaf as a way to describe behaviors, attitudes, or feelings that may be harmful to themselves or to others. On one side of the leaf, they write down the behavior, thought, or feeling to be changed; on the other side of the leaf, they write down an alternative, more adaptive behavior, thought, or feeling.

In a different approach, Wolfe et al. (1996) suggested using a panel of past group participants to talk about what they learned, what effect the group had on them, what they enjoyed most about the group, how they felt at their first session, and what feelings developed across the group sessions. Then, new group members could be allowed to ask former group members specific questions.

Dossick and Shea's (1990) activity titled "The State Lottery" asks group members to self-disclose through fantasy about what they would do with the money if they won the lottery and then how it would change their lives, helping to identify potential goals for the group.

There are many good activities to illustrate group process. Using cooking as a metaphor, the group can be described in terms of spices, and each member can be asked to describe how he or she contributes to a recipe, like a spice. To make it concrete, each group member can be given an ingredient to make chili or a Chex®-mix-like creation so that group members can see (and taste) how each ingredient (like a member) contributes uniquely to the group. Musical chairs can be used as an analogy of what it is like to be left out, followed by a discussion of how to make sure that it does not happen in group. The hot potato game can be used as a metaphor of what it is like to be put on the spot in group, and group members can then discuss how they can help each other learn and try out new behaviors by giving constructive feedback and making comments about what happens in group, but in a way that is respectful and that the group member can hear and use.

Summary

The initial session is critical to establishing trust and rapport between group members and creating a safe atmosphere that encourages students to examine and try out new behaviors. Group members' anxiety lessens when they begin to understand how groups work and the role of the leaders and members in this process. Group members begin to learn about the other group members and themselves in relation to the group goals, and begin to develop an individual plan of action. Group leader interventions emphasize caring and executive function leadership behaviors to provide structure and support with some meaning attribution to help group members understand how they will learn from participation in this group.

Suggested Training Activities

1. Identify and Adapt Icebreaker Activities

- Examine group literature in general and specific to one type of psychoeducational group for activities that may be used as part of the initial session. Figure 2.1 in Chapter 2 and Appendix G contain some suggested resources.
- For each activity, identify the task(s) for the initial stage that this activity would accomplish.
- For each activity, identify therapeutic factors that this activity would promote.
- For each activity, write two or three processing questions directed at meaning attribution for this activity.

2. Identify and Adapt Existing Initial Sessions

- Examine group literature in general and specific to one type of psychoeducational group for existing sessions. Figure 2.1 in Chapter 2 and Appendix G contain some suggested resources.
- For each session, identify the task(s) for the initial stage that this activity would meet.
- For each session, identify therapeutic factors that this activity would promote.
- For each session, write two or three processing questions directed at meaning attribution for the processing part of the session.

3. Observation of an Initial Session for a Psychoeducational Group

- View Part 1 of the Smead (1996) videotape.
- Identify the task(s) for the initial stage that was (were) addressed and how.
- Identify leadership behaviors in all four categories: Executive Function, Caring, Emotional Stimulation, and Meaning Attribution.
- Identify therapeutic factors that occurred.

4. Design and Implement a First Group Session

- Choose a specific type of psychoeducational group and a population.
- Choose goals for the group and make procedural decisions.
- Design a first group session that includes opening, working, processing, and closing parts.
- Make sure that all the major tasks of an initial session are addressed.
- Select an evaluation measure that includes goals for group and assesses progress toward the specific goals of the group at the beginning of the group and how group will help work on this goal.
- Complete the Group Planning Sheet in Appendix D, and include the information about each member based on screening interviews.
- Implement the session as a role-play, videotaping the session. (This could be an in-class role-play.)
- After the session is over, ask your members to talk about the following:
  - What was helpful in making them feel comfortable?
  - Interacting with other members?
  - Establishing a goal?
  - Wanting to come back to group again?

- Administer the evaluation measures.
- Evaluate the session using the tape, feedback from members, and one or more of the group leadership assessment forms discussed in Chapter 4.
- Complete the Group Processing Sheet in Appendix E for this session.
- Meet with your co-leader using the model of Reporting, Reflection, Integration, Planning, and Evaluation (DeLucia-Waack, 2001) and the CLINICKING section of the Co-Facilitating Inventory (Pfeiffer & Jones, 1975).
- Complete the planning sheet for the next session.

5. Processing of a First Class Session as a Parallel to a First Task Group Session (for Instructors)

- Conduct a first class session as you would typically. Perhaps include an icebreaker that emphasizes self-disclosure and setting of goals.
- Ten minutes before the class ends, ask the class to reflect on some or all of the following questions for themselves personally:
  - How are you feeling?
  - What made you anxious?

- What helped lessen your anxiety?
  - What did the instructor do specifically to help you feel more comfortable?
  - What did others do to lessen your anxiety?
  - What have you learned?
  - What do you need to think about and do before next week?
  - What are your goals for this class?
  - What do you need to do to make them happen?
  - How can others in the room help you achieve your goals?

- Then ask them to switch into the role of the potential group leader. Ask them to discuss the following based on their observations:
  - How will you provide safety and structure for your members?
  - How will you establish norms?
  - How will you help develop group and individual goals?
  - How will you address anxiety and help lessen it?
  - How will you promote interactions between members?
  - How will you promote connections between members?

6. Design and Implementation of a Second Group Session

- Design a second group session that includes the following:
  - Quick review of names
  - Quick review of ground rules
  - A goal-setting activity
  - Processing
  - Closing

- Complete a Group Planning Sheet, found in Appendix D.
- Implement the session as a role-play, videotaping the session. (This could be an in-class role-play.)
- After the session is over, ask your members to talk about the following:
  - What was helpful in making them feel comfortable?
  - Interacting with other members?
  - Establishing a goal?
  - Wanting to come back to group again?

- Administer the evaluation measures.
- Evaluate the session using the tape, feedback from members, and one or more of the group leadership assessment forms discussed in Chapter 4.
- Complete the Group Processing Sheet in Appendix E for this session.
- Meet with your co-leader using the model of Reporting, Reflection, Integration, Planning, and Evaluation (DeLucia-Waack, 2001) and the CLINICKING section of the Co-Facilitating Inventory (Pfeiffer & Jones, 1975).
- Complete the Group Planning Sheet in Appendix D for the next session.

CHAPTER 6

Middle Sessions

O nce group members have a chance to get to know each other and begin to understand how groups work and how to participate, psychoeducational groups for children and adolescents really get going. This is the fun part. Group members have begun to get over the awkwardness of being in group, which has different rules of participation and interaction from the rest of their lives, and have truly started to be themselves and interact as they normally do in other settings. And this is what we want them to do. As group leaders, you begin to see how they normally interact, what their strengths are, what areas they need to work on, and what skills they need to learn or develop more fully. Group members take risks, try out new behaviors, and work together. They also display their reluctance and what intimidates or worries them, and they may not fully participate because of peer pressure. This is OK because what is important is that group members are interacting in group in a way that is typical of how they interact in the rest of their lives. Role-plays are useful to practice new skills because group members learn the most when they use their new skills in meaningful actions in group. Thus, as they plan for the middle stages, group leaders need to think carefully about how to integrate, particularly in the processing and closing of a group session and in homework assignments, interactions that ask group members to use their new skills in realistic situations.

The middle stages are the action stages of group, sometimes called the working or performing stages. In psychoeducational groups, this is where group members learn new behaviors and try them out, using the group process to suggest a wide range of alternatives, practice in a number of different situations, and receive feedback from various perspectives.

Goals and Tasks

Working-stage activities focus on identifying behaviors, attitudes, and cognitions that negatively affect group members' affect and relationships, as well as identifying, learning, and practicing potentially new and more effective skills and ways of thinking. In psychoeducational groups, most working group sessions will use brainstorming, role-playing, problem-solving, and decision-making interventions to teach and practice new skills and interactional styles. All psychoeducational groups, to some extent, focus on the development of communication and relationship skills and self-instructional training to meet specific content group goals. These skills help group members work effectively in group as well as facilitate relationships outside of group. Middle-stage activities should then include information about these topics, as well as activities to practice these new behaviors and skills. The goals of the middle sessions should be directly related to the goals of the group. Each session should have a goal that specifically teaches new skills, behaviors, or cognitive strategies to meet the goal of the psychoeducational group.

Group Leadership Skills

In the middle stages of a psychoeducational group, the focus of group leadership interventions is on creating a safe atmosphere where group members can identify and practice new behaviors, and give and receive feedback that is directed at skill development.

Caring

Group leadership interventions in the area of caring during the middle stage focus on supporting group members and helping them to identify strengths and take risks. Much of the caring that occurs at this stage comes from other group members. Leaders facilitate cohesiveness, connections, and giving of positive feedback by asking questions or making comments that focus on similarities between members, how they connect to each other, and how they have taken risks for each other, and the leaders also help to structure feedback in a way that group members can hear and use.

Executive Function

During the middle stage of psychoeducational groups, the executive functions are leadership behaviors focused on creating an atmosphere through structure in which members feel safe enough to try out new behaviors, participate in group activities, and give feedback to each other.

Structuring of Interactions. The structure of group interactions should help members to feel safe and know what will happen without preventing them from being spontaneous or sharing important information. Smead (2000b) suggests using dyadic activities in early group sessions to help members get comfortable self-disclosing to one member in preparation for sharing with the whole group. She suggests using other combinations of clusters of group members later on, depending on the activity. Sometimes, it is useful to have two or three group members role-play a situation, with additional members serving as coaches to suggest interventions. The rest of the group may serve as observers and ask questions and give feedback after the role-play. Other times, it may make more sense to bring groups of two or three to role-play, with all group members sharing feedback and insight as a large group after the role-play.

A structured intervention throughout the session to assess group members' feelings, reactions, thoughts, or plans for action is particularly useful—during the opening to gauge members' mood that day and what progress they have made on homework; during processing of an activity to give members feedback, suggest alternatives, and plan for the future; during processing of a group session to identify what has been learned and how members will apply it; and during closing to identify commitments toward homework and behavior change for the next week. Go-rounds, or share-arounds as Smead (2000b) prefers to call them, are an invitation to group members to respond to a specific stimulus question or statement and suggests stating that everyone needs to speak, but people can go when they are ready rather than in a prescribed fashion. Carrell (2000) advocates for the round-robin approach because "teens are not skilled in social intercourse, and unstructured interaction can be threatening. In round-robin, each member knows when it is his or her turn to speak" (p. 6). Such go-rounds can focus on content and process. The content might be what group members have learned from the session and how they will use that new information, skill, or attitude in the coming week. Process can focus on who or what was most helpful in the group session that day in an effort to identify connections and promote learning about what is helpful in group.

Mathis and Tanner (2000) suggested the use of rounds as an activity to promote insight and gain information to work toward skill development. They suggested the value of rounds for "gathering information, involving members, and controlling overparticipators" (p. 92). Group members should be informed at the beginning of a round that the goal is to be specific but concise (one or two sentences at the most). Rounds can then be processed in terms of what was learned about themselves, what was learned about others, similarities and differences in responses, and future coping strategies. Mathis and Tanner suggested a series of four rounds designed to help group members become aware of their family norms, how they communicate in their families, and then what they want to change or what new skills they want to learn.

The part of the session, group members' anxiety level, and the goal of the intervention determine which approach to use. If it is essential to have all group members speak, then group leaders should state this when they introduce the question or statement to be finished. As a check-in during the opening on mood or goals, everyone should speak, and it may be easiest to go in order. Similarly, during processing or closing to assess learning and to perhaps identify homework assignments, going around the circle in an orderly fashion is recommended so that no one is missed and everyone has a turn. During a feedback session for a particular activity, however, it may not be critical that every member speaks. Observing who speaks first, who agrees with whom, and/or who jumps in gives the group leaders information about group members' interactional styles. After an activity, a group leader may ask, "Who has feedback for the participants?" If positive feedback is given by several members, the group leaders may then ask if there are any constructive comments. If several are made but a few group members still haven't spoken, the group leaders may ask, "Does anyone else have something to add? There are several of you who haven't spoken up yet." If one or two group members consistently do not offer feedback during several activities, group leaders may speak to them directly: "You haven't offered any feedback in the past few feedback sessions. It is important that you practice giving feedback and that group members hear your feedback. What would you like to say?"

Building a Group Culture. Underlying all groups is the assumption that honest feedback, risk taking, and direct communication are important and valued skills both to promote effective group process and also to develop relationship skills outside of group. Interventions that highlight when someone discloses and how it affects other group members, compliment risk taking and identify the risks, and acknowledge the difficulty of being direct but that it gets results all build the culture that group members are going to be honest with each other, give feedback, and be supportive but challenging.

Emotional Stimulation

Many of the group leader interventions in the area of emotional stimulation during the middle stage of psychoeducational groups are directed at helping group members identify and explore their emotions, and how these emotions are interconnected with their thoughts and behaviors. Identification of positive emotions such as happiness, joy, satisfaction, and contentment is important so that positive interactions can be labeled and then analyzed for what made them positive, and strategies planned that will reinforce these interactions and encourage them to occur again. Identification of negative emotions is also important because it often leads to the identification of negative self-talk or behaviors that are not effective in social situations. Psychoeducational groups create an atmosphere that is relatively safe but produces some of the anxiety, hesitation, and reluctance that occurs in other social situations by virtue of what it asks group members to do: self-disclose, self-assess, share personal thoughts and feelings, give and receive feedback, take risks, and try out new behaviors. It is the emphasis on identification of feelings in the group that is important. Group members may discount or downplay what they are feeling by saying, "This isn't a real group . . . These aren't my friends . . . I do not care if they like me or not." Group leaders can respond by acknowledging that this is different from most situations, and then asking them to infer, role-play, or play "What if?" "OK, maybe you do not care, but if you did, what would you feel? What would you think? What might you do differently so that they would like you?"

Emphasizing throughout the life of the group the connections between thoughts, feelings, and behaviors is essential. Smead (2000b) suggests using an activity early in the middle stage of group that identifies and explains thoughts, feelings, and behaviors and how they are interconnected. At some point during each session, it is essential to check in with members about their feelings. Sometimes, it is useful during the opening, and often during processing of an activity or during the processing part of a group session. Almost always, it is important to assess group members' feelings as they leave group.

Meaning Attribution

Challenging. Challenging helps group members look at new behaviors, try out new behaviors, and assess what works and what does not in an effort to help them work in the group and use the group most effectively. Often, challenging asks group members to take a step further than they have before. It may ask them to try out a behavior that they have been edging toward but haven't quite done yet: "OK, you have a good sense of what you want to say. So look at the member and say it directly. You can do it." Challenging may ask group members to look at the discrepancy between their verbal and nonverbal behavior: "You say you are OK with the feedback you just got, but you have your arms crossed and you have pulled your chair out of the circle." Challenging may ask them to think about a situation or a behavior from a different perspective: "You are very insulted that these people would ask you to look at them when they are speaking. But I hear them saying that they want to know that you are interested in them and listening to them because they want your feedback."

Making Process Comments. Commenting on the process of the groups—what is happening, patterns of interaction and communication—is essential to any type of group. And such comments are essential to facilitating emotional stimulation and meaning attribution in psychoeducational groups because they take the focus in group from role-playing and practicing to relating to real situations with real emotions, thoughts, and behaviors. Carroll (2001) emphasizes how linking is used to connect members in the present based on their interactions in group. One important impact that Carroll stressed is how questions asked by group members usually have as much to do with the group member who is asking the question as the one to whom the question is directed. Her example, "Do your parents require you to be in at a certain time on Saturday nights?" suggests that the group member may be trying to see how universal his or her situation is, make a connection, or perhaps share something about him- or herself. Carroll recommends clearly stating that such questions often have a dual meaning, and that group members should be asked to reflect on why they are asking this particular question. This may lower the anxiety of the group member who is being put on the spot; explain more about the group member who is asking and his or her reasons; and also serve as a context for the question, which may make it easier for the group member to answer. She suggests three goals for here-and-now comments: (a) bringing the content into the present ("I hear you saying that you get anxious when others look at you. What do you think others are thinking as they are looking at you in group?"); (b) helping members to look inward ("What was it like to do this activity? What feelings did you have? What thoughts?"); and (c) personalizing the experience ("Can you speak directly to one person and use 'I' statements?").

In psychoeducational groups, it is important to ask group members to reflect on the here and now, or what happens for them in groups, at three different times.

The first time should be when the group is working well so that they can identify specifically what works and how to continue doing it ("What helped us to disclose? What helped us to problem solve tonight? How can we continue to do it? How can you do it outside of group?"). Early activities that focus on problem solving, such as the "Human Knot," are good instances of activities to comment on how well the process worked and the creation of ground rules. This discussion of positive inter-actions sets the stage for the second set of circumstances when group leaders need to comment on the process.

The second instance should be when the group is not working well so that group members can identify and evaluate what the problem is and suggest solutions to resolve it. Group members may not give feedback after a particular activity, or it may be shallow and not what they typically do. This is a good time to comment: "Something seems different this session. The feedback didn't seem as specific as the group usually gives. What do you think is happening?" Even if the group leaders are pretty certain that they know what the obstacle may be (e.g., the person who role-played is perceived as very delicate and they do not want to hurt her feelings), it is useful to start out by commenting only on what has been observed. It is much more helpful if group members can identify what the obstacle is and then come up with a solution. If the group leaders were to push through the resistance by asking very specific questions that ended up in the person who role-played being given specific feedback, the group leaders would have lost the opportunity to help group members identify their reluctance and resistance and might have resulted in group members feeling pushed too far.

The third instance when the here-and-now interpersonal process should be brought up in the group session is related to members' goals. Continuing with the example above, it would be all the more important to discuss what was happening if several group members had goals related to being honest with other people, especially in giving constructive feedback. Particularly when a thought, feeling, behavior, or group interaction interferes with a group member making progress on his or her goals, then it must be discussed. However, some caution must be used. Group members tend to feel overanalyzed if group leaders are constantly pointing out problems.

My guideline is that once is a coincidence, but two or three times is probably more of a pattern, and I will comment on that. Sometimes, when I talk about my role as a group leader, I may even give an example, such as that people might be late to group the first time we meet because they aren't sure exactly where we are meeting, but after that, they should have figured out how to get here on time. So, if they are continually late, I would probably ask what gets in the way of being here on time.

Just commenting about the pattern brings attention to it and asks the group to stop and reflect on it. "I hear a lot of yesbutting to suggestions." "A lot of people had trouble doing (or committing to homework) today." "You look like you want to cry but won't let yourself."

Reflecting on your feelings as a group leader also emphasizes the immediacy of group interactions: "Right now I am feeling . . ." Noticing someone else's feelings toward you as the group leader encourages the projection of feeling onto a relatively safe topic: "You seem angry with me."

Some other examples of here-and-now statements are as follows:

- This silence doesn't feel good to me.
- I've noticed that you have been very quiet during this session, and I'd like to know how you feel.
- What would you like to do?
- Have any of you had any thoughts about our previous session that you'd like to share?
- What else needs to be said?
- How were you affected by _____?
- How does this issue relate to you?

Silence, in and of itself, is a powerful process statement. Silence allows group members to reflect and figure out what they want to say. Some group members process faster than others, and so silence allows all members a chance to gather their thoughts. Silence also makes the statement that the group leaders will not be responsible for engaging the group constantly; all group members need some moments of silence. Silence enhances a powerful statement, such as a process comment: "We all seem really edgy today." Silence also allows group members to engage in their typical behaviors; group members who need to fill every waking moment will be uncomfortable with silence and will break it quickly. Group leaders should process what happens for group members, what they are thinking and feeling, how they choose to stay quiet or break the silence, and whom they are taking care of by their actions—themselves or the group.

Moving From Affect to Action or From Action to Affect. Identification of feelings is a key part of decision-making, problem-solving, and brainstorming activities. As group members acknowledge one or more emotions, they are less likely to be swayed by the feelings. However, it is important to understand the importance of identifying feelings as part of the process toward developing a plan of action, not a goal in itself. People sometimes get stuck in the affect and can't move on to developing a plan. Group leaders need to help group members see the value of identifying and expressing feelings as part of the context of planning future strategies. Identifying anger may then lead to identifying irrational beliefs about how one is supposed to act that need to be disputed in order to lessen the anger.

In contrast, some group members may be more comfortable with a cognitive style and jump into the cognitive part of decision making or problem solving without first identifying feelings. It is up to the group leaders to comment on the overemphasis on problem solving without the identification of emotions. The role of the group leader is to help group members to both think and feel as they problem solve, brainstorm, and develop coping strategies. The advantage of group members who have different styles and emphasize thoughts and feelings differently is the variety of feedback, perspectives, and suggestions to help the person look at the situation from various angles.

Encouraging the Group to Give Feedback. Group member feedback is the key ingredient in successful psychoeducational groups. If group members could learn what they needed to know by just participating in an activity, they could do it on their own or with one counselor. But the importance of group member feedback to the group process cannot be underestimated. I cannot tell you how many times I have been told as a group leader, "Of course you care. You are being paid to care." Or, "Of course you will say nice things. You are the leader. You have to. You can't get angry and yell at us." To which I say, "Although I am paid, I do care about my group members, or I would suggest that they work with someone else as I believe caring is a key ingredient in groups." I also tell group members, "I can get angry, but I will do my best to model appropriate expression of my feelings, and if I do not, I would like feedback from you about it." That being said, honest feedback from group members is so valuable in psychoeducational groups from both the giving and receiving perspectives. Honest feedback is something that members can't get most places, and it means so much more from a member than from a group leader. Friends, or ex-friends, are more likely to stop hanging around with you than tell you what you have done to make them mad or make them think you are an uncaring person. Furthermore, having a place to practice giving more supportive and constructive feedback is a benefit of psychoeducational groups. Children and adolescents often do not have a place to try out these behaviors without the stakes being very high (e.g., losing a friend, offending a teacher). Groups allow members to make mistakes, get feedback, and try again. Mistakes are expected, and group members are expected to be clear about what they heard, what they perceived, and how the message was received. In addition, group members are asked to be specific about how the group member could phrase it differently so that the message can be heard without offending someone. Group leaders need to start slowly in the first session, asking for comments, reactions to the group as a whole, the process, and specific incidents, and then move to people and their behavior. In the first session, group members are typically asked with whom they connect and from whom they heard something that affected them (positive feedback). In the middle stages, group members participate in activities where they give specific feedback on role-plays and other practice activities: How would you have felt if they said that or did that to you? Would you be OK with it? Why? Would you be offended? Why? What could they change? How might you say it? Then, as group interactions occur between group members where there is some disagreement or difference of opinion, group leaders can ask them to talk to each other directly, use "I" statements, describe their feelings, identify what specifically is upsetting to them, and state how they would like it to be different. The group leaders can encourage and coach members through the discussion. It is essential after such a discussion is finished that group leaders process with the whole group what that interaction was like, what they were thinking and feeling, what worked to help facilitate the discussion, and how each group member will work toward using these behaviors in group in the future when they are upset or uncomfortable, or when they disagree.

Advice is discouraged, and Carroll's (2001) suggestions about questions may be relevant here as well. What is the person who is asking the question (or giving advice) trying to communicate? Sometimes, as group members try to establish themselves as important or all-knowing in the group, they may give advice. Usually, it feels like the person giving the advice does not understand the person discussing his or her situation very well because the advice does not fit or the advice feels condescending: "Of course I already tried that. Do you think I am stupid?" It is helpful, if possible, to include "no advice giving" as a ground rule, or speak early on about the difference between giving advice—"You should do this"—and making a suggestion—"Have you considered this?"

Possible Pitfalls

I began this chapter saying that the middle stage of group is the most fun, and it is by far. Group members are changing; expressing themselves; energized by activities; and usually trying out new behaviors, some of which work and some of which do not. The group members act most like they do outside of group and although this makes groups fun, it also makes the middle stage the most challenging as well. All people make mistakes in social interactions, get anxious, do not want to participate, and occasionally are insensitive to other people. So, in group, this means that sometimes members may be silent, rude, talkative, or distracting. This part of the chapter will discuss some of the possibly trying situations that may occur in the middle stages of psychoeducational groups and present a framework within which to conceptualize the behaviors and interventions.

Even though psychoeducational groups are being discussed, an old psychodynamic phrase comes to mind: "Everything is grist for the therapeutic mill." What does this mean for psychoeducational groups? For me, it means that my goal as a group leader is to help the groups work together so that individuals benefit from participation in the group. So, whatever happens in group, I may comment on it. As mentioned earlier in the section Making Process Comments, it is helpful to comment when things are going well to encourage these same behaviors to recur. It is even more important to comment on something that is interfering with effective group processes that help members to learn and change and grow. Sometimes, the group member's impact on the group is related to his or her goal (he or she does not want to talk about his or her feelings, so he or she tries to change the topic when feelings are being discussed). Other times, peer pressure makes a member want to be the center of attention, so he or she tells jokes. This is still related to how this person interacts, and it is important that he or she sees both the short- and long-term consequences of such behavior. (Right now the group members think the person is funny, but when group is ending and members realize how much time they wasted being distracted that could have been focused on their goals, they may be angry or disappointed.) The same foresight should go into group leadership decisions. Beginning group leaders often want to be liked, and so they do lots of things to be caring and supportive but do not challenge their members or keep them on task as often as they should. The short-term consequence is that the group members like them, but the long-term consequence is that group members do not get as much out of group as they could.

Thus, it is important for group leaders to think about all behaviors that group members exhibit in group as related to who they are, their strengths and weaknesses, and their goals. In addition, all behaviors exhibited in group speak to the group in some way. People aren't mean and nasty just to be mean and nasty, nor did they just wake up one morning and decide to be mean and nasty. Everyone has a history, a context, a story, and how he or she acts in group communicates that story in some way. This is especially important to remember when working with adolescents, particularly angry adolescents. But then, aren't all adolescents angry to some extent? Or shouldn't they be? They are expected to act like adults, and to go to school and work, but they have none of the privileges of adults. It's tough to be a teenager these days. Furthermore, remember the basic premise of psychoeducational groups: skill development (whether behavioral, cognitive, or affective). Most likely, group members are not exhibiting positive social skills and adaptive behaviors out of resistance but because of a skill deficit. They simply haven't learned the skills they need to express themselves, communicate, reframe a situation, problem solve, or resolve conflict. It is helpful for me to remind myself that I haven't mastered all those skills as an adult, so how can I expect children and adolescents to do so? I also like to remember that an occasional self-help book on feelings, anger, or relationships is a good refresher for me on these skills (I particularly like Harriet Lerner's series of books that begins with *The Dance of Anger,* 1985, because they are skill-based but easy to read because of her self-disclosing vignettes).

Dr. Arthur Horne, who has written extensively about group work, particularly for adolescents and teenage boys specifically, likes to emphasize the importance of paying attention to what group members are trying to tell us with their resistant behaviors, which he reframes as reluctance. They are not resistant to our interventions, but reluctant in some way. And that reluctance has to do with who they are as people—their strengths, skills, and anxieties, as well as what is happening in group interactions and how it may be representative of other relationships in their lives. Some group members might be reluctant to speak at all in group, or in any social situation, whereas another group member may not feel comfortable speaking in this particular group because of previous interactions with other group members. These differences are important to discover so that solutions can be devised. If one can conceptualize the reluctance as a message about what is happening in group, it is much easier to think about how to work with the group members rather than dismissing them as angry or rebellious teenagers. Horne and Campbell (1997) suggested that the message is often related to the group member's needs not being met in some way, and he offers several possible reasons: What we are doing or offering is not perceived as relevant, we do not understand (or do not communicate understanding of) the group member or his or her situation, the solution presented to the group members is too complex or irrelevant, or the group member hasn't "bought into" the interventions specifically or the group as a whole. Based on this conceptualization of reluctance, several suggestions are offered as interventions within psychoeducational groups. First is to acknowledge directly to the group member who is reluctant that the behavior, attitude, and/or feelings are noticed. Second is to facilitate a discussion of the group member's experiences in and outside of group as they relate to the behavior. *Facilitate* is the key word, not telling the group member what is probably going on. Third is to then discuss with the group member how, collaboratively, you and the group member (and the group) can work through this. As a group leader, it is important to point out the parallels between what happens in group and in outside relationships, how group members can both give and receive in group, and how you can guide and support but not direct them what to do.

Some of what happens in groups related to reluctant behaviors also has to do with setting up and following specific ground rules from the first minute that group members enter the group room. It is essential to begin to develop norms and be consistent about them as much as possible. If there are inconsistencies, group members pick up on them. In the earlier discussions on setting group guidelines, it was emphasized that all activities should be directed at self-disclosure, cohesiveness, and group goals. I have often had group members say, "Let's talk about this or do this." My standard response is, "How will this help you with your group goals?" If they can relate what they want to do to group goals, then the group can do it. It is much better to go with the flow of the group if the members are moving in the right direction, because they feel more in control, internalize the norms, and are much more invested. I like to use the analogy of sheepdogs herding sheep. At the beginning, as they start to move the sheep from one pasture to another, the dogs work very hard at getting the sheep to go in the right direction at the right speed in the right formation (the beginning stage). Once the sheep begin to move in that direction, the momentum is there, and the dogs just need to keep the sheep moving in that general direction, occasionally herding a straggler back in the right direction (middle stage). As the sheep get to the new pasture and need to enter through a narrow gate, the dogs need to work hard again to make sure that all the sheep are successful and accounted for (termination).

Group members sometimes initially balk about being called sheep, but when I admit that talking about myself as a "big old sheepdog with lots of hair in my face, bounding all over the place" isn't the way I want to be remembered, they laugh. This is usually a joining moment, and the concept of the dog herding the sheep can now be used in the group. I can say things like, "I think the sheep are getting off their path. What can they do to get back on it?" or "What does the dog need to do?" or "We're getting close to the gate. I'm going to have to start herding you a bit."

Going back to the earlier example of the group member who is hesitant to speak in any social situation, the group leaders might meet with the group member individually and discuss how they can help the member to begin to speak in group. Can they ask the person directly, does it help to sit next to a particular person, can they look at the member? Although it is important to conduct as much discussion with group members in group as possible to facilitate group interactions, reactions, and subsequent processing, sometimes it is beneficial to meet with group members individually. When working in the schools or also seeing an adolescent for individual counseling, group leaders have the luxury of being able to check in with group members individually. Some things are better said privately because of the shame and embarrassment factor. Embarrassing a group member in front of peers may make the person become defensive and get aggressive; a one-on-one conversation may likely result in some self-disclosure and willingness to connect on his or her part. Most times, it is helpful to suggest to the group member that it probably should be shared with the group that there was a meeting outside of group. Therapeutically, it is helpful to talk with the group member about how this should be done. Does he or she want to bring it up? What should be said? What shouldn't? This discussion emphasizes setting appropriate boundaries at the same time that it reinforces the commitment about out-of-group contact.

For the second example of a person whose nonparticipation is more related to previous negative interactions with group members, the group leaders might ask directly what has happened and how it can be resolved so that all members can participate in group. Again, depending on how the intervention might be received in group, the group leaders may want to talk with the person outside of group and perhaps ask if they can bring it up in group. If the group member says no, the group leaders may still want to say, "OK, but if it interferes in group, we are going to have to talk about it," allowing the group member the option of resolving it for himself or herself and/or changing his or her behavior without it becoming a topic of group. If the topic does come up in group, some coaching might focus on how to use "I" statements and feeling words, how to be specific about what was upsetting, and how the member would like it to be different. It would also be very important to thank the members involved for their willingness to take risks, be honest, share and self-disclose, and try to resolve their differences with the group.

Monopolizers (or Group Members Who Have Lots of Words). There are lots of reasons why people talk too much: They do not feel understood, they do not like silence, they want to take care of the other group members, they have a lot to say, and probably many more reasons. Some of the structuring techniques will help with this behavior, such as the use of go-rounds and round robins with specific directions about answering with one word, one sentence, or in one minute. If group members are able to follow these guidelines but with much restraint, it is important to process with them what it was like to behave differently, and what happened for them that helped them do this. When group members consistently are the first to speak up, at some point it is useful to observe the pattern and ask the group to discuss the benefits and consequences of this interaction, how they feel about what happens, and how they allow it to continue. Group responsibility is important to discuss because group members may be irritated by the behavior but do not acknowledge that, on some level, they allow it to continue by not speaking up themselves. Overactive group members need to understand their motivations as well as the ramifications in terms of how they are perceived by other group members. For those who talk a lot and often in circles, it may be because they do not feel understood. It is helpful for group leaders to help them to speak more effectively, to make their point and then ask for a response from group members rather than continuing to talk because no one else says anything. If the group member is verbalizing his or her thoughts as a way to organize and process them, he or she needs to ask for assistance from the group with these tasks so that it becomes a discussion, not a monologue.

Attention Seeking (Usually the Class Clown). It is helpful to think about this group member from the perspective of what he or she wants: the group's attention. From a behavioral perspective, positive behavior is to be rewarded and negative behavior ignored. Remember the goals of psychoeducational groups: to teach and practice new skills. Assume that the group member is not sure how to participate in a way that is effective and engaging. Carroll (2001) suggests circumventing the problem by asking group members who need a lot of attention to be responsible for some important task that gives them positive attention, such as reading a statement to open the session, distributing materials, writing on the board, or keeping time. To further reinforce and internalize group norms and consolidation of learning, group members might be asked to create the go-round for the processing section of the group so that throughout the group, they must be paying attention to what is happening in order to select an appropriate statement to finish or question to answer.

Attend to the distracting behaviors only when necessary, and then only to ask the group member to stop. Use nonverbals whenever possible to lessen the distraction to other group members (gently touching a member, motioning for silence, etc.). It is sometimes useful to deflect the intent of the disruption if confronting the group member. For example, "Johnny, I am noticing that you are playing a video game while Susie is talking. If I were Susie, I would be uncomfortable and might wonder why you are not paying attention to me. As a group leader, I am aware that there are lots of reasons why you might not be focusing on what is happening in group right now. Maybe you aren't interested in the topic, or you are feeling off today in general. We all are a little off sometimes. Is there something that we can talk about, like how to get you more involved? Or maybe just get your attention for now?" This has the impact of letting Johnny know that the behavior is unacceptable, allowing him a lead-in if he is unhappy with group in some way, but also just giving him the out to put the game away and pay attention without saying anything.

Tardiness. Again, the strategy is to ignore the negative behavior. Do not stop the group or allow the group to be distracted by the person arriving, but continue to give the group member who is speaking your full attention. The implicit message is that the group attends to those who are contributing to the group and not to those who are distracting. Motioning to the group member to come in and sit down quietly acknowledges that he or she is there but does not allow the group to focus on him or her. It is helpful at some point either during the initial discussion of ground rules, or when it has occurred, to talk about how the group wants to deal with latecomers. It makes sense to frame the situation as yes, we want you to come to group, even if you are late, but enter quietly so that whoever is working can continue and finish and then you will be brought into the conversation. Being clear about this sets this as a norm for how all group members will be treated if they are late, and it does not allow individual group members to say they're being treated disrespectfully if they do not get the group's full attention when they enter group late.

Yesbutters (or Woe Is Me . . . Nothing Can Help Me). Group members may be reluctant to engage in an intervention or activity, or to try out suggestions or feedback given by group members, for a variety of reasons. Some of the reasons may be related to the individual group member: He or she may not be ready to change, may not believe anybody can help him or her, or may not have the skills to try out the new behaviors. Other reasons may be related to the group and/or specific group members: The group member does not feel understood by the group, and so the suggestions or interventions are irrelevant, or he or she may feel judged by the others and isn't comfortable taking a risk in front of them. Thus, probably the most effective intervention is to ask the group as a whole what is happening. "We're giving Allison a lot of suggestions, but none of them seems to fit for her. What do you think is happening?" The whole group, including Allison, has been invited to comment on what it is like to be in this situation. Maybe she will talk about how the interventions do not fit for her, maybe group members will talk about how they always make suggestions to her and she never takes any of them, or other group members will talk about not really having a sense of what is happening for Allison so it is hard to make suggestions to her. It is helpful to reinforce from the beginning that all efforts directed at brainstorming, problem solving, and generating alternatives must involve the group member himself or herself at some point selecting which alternatives are most feasible for him or her based on the situation. The group cannot make the decision for that member; however, the group should have enough information and understanding of the group member to suggest some viable options.

Side Conversations. Side conversations in group probably most often suggest that at least one group member, if not more, finds what is happening in the group irrelevant to him or her either for this specific intervention or the group in general. Occasionally, a side conversation indicates insensitivity or disrespect for the group member who is talking. Either of the situations has a substantial impact on the group, and both need to be addressed. The first time, frame it as everyone occasionally makes a mistake, and gently ask members to stop the conversation and focus on the group topic. The second time, group leaders might want to wonder about whether the group topic seems relevant to these group members and frame it as, if it is not, then what would be relevant? If group members suggest that they do not find the group activities interesting or relevant, disclose the goals of what the activity was intended to do and ask the group to generate its own activities to accomplish these goals. Members' activities are often more interesting and applicable. In addition, because they have to decide upon the activities as a group, group members internalize the goals of the group, take responsibility for the group, and have to use problem-solving and conflict-resolution strategies to make a decision.

It is rarely wise to ask the group members directly if they are being disrespectful to a certain group member. Only if they bring it up specifically should it be addressed in group, and then the discussion should be between the group leaders and the offending group members, bringing in the group member who was being disrespected only when necessary. Another strategy would be to call in each of the group members who is participating in the side conversations and state clearly the pattern that has been observed. Ask them why this is occurring and how, as a group leader, you could help to facilitate more respect and understanding between group members in the group.

Arguments and Fighting. Careful articulation of how to make interactions respectful, even when group members disagree, will lay the foundation for group leaders to intervene but will not prevent arguments from occurring in group. Disagreements and conflict are inherent in groups, as they are in relationships, and so the implicit goal of group leaders in the middle stages of group is to teach communication and conflict-resolution skills to facilitate conflicts and disagreements when they occur. Asking group members if they are willing to try to resolve this in group; how the group can help them do this; reminding group members of strategies to communicate effectively but respectfully; and being very active in directing, reframing, and reshaping statements is helpful. When the conflict has been resolved, process it thoroughly with the whole group by discussing how it happened, what helped to resolve it, what each group member did to help resolve it, and how all group members can do this in the future. Asking how it could have been prevented or discussed before it got to this critical point encourages group members to not suppress conflicts and to express them as they occur, rather than letting them simmer.

Examples of Activities

The middle stage of psychoeducational groups includes more expression of affect, increased self-disclosure, and more motivation and willingness to participate in activities to increase self-awareness and learn new skills and patterns of thinking related to group and individual goals. As the group moves past the initial conflicts of safety and trust, a higher sense of cohesion develops, allowing for increased self-exploration and expression, and willingness to take risks and try out new behaviors. Activities for this stage of group should be challenging for members and sometimes may be anxiety provoking as well. Through this, members will be assisted in contributing the appropriate amount of disclosure within the group. More intense activities will match the group members' increased willingness and eagerness to become more self-aware. Activities at this stage might also assist members in working with conflict and recognizing a wider range of emotions and expressions, as well as focusing on the here and now as these relate and contribute to the achievement of group and individual goals.

Behavioral Changes

Interventions to develop new behaviors and change existing behaviors are a major component of the interventions in the middle stage of psychoeducational groups. Because skill development and the promotion of positive relationship behaviors are integral parts of psychoeducational groups, most activities contain some aspect of identification and practice of new behaviors and new ways of thinking and feeling.

Role-plays facilitate behavior change, particularly in interpersonal situations, by allowing participants to rehearse new behaviors in a supportive environment and to receive feedback in a constructive way. One useful format is the following:

- Discussion and demonstration of the targeted behaviors
- Discussion and demonstration of ineffective behaviors
- Identification of situations where a targeted behavior would be useful

- Selection of a specific situation to role-play
- Discussion of how to use the skills effectively in this situation
- Role-play of the targeted behaviors in this situation
- Feedback from the audience about how the targeted behavior was executed
- Feedback from the audience about any ineffective behaviors
- Suggestions from the audience about other ways to use the targeted behavior in a situation
- Discussion from the participants in the role-play of what it was like to use the targeted behaviors, how they made decisions about what to do and what not to do, and how they might do it differently next time.

Role-play situations can come from a variety of sources: those identified by the group leaders based on the literature and their knowledge of the group members' environment, identification of situations to practice by group members anonymously, or identification of situations by group members asking to practice a particular role-play. As the role-plays approximate real situations for group members, they become more anxiety producing, so it may be useful to introduce situations in the order above. Smead (2000b) includes some examples of role-play situations for anger (p. 252), compromising and negotiating (pp. 214–215), and listening (pp. 62–63).

Problem-solving activities include interventions that both teach strategies for problem solving and then apply the problem-solving strategies to different situations. Sommers-Flanagan et al. (2000) suggested five basic cognitive steps to problem solving:

1. What is the problem?

2. What are the different things I can do about it?

3. Which of my possible solutions will work best?

4. Try a solution.

5. Evaluate. Did the solution work?

Other activities help group members to identify places where they want to make changes and what alternatives they have. Activities such as "Strength Bombardment" (Sommers-Flanagan et al., 2000) help students to identify strengths in themselves that they may not otherwise notice, as well as give them practice in giving positive feedback to others and receiving positive feedback. One common activity is to ask group members to draw the family dining table and to identify all communication patterns, then identify which ones are effective and which ones they might want to change. The "Human Knot," in which all group members clasp hands (each with two different persons) and then have to untangle themselves into a circle without letting go, involves movement and energy. It also encourages them to communicate and problem solve. Processing can then focus on how they worked together as a group and how they want to problem solve effectively in other situations. Family sculpting can be used to depict family (or friend) situations, identify what the group member would like to be different, and then role-play new strategies.

Cognitive Changes

Most people, and particularly adolescents, adhere to at least one, if not more, irrational beliefs or faulty assumptions that, at least in the short term, lead to negative affect; in the long term, they may lead to depression. Thus, interventions to help students assess whether their perceptions of the world, their self-talk, and the meanings they attach to behavior are realistic can be very useful. A major component in psychoeducational groups is the use of interventions to change cognitions. Cognitive restructuring exercises concentrate on changing self-talk and disputing irrational beliefs. Self-talk consists of the thoughts and verbal statements that people say to themselves that usually direct actions and evaluate behavior, which may also result in emotion. The goal of changing cognitions is to have a positive impact on affect and/or behavior. Furr (2000) suggested that psychoeducational groups must help group members to first recognize inappropriate self-talk, then restructure the content of the self-talk to be more adaptive, and then practice the readjusted self-statements (p. 39).

Merrill (2001) suggested four major steps in cognitive therapy related to depression but that are applicable to many topics for psychoeducational groups, such as self-esteem, body image, social skills, anger management, and relationship skills. The steps could also serve as the basis for an individual guidance lesson or a series of classroom guidance lessons. Step 1, Developing Awareness of Emotional Variability, teaches students to become aware of their own emotional variability and then to connect that variability to specific cognitions and behavior. Activities such as the "Emotional Thermometer" ask students to identify certain situations that they might experience that involve particular emotions (such as anger, sadness, or fear) and then to select the appropriate level of emotional intensity for that situation. The "Emotional Pie" activity uses pictures to help students identify different mood states experienced during a certain period of time. "Feeling Charts and Cards" can be used to help students identify their range of feelings. It is important in processing these activities in a group setting to help students serve as role models for each other in identifying and expressing the emotions and normalizing the range and intensity of the emotions.

Step 2, Detecting Automatic Thoughts and Identifying Beliefs (Merrill, 2001), focuses on the identification of individual patterns of thinking, both positive and negative, and the belief systems that underlie thought processes and influence emotions. Persons who are depressed often have developed patterns of negative automatic thoughts in response to many situations; these negative automatic thoughts are often distorted and unrealistic, and further fuel the depression.

Step 3, Evaluating Automatic Thoughts and Beliefs (Merrill, 2001), teaches skills to evaluate whether one's adopted automatic thoughts and belief systems are realistic. Step 4, Changing Negative Automatic Thoughts and Maladaptive Beliefs, focuses on the process of actively attempting to change maladaptive thoughts and beliefs identified in the previous steps. The goal of this step is not only to eliminate maladaptive thoughts and beliefs but also to replace them with more positive statements and beliefs.

Merrill (2001) suggested additional activities and techniques that group leaders may find helpful. "Thought Charts" are used to help students identify specific situations, and then the thoughts and emotions associated with the situations. The "Cognitive Replay Technique" helps the student identify automatic thoughts by discussing out loud the particular problem situation. "Thought Forecasting," based on an imaginary but realistic situation, asks students to forecast what might happen and what they might be thinking. The "Hypothesizing/Guessing" activity asks the group members to offer guesses about what negative thoughts a person may have in a particular situation to help that person begin to identify his or her thoughts. The "Down Arrow" technique helps student identify thoughts and irrational beliefs by asking a series of questions such as "So what?" "What?" and "What does that mean?" to identify the core beliefs that may fuel the depressive thinking.

Identifying thinking errors, based on Beck's (1967) six basic errors in processing information, is also useful. The six basic errors are arbitrary inferences, selective abstraction, overgeneralization, magnification and minimization, personalization, and absolute dichotomous thinking. Burns (1980) described them in a more simple way and expanded the types of errors to include binocular vision, black-and-white thinking, dark glasses, fortune-telling, making it personal, overgeneralizing, labeling, discounting the positive, and "beating up" yourself or others. Similarly, Ellis's (1962) list of common irrational beliefs is useful with children and adolescents. Typical negative thoughts to be disputed include the following:

There's something wrong with me.

Something bad is going to happen.

What's the use of trying?

I am no good.

I always say dumb things.

I'll never make any good friends.

I am stupid.

I cannot try this because I would be really embarrassed.

I'll never feel good again.

I'm worthless.

There's no point in getting up in the morning.

The "Examining the Evidence" (Merrill, 2001) intervention asks three questions to determine whether an automatic thought is realistic: "What's the evidence?" "Is there any alternative evidence?" and "What if?" The "Evaluating Positives and Negatives" activity helps the student evaluate his or her cognitions by developing a list of advantages and disadvantages of particular situations. The "Reframing and Relabeling" activity (Merrill, 2001) helps students to generate new labels for problem situations perceived as catastrophic. At times, simply putting a new label on the problem will make it seem more possible to cope. Sommers-Flanagan et al. (2000)

suggested having students make a list of thoughts, feelings, and/or behaviors that they find troubling in their lives. From this list, the concept of a negative spiral is illustrated showing how students may move from a relatively small event to the "pit of doom" or "the black hole of helplessness" based on what they tell themselves about the situation. Conversely, students are then helped to talk themselves out of an event that may feel troubling, and to not let it get out of control.

People in general tend to focus on the negative more than the positive. Several activities are suggested to emphasize the positive and create a positive mood set. Making a list of activities and events that a student finds pleasing, as well as keeping a list of the activities in which a student engages during a week that they find pleasurable, is helpful. Teaching relaxation techniques as well as identifying situations where students may want to use such techniques is very useful. Activity-scheduling interventions are based on the theory that as engagement in positive activities increases, depressed mood state decreases. Thus, students are asked to decrease the amount of time that they spend in isolation, without purpose, or in activities where they are likely to ruminate about problems, and to increase the amount of time that they spend in pleasant activities.

Several activities are suggested to put new, more realistic thoughts into practice. Beck, Rush, Shaw, and Emery (1979) suggested a "Daily Record of Thoughts" to identify the situation, emotion, automatic thought, thinking error, rational response, and outcome. A simpler version is called the "Triple-Column Technique," which has columns for maladaptive thought, thinking errors, and more realistic thoughts. "Cognitive Rehearsal" activities and role-plays help to identify automatic thoughts that may interfere with a particular situation, generate new ways of thinking, and practice effective behaviors related to the situation. The incorporation of increasing and practicing positive self-statements within role-plays is also useful.

Reynolds's (2002) "Meta-Cognition to Reduce Test-Taking Stress" could be useful in test anxiety groups, stress reduction, school survival, and relationship skills groups because it helps to identify and then dispute negative statements that students make to themselves. For all of these activities, group interventions help students identify specific situations in which they are telling themselves negative thoughts, assess how realistic the thoughts are, and generate more adaptive thoughts with regard to the situation.

Affective Changes

Helping group members to develop and express appropriate affect is an important part of psychoeducational groups. Group members need to learn to feel good about themselves, identify their strengths, and take pride in themselves and their work. In addition, they need to learn to view negative affect as a signal, a sign that something is amiss. If they are depressed, they need to look at their situation: Are they telling themselves negative things? Are they interacting with people in ways that do not feel good? Are they doing things behaviorally that are not good for themselves physically or emotionally? Martin's (2002) "Masks of Shyness" activity can be used in most psychoeducational groups to help group members identify which feelings they try to hide in public situations; identify similarities in fears, anxieties, and feelings; and then generate alternative behaviors. Gerrity's (2002) "Our Two Faces" also emphasizes which feelings people share with others and which ones they hide. Processing focuses on similarities in masks and how more of the inner masks can be shared with others. Halbur and Nowparvar's (2002) "Set My Life to Music" uses music to suggest a feeling and then has group members write about the feelings in response to the music. "The Kids' Grief Kit" (LeGrand, 2002) clearly identifies feelings as well as coping strategies to deal with grief and loss. Pederson's (2002) "Nested Emotions" asks group members to identify both their own feelings and what they think others will feel in a certain situation, emphasizing the similarities, differences, and range of feelings to one situation. Gladding's (2002) "Lines of Feelings" helps group members express their feelings in a non-threatening but concrete way by using a visual representation of a line using color and design.

Summary

Activities to teach new ways of thinking, feeling, and behaving are a large part of the substance of the middle stages in psychoeducational groups. Structure must be provided to help group members feel safe so that they participate, self-disclose, share, try out new behaviors, and give feedback. Group leaders model expected behaviors implicitly and explicitly, gently shaping and encouraging more positive and adaptive behaviors from group members.

Suggested Training Activity

1. Design a 1-Hour Group Session for the Middle Stage of a Psychoeducational Group

- Choose a specific type of psychoeducational group and a population.
- Choose goals for the group and procedural decisions.
- Choose one of the goals and design three group sessions that include opening, working, processing, and closing.
- Make sure that all the major tasks of the middle stage are addressed.
- Select an evaluation measure that reflects the goals you have chosen.
- Complete the Group Planning Sheet in Appendix D, including the information about each member based on screening interviews.
- Implement the sessions as a role-play, videotaping the session.
- After each session is over, ask your members to talk about the following:
  - What was helpful in making them feel comfortable?
  - Interacting with other members?
  - Working on a goal?
  - Wanting to come back to group again?

- Administer the evaluation measures.
- Evaluate the sessions using the tapes, feedback from members, and one or more of the group leadership assessment forms discussed in Chapter 4.
- Complete the Group Processing Sheet for each session in Appendix E.
- Meet with your co-leader after each session using the model of Reporting, Reflection, Integration, Planning, and Evaluation (DeLucia-Waack, 2001) and the CLINICKING section of the Co-Facilitating Inventory (Pfeiffer & Jones, 1975).
- Complete the Group Planning Sheet for the next session in Appendix D.

CHAPTER 7

Termination Sessions

ctivities in the ending stage assist members in termination and in bringing together what they have learned to use once the group has ended. Group members need to leave group with a clear sense of what they have learned from group and how they will use it, how they have learned what they have learned, and who was influential in the learning process. At least one session, if not two, is devoted to termination with the goals of helping group members (a) summarize what they have learned and how they learned it, (b) express their feelings about the group and group members, and (c) discuss how they will use what they have learned in their families and outside situations.

Group leaders often underestimate the importance of the termination session and the consolidation of learning for a variety of different reasons. One is that psychoeducational groups tend to be so brief that it is difficult to consider giving a whole session to a topic that is not teaching a new skill or strategy. Another is that much of the addiction literature has focused extensively on planning for the future, identifying specific situations where new skills can be used. However, the term often used is *relapse planning,* which does not seem to fit with the emphasis on prevention, wellness, and skill development in psychoeducational groups. However, if one looks more closely, relapse-planning strategies are useful in helping group members to assess critically what they have learned and plan specifically how they will incorporate these new skills into their lives. If you go back to the analogy suggested in the chapter on initial sessions, that of planting seeds and pulling weeds, this analogy can be used at the end of group as well. Members can talk about what seeds they have planted (the new skills that they have learned) and the weeds that they have pulled up (the bad habits that they have identified and tried to extinguish, particularly negative thoughts that interfere with positive behaviors). In the spirit of relapse planning, they can talk about in which situations they want to use their new skills, in which situations they think that their weeds might return, and what they will do to keep their seeds growing and their weeds from returning. Third, termination brings up grief and loss issues, and sometimes group leaders may not want to experience emotions that go along with this stage, so they avoid it if at all possible.

Goals and Tasks

Termination is a time for members to go beyond the specific skills and strategies they learned and to begin to develop a sense of how learning occurred, what learning strategies work best for them, and how the group created these effective interventions. There are several levels to the discussion that happens during termination about what group members learned and how they learned it. The consolidation, integration, and application of learning are facilitated by these discussions. On the concrete and intrapersonal levels, members are identifying how they learn, whether it is through cognitive strategies, affective strategies, experiential strategies, feedback from others, and so on. It is important for group members to begin to understand how they learn best so that they can incorporate the strategies into their academic and personal skills. If a group member recognizes that the writing activities in particular were what helped to clarify thinking patterns and alternatives in different situations, group leaders might ask how such activities can be used in day-to-day school assignments. On a more personal level, the group leaders might ask the member to explore, when he or she has a problem or a difficult situation in the future, which strategies could be applied based on what he or she learned in the group to solve the problem. Hopefully, the group member identifies something like writing down the problem, brainstorming about alternatives, writing down pros and cons of each alternative, and writing out a strategy to solve the problem.

On the interpersonal level, group members have the chance to practice some of the skills they have been working on in the group: communications skills, expression of feelings, and giving feedback to other group members. The importance of modeling and altruism is highlighted in these discussions. Group members often hear for the first time how helpful they have been in different situations.

Sometimes, the themes of grief and loss are intertwined with the tasks of the termination stage. It is hard to say goodbye to group members without remembering other people who have left their lives. Psychoeducational groups in the schools often present the dilemma that the group members will say that this isn't really goodbye because we are going to still continue to see each other in classes and other places. Although I do not tend to be very Adlerian or Gestalt in much of my approach to group work, some of the themes of those theories resonate in the termination stage. People must finish one relationship in order to move on to another relationship. Unfinished relationships cause the most grief, loss, and pain for people. I cannot count how many times I have heard clients (and friends and family) say about people who had died, "I wish that I had told them that I love them. I do not think they know how much they meant to me." This is probably why the empty-chair and two-chair techniques are so useful as interventions—they allow people to express the things they didn't get a chance to say to people.

Group leaders can take these ideas of unfinished relationships and the need to say goodbye (and thank you) and use them as a framework for the tasks of the termination stage. Group members need to finish their relationships within the group so that they can move on to new relationships with other people or different relationships with group members. I often acknowledge to adolescents in a psychoeducational group I am leading (or graduate students in a training group) that "yes, you probably will see each other again, and yes, you probably will continue to have some kind of relationship with this person. However, the relationship now between the two of you is as group members, which is different from classmates or friends. So let's finish this relationship as group members so that if you choose to you can move on to being friends. Or at the very least you can be classmates who are comfortable with each other. And how we do this is by being very clear about how each person in group helped you to learn, what he or she did specifically, what he or she said, so that if you never see this person again, he or she knows how helpful he or she was to you."

In addition, it is useful to frame one of the tasks of termination as practicing the skills involved in saying goodbye to people and acknowledging how helpful they were to you and how they affected you. Leaders can frame it by saying that people in general do not do a very good job of saying goodbye to other people and thanking them for how helpful they have been. This is a chance for group members to practice these skills in a situation that is relatively nonthreatening so that when there are times in their lives when they need to say goodbye to people (e.g., when a family member is dying, when friends move away, when they go off to college), they will know how to do this and feel comfortable doing it.

It is also essential for group members to give feedback to the group as a whole and to group leaders about the effectiveness of the group interventions, activities, and leadership behaviors. Again, there are three major reasons for this to occur. First is the need for group leaders to have specific information about what makes groups effective so that they can plan for the future. The second reason is related to something that was discussed earlier in this section—the need for group members to begin to understand how they learn. Group members need to be able to assess strategies and interventions systematically to determine which ones are helpful to them and which ones are not. They will have participated in activities related to problem solving, decision making, and brainstorming, where they have identified options that work for them and options that don't, and the reasons for each. Now they need to begin to analyze real-life situations for their usefulness to themselves as individuals. In some ways, it is nice if all group members can find something positive about each activity that the group has done. Optimism and "finding the silver lining in every cloud" are useful strategies. However, it is also important for group members to develop strategies to evaluate systematically the usefulness of activities, interventions, and events that happen in order to make decisions about which of these things they will actively seek out.

The third reason is related to the development and practice of interpersonal skills. Expressing to the group as a whole and specifically to the group leaders what activities and events each member found to be particularly helpful serves as practice for giving positive feedback. Identifying activities and events that were not as helpful or not helpful at all, and giving reasons for why they weren't, serves as practice for giving constructive feedback. Frame the issue by saying that people will always find some activities or events to be more helpful than others. It is useful to categorize these events on a continuum from *very helpful* to *not helpful at all,* so that if people have choices about in which activities they want to engage, they have a clear schema of how to make these choices.

Group Leadership Skills

During the termination stage, group leader interventions should be focused on the meaning attribution, caring, and executive functions. To some extent, emotional stimulation should be deemphasized because there is insufficient time to process the events in a way that leads to meaning attribution and closure for the group.

Caring

Group leadership behaviors in the area of caring emphasize instillation of hope, modeling, altruism, feedback, and cohesion, so the group members leave feeling connected and that they have contributed to the effectiveness of the group. In order to do this, group leaders need to think systematically about each group member:

- What did this person learn as a result of participation in the group?
- What progress has he or she made on his or her goals?
- What has this person learned about him- or herself? Relationships? How he or she interacts with others?
- What are specific behaviors and examples of how this person changed his or her behavior in the group?
- What are specific examples of different cognitive strategies he or she displayed in the group?
- What are specific examples of how this person displayed his or her feelings in the group?
- What does this person want to continue to work on? How might he or she do this?
- How was this person a good group member?
- What did he or she do specifically to contribute to the group?
- How has this person learned what he or she learned in group?
  - From which members?
  - From which activities?
  - From what things leaders said?
  - From what things members said?
  - What were the critical incidents? Inspirational moments for each one?

- For what does this person want to thank other members? How have these members affected each other?
- What did this person do to help other group members? Give specific examples.
- What did he or she do to learn new skills? Give specific examples.
- What did he or she do to try out new behaviors? Give specific examples.
- What did this person do to take risks? Give specific examples.
- When did he or she get helpful feedback? Give specific examples.

Group leaders need to know the answers to all these questions, but they may not necessarily need to share all of this information with the group. The idea is that group leaders should have a comprehensive sense of what group members need to leave the group thinking about in terms of consolidation and application of learning, and their contributions to group. The analogy of a jigsaw puzzle is useful here. Each group member begins his or her own jigsaw puzzle by talking about what he or she has learned, how he or she acted differently in group, and what he or she will continue to work on. Group members then fill in additional pieces of the puzzle with their comments about what they think the group member has learned by giving specific examples of changes that they have seen in group (and outside of group if they have that information) and also making suggestions about how the member might want to work on his or her goals. Group leaders fill in the final pieces of the jigsaw puzzle by adding comments that the other group members have left out. This framework is parallel to the framework that was suggested during the initial stage to help the group members talk about what their goals are, how they want to work on them in group, and how the group can help them to do this. This idea of a jigsaw puzzle creates a conversation between group members, rather than one group member giving a soliloquy (or diatribe) of what he or she has learned.

Executive Functions

The termination stage of group is the other stage of group, besides the initial stage, where structure is absolutely essential. Structure is critical to helping members feel safe enough to assess progress and identify elements of the group that have been helpful for them. In addition, ending and saying goodbye may be new activities for children and adolescents, and so it is useful for them to understand what will happen and what will be expected of them. As with other groups, termination should never feel sudden for members of a psychoeducational group. Screening interviews and initial sessions should clearly delineate the length of the group. About halfway through the group, group leaders should announce that the group is almost half over and facilitate a discussion of what progress members have made so far as a result of being in the group, and what they want to continue to work on related to their goals. After that, group leaders should announce routinely, "We have x number of working sessions left. The last session (or last two sessions) will be reserved for termination, to say goodbye, assess progress, and talk about how the group and specific group members have helped each other." Related to structure, group leaders also need to make it clear that members do need to participate in closure activities as it is essential that all group members leave with a sense of what people have learned and how group members have been helpful to each other.

Keeping Members on Task. Because of time constraints and the importance of having each group member talk, it is helpful to identify clearly what group members need to do, and also that the group leader's job in the last session(s) will be to keep members focused. It is particularly useful to preview in the session before termination what will happen in the termination session(s). Sometimes, homework can focus on helping group members to prepare for the activities. Another strategy is to clearly state the goals of termination for group members and ask them how they want to accomplish those goals. Designing an ending activity helps group members to internalize the tasks and invest in the termination process. Group members have come up with some great ideas about how to say goodbye, everything from creating big posters for members to take home with comments from each member on them, to giving symbolic gifts, to writing a group poem.

Cutting Off. There is a caveat, and a big one, to this request for constructive feedback. In psychoeducational groups, the constructive feedback needs to be focused on one of two topics: a specific intervention or activity, or something that a group leader said or did. Group members need to leave the group with a positive sense of how the group has worked for them. If a group member attacks another group member, often referred to as a "hit-and-run," in the last session, the impact on the group can be devastating. Thus, it is important to remind, and encourage, group members to give any feedback that might be negative when the incident or reaction occurs, or as close to it as possible. Group leaders need to do all they can to prevent hit-and-runs at the end of the group by noticing when group members appear to be reacting to another group member. For instance, if the group leader notices that one group member is particularly quiet during a feedback discussion after a role-play, the group leader may comment, "You are pretty quiet. Anything you want to say?" If the member says no but his or her nonverbals suggest that something is going on, the group leader may continue by commenting on the nonverbal behavior. The group member still may not want to talk about it, either because it isn't a reaction to what is going on in the group or because he or she is not ready to talk about it.

It is helpful for group leaders to think about one instance of any behavior that looks like resistance or reluctance as a coincidence and frame it as such. If the behavior continues, however, then the group leaders may perceive it as a pattern and comment on it. Continuing with the example, if the same group member who was quiet during the role-play discussion was either quiet during the first half of the next group session or became quiet when the people who were in the previous role-play started to talk, group leaders may want to intervene in a way that questions and comments on what they noticed, rather than interpreting the behavior or confronting the group member. They might comment, "You have been pretty quiet most of today, and you were last week, too. What's going on?" If the member says that everything is OK in his or her life, the group leaders might push a little further: "This is just an observation, and it may not be correct, but you seem to be most quiet when John and Susan are talking. Did you notice that?"

The best way to prevent group members from doing a hit-and-run in a termination session is by gently encouraging members to give feedback as it occurs. There may be some instances, however, when group members may still bring up new and negative feedback in the termination session. If the group member is someone like the group member in the earlier example who has been encouraged gently and consistently to share his or her reactions but has not, the response from the group leaders should focus on cutting off the group member from further disclosure.

Refocusing. Another intervention that is useful when group members begin to disclose in the termination session something that cannot be resolved then is refocusing. Refocusing is shifting the focus from the content of what the group member is saying to the context in which it is occurring. Going back to the previous example, group leaders focus the group member who was trying to attack another group member by asking why the person feels safe in disclosing this problem now, but not at other points in the group. The goal of the intervention is to protect the group member who is being attacked, and the group as a whole, by not allowing conflict to come up in the last session that cannot be resolved. For the group member who brings up this new self-disclosure, it is more important for this person to explore why he or she feels safe in bringing up the problem now, but not earlier. How is this protective for him or her? What does he or she get out of it? Is the person afraid of this interaction in some way, so he or she waits until there is no time to resolve it? Or is it too uncomfortable for him or her to focus on the positive, so he or she has to start a conflict?

Meaning Attribution

Meaning attribution in the termination stage encompasses the major focus of this stage: the consolidation, integration, and application of what is been learned in group to what group members will continue to do in their real lives outside of group. As with how specific activities and interventions are typically processed in psychoeducational groups, it is best to focus on two levels:

1. What has been learned and how it will be applied
    - Behaviorally
    - Attitudinally
    - Cognitively
    - Affectively
    - In what situations will these new skills be used?
    - What will serve as reminders of when and how to use these new skills?
    - What does the group member want to continue to learn?

2. How learning has occurred in group
    - As the result of which interventions and activities?
    - As a result of what specific things other group members did or said?
    - As a result of what specific things the group leaders did or said?
    - As the result of which critical incidents in the group?

Remember the analogy of the jigsaw puzzle here. Each group member starts the conversation, followed by other group members filling in other pieces of the puzzle and ending with group leaders filling in the final pieces. It is also important to emphasize here again that research suggests that feedback is much more willingly received and has greater value when it comes from other group members than from group leaders. Group leaders might want to gently remind group members of interventions and events that seemed particularly important for them and ask them to comment on how they were affected by them. As a preview at the end of the session prior to termination, or as part of the opening for the termination session, leaders may want to review briefly the topic of each session and activities used. A list could be distributed to refresh group members' memories. If group leaders have used the

Critical Incident Questionnaire either in writing or as part of the processing of group sessions, they may want to review group members' responses to remind them of what group members had mentioned previously as important and helpful.

Typical questions or statements that group leaders might use to facilitate the discussion of what has been learned and how it will be applied include the following:

- How do you think you are different as a result of this group? Behaviorally? Cognitively? Affectively?
- What has this group meant to you?
- What are some of the most important things you learned about yourself?
- Are there any things you want to say to anyone in here?
- I'm aware of the tendency to forget what we learn in group, so I'd like to talk about ways that you can remember what you did learn.
- How can you practice what you learned in here?
- How do you think you'll be different? Don't tell them, show them!
- With whom do you need to talk outside of the group? What is the essence of what you want them to hear?
- What decisions have you made? What will you do about them? When?
- If we were to meet 1 year from now as a group, what would you want to say that you've accomplished?
- If you had to say your message in *one sentence,* what would it be?
- Where can you go from here, now that the group is ending?
- How might you discount what you've learned in here?
- How can you translate insight into action?

Questions that focus on how learning has occurred as the result of interventions and activities within the group include the following:

- How did the group help you to make these changes?
- Which events and activities were most helpful to you in this group? How?
- Which events and activities were least helpful to you in this group? Why?
- Were there times when the leaders could have intervened to help you, and they did not? When? How?
- Were there times that the leaders should not have intervened? When? Why?

One of the tasks of this stage is for group members to demonstrate some of the new communication skills and self-assessment skills that they have learned as a result of participation in a psychoeducational group. It is very important for members to take risks and try to be very specific about how group members were helpful, to talk directly to them, and to identify how situations might be changed to be more useful to them. Although many activities designed for the termination stage use writing, it is also essential for group members to express verbally their thoughts, feelings, and wishes for change to group members, group leaders, and the group as a whole. Writing is important as a preview because it helps group members organize, integrate, and clarify their thoughts and feelings, and also because many of the writing activities result in a project that group members can take home to remind them of the cohesiveness and connections in the group, the things they have learned, new coping strategies, and their positive attributes. All this being said, it is absolutely critical that members verbalize to each other how they have helped each other in order to facilitate closure for the entire group.

Acknowledgment of the Content and the Process. I often talk with my group members about how, in some ways, the process of termination is more important than the content. What they say is certainly important, but being able to practice these new skills in a real setting is critical. Acknowledge again that the key differences between individual counseling and groups are the altruism, self-esteem, and learning and practice of helping skills that occur as a result of the group interactions.

Acknowledgment of the Feelings of Loss, Change, and Separation. It is also important to acknowledge that group members may feel a number of emotions related to the ending of the group, and although some of these emotions may seem contradictory, this experience often happens in real life, emphasizing universality and existential factors. The "silver lining in a cloud" is more common than we may realize, with most negative situations having some positive benefit. In contrast, even good things have some negative aspects. For example, going off to college means leaving your friends. In contrast, some children of divorce admit that although they do not like the divorce or separation, it feels good that their parents aren't fighting any more. It is important to model and to acknowledge to the group members that it is common to have more than one emotion, and sometimes contradictory emotions, regarding a situation. Acknowledging the range of emotions is useful in problem solving, decision making, brainstorming, and conflict resolution. Acknowledging conflicting feelings identifies why a decision has been hard to make and frees the individual to consider other alternatives to solve the problem.

Some group members may express relief at the group ending. This is perfectly understandable, because learning about oneself and trying out new behaviors is emotionally demanding and sometimes just plain hard work. Group leaders might acknowledge that improving oneself is like working on a project; taking periodic breaks is useful.

Group members who talk about how much they will miss the group and what they got from it—cohesiveness, universality, modeling, a new perspective—may be encouraged to think about places in their outside lives where they may get the same thing. With whom can they talk? Who listens to them without judging? Who has good ideas? Who might be able to help brainstorm and problem solve without giving advice? If the group members express how good it felt to work as part of a team on a specific goal, can they identify other activities (e.g., sports, clubs, community service programs) where they can also experience cohesion, purpose, and teamwork?

Possible Pitfalls

For many children and adolescents, grief and loss are not significant issues. For others, however, termination of the group often may bring up feelings of grief, abandonment, and loss. In psychoeducational groups with topics related to grief and loss, such as children-of-divorce groups, groups for students whose parents are ill, or groups for students who are grieving, it is essential to acknowledge the feelings and discuss how to express them. This is a time to intervene through modeling, expression of feeling, and development of coping plans. As a preview for termination, group members might be asked the following:

How do they typically say goodbye?

Has this way of saying goodbye been effective in the past?

Are there people to whom they wish they could have said goodbye?

What would they have said?

At this point, group leaders might talk about how it is useful for a person to tell other people clearly how they have affected that person and how much that person cares about them. They might then ask group members to think about group as a chance to practice these skills. Based on this, group members are asked to identify what they usually do well that is related to saying goodbye and what they also want to do differently in this termination as practice for future endings. It is helpful for group leaders to disclose at this point about how they might have wished they had said goodbye to people. To illustrate this point in a relatively nonthreatening way, I often tell the story of moving and waiting for my roommate to arrive home so I could say goodbye to her. However, she got caught in a meeting, and my goodbye to her was waving as our cars passed in the street. For several years, I felt bad about this ending. She had been a good roommate and a good friend, and I didn't have a chance to tell her. So, when I finished my doctorate and was ready to move, I made a conscious decision. I was to move in August, so I took the whole summer to say goodbye to the friends I had made in graduate school. I went out to dinner with each of them and thanked each for being a good friend; I threw a going-away party to say goodbye.

Members who have trouble with saying goodbye and with endings may not show up for the last session. Group leaders may anticipate this and prescribe it:

It is important that everyone has a chance to say goodbye to everyone else. It is important for closure and to practice our new skills. Group members also need to know how they have helped others. If you cannot be at the last session, please tell us so we can say goodbye before then. If you are not at the last session and we do not have a chance to say goodbye to you in person, we will say our good-byes to an empty chair as a symbolic representation. It would be nice if every-one could be here to hear and respond to the comments.

Group members are often more anxious about other group members talking about them in their absence than they are about termination, so that may motivate them to attend. For others, it may be helpful to ask directly when you talk about how they typically say goodbye: "Who usually does say goodbye? Who waves and runs? Who might be likely not to show?" You might even ask group members who might not show up and then discuss why they are concerned about this.

Other members may discount the group experience by announcing that they have learned nothing at all. Again, the process is more important than the content. Group leaders may refocus and ask the group member to discuss why he or she would share this now and not earlier in the group when changes could have been made. Or, group leaders may want to address the group as part of the jigsaw puzzle with the notion that the group member is having difficulty finding the first puzzle piece, so the group members must begin the puzzle for that person by commenting on how they have seen the group member learn, change, and grow.

Group leaders' personal reactions may also present obstacles to termination. Grief and loss are difficult issues for all of us, and as adults, group leaders may have experienced more or more recent instances of grief and loss. It is painful to experience these feelings, and group leaders may want to avoid them, focusing much more on the cognitive aspects of the termination process. Co-leaders may not want to acknowledge the ending of the group because it means the ending of their relationship.

To prevent group leaders' personal issues from interfering with effective termination, it is helpful for co-leaders to reflect on their own experiences with saying goodbye and ending. How do they typically say goodbye? Do they avoid it? Do they tell the person how much he or she meant to them? It is important in supervision to discuss how co-leaders typically end relationships because that might have an impact on their reactions toward and interventions during the termination stage. If they typically avoid saying goodbye, then they might collude with the group members to put off discussion of termination because "it isn't important."

It is important to begin to discuss termination several weeks prior to the termination sessions so that co-leaders have adequate time to examine their own feelings and personal issues related to termination, understand the impact of these feelings and issues on their behavior in group, and plan specifically so that these feelings and issues don't affect the group's closure activities negatively.

Examples of Activities

The termination stage of group is the other stage of group work where structure is important. Group members need to leave group with a clear sense of what they've learned from group, how they have learned what they've learned, who has been influential in the learning process, and what changes they will make upon leaving group. There are many activities in the literature that would be useful in facilitating closure for group members. Adaptations of "Tic Tac Toe" and "Jeopardy" can be used to reinforce and remind group members of activities, interventions, and themes of previous group sessions. Bob Wilson's (2002) "Feedback as Poetry" could be used in the middle stages of group to assess what members have learned and what they need to continue to learn. This activity, however, could also be a powerful closing activity, with each member summarizing what he or she has learned and leaving with a concrete reminder, a poem, of what he or she has gotten out of group. "Closing: What Have We Learned About Ourselves?" (DeLucia-Waack, 2002b) and "Closing: Thanking Others" (DeLucia-Waack, 2002a) help group members identify the changes they will make upon leaving group specifically based on what they have learned in group. The

"Where in the World Can I Be?" (Johnson, 2002) and "Paper Quilt" (Paisley, 2002) activities can be used in closing sessions to help members say goodbye, summarize what they have learned, and make plans for future change. Dossick and Shea (1990) suggested an activity called "The Gift," where group members give other group members symbolic gifts by writing the gift on a piece of paper and then explaining verbally why the gift was chosen for that person. In my children-of-divorce groups, I create two characters early on, Kelly and Corey, to represent children who are going through a parental divorce. (Kelly and Corey are named in many of the songs that we use, and they actually sing on the tape.) I often ask group members to project their thoughts, feelings, and beliefs onto Kelly and Corey, and then, in the reverse, ask group members to generate solutions to problems and situations based on what they think Kelly and Corey might do. So, as a closing activity, group members write a letter to Kelly and Corey summarizing what they have learned, how they will continue to practice their new skills, and what other children who are experiencing a parental divorce or separation should know in order to survive. Group members then read their letters out loud to the group, with processing comments focusing on similarities in what was written and identification of coping strategies.

Summary

Termination, though a relatively brief stage in a psychoeducational group for children and adolescents, is an essential part of the consolidation and application of learning for group members. Not completing termination is in some ways analogous to doing activities throughout the group but not processing them. Leaving group members to make sense of what they have done, what they have learned, and how they may use it on their own is probably not an effective strategy in psychoeducational groups. The analogy of test-taking strategies may be useful here. Students learn some pieces of the material on which they will be tested in class, through readings, and through homework assignments. But it is by systematically studying the material in preparation for a test that they truly begin to integrate, understand, and apply it. The termination stage is analogous to studying for a test. Asking group members to reflect on their experiences and to pull them together to define and identify clearly what they have learned, how they have learned it, and how they want to continue to integrate these new skills into their lives is the preparation for the big test—their real lives.

Suggested Training Activities

1. Identify and Adapt Termination Activities

- Examine group literature in general and the literature specific to one type of psychoeducational group for activities that may be used to facilitate termination. Figure 1 in Chapter 2, as well as Appendix G, contain some suggested resources.

- For each activity, identify the task(s) for termination that this activity would accomplish.
- For each activity, identify therapeutic factors that this activity would promote.
- For each activity, write two or three processing questions directed at meaning attribution for this activity.

2. Identify and Adapt Existing Termination Sessions

- Examine group literature in general for existing termination sessions, regardless of the topic of the psychoeducational group. Figure 1 in Chapter 2, as well as Appendix G, contain some suggested resources.
- For each session, identify the task(s) for termination that this activity would meet.
- For each session, identify therapeutic factors that this activity would promote.
- Adapt it to the topic of your psychoeducational group.
- For each session, write two or three processing questions directed at meaning attribution for the processing part of the session.

3. Design a Termination Session

- Design a 1-hour group session that includes activities that address the following:
  - What progress have members made on their goals? What have they learned about themselves? Relationships? How they interact with others? How have they learned it? From which members? From which activities? From which things leaders or other members said?
  - What were the critical incidents? Inspirational moments for each one?
  - What do they want to continue to work on?
  - For what do they want to thank other members? How have they had an impact on each other?
  - How will they continue to interact now that group is over?
  - Complete an evaluation measure that assesses progress toward the specific goals of the group.
- With your co-leader, write a Group Planning Sheet for this session in Appendix D.
- As a part of planning for this session, discuss the following with your co-leader:
  - How do you typically say goodbye?
  - Has this way of saying goodbye been effective in the past?
  - Are there people to whom you wish you could have said goodbye?
  - What would you have said?
  - What feelings do you have as you approach termination?
  - How might they interfere with effective termination?
  - How can you work together to prevent this from happening?

- Enlist the help of six people to role-play, and give them a brief history of what the group has been working on and doing in activities so far. (If possible, use a group of people who know each other and who can talk specifically about their interactions. This will be much more realistic for you as group leaders. I have sometimes done this as a last class, and it gives students a chance to say goodbye and consolidate what they have learned as a group.)
- Choose an outcome assessment measure specifically related to the goals of a psychoeducational group.
- Choose a measure designed to assess group climate.
- Role-play a 30- to 40-minute group session complete with opening, working, processing, and ending.
- After the session, ask group members to complete the following:
  - Posttest of the outcome measure
  - Assessment of group climate
  - The Critical Incident Questionnaire

- Then ask them to discuss the following:
  - How did you feel during this session?
  - What were you thinking?
  - What did the leaders do that made you feel comfortable? Be specific.
  - What did the leaders do that helped you to learn something about yourself? Be specific.
  - What did the leaders do that helped you learn something about others in the group? Be specific.
  - What did the leaders do that helped you learn something about how groups work? Be specific.
  - What did the leaders do that helped you interact with other members?
  - What did the leaders do that helped you work on your goal?
  - What did the leaders do that wasn't helpful?
  - What else could they have talked about that would have been helpful?
  - Anything else you want to tell us?

- Complete the Group Environment Form and Processing Sheet.
- Evaluate the session using the tape, the feedback from members, and the written forms. Meet with your co-leader using the model of Reporting, Reflection, Integration, Planning, and Evaluation (DeLucia-Waack, 2001, pp. 17–18) and the CLINICKING section of the Co-Facilitating Inventory.

CHAPTER 8

Using Activities Effectively in Group Sessions

T here are several ways to think about the use of activities within the context of group work. Based on the type of group, individual and group goals, and the group's structure and format, the use of activities will vary significantly. In this chapter, guidelines are suggested for choosing activities based on the type of group, group goals, goals of the specific intervention, and therapeutic factors. The use of creative activities as a way to engage group members and help internalize knowledge and skills will be discussed as well as guidelines for processing activities. Meaning attribution is a key component in the effectiveness of activities; group members must understand why they participated in an activity, what they did, and what they learned from it.

Common Mistakes in Using Activities

One of the most common mistakes made in the selection of an activity is that the activity is chosen just because it is fun or because group members would like it. Remember that always implicit in effective groups is a focus on communication, conflict resolution, and problem solving. Also important to remember is that one of the executive functions of group leadership is to keep members on task to provide structure and safety and to use time effectively. Thus, a group leader wastes time and diverts attention from the group goals and tasks by introducing an activity that does not clearly relate to group tasks. Having said that, two issues need to be considered. One, sometimes groups do need to connect and laugh and share some common experiences without a lot of emotion or seriousness. Two, just about any activity can be useful if it is processed in such a way that it facilitates the group tasks at hand. A later section in this chapter will provide guidelines for how to process activities effectively and will suggest several frameworks for generating processing questions.

Michael Hutchins's (2002) activity titled "A What?" is a good example of an activity that encourages levity, humor, and laughter within group work, as well as asking group members to think about how groups work effectively in a nonthreatening way. Group members are given an object (or objects) to pass around the group with directions on how to describe the object. Hutchins suggested different processing questions depending on the type of group, the group stage, and the population, such as, "How did you and your group address chaos and confusion when it occurred?" "What enhanced or inhibited how this group functioned?" "What enhanced or inhibited what you did to make this activity work in this group?" "What did you learn about how groups function?" (p. 80). Later sections in this chapter focus on the selection of activities based on group stage and group goals.

Several common mistakes occur related to how activities are conducted. Directions need to be very clear, specific to the age group, and sequenced appropriately. It is helpful to write directions ahead of time and to make sure that all words will be understood by the group members. Evaluation of the order and sequencing of the directions is also helpful. For older group members, you may be able to give them three directions at once. For elementary school students, you might give one direction, let them complete the task, give another direction, and so on (draw a circle on the paper, wait, draw a symbol that represents you in the middle of the circle).

Underestimation and overestimation of time are two other common mistakes, ones that I still commit on a regular basis. Even with practice of specific activities, the amount of time needed to complete a particular activity varies significantly depending on the group. My solution to overestimation is to be overprepared and always have another activity with the same goals and topic ready if there is more time available. I also usually plan four to five processing questions for each activity, with the understanding that I will choose the two or three that are most relevant based on what happens in this activity for that particular group. If an activity takes less time than I anticipated, the group may discuss all of the processing activities related to that activity.

My solution to the problem of underestimation of time for a specific intervention is less than ideal. When planning an activity, it is helpful to consider if any steps can be omitted, or if members can be asked to think about any steps over the next week for discussion in the next group session. Again, to save time, the focus of processing may be on only one or two directed questions as opposed to all prepared.

There may be some temptation, and some pressure, to conduct the group around a table. In schools, groups are often conducted in classrooms or in the lunchroom. If at all possible, use a circle of chairs or sit on the floor in a circle, again emphasizing that this is a different atmosphere with different guidelines from other situations within the school. Others (Carrell, 2000; Smead, 2000b) suggest using a table for creative endeavors but moving back to the circle to discuss and process. Tables sometimes serve as a barrier to effective communication.

If at all possible, practice the activity ahead of time. Even if you participate as both group leader and member, you will have the experience of saying the directions out loud, gaining an estimate of how long an action takes, and recognizing potential problems.

Be prepared that the activity may not go as planned. Always consider the use of one or two processing questions that are directed at understanding why the activity did not work. For example, the group leader might ask, "The goal of this activity was to help group members to identify strengths that they could use to help other group members in this group. But most of you had a very hard time saying that you did anything well. What happened? What was it like to think about things that you did well? Could you think of any? If you could, what made it difficult to share with the group? What things inside of you made it difficult to share with this group? What things that have happened in this group made it difficult to share with the group?"

One of the most common mistakes group leaders make is to not process an activity. Indeed, most books on group exercises and activities do not include the direction or guidance that is necessary for effective processing of activities (Kees & Jacobs, 1990). This is ironic, because processing has been described as the most important phase in using group exercises. Yalom (1995) further emphasized that the experiencing of events in group is not sufficient for the facilitation of change. Rather, an in-depth process examination of the experience is necessary to be able to retain, integrate, and generalize these experiences. Processing helps group members understand what they have done, how they have contributed to effective group process, what new skills and behaviors they have learned, and how they can apply what they have learned to their outside lives. A later section in this chapter will discuss guidelines and models for processing activities effectively.

Uses of Activities Related to Group Tasks

Although many activities can be used to develop several therapeutic factors and address different group goals and tasks, it is how group leaders process the activity that determines the focus, direction, and application of learning for the group members. This section will discuss different uses of activities in groups, provide suggestions on how to process these activities, and also provide examples of specific activities that could be used in psychoeducational groups for children and adolescents.

Introduce Group Members to Each Other

In the initial stage, one of the primary tasks is to introduce group members to each other, focusing on both the uniqueness and the strengths of group members, as well as connections and similarities between group members. Anxiety is high, given the newness of the experience and the apprehension of sharing in a group of strangers. Activities used at this point should help members to self-disclose safely and then ask members to discuss what it is like to share, how they chose to take risks in group, and how they will continue to do this throughout the group.

Examples of activities that might be useful in this stage include Asner-Self's (2002b) "No Question About It Ice-Breaker," which asks group members to get to know each other, but the one caveat is that they're not allowed to ask questions of each other. Processing questions focus on what they learned about each other, possible connections, and what they have learned about how to interact with each other. In Conroy's (2002) "Getting to Know You" exercise, group members introduce themselves as a friend would introduce them, emphasizing their positive qualities.

In groups where children and adolescents may already know each other, it is important to use activities that will help group members get to know a side of each other that they would have not known from previous interactions. Doughty's (2002) "Guess Who?" activity asks group members to write down on a card a fact or personal experience that the group probably would not know about them. Cards are then shuffled and read to the group, with the group trying to guess whose disclosure it is. Hulse-Killacky's (2002) "The Names Activity" is a short but useful activity that asks members to talk about what their name is; how they got their name; whether they like their name; and if not, what name they would choose. Processing can focus on what they learned about each other, what it was like to share this information with each other, and connections.

Guth's (2002) "Getting to Know Each Other" activity could also be used. Processing questions that might be adapted for any of these activities are "How did you feel sharing with the group?" "How do you feel now that you shared?" and "How do you feel about sharing in the future?" Processing comments made during the forming stage should focus on how members feel about trusting each other and how safe members feel in relation to each other. The focus should also be on helping members to make connections between each other. Questions to facilitate such linking are "To whom did you feel connected as others shared?" and "Who shared feelings or thoughts similar to yours?"

Reduce Anxiety Through the Illumination of Group Process

The activities suggested in the above section are designed to help members get to know each other and reduce their anxiety as they start to make connections and feel more comfortable. Other activities that define group process and identify concrete goals for group members also help reduce anxiety.

Examples of such activities include Brown's (2002) exercise "Looking at Process," which encourages members to focus on group process while deciding on a get-acquainted activity. Other activities ask members to focus on their relationships with others in the group and how they affect productivity. Bree Hayes's (2002) activity titled "More or Less" is another good example of an icebreaker activity to facilitate self-disclosure, cohesiveness, and a discussion of how groups work without being overly intrusive. Dossick and Shea (1990) suggest an activity called "The Helping Hand" that focuses on situations when group members may need help, and how others can offer suggestions and help in the group and to people in general.

Richard Hayes's (2002) activity "Why Are We Meeting Like This?" encourages group members to display resistant behaviors that interfere with effective group process. Adolescents love this activity because it allows them—in essence, demands them—to act out and be resistant, defiant, and interfering. It also clearly illustrates how one member, and very specific behaviors, can interfere with a whole group process. Processing of this activity focuses on what group members individually and as a group can do to make sessions and activities productive, and it also emphasizes the role of the group leader as facilitator, not the person in charge of the group. The "M&M Game" (Darst & Drury, 2002) emphasizes the importance of cooperation and working together in a fun way while using M&Ms, and Halbur's (2002) "Ball in Play" asks group members to reflect on the process of how they created a game using a ball and ground rules for how they will interact productively in the group.

Provide Structure

Psychoeducational groups for children and adolescents require more structure than adult counseling and therapy groups. Younger group members seem less able to make the transition from group session to group session. Using a similar structure for each group session that includes opening, working, processing, and closing is very helpful to provide continuity and safety. Group members have a good idea of how long each activity may last and what is coming next. The content of the questions used to process an activity or in the processing and closing sections may differ, but the focus and the structure usually will be familiar.

Role-plays are particularly helpful in providing structure in that scenarios can be predetermined either by the leader or anonymously by the group members, but the safety of knowing that it is a role-play allows group members the freedom to take risks and try out new behaviors that they might not do otherwise. It is helpful to give very clear directions about what kinds of behaviors you want the people in the role-play to enact; how long the role-play will last; what the role of the group leader may be (e.g., asking questions, directing, coaching, not involved); and what the focus of processing will be afterwards.

Teach and Practice New Skills

Activities designed to teach and practice new skills often include an instructional component along with a practice component. Sometimes, it is useful to have students discuss and write down what their strengths are in a particular area, potential strategies, and new skills, and then lead into experiential activities such as role-plays and drama to practice the new skills. Children and adolescents may already have skills in the area of communication, conflict resolution, and assertiveness, yet they may not choose to use them. When group members possess essential skills and actively choose not to display them, one of the goals of the intervention is to help group members examine why they would choose not to use effective behaviors. Irrational beliefs, family concerns, and peer issues may all influence group members' attitudes and behaviors.

Activities specifically designed to promote creative thinking and brainstorming may be useful as introductory activities to create a framework of effective problem solving that facilitates accomplishment of the group goal. "Agenda Setting" (Conyne, 2002) is specifically designed for task and work groups and provides a very clear framework within which members set goals, generate solutions, and decide on a plan of action. "Painting Yourself Into a Corner" (Dossick & Shea, 1990) helps group members identify potentially problematic situations and multiple solutions to them.

"Your Personal Board of Directors" (Jacobs, 2002) and "Fiddler on the Roof" (Horne, 2002) are exercises that could be used to help adolescents focus on how to make decisions, and who has influenced their decisions, both currently and in the past, as a lead-in to developing their own effective strategy for decision making. Examples of process questions might include "How did the group help you handle this situation?" and "What was useful/not useful?" Dossick and Shea (1990) suggest an activity called "The Road Not Taken" to evaluate choices that group members have made, which choices they made that did not work (and why), and what they could have done differently.

Sam Gladding's (2002) activity titled "Lines of Feelings" is useful in psychoeducational groups to get members to explore feelings related to the current group situation or topic. Karp et al. (1998) suggested several activities specifically for adolescents designed to identify feelings and practice expressing them. "Feeling Charades" is a particularly good one because it emphasizes nonverbal and verbal expression.

Jacobs (2002) suggests several multisensory activities designed to help group members reflect on their experiences and strengths, and to teach new skills. "The Shield" uses a 12 in. × 12 in. piece of plexiglass to illustrate the hurtfulness of certain comments or actions, and then group members practice deflecting or responding assertively to such comments. The "Small Chair" examines how group members put themselves down, identifies situations where they do this, and then suggests different ways of responding. The analogy of Eeyore and Tigger is suggested as a metaphor for how group members may approach life (positive vs. pessimistic attitudes) and how they can change their approach, which in turn changes events. The "Masks of Shyness" (Martin, 2002) and "Meta-Cognition to Reduce Test-Taking Stress" (Reynolds, 2002) are both activities designed for specific psychoeducational groups, shyness and test anxiety, that identify and dispute irrational beliefs and cognitive distortions that may interfere with affective behaviors.

For children and adolescent grief groups, "The Kids' Grief Kit" (LeGrand, 2002) may be a useful introduction to several topics related to grief. Halbur and Nowparvar's (2002) "Set My Life to Music" is another good example of an activity using music to begin a discussion on a particular topic or theme for adolescents. Karp et al. (1998) also suggest several activities related to the identification of personal boundaries and space, and practice scenarios to establish boundaries with friends and families.

Provide Members With Feedback

Activities that focus on feedback have several different foci. The first is very specific, asking group members to comment on a very specific interaction, whether a role-play or activity, with feedback given to all group members. Sometimes, feedback is given to members based on perceptions over a series of group sessions and is focused less concretely on specific situations. It is also useful at various points in the group to reflect on how the group works together as a whole and to give the group as a whole feedback on what things to continue to do to make the group effective, and also what things might need to be changed to make the group more effective.

Dossick and Shea (1990) suggest an activity called "Actions Speak Louder Than Words" that focuses on how people communicate both verbally and nonverbally, with members encouraged to give feedback about the double messages that they may be receiving. They also suggest an activity titled "Best Foot Forward," which asks group members to identify some personal strengths of each group member when his or her name is called. Processing of this activity includes discussion of what it was like to receive positive comments and also asks group members to be specific about which interactions in group they used to determine the attributes they named.

Rapin's (2002) "What Is My Relationship to the Group?" asks members to describe their relationship to the group, and "A Group Image" (Brown, 2002) also asks group members to examine their perceptions of how the group works together and to identify potential areas of difficulty. Trotzer's (2002) "Boxed in: An Activity for Overcoming Resistance and Obstacles to Problem-Solving in Groups" as well as the "Sibling Position" activity (Trotzer, 2000) and "Diamond and 4 Activity" (Trotzer, 2000) all emphasize feedback, problem solving, and how to work together as a group.

Wilson's (2002) "Feedback as Poetry" exercise uses creativity to resolve an impasse and further define how to work together as a group. Examples of processing questions in this stage might be "What makes it difficult to understand each other?" and "How would you like for things to be different in the group?" Other examples of process questions might include asking members about their negative reactions toward the leader's authority and influence. Such comments typically evolve as members complain about other authority figures in their lives outside of the group or when their resentment gets displaced onto other members.

Increase Self-Awareness

Useful activities to increase self-awareness include "Group Exploration of a Member's Dream" (Provost, 2002) and "Country of Origin Fairy Tales" (Asner-Self, 2002a). "Power Line" (Comstock, 2002) helps group members examine sources of privilege and/or marginalization in a person's life that affect an individual's sense of agency and relational mutuality, as well as how these experiences affect group dynamics and relationships outside of group. Mathis and Tanner (2000) suggest a series of structured activities that is appropriate for use in most psychoeducational groups for children and adolescents. The focus of the activities is on family-of-origin concepts, highlighting and emphasizing the differences in how families work, communicate, and change. Each of the activities uses a series of four rounds where group members respond to a specific question or request for information, and then processing occurs at the end. One activity asks group members to describe their cast of family characters in terms of structure (e.g., I live with my mother, father, and sister); names and faces of family (My sister Julie is 10 and we call her "Jul." She likes to dance and play the flute. She is always with her friend Missy); one word that best describes the family when group members were a certain age (e.g., the word I would use to describe my family when I was 10 is "busy"); and who they identify as the family star (e.g., my brother because he is smart). Processing would focus on what group members learned about their own families, similarities they noted between themselves and other group members, and what it was like to talk about their families.

Important processing questions for such activities are the following: What is it like to talk about the influences on who you are? What did you learn that surprised you? What do you need to think about further? How will what we talked about today affect your life? What will you do differently? How will you think differently?

Facilitate Closure and Consolidation of Learning

As members contemplate leaving the group, examples of process comments relate to how their leaving might reflect familiar patterns of leaving and loss or how they will apply the insights they have learned in the group to both how they choose to leave and their lives outside of the group. Group members might write letters to themselves, which can be mailed to them, detailing what they have learned from the group and how they will continue to use their new skills. Group members may also go back to their original goals and evaluate their progress. Useful activities include "Closing: What Have We Learned About Ourselves?" (DeLucia-Waack, 2002b) and "Closing: Thanking Others" (DeLucia-Waack, 2002a). Dossick and Shea (1990) use an activity titled "The Scrapbook" to create a collage that shows the impact that the group has had on each group member. Group members can also create a poster for themselves decorated with their name and some symbols of themselves. Other group members are then asked to add to the poster with comments and descriptions of how that group member has affected them during the group. Each group member leaves with a concrete representation of his or her impact on other group members. A modified version of this is to ask each group member to write a positive attribute about every other group member on individual index cards, which the group members can then carry with them to remind them of their strengths and uniqueness.

Creative Arts Activities

"Life difficulties are reflected in counseling through dramatic means and therefore, the language and action of counseling should be expressed in dramatic terms" (Gladding, 1998, p. 88). Creativity in activities—particularly singing, writing, dancing, and music—are ways to identify and express feelings and to brainstorm and practice new behaviors and coping skills (DeLucia-Waack, 2001; Gladding, 1998). Gladding suggested that the use of creative arts in counseling is beneficial to (a) experience the connectedness between mind and body, (b) increase energy flow, (c) focus on goals, (d) increase creativity, (e) establish a new sense of self, (f) provide concrete interventions that are beneficial, (g) provide insight, and (h) promote socialization. Traditional methods of talk therapy just do not work for children and adolescents, and so the more activities involve creativity and movement in the group process, the more likely it is that group members will be motivated to attend and participate, and, hopefully, apply what they have learned. Counseling and psychoeducational inventions should assist group members in sharing and developing coping skills and behaviors to deal with problematic situations. Children in particular often respond better to nonverbal techniques than they do to verbal exercises because of their limited vocabularies, so songs may provide a way for them to express themselves. Gladding (2000) later identified several other benefits of using creative arts in groups, particularly with children and adolescents: they are multicultural, energize, communicate messages on multiple levels, are playful and nonthreatening, and open up options (p. 8).

Creative arts activities often result in a concrete product, something that group members can take home as a reminder and reinforcement of what they have learned in group. Songs reverberate in their heads, and banners and note cards can be displayed in public (in their lockers, on the mirror at home) and in private places (inside their notebooks, in their wallets) to remind them of their strengths, their new skills, and new positive thoughts.

Jacobs (2002) emphasizes the use of multisensory techniques with children and adolescents in groups. Multisensory techniques engage group members' senses with techniques that members can see, do, and/or touch. His reasons for this emphasis are that such techniques help to focus members because they access more parts of the brain, make concepts more concrete by visual or experiential experiences, are useful when language may be a problem, and keep members engaged (p. 9).

Music

Music is particularly important when trying to help children and adolescents express their feelings. Music helps link people and gives them a common basis for discussion. Music may be added to traditional methods and interventions to serve a variety of functions. It is also used in group sessions to introduce topics, get the session started, change topics, and end the sessions on an upbeat note. Music serves as a concrete reminder and reinforcement of what has been learned in group with specific songs that may serve as a reminder of the coping strategies that have been discussed in group.

Research has suggested that music increases group cohesion (Cassity, 1976), emotional or effective responses (Ashida, 2000; Henderson, 1983; Hilliard, 2001), and self-disclosure (de l'Etoile, 2002; Jensen, 2001). Effective music therapy interventions include group guitar lessons, music to encourage reminiscences, group singing, song writing, group drumming, listening to music, lyric analysis and improvisation, and writing stories while listening to music. Listening to a song and then discussing the message of the song and what the person who wrote it might have been feeling or thinking is often very useful. This one-step technique identifies potential feelings and thoughts without attaching them to a specific group member—something that can be threatening for a child. Such a technique also helps to normalize experiences as children realize that others have similar thoughts and feelings.

Vines (2004) suggested several questions to be used to stimulate discussion after students listen to a specific song: "What is the meaning of the song? What did the author mean when he said XXXX? What feelings did you experience when he repeated the chorus? Why do you think he sang those words over and over?" (pp. 12–13). She also suggested the following songs to address specific topics: "Faith of the Heart," by Rod Stewart, for motivation to reach goals; "It's My Life," by Bon Jovi, for career choices; "Drive," by Incubus, for motivation to make good life choices; "Superman," by Five For Fighting, for personal awareness; "Do Not Laugh at Me," by Peter, Paul, and Mary, for accepting differences; "A Song for Mama," by Boyz II Men, for family relationships; "I Hope You Dance," by Lee Ann Womack, for motivation and making good choices; "The Change," by Garth Brooks, for peaceful living; "I Will Remember You," by Sarah MacLachlan, for interpersonal skills; and "Bug-a-boo," by Destiny's Child, for sexual harassment. "Troubles," by Alicia Keyes, and "Message in a Bottle," by The Police, were also songs that Vines used in a self-mutilation group. Halbur and Nowparvar (2002) suggest the use of songs such as "Climbing," by Lionel Richie; "Drops of Jupiter," by Train; and "Hold on," by Wilson Phillips, to promote self-discovery or reflection within the group.

Music helps to link group members and gives them a common denominator with which to relate. Children, in particular, relate to music because they may not have the vocabulary to express certain feelings and/or thoughts, and the words to a song do it for them. For adolescents, connecting to the words of a song helps them to feel understood and not so alone in the world. Songs may be used in psychoeducational groups to introduce a topic and to identify important themes and issues related to the group goals. Dan Conley (1994) has produced an album of songs titled *If You Believe in You* for elementary students focusing on self-esteem, coping skills, and communications skills. About half of the songs on the album focus specifically on issues related to children whose parents are separating or divorcing. So, as an example, the song "Divorce" is often used in initial sessions of the children-of-divorce group to introduce the topic of divorce and identify potential thoughts and feelings related to it. Group members can identify with those characters in the song whose parents are divorced and then continue to identify other people they know whose parents are divorced, emphasizing the universality and normality of the situation. The song "Is It My Fault?" identifies some of the fears and anxieties the children often have related to the divorce that they have difficulty verbalizing.

Songs can also be used to channel energy. If group members are particularly lethargic when they come in, group leaders may play something energizing to get them up and moving. If group members are agitated when they arrive for group, a calming song may be played. A calming song may also be useful to close a group. Songs that reinforce communication skills, working together, helping each other, and coping skills may be used to introduce skills and also as a reminder of what skills they have learned. Group members in my children-of-divorce groups take home tapes of Dan Conley's music and are asked to listen to a song or songs when they are having a bad day or want to be reminded of what they have learned in group. One of my own favorite personal interventions is to play the song "Bad Mood" (Conley, 1994) when I am in a bad mood. I can't help but sing along; it makes me laugh, and within a few minutes I feel better.

Group members may write their own verses to a song to identify their own experiences, or they may want to choose a song (and bring it to group) that exemplifies their feelings, thoughts, and experiences. It is also helpful to have group members choose a song that is motivational and inspirational for them to which they can listen for guidance and support. Pack-Brown (2002) suggests an activity call "Drumming," based on Afrocentric principles, to promote connections between group members and also connections between affect and behavior for group members.

Visual Arts

Visual arts activities in groups include both the discussion and the creation of art to help members learn about themselves. Gladding (1998) suggested that visual arts activities tap into the unconscious, help individuals express a multitude of emotions, and assist people in picturing themselves and their situations in a concrete manner. Because these activities are often perceived as nonthreatening, they may overcome resistance to self-disclosure and self-exploration. Gladding suggested several different art activities: reacting to pictures with a theme related to a group topic, body outline drawings that are then decorated and discussed, serial drawings to symbolically represent a group member and his or her problems, and the use of paint and clay.

In most psychoeducational groups for children and adolescents, it is helpful to ask group members to draw a picture of their family and typical activities that they do together. Group members use the pictures as a starting point to self-disclose a little bit about their family and what kinds of things they like to do, and also give group leaders some sense of strengths and potential problems within the family.

"A Group Image" (Brown, 2002) and "What Is My Relationship With the Group?" (Rapin, 2002) both ask group members to create images to symbolize their connectedness to and structure of their group. Dossick and Shea (1990) suggested the activity "The Group Quilt," in which each member identifies and depicts through drawing his or her role in the group and how he or she contributes uniquely. Pictures are then fastened together to form the group quilt. The "Masks of Shyness" (Martin, 2002) uses paper bag masks to highlight behaviors that accentuate shyness and potential behaviors to connect with others, whereas Rhine, Schoenfeld, and O'Shaben (2002) create a puzzle to emphasize uniqueness and connections among group members.

It is important to clarify with visual art activities, as with most other creative activities, if group members will be asked to share some or all of what they have created. Most of the time, it makes sense to allow group members to share some or all depending on their comfort level. Telling group members that they will be expected to say something, particularly if they are going to be asked to display or describe their drawing, before the activity starts is helpful so that they can edit what they want to put down on paper and share with other group members.

Writing

Wenz and McWhirter (1990) suggested that creative writing such as free-form poetry and prose and personal journal logs are effective interventions in groups, particularly to increase self-disclosure and self-acceptance of feelings and experience, and to promote group interaction and cohesion:

> Creating and sharing writing seems to improve and increase self-disclosure, self-actualizing behaviors, and self-acceptance of feelings and experience. . . . The function of writing as a way to express ideas, attitudes, and feelings in an indirect manner as though they are abstract or belonging to someone else . . . may elicit new and significant insights that may not surface through other therapeutic modalities. (p. 38)

Brand (1979) suggested several therapeutic benefits of writing in counseling that Wenz and McWhirter extended to groups: (a) Writing is a creative art that counters repressive and regressive factors, (b) writing provides material to be analyzed and discussed in group as a projective medium, and (c) writing amplifies the therapeutic effect through the opportunity for rehearsal and self-reflection.

Group leaders may present a poem to introduce a topic and then ask members to react to it indirectly or directly. Group members may use poetry as a way to "focus their attention on images, thoughts, and emotions . . . to encourage a deeper expression of hidden information that can stimulate the group interaction" (Wenz & McWhirter, 1990, p. 38), either as an icebreaker to facilitate trust, affiliation, and self-disclosure, or as an assessment of perceptions of group process and stage (Wilson, 2002). Wenz and McWhirter suggested three writing activities to be used in psychoeducational groups. The goal of the "Stain Glass" poem is to ask group members to get in touch with current emotions, thoughts, and goals through responding to a series of six questions and then organizing the responses into a poem. The "Personal Logo" asks group members to doodle until they come upon a symbol that feels right for them, then tell a story about the symbol, with the goal of illuminating positive themes and goals for group members. The "Epigram" asks group members to identify an epigram (short, witty sayings that appear everywhere these days from books of quotations to fortune cookies and tea boxes) that has held meaning for them personally and then to write about it.

Group members may be asked to journal in group or as a homework assignment to focus them on what is helpful in group sessions, what progress they are making toward group goals, and the identification of potential situations that they may want to discuss or role-play to practice coping skills or new behaviors. Sometimes, it may be helpful to assign a specific theme about which group members write in their journal, and sometimes a format may be suggested. Cognitive interventions often use a thought diary in which specific situations are recorded that trigger negative thoughts along with what the thoughts are, how realistic they are, and eventually how they can be disputed.

The "Autobiography" (Bridbord, 2002) asks group members, based on their lives, to create a title, define the type of book it would be (e.g., fiction, romance, etc.), and identify past and future events in an effort to identify the uniqueness of each group member and to connect group members as well. "What a Character" (Gillam, 2002) directs group members to identify in writing their favorite fictional character along with descriptions of the character to help group members identify how they contribute to the group.

Writing activities encourage group members to be self-reflective and may help them to get in touch with thoughts, feelings, goals, and motivations that they were relatively unaware of. However, it is important to choose writing activities that are relevant to the group goals and stage, and to process them so that group members gain insight and meaning from them.

Drama and Role-Playing

Other creative arts interventions include the use of puppets, drama, and role-plays. Because young children are often unable to express their feelings directly, using puppets may help to express their feelings, thoughts, and potential fears. Used along with songs and bibliotherapy, puppets help take the information and situations in the songs and books and make them real for children. After listening to a song or reading a book, the group leader may say to the children, "Let's act out that story now."

For instance, in one of the early sessions of a children-of-divorce group, children may listen to a song or read a book about how children find out that their parents are getting a divorce. The children may then act out the situation, with each child choosing a puppet to portray a specific person: mother, father, children, and/or other important figures in the situation. The group leader can act as a facilitator of the puppet show, instructing the parents to disclose certain information (i.e., reasons for the divorce, that they will still see them every week), and encouraging the children to express feelings or ask certain questions, or to back up and replay a situation in a different way (now react with anger or sadness instead of saying everything is OK).

It is essential to have a variety of puppets to act out situations. Group leaders can be creative in their collection of puppets: bath mats, oven mitts, as well as puppets made by the children as an activity all work well. To encourage the expression of a wide range of thoughts, feelings, and verbalizations, it is important to include some puppets that are scary, fuzzy, and furry, as well as those that represent lots of different roles: queens, kings, princesses, firefighters, police officers, and so on. Law (2004) theorized that by using puppets and props in your lessons, students have a chance to focus attention away from themselves and onto the puppets. This removes tension from the situation but allows students to work through problems with the puppets. "The problems are voiced and shown through the puppet's acts. Not only does this tool help students better understand the situation but it also helps them process the problem" (p. 16). Smead (2003) emphasizes the use of stuffed animals for group members to hold to feel safe and loved, and also as metaphors for coping skills and adaptive behaviors: "Frogs are patient and flexible when waiting for the dragonfly to come along. How can you be patient and flexible in your situation?"

Role-plays are essential activities in psychoeducational groups for children and adolescents. They can be structured in that the group leaders provide scenarios and roles for group members, and include coaching to increase risk taking and trying out of new behaviors. It is also useful to ask group members to identify in writing, anonymously, situations on which they would like to work. The pieces of paper can be shuffled and then distributed randomly to group members, who then enact the role-play. Choosing other group members as coaches for those group members who will role-play the situation also helps to lesson anxiety and increase the number of potential behaviors and strategies that may be tried. Role-plays can be more realistic and somewhat unstructured, re-enacting a current situation to identify relevant issues and feelings, and practicing new behaviors and skills.

Gestalt empty- and two-chair techniques also may be used to clarify thoughts and feelings and practice new behaviors. An empty-chair technique may be used for a child who is angry at a parent because the parents are getting divorced. The group member may be urged to say whatever he or she wants to say to the parent. It may then be helpful to process the activity, focusing on how the child felt, what it was like to say this, and then how he or she can express anger realistically to his or her parent in a way that invites discussion rather than offends the parent. Whenever role-plays involve only one or two group members, it is helpful to ask the rest of the group members to discuss their reactions, as much vicarious learning may occur. Group members may support and validate the group member's feelings, or they may suggest a different perspective or way to communicate. Observing group members may also notice emotional reactions or new behaviors that they want to discuss or practice in future group sessions or activities.

Bibliotherapy

Bibliotherapy, or the use of books and films in therapy, has been particularly effective in helping children and adolescents express their feelings and concerns about particular situations, and also to learn new skills. Children can deal with their feelings indirectly through the use of books and films. In early sessions of groups, books and videos can be used so group members can view, listen, and then reflect. For example, after reading a book about a family whose parents get divorced, the group leader might begin a discussion with questions such as, How did the children in the book feel? How did they express their feelings verbally? Behaviorally? Nonverbally? In later sessions, group members may be encouraged to write their own books to suggest for other children how to express their feelings, and then to actively prescribe ways to cope with the feelings and the situations that they have encountered. The Resource Guide in Appendix G suggests specific books and stories that may be used in different types of psychoeducational groups for children and adolescents.

Games

Games are often very effective interventions in psychoeducational groups. All children, and even most adolescents, like to play games. Games are often helpful in teaching rules of interaction, such as taking turns, listening, speaking directly to another person, and following directions. Carlson (1999) suggested that counselors for children and adolescents "do well when they break from traditional, therapeutic rituals, habits, and routines and learn to encompass a spectrum of multi-modal strategies such as games and exercise. Counselors experience less resistance to physical exercise interventions than to regular therapeutic procedures" (p. 231). He suggests cooperative games that are noncompetitive physical activities that incorporate exercise, movement, and coordination. The benefits of cooperative games include health, expression of feelings, relaxation, fun and enjoyment, learning physical skills, forming positive peer relationships, increasing positive self-image, developing problem-solving and goal-setting skills, and learning self-control behavior (p. 232). Carlson suggested the adaptation of many commonly known games such as tag, telephone, hot potato, and red rover to emphasize corporation, inclusion, and friendship skills.

In addition, there are some games specifically designed to be therapeutic. The UnGame (Zakich, 1987) has been around for a very long time and has many versions, some for teens, some for parents, some for parents and adolescents, and so on. What makes the UnGame different is that there is no competition, there is no way to win; the game ends after a predetermined amount of time. This is useful in psychoeducational groups because it can teach communication skills but also can be played for a relatively short time and used as a reward for good session; often, I would say, "We can play the UnGame for the last 5 minutes of group if we get our activities done." Group members move around the UnGame board, landing on squares that ask them to describe experiences related to specific feelings. Group members can make comments or ask questions of other members, but only at specified times.

Other available games include Anger Bingo for Teens (Driscoll, 2002); From Rage to Reason Game (2000); Hidden Treasure of Assets: For Children and Adolescents (Curtis & Whitman, n.d.); Drug Prevention Bingo (n.d.); and Two-in-One Pregnancy Bingo (Smallwood, 2000). The Resource Guide in Appendix G includes games that may be used in different types of psychoeducational groups for children and adolescents.

Processing Activities Effectively

Goals of Processing

Processing has been characterized throughout this book as a key component of meaning attribution group leadership behavior to help members make sense of group events and then subsequently apply what they have learned to their lives outside of the group. What exactly is processing? According to Stockton, Morran, and Nitza (2000), processing can be described as

> capitalizing on significant happenings in the here-and-now interactions of the group to help members reflect on the meaning of their experience; better understand their own thoughts, feelings and actions; and generalize what is learned to their life outside of the group. (p. 345)

Jacobs, Harvill, and Masson (1988) described processing as the most important phase in using group exercises. To be effective, processing needs to take into consideration group stage, group goals, and goals of individual group members.

Processing is important because it allows participants to create meaning through reflection, sharing, connecting, and extrapolating. It is a creative endeavor that uses all of the participants' experiences. Philosophically, processing is a means of translating the concrete to the abstract, and it is an invitation to participants to co-create meaning and to be active in their own process of growth. Effective group leaders listen for themes (including those that come in metaphors) that are interpersonal, intrapersonal, and whole-group. A group leader who processes is much like a conductor of a symphony. Each member plays his or her own instrument, and it is up to the conductor to make sure that each musician is on key; notice when he or she is not; and help the orchestra function as a whole for the benefit of each individual musician, as well as for the benefit of the composition (Lugris & Bridbord, 2002).

Processing can be directed at various levels of interaction: interpersonal, intrapersonal, and whole-group. Processing questions are intended to help members reflect on their reactions to the exercise, learn about themselves, and transfer their learning to their real lives. Intrapersonally based questions are intended to help members gain personal insight. Examples of questions are, "What have you learned about yourself?" "Were you surprised by your reaction to the activity?" "How did you feel disclosing the information about yourself?" and "How does that relate to your life outside of the group?"

Processing questions that are interpersonally targeted allow members to learn about their interactions with others, such as, "What did you learn about others?" "How will this learning affect your interactions with group members?" "What similarities did you notice between your responses and others' in the group? Differences?" and "How will you apply this outside of group?"

Whole-group processing questions are intended to help members learn about group dynamics and how they operate within groups; for example, "What did you notice about how the group interacts?" and "How will conducting this activity affect how we work together?"

Processing to Facilitate Therapeutic Factors

The group leader intentionally facilitates the occurrence of one or more of the therapeutic factors as the result of processing of an activity. For example, regarding the therapeutic factor Interpersonal Learning, Yalom (1995) stated,

> If the powerful therapeutic factor of interpersonal learning is to be set in motion, the group must recognize, examine and understand group process. It must examine itself; it must study its own transactions; it must transcend experience and apply itself to the integration of that experience. (p. 129)

Engaging members in processing encourages them to learn about themselves and one another. Although the goal of an activity and what members have learned may seem obvious to group leaders, that is not always the case with children and adolescents. The underlying goal of processing any activity (or critical incident) in a psychoeducational group is always interpersonal—helping group members learn something about themselves so that they can, in turn, act, feel, or think more adaptively. However, as Yalom has often reminded the field, other therapeutic factors must be present in order for interpersonal learning to occur. Thus, processing emphasizes different therapeutic factors depending on the goals and needs of group members in any particular session.

In early sessions of a psychoeducational group, instillation of hope must be emphasized by focusing on how the group will help members and what they will learn from it; specifically, how they will change outside of group as a result of learning in the group. The development of a clear goal (with a specific criterion of when they have reached their goal) and a definition of how groups work helps to instill hope. Processing questions for a goal-setting activity during the first session or, in general, at the end of the first session might include the following:

- What have you learned about how groups work?
- Specifically, how will this group help you?
- What have you heard today that makes you think you can learn new behaviors or new ways of thinking or feeling?
- How does it feel to have a clear and specific goal?
- Who have you identified in this group to help you with your goal?

In later sessions, instillation of hope can be emphasized by focusing on what members can learn from each other. Typically, group members have been chosen so that they have different skills and experiences that can be used in brainstorming, problem-solving, and role-play activities within the group. Processing questions to emphasize learning from other members might include, What did you learn from other members today? Who seems to be a little bit farther along in their situations than you? How are they different from you? What do you want to ask them? What can you learn from them that will help you progress?

In psychoeducational children-of-divorce groups, this instillation of hope often occurs when members whose parents have been divorced for awhile can share experiences with members whose parents have just separated or divorced, and say things like, "I used to feel that way, too. I thought it would never get better, but things have settled down. I used to spend all of my time wishing that my parents would get back together, and now I know they won't. So I just try to enjoy the time I get with each one of them."

Altruism is often engendered in group members as a result of similar processing questions. Helping one group member to identify someone who can be helpful to him or her also identifies a group member who can be altruistic and feels that he or she has something to offer the group. Questions that focus on identifying how group members have helped each other serve to increase altruism. An important part of groups as opposed to individual counseling is that group members are allowed—in fact, encouraged—to play the roles of both helper and helpee. In individual counseling, the client is always the client, and trying to help the counselor probably would be interpreted as resistance in some way. However, in groups, as in real-life relationships, sometimes you need help and sometimes you give help. Thus, group members learn from their group experiences to both give and receive. Possible questions to facilitate the development of altruism and group members include the following:

Who was helpful to you today, and why?

To whom would you like to say "thank you" for helping you today?

As you reflect back on the activities today, what comments and suggestions were most helpful? Why? What did you learn from them?

Similar processing questions can be used to emphasize universality among group members—universality both in terms of experiences and in terms of feelings and thoughts. For adolescents in particular, it is important to emphasize questioning of self-worth, concerns about fitting in, mood swings, uncertainty about friendships and romantic relationships, and negative body images that are typical of most adolescents. Processing questions and comments that focus on similarities and make connections between group members are important goals. In the initial sessions, linking and connections may be focused more on common experiences to allow the connections to occur quickly. In the later sessions, the universality of thoughts and feelings, regardless of the experience, should be emphasized. Processing questions to emphasize universality might include the following:

To whom do you feel most close at the end of the session today?

With whom can you identify most closely today?

Whose behavior was most like yours today?

Who revealed thoughts and feelings most similar to yours?

Based on what people have said in this group today, whom might you ask for suggestions?

Even though people's situations are different, who expressed feelings similar to yours today?

What was the theme for today in terms of thoughts?

What was the theme for today in terms of feelings?

What was the theme for today in terms of new behaviors?

Cohesion is facilitated when processing creates a shared reality and members feel part of the group. Process comments and questions that focus on connections between members and how closeness helps members to take risks and contemplate changes are useful, particularly in the early sessions. It is important to emphasize cohesion without emphasizing the group so much that members feel like they can't be different. Processing questions and comments to facilitate cohesion might include the following:

- What was it like to be in group today?
- What things happened that help members feel closer to each other?
- What things do we need to continue to do to feel safe so that people can take risks and make changes?
- What made it possible to take that risk?
- What kinds of things do we do in this group to make group members feel safe?

The corrective recapitulation of the primary family group emerges by virtue of the group's dynamics; members often represent siblings and leader(s) often represent parents. Group members come to realize that there are enough opportunities for each individual to have his or her own contributing role and also gain from the group. Possible processing questions might focus on the unique contribution of each person in group, how peers relate to each other, and how group members relate to group leaders. Possible questions and process comments include the following:

- How did each of you contribute to this activity?
- Look at the person next to you and tell him or her how he or she contributed to this activity today.
- Identify one person in this group today who you think contributed, and tell him or her how he or she contributed.
- We worked really well as a group today. Let's talk about how that happened. How did we work together? What did we do to make this work?
- How did you all interact today in group differently from how you interact with your peers outside of this group? What are you willing to change with your peers to make those relationships more effective?
- How did group members and group leaders interact today differently from how you typically act with your parents or your teachers? What did you learn about these interactions that you can take outside of this group? What can you do differently this week with your parents and teachers?

Because processing often brings group members' feelings to the forefront, catharsis often can be a by-product of the experience. Sometimes, it is important to help group members who were focusing much more on their thoughts to specifically identify their feelings. Other times, it is important to identify feelings as one part of the problem-solving or brainstorming activity. Often, it is useful to identify feelings as part of asking group members to discuss group process. Useful questions include the following:

- How did it feel to do this activity?
- How did your feelings change as we did this activity? What influenced the change?
- How did you feel as you tried out this new behavior?
- When you tried out those new thoughts and self-instructions, did you feel differently?

Imparting information can be a large part of processing activities, because feedback is a tool used to help members understand themselves as a lead-in to interpersonal learning. Group leaders typically will impart a great deal of information in the form of directions about how to participate in specific activities, and also provide content information related to the group topic, such as a definition of self-esteem, different types of self-esteem, and cognitive thoughts that people tell themselves that make them feel bad. In addition, group leaders may provide specific instructions about communication skills, decision-making skills, brainstorming, and conflict resolution. Psychoeducational groups have the goal of providing information to teach skills, so part of the group leaders' role is imparting information. In addition, group leaders need to facilitate the imparting of information by group members. Research suggests that feedback, when given constructively, is more useful from other group members than from leaders. Thus, group leaders must intervene actively to teach members of psychoeducational groups how to give constructive interpersonal feedback and also include specific processing questions, when relevant, at the end of activities. Potential processing comments and questions might include the following:

- Susan has been trying out some new behaviors today. It would be helpful if people shared with her what they noticed her doing differently.
- Mark has been working on being more assertive today. Can people tell him what it was like when he specifically asked them to do something?
- Mark, would you like some feedback on your behavior today? From whom would you like to hear?

Development of socializing techniques is an implicit goal in all psychoeducational groups. Psychoeducational groups are designed to help children and adolescents develop new skills by using activities that teach and provide practice opportunities for new skills. Thus, most processing of activities in psychoeducational groups will focus on this therapeutic factor. Useful questions include the following:

- What new skills did you learn today?
- What new behaviors did you practice today?
- How did you think differently today?
- What new feelings did you have today?
- What did we do as a group to help you learn the skills?
- How are you going to carry these new skills outside in other situations?

Modeling, or imitative behavior, is another key component of psychoeducational groups. Group members learn from observing both group leaders and other group members modeling participation in the group and skills to be mastered. In the beginning, modeling of self-disclosure, expression of feelings, and identification of goals is important. In the middle stages of group, modeling of problem solving, brainstorming, constant communication skills, conflict resolution skills, and practicing of new behaviors is essential. In the termination stage, modeling of identification of what has been learned and how others have helped in this learning process, as well as application of newly learned behavior to outside situations, is to be emphasized. Process comments and questions that emphasize the importance of modeling include the following:

- Today in group, lots of good things happened. How did you see group members interacting in ways that got the group going? What is one thing that you saw someone do today that you want to try to do next week?
- In this activity, several members practiced new behaviors. What were they? What behaviors do you think you might want to try sometime? In what situations?
- In this activity, several members displayed positive thinking statements. Which ones do you think might be helpful to you at some point? When would you use them?

Existential factors arise as the uncertainty of life and certainty of loss emerge. Although these factors are not critical in many psychoeducational groups, the themes are still there. Themes such as "life isn't fair"; "some people have to work harder to do a good job"; "everyone is good at something"; "there will always be somebody better than you" (and conversely, "there will always be somebody worse than you"); and "everyone has bad days" all come up quite often in psychoeducational groups. It is important to identify and reinforce these themes. Sometimes, just commenting on the theme is enough: "It sounds like a lot of people are having a bad day today." Other times, it is important to explore the underlying roots of the belief. For example, in a group in which group members have all identified that they feel bad about themselves because they need to work so much harder to get an A than other students, a group leader might comment, "It sounds like this is a theme for everybody. My experience is that there are always people who make it look easy. So what do you want to do about it? Do you want to continue to make yourself feel bad, or do you want to think about changing your perception of the situation?"

As you have probably surmised as you read this section about using processing questions and comments to facilitate the development of therapeutic factors in psychoeducational groups, probably the most important therapeutic factor, interpersonal learning, is intertwined with all that has been discussed. The goal of all processing questions and comments is to help students think about what they have learned and apply it to future situations.

Models of Processing

Processing needs to be included from the outset of groups so that the leader(s) can model its significance and teach members how to facilitate it themselves. Each activity used in a psychoeducational group session should be processed. In addition, a small amount of time toward the end of each group session should be spent on processing the group session as a whole. One of the goals for effective group leadership is to discourage the group's initial tendency to expect an authoritative leader to provide answers and make sense of what happens for them, and to move the group toward a more dynamic interpersonal approach in which member-to-member interaction is encouraged and where members construct their own meaning and application for what happens in the group.

When observed, processing of group activities often appears to be spontaneous and made up on the spot. In reality, careful attention must be paid to the selection of processing questions. In general, processing questions should be directly related to the goals of the group, the goals of the activity, and the group stage. The questions or comments should start slowly and build in intensity so as not to create undue anxiety in group members. If group members get extremely anxious, they may shut down. This section describes some general goals and guidelines for processing activities, and also presents three different models for the selection and sequencing of processing questions.

Focus and Skills. Kees and Jacobs (1990) identified three critical elements involved in processing activities: good questioning skills; advanced accurate empathy (Egan, 1986); and an awareness of the focus on the group with the ability to hold, shift, and deepen the focus (Jacobs et al., 1988). Good questioning skills involve using open-ended questions that help group members develop new insights and awareness (Kees & Jacobs, 1990). For example, group leaders are much more apt to get more descriptive information if they ask questions such as, "What has helped your anxiety level decrease as you went through the session?" as opposed to "Has your anxiety level decreased?"

Advanced accurate empathy involves being fully present for the client and mirroring and reflecting anticipated feelings and reactions that may be unstated or understated by the members themselves. Empathy serves to communicate understanding and validation on interpersonal, intrapersonal, and whole-group levels. It also serves to model empathic attunement for members and facilitate cohesiveness. Such interventions are particularly useful when members appear anxious or when someone is unwilling to talk about what is making him or her anxious. For example, in the first session of the group, a group leader might say, "I'm feeling a little anxious right now wondering how this group will work out. I'm wondering if others are having the same kinds of feelings. It might be helpful to talk about them. If we can identify concerns, maybe we can address them."

Kees and Jacobs (1990) described the importance of awareness of the focus on the group with the ability to hold, shift, and deepen the focus. It can be very helpful to comment on what seems obvious in the group as a way to acknowledge potential difficulties and resistance, and then to help the group move on. For example, a group leader might notice that the group members are very quiet as they come in. He or she might say, "You seem pretty quiet. What's going on?" If the answer is that they just came from a test, the group leader might introduce a brief relaxation exercise to shake off the tension, or put some music on and ask the group members to dance for a minute or two to get rid of the tension. If the answer is that two group members had a conflict in the hallway before group, the group leader might say, "We've been practicing conflict resolution skills. This might be a good opportunity to try them out for real. Would you be willing to do this?" If group members appear to be having difficulty doing a particular activity, such as writing down their strengths or drawing something, it is often more important to talk about where the difficulty originates, rather than urging them to finish the activity. If members are having difficulty identifying what they do well, self-esteem is an issue and should be discussed. If the group members are self-conscious about drawing, the group leaders may want to ask what this is about. Often, group members express concern that they do not draw very well, they are afraid people will make fun of them, or they do not like to do things that they are not good at. All comments are important to discuss within the group framework of identifying strengths, developing new skills, and feeling good about themselves.

Hammell (1986) divided processing skills into concrete (knowledge, comprehension, and application) or abstract (analysis, synthesis, and evaluation) thought processes. Concrete processing questions aim to review and describe events, feelings, thoughts, and problems (e.g., "What were you feeling?" and "What did you see?"). Abstract processing questions aim to identify patterns, make comparisons, relate learning to daily life, propose solutions, and examine values (e.g., "How does this exercise relate to your life outside group?" and "What insights have you made about yourself?").

Stockton, Morran, and Nitza (2000). Stockton et al. (2000) created a conceptual map to provide general guidelines for effective processing. Specifically, they conceptualized processing as four interrelated stages: identifying critical incidents of importance to group members, examining the event and member reactions, deriving meaning and self-understanding from the event, and applying new understandings toward personal change (p. 347).

Identifying critical incidents involves the group leader deciding what aspect of the process he or she will address. The group leader must ultimately use his or her empathic attunement to decide the "process direction," but Stockton et al. (2000) list some indicators that may help the leader make this choice. Examples of these indicators include heightened emotional or behavioral reactions from group members, conflict in the group, emotional self-disclosure, or body language that suggests unspoken reaction to an event/activity. The goal for processing most activities in psychoeducational groups is identifying what parts of an activity, or what parts of the session, are most useful to group members. In order to identify the critical events, group leaders might ask questions such as, "What was most helpful about this activity?" "What did you learn from this activity?" "From which activity did you learn the most?"

At the end of a group session, as part of processing for the entire series of sessions, group leaders might ask questions such as, "What was most helpful about what we did today?" "What were the critical events today?" "From which activity did you learn the most?" "To which activity did you have the most emotional reaction?" "Which activity did you like the most?"

Examining the event and member reactions involves the leader engaging the group in a here-and-now discussion. Once a critical incident or the important part of an activity has been identified, Stockton et al. make several suggestions to help clarify group member reactions to critical incidents and activities, including posing direct questions to members, encouraging members to address each other directly, and using "I" statements. Processing questions here are usually very specific: "What did we do?" "What was it like to do it?" "What were you thinking as we did it?" "What were you feeling?" "What new behaviors did you use?"

Deriving meaning and self-understanding from the event or activity involves helping group members apply the critical incident to their personal lives, interactions, and experiences. Stockton et al. encourage the use of feedback as a way of helping members see themselves as they are, with leaders modeling giving, asking for, and receiving feedback. Most importantly, when other members are not directly involved in the critical incident, it is important to engage them as part of the processing so they can share their vicarious learning experiences. Examples of questions directed at deriving meaning and self-understanding are, "What did you learn as a result of participation?" "What did you learn as a result of observing others?" "What are you willing to do differently?" "How do you want to think differently?" "How will doing some of this help you to feel differently?" "How does what you learned today help you to meet your goal?" "What did you see others do today that you can use toward your goal?" "I'm noticing that several of you were quiet when I gave the directions. Can you tell me what you were thinking? Were my directions clear? How could I have worded them differently so that you would have been more willing to do them?"

Promoting change involves helping members apply what they have learned in the here-and-now interactions of group to their everyday lives. Stockton et al. also suggested several strategies for promoting change, including journaling, members restating their goals and clarifying their learning, and role-playing. Group leaders might use processing comments as well as questions and invitations to promote change, such as the following: "Who is willing to work on his or her goals outside of group this week? What would you do specifically?" "Who is making progress toward his or her goals? How?" "What have you been doing to change? What do you need to continue to do? What do we need to do in group to help you? What will you do when you need to change outside of group?" "You have identified several really good ideas on how you want to think and behave differently. Would you be willing to try them out in a role-play?" "When can you specifically act and think differently in the next week? How will you remind yourself to do this?"

Glass and Benshoff (1999). Glass and Benshoff (1999) developed the Processing: Activity, Relationships, Self (PARS) model to serve as a road map for processing group activities. They suggest that "processing of activities becomes the 'bridge' from exercise to insight, from experience to behavior change" (p. 16). Their model includes three foci of processing (Activity, Relationships, Self) and three steps (Reflecting, Understanding, Applying).

Step 1, Reflecting, focuses group members on what happened during an activity. To reflect on the activity, one might ask, "What did we do?" To reflect on relationships, the question might be, "How well did we work together?" To reflect on self, the question might be, "What role did you play as an individual member?"

Step 2, Understanding, focuses on helping members gain insight into the group processes and individual learning that occurred during the activity. To facilitate understanding of the activity, one might ask, "How did this activity help us?" The question "What did we do to make this activity work (or not work)?" would focus group members on relationships. To facilitate understanding of self, a group leader might ask, "What did you do individually that influenced the outcome of the activity?"

Step 3, Applying, challenges and helps group members to apply what they have learned during their activity to their relationships outside of group and their goals. The question "How can you apply what we did in this to your everyday life?" focuses on the activity. To emphasize relationships, one might ask, "What did you do differently with group members in here that you can do with friends?" To focus on self, one can ask, "What did you learn about yourself that you can do differently next time?"

Conyne (1997). Conyne (1997) developed the Grid for Processing Experiences and Events in Group Work to facilitate understanding, meaning attribution, and application. The grid includes two columns of focus: What and How. Interventions in the What column are aimed at content, identifying what people and what topics group members are discussing. Interventions in the How column are aimed at helping group members understand how they deal with the content and how they deal with each other. The four levels of interaction are represented as rows in the grade:

I, You, We, and *Us.* Comments in the *I* row are typically self-disclosures, whereas *You* comments are typically feedback to another member in the group or about activity, both vital parts of the psychoeducational groups. *We* comments are about interactions between two or more group members or between group members and group leaders. *Us* comments focus on the group as a whole.

Conyne suggests that group leaders think about what kinds of interactions are occurring in the group at a specific time based on the grid and then develop processing questions to facilitate understanding and application. For example, if a role-play that involves two members practicing new skills does not seem to be working, the group leader may ask the two members first (and then later the rest of the group members) to comment on the What: "What were you trying to say to each other?" "What was your message to the other person?" "What message did you hear from the other person?" "What were the two group members trying to say to each other?" Then, the group leader could focus on the How: "How were you trying to get your message across? Did it seem to work?" "What did you hear the other group members saying? Could you hear it without getting defensive? If not, how could they have said it so you wouldn't get so defensive?" "If the group members were talking to you, how could they have spoken in a way that you could have heard? How do you think they could have spoken more respectfully?"

Cautions

Even in psychoeducational groups, activities can be overused. Leaders may become overly dependent on activities, using them in rapid-fire succession rather than recognizing the value of properly processing an activity. Allowing sufficient time for one activity and the careful processing of that activity to promote interpersonal learning, self-understanding, and practice of new skills and behaviors may be much more effective than quick completion of four activities on the same topic.

Creative arts activities, particularly those that involve drawing, cutting, and pasting, are very time intensive. Group time is valuable, so if time-intensive projects can be assigned as homework, so much the better (e.g., hand out paper bags and magazines and ask members to represent themselves on the inside and outside of the bag to share in the next group session). Work outside of group reminds group members of what has happened in previous sessions and also helps them to prepare for future sessions. (Yalom used to send process notes to his group members between group sessions to make them think of group between sessions.)

Activities and exercises may appear gimmicky (Gladding, 2000) to group members if they are overused and if they are not properly processed. Children and adolescents begin to see group as the place that they go to make things, not the place that they go to learn about themselves and make changes. Again, meaning attribution for all activities is essential. Also, because the activities are used in groups, the goals of the activities should be, in order, learning about oneself, learning about how one relates to others, and learning about oneself as perceived by others. Thus, processing of activities should focus on the multiple levels of learning and activities. The earlier section that describes modeling of processing addresses this issue and makes suggestions on how to select processing questions that focus on the group members, interactions between group members, and the group as a whole.

It is also important when leading psychoeducational groups for children and adolescents that there be a balance of information delivery, skill development, and group processes (Conyne, 2003). Ideally, as part of the working part of a group session, there should be a brief provision of information—sometimes a refresher of information previously discussed and sometimes introduction of new information (3 to 5 minutes)—some activity focused on practicing the skills, and then some time spent on processing the activity directed at identification of what group members have learned and how they will apply it.

Summary

Activities are an essential and very effective component of psychoeducational groups. The goals of the activity must match the overall goals of the group, the goals of individual group members, and the group stage. In addition, the interventions must be processed sufficiently to facilitate learning related to group and individual member goals. Processing group activities is an essential aspect of effective group work. It is during processing that group members reflect and learn about the effects of their thoughts, feelings, and behaviors on their interactions; how their thoughts, feelings, and behaviors have been replicated in group interactions; and alternative ways of behaving, feeling, and thinking in the future. The beauty of processing is that members learn the skills to process and thereby better understand their relationships and themselves.

Suggested Training Activities

1. Identify and Outline Potential Group Activities for Group in a Particular Stage

- Choose with your co-leader your group topic, population, and for which stage of group you want to develop activities.
- Select several activities from the literature or that you have observed.
- Develop an outline based on the Group Planning Sheet in Appendix D.
- Choose one model of processing and write five to seven processing questions. Order them in sequence of how you might ask them in a group session.
- Implement the session as a role-play, videotaping the session. (This could be an in-class role-play.)
- After the session is over, ask your members to talk about the following:
  - What was helpful in making them feel comfortable?
  - Interacting with other members?
  - Establishing a goal?

    – Working on their goal?
    – Wanting to come back to group again?

- Administer the evaluation measures.
- Evaluate the session using the tape, feedback from members, and one or more of the group leadership assessment forms discussed in Chapter 4.
- Complete the Group Processing Sheet for this session in Appendix E.
- Meet with your co-leader using the model of Reporting, Reflection, Integration, Planning, and Evaluation (DeLucia-Waack, 2001) and the CLINICKING section of the Co-Facilitating Inventory (Pfeiffer & Jones, 1975).
- Complete the Group Planning Sheet for the next session in Appendix D.

2. Identify and Outline Potential Group Activities That Meet Specific Group Goals

- Choose with your co-leader your group topic, population, and the goal of the intervention for which you want to develop activities.
- Select several activities from the literature or that you have observed.
- Develop an outline based on the Group Planning Sheet in Appendix D.
- Choose one model of processing and write five to seven processing questions. Order them in sequence of how you might ask them in a group session.
- Implement the session as a role-play, videotaping the session. (This could be an in-class role-play.)
- After the session is over, ask your members to talk about the following:
    – What was helpful in making them feel comfortable?
    – Interacting with other members?
    – Establishing a goal?
    – Working on the goal?
    – Wanting to come back to group again?

- Administer the evaluation measures.
- Evaluate the session using the tape, feedback from members, and one or more of the group leadership assessment forms discussed in Chapter 4.
- Complete the Group Processing Sheet for this session in Appendix E.
- Meet with your co-leader using the model of Reporting, Reflection, Integration, Planning, and Evaluation (DeLucia-Waack, 2001) and the CLINICKING section of the Co-Facilitating Inventory (Pfeiffer & Jones, 1975).
- Complete the Group Planning Sheet for the next session in Appendix D.

CHAPTER 9

Follow-Up After Group Ends

The Association for Specialists in Group Work (1998) *Best Practice Guidelines* emphasize two major considerations for group leaders as a group ends. One is that evaluations (both formal and informal) be conducted at the conclusion of the group, and the second is that follow-up contact should occur with group members, as appropriate, to assess outcomes or when requested by a group member. This chapter will discuss guidelines for how to provide appropriate follow-up after a psychoeducational group for children and adolescents.

Assessment of Progress

One the major tasks of the termination stage, as discussed in the earlier chapter on termination sessions, is an assessment of each member's progress toward individual and group goals as well as a focus on how group members will maintain these changes after group ends. Thus, group leaders often have a very clear sense of progress from the members' perspective when group ends. Because perceptions of progress are subjective, it is helpful to gather data from a variety of sources to assess progress. Because much of the focus in psychoeducational groups is on teaching skills, it may be useful to use questionnaires to assess attitudes, thoughts, feelings, and behaviors that were targeted in the group. Comparing questionnaires completed before the group to questionnaires completed after the group provides data about individual member progress as well as an overall estimate of the group's success. Smead (2000b) created "Pretests/Posttests" for a variety of different psychoeducational groups. It is often useful to ask group members to complete the final questionnaire before the last group session so that they can discuss the following in the last session: what they have learned, what new skills they have developed, and what they may still need to work on. Group members are much more likely to complete such questionnaires if they see a use for it; the questionnaires can be framed as an aid to help them to assess progress in the group. The following chapter will also discuss useful process and outcome measures for assessment of group effectiveness.

Group leaders may also want to get feedback from teachers and parents about progress and potential changes that they have noticed. Teacher and parent rating forms with proven reliability and validity are available, but often they are used more for remedial purposes. Simply adapting one of the questionnaires that group members use to assess their progress might be a more viable solution. The goals of psychoeducational groups often are very specific in terms of changes in behaviors, affect, attitude, and cognition. Parents and teachers may be asked to rate progress on group goals.

Assessment of Need for Further Treatment

There is always room for improvement in one's interpersonal skills (I tell my group members this all the time when I do something in group that is insensitive or I do not communicate my feelings very well; I frame it as modeling imperfection and how to admit mistakes). However, because the goals of most psychoeducational groups are preventive and designed to teach skills rather than provide remediation, most students will not need further counseling interventions upon the termination of a group. Leaders will occasionally identify one or two students who need further support and/or counseling. The students may have self-disclosed in group intense emotions, potential acting-out behaviors, or maybe distressing family situations or relationships. They may be the students who have taken up a lot of time in group because they appear needy, or they had a concern related to a topic in group, or they had extreme difficulty in sharing or connecting with other group members.

Interview Sessions

Similar to the beginning of group, it is essential for group leaders to meet individually with each group member for closure. Some of the time, group members may not say anything different in a closing interview with group leaders than what was already said in the last group sessions. However, this is often another chance for group members to consolidate and apply what they have learned, not only about their goals but also about group process and relationships. Group members may be more honest in the closing interview with group leaders about fears and concerns they have, their actual progress toward goals, and issues and concerns that they may want to continue to work on. Group members might have felt some implicit pressure within the last group sessions to emphasize the positive, and perhaps to overemphasize the changes that they have made and how helpful group was to them. Group leaders might frame this closing interview session as a chance for the group members to further discuss progress and changes still to be made as well as provide group leaders with valuable information about the effectiveness of the group techniques and interventions used in this group. Possible questions to structure the interview include the following:

- How do you think you are different behaviorally as a result of this group? Cognitively? Affectively?
- How did the group help you to make these changes?
- Which events and activities were most helpful to you in this group? How?
- Which events and activities were least helpful to you in this group? Why?
- Were there times that the leaders could have intervened to help you, and they did not? When? How?
- Were there times that the leaders should not have intervened? When? Why?

To begin to discuss with a group member the need for further interventions, group leaders might comment that the goals of psychoeducational groups are preventive and teach skills and coping strategies. However, most new habits and behaviors take at least 10 weeks to be fully learned and integrated, and so the process of change and growth often has just begun. With an introduction like this, group leaders might ask another series of questions:

- What do you still need to work on related to the goals and topics of this group?
- How do you think you might do that?
- Would another group help to do this? On the same topic? On a different topic?
- Do you think that individual counseling might help?
- Have you ever seen an individual counselor before? Was that helpful? Could you go back to see the same counselor?
- Are there other problems or topics of concern for you that you could work on in counseling or in a group?

Referral for Further Treatment

It is certainly easier if a group member requests further interventions, whether individual counseling or another group. Before the group ends, group leaders should be gathering information about school resources, community resources, and other sources of support and intervention available for children and adolescents in their community. In a school, the group leaders need to know specifically what resources for individual counseling and group work are available for students within the school and how to make appropriate referrals if the group leader would not be providing the intervention. Parents may also need to be notified about further interventions. If there are no other resources within the school, or if the resources available are not appropriate for the needs of a particular student, group leaders will need to make a referral to outside agencies in the community.

It is helpful for counselors to have a list of social workers, psychologists, and counselors who specialize in working with children, adolescents, and families; referral procedures; and financial costs such as fees and insurance coverage. Some school counselors who refer a large number of students to outside agencies for individual counseling recommend developing a relationship with these counseling practitioners, with regular communication about the students who are being seen (with consent) and about the counseling practitioners' areas of expertise and procedural considerations. It is generally recommended to give three referrals and to suggest to parents that they may want to discuss with each of the counselors his or her theoretical orientation, counseling philosophy, typical interventions for children and adolescents, and fees and insurance reimbursement prior to scheduling the first appointment or during the first appointment. Sometimes, parents are hesitant, and so group leaders may schedule the appointment for them. Following up with both group member and parents is helpful to make sure that they got to the appointment. Parents are often reluctant to have their child see a counseling practitioner outside of the school. Their hesitancy is well-founded: They already know the school counselor, there is less stigma attached to seeing a counseling professional within the school, and it is more convenient to have the student seen during school hours. However, when a referral is made for outside counseling for a student, the necessity justifies the referral. School counseling professionals, by virtue of the school calendar, cannot work with students 2 months a year or, usually, for more than 30 minutes every week at the most. Moreover, the likelihood of getting family members involved in counseling sessions is much less likely in the schools. Thus, most referrals to outside counseling agencies are made because students need a longer counseling session each week, they need continuity of care that may extend into the summer, and it may be useful to involve family members in the sessions.

Summary

It is useful to meet briefly with each group member after the final session of the psychoeducational group. The focus of the closing interview is on helping the group member to assess and apply what he or she has learned in the group as well as give group leaders feedback about the usefulness of activities, interventions, and the group in general for future planning. Prior to the end of the group, leaders should compile a list of resources within their school or agency that is available to group members if they need further support or interventions, and also a list of resources available in the community. Information about the referral process as well as costs should be identified prior to making a referral, so that when a group leader refers a group member to outside resources, he or she will be able to give parents detailed information about these resources.

Suggested Training Activities

1. Design a Closing Interview

- With your co-leader, prepare for and conduct at least two closing interviews.
- Create an outline for the closing interview with questions to be asked and who will ask them.

- Choose an established measure or create a questionnaire to assess progress. Ask your interviewee to complete it prior to the closing interview.
- Discuss with your co-leader what progress you think each interviewee has made toward his or her goals, as well as other positive changes you have noted.
- Conduct the two closing interview sessions, videotaping the sessions.
- Evaluate each session using the tape and one or more of the group leadership assessment forms discussed in Chapter 4.
- Meet with your co-leader using the model of Reporting, Reflection, Integration, Planning, and Evaluation (DeLucia-Waack, 2001) and the CLINICKING section of the Co-Facilitating Inventory (Pfeiffer & Jones, 1975).

2. Prepare for Closing Interview Sessions

- Brainstorm with fellow group leaders possible group member responses that you typically wouldn't expect (e.g., "I really didn't get anything done in this group," "I just said it to make people feel better," "I have been really suicidal for the past 6 weeks but did not want to tell anybody," "I think you were the worst leaders I've ever seen and the group would have been better if you just hadn't done anything," etc.).
- Generate possible therapeutic responses to the group member responses.
- Role-play the scenarios to practice the therapeutic responses.

CHAPTER 10

Assessment of Group Effectiveness

Hopefully, you are not reading this chapter as you are finishing leading a psychoeducational group. If you are, you might get a quick idea of what you can still do to evaluate your group but will have much better ideas for the next group you lead. Part of accurate assessment of group effectiveness begins in the preplanning stage. In Chapter 2, it was briefly suggested that some sort of assessment measure should be chosen to assess where group members are with regard to group goals and related skills prior to their selection for group. It is also useful to use the same assessment at the end of the group to assess progress as a result of the group effort. This chapter will begin with general guidelines on how to choose and use assessment measures to assess group effectiveness. The goal is to go beyond the traditional question of "Did this group work?" and to also ask, "What were the therapeutic factors and group leader interventions that helped group members to learn and change and grow?" Thus, this chapter will also include a discussion of measures designed to assess group interactions and group and leader interventions as they occur in specific groups, and their relationship to group effectiveness. Self-report from group members and leaders is recommended as well as systematic analyses using videotapes and/or observations of group sessions.

Guidelines

It is important to get both positive and negative feedback from group members. In their quest to create the perfect group, group leaders may not pay sufficient attention to what they are already doing well, so sometimes, they change things that are working in the hope of making a group more effective. Thus, the focus of evaluation of intervention effectiveness is to identify both the activities, interventions, and leader behaviors that were deemed useful by group members (and how these factors contributed to group member change and learning) and also the activities and interventions that were not perceived as useful to group members. Group leaders may also identify through processing of activities and at the end of group sessions times in the group when they could have intervened, not intervened, or perhaps intervened differently. This evaluation is focused on the future, both for the development of group leadership skills and the development of more effective interventions for psychoeducational groups.

Collect Data From Multiple Sources. Group members' perspectives on how they changed as a result of being in group, as well as the group processes, activities, and interventions that helped them to change, are very important. In addition, information from people who interact with the group members (e.g., teachers, parents, and sometimes peers) about changes in group members' behavior, attitudes and thinking patterns, and emotions is also useful in evaluating the effectiveness of a psychoeducational group. The group leaders' perspective on group members' change is important because group members may overestimate or underestimate how much they have changed depending on the situation. Group members often forget where they were when they began in group, and so they underestimate how much progress they have made; group leaders can remind them of the changes they have made using information from early goal-setting activities and also examples of their participation and behavior in early group sessions. Group members may sometimes overestimate the progress because, compared to other group members, they have made a great deal of progress, or because they do not have an accurate sense of the severity of their problems or issues when they began.

Comparison of the data from different sources can be interesting and enlightening. Group members' and leaders' perceptions of events, and specifically of what is helpful and not helpful, may differ significantly. A student of mine (Horrocks & DeLucia-Waack, 2006) is conducting a program evaluation of a year-long psychoeducational group for adolescents at an alternative middle school based on a structured curriculum. Borrowing from Kivlighan and Goldfine's (1991) Critical Incident Questionnaire, she asked students to identify the five sessions that were most helpful and the five sessions that were least helpful to them, followed by an interview focused on why these sessions were helpful or not helpful and what the students learned from them. Surprisingly, the list of most helpful sessions significantly overlapped with the list of least helpful sessions, strongly suggesting the wide range of variability in adolescents' perceptions and learning styles.

A slightly more humorous and lengthy, but enlightening, illustration of the differences in therapist and client perspective is the book that Yalom co-wrote with his client, Ginny Elkin, *Every Day Gets a Little Closer: A Twice-Told Therapy* (1991). Both therapist and client wrote reactions to each individual counseling session. It is amusing to see how different their perceptions were of the same counseling session. Yalom, as with most therapists, perceived a certain session as therapeutic because he had shared some insight that he thought would be particularly helpful to the client. More often than not, Ginny reported not getting anything out of a session like that. In contrast, Yalom might make some off-the-cuff comment as Ginny was walking out the door that she would contemplate all week and come back with some wonderful insight (and, sometimes, behavior change). Thus, it is important to get multiple perceptions of what makes groups effective.

Collect Data at Multiple Times. It is important to collect data at various points in the group to compare how group members were before they start a group to how they are after group ends, and sometimes 3 or 6 months later to see if they maintain their progress. At midpoint, it is helpful to ask members to complete a rating scale related to their goals as a starting point for discussion of progress, what changes group members have made, and what they want to continue to work on for the rest of the group. Often, group members have this perception, even in very short groups such as eight sessions, that they have lots of time to work on their goals. It is then a "wake-up call" when leaders ask group members to evaluate their progress on a scale of 1 to 10 and then ask group members specifically what they want to work on in the next three sessions (recognizing that the last session is used for consolidation of learning and saying good-bye). With regard to group process, dynamics, and interventions, it is useful to collect a group member's perceptions at various stages so that that information can be used to assess effectiveness and also to plan for future group sessions.

Decision Making in the Preplanning Stage. Decide on how group process and outcome will be assessed as part of the preplanning process. There is nothing more frustrating than frantically searching for a measure that you know exists or trying to find a measure to assess the behaviors and skills that you have been targeting 1 hour before the last group session (or if you are somewhat organized, 1 hour before the second-to-last group session so that group members can complete the measure before they come back to the last group session). Plan ahead, because you may need to modify the wording to be more appropriate for children and adolescents, contact someone to get the scoring key, or purchase copyrighted measures and scoring keys.

Integrate the Assessment Into the Group Activities. Find a way to integrate the assessment measures into the structure of the group. Several of the implicit goals of all psychoeducational groups are met when group members assess their progress in group and give feedback on specific interventions and activities that were and were not helpful to them. The implicit goals of all psychoeducational groups are self-awareness, specifically with regard to changes in self-esteem, strengths, and areas to work on; direct expression of thoughts, feelings, and wants and needs; and evaluation of problem-solving, decision-making, coping skills, and conflict-resolution strategies specifically related to effectiveness for each individual group member. Written evaluation often helps group members clarify, integrate, and organize their thoughts and perceptions, which helps them to verbalize these ideas more accurately and comfortably in group. However, if children and adolescents do not see a direct connection or relevance to the group, it is very likely that they may not complete evaluation measures.

As mentioned previously, group leaders of a children-of-divorce group were able to integrate the Critical Incident Questionnaire (Kivlighan & Goldfine, 1991) as part of the processing time at the end of the group session by asking members,

"Of the events that occurred in this group session today, which one do you feel was the most important to/for you personally? Describe the event—what actually took place, the group members involved, and their reactions. Why was this important to you?" The results of integrating this questionnaire into each group session were threefold. First, group members knew what to expect during processing, so they could think about what their answers would be prior to that part of the session. Second, group leaders were able to assess effective components of each group session and get immediate feedback from group members. Third, researchers studying the effectiveness of interventions for children of divorce were able to analyze the answers in terms of therapeutic factors to gain a more in-depth understanding of therapeutic factors in children's groups in general, and specifically for children-of-divorce groups that use music.

Be Clear About What You Want to Measure. It is much easier to find an instrument to assess outcome if you clearly define the construct to be measured. The easiest way is to go back and look at the goals of the psychoeducational group. What new behaviors are you teaching? What cognitive strategies are you teaching? What affective changes might group members experience as a result of participation in the group? For a children-of-divorce group, it is generally expected that anxiety and depression will lessen as a result of the group (e.g., Revised Children's Manifest Anxiety Scale, Reynolds & Richmond, 1985; Children's Depression Inventory, Kovacs, 1981, 1992). The Perceived Competence Scale (Harter, 1982) also could be used to measure self-esteem in children. In addition, if a specific children-of-divorce group is going to address some of the irrational beliefs that children may hold related to divorce (e.g., it was my fault that they got divorced; I want my parents to get back together again; children will make fun of me if they know about my parents; because one of my parents left, the other parent may leave as well), then the Children's Beliefs About Parental Divorce Scale (Kurdek & Berg, 1987) might be useful to assess changes in cognitions. In a body image group, it might be helpful to assess body image, self-esteem, and perhaps depression and anxiety.

Use Established Measures of Process and Outcome. Although not many instruments have established reliability and validity, are relevant to groups, and are designed for children and adolescents, it is wise to use one whenever possible. There are many more reliable and valid outcome measures (e.g., anxiety, depression, social skills, self-esteem, body image) than measures of group process.

As you choose outcome measures specific to the goals of the psychoeducational group, consider how they might be used as part of the pregroup screening process to help select (or deselect) group members who are appropriate for the focus of the group along with providing information about which sessions would be most useful. Several good, reliable measures are available that assess social skills in general, can be used with middle school and high school students, and can serve as a baseline but also help the students to develop specific interpersonal goals for themselves. The Inventory of Interpersonal Problems (Barkham, Hardy, & Startup, 1996) is self-scoring, with 12 scales such as too controlling, too involved, too caring, too easily influenced, problems with competition, and hard to be assertive.

The Group Expectations Questionnaire (Lieberman et al., 1973) focuses even more specifically on areas of social difficulty by asking potential group members to identify their current interpersonal functioning and also where they would expect to be after the group experience (e.g., *frequently do not understand my inner feelings* to *usually understand my inner feelings*) along an 8-point continuum.

Take into consideration the length of the instrument, because children and adolescents probably will not have the attention span to complete long assessments. It is also helpful to use instruments that are designed and validated specifically for children and adolescents because the wording level will be appropriate and also because such measures usually will have normative data upon which specific group members can be compared.

Examination of the manual for the instrument will also provide helpful information on the reactivity of the measure. Psychoeducational groups are relatively short interventions, and so instruments must be relatively sensitive to change in order to be useful in assessing changes over 8 weeks. For instance, the Trait part of the State Trait anxiety measure is known to be extremely resistant to change, and so that probably would not be a good measure to assess anxiety in children and adolescents. However, the State part of that measure is much more situational; thus, it is much more reactive and more likely to show change over a short time period.

Summary. The field of group work recently has begun to emphasize the importance of reliable and valid measures in assessing group process and dynamics, and so more measures have begun to appear in the literature. What follows is a brief discussion of some measures that may be useful. Some suggestions are also provided about how group practitioners may use these measures to assess group member change and progress, and the effectiveness of specific group interventions, activities, and leadership behaviors.

Assessment of Group Climate

It may be helpful to assess group members' perceptions of the group climate related to cohesion and safety at various points during the group. If there appear to be some problems in the group (e.g., sporadic attendance; resistance to sharing or disclosing, or to trying new behaviors; lots of discussion of feeling unsafe in other places), it might be useful formally or informally to assess group members' perceptions of group climate. Many of these measures are more appropriate with adolescents with reading ability.

Group Climate Questionnaire-Short

The Group Climate Questionnaire-Short (GCQ-S) (MacKenzie, 1983, 1990) is designed to be sufficiently short to be administered after every session. Consequently, the GCQ-S consists of 12 items rated on a 6-point scale from 1 = *not at all* to 6 = *extremely*, and can be completed by both group leaders and members. High scores indicate higher perceived levels of that construct. Engaging is the degree of cohesion and work orientation of the group, and consists of the subscales Cohesion, Self-Disclosure, and Willingness to Confront. Avoiding is the degree to which individuals rely on group members and leaders, consisting of the subscales Conformity, Superficiality, and Denial of Responsibility. Conflict consists of the subscales Friction, Distrust, and Mutual Withdrawal.

MacKenzie (1983) suggested that the GCQ-S provides leaders with information regarding group members' perspectives; specifically, the GCQ-S may identify members who view their group so differently from their peers that they end up being scapegoated. The GCQ-S is probably most appropriate for high school students because of word usage.

Group Environment Scale

The Group Environment Scale (GES) (Moos, 1986) assesses group functioning and the social environment of groups, such as task-oriented, social, psychotherapy, or mutual support groups (Littlepage, Cowart, & Kerr, 1989). This measure is used to assess group member perception of climate both over time and after individual sessions. The GES consists of 90 items rated as true or false. Ten subscales, composed of nine questions each, assess three underlying dimensions: Relationship, Personal Growth, and Systems Maintenance/Systems Change. Higher scores indicate greater levels of that subscale. The Relationship dimension includes the subscales Cohesion, Leader Support, and Expressiveness. The Personal Growth dimension includes the subscales Independence, Task Orientation, Self-Discovery, and Anger and Aggression. The System Maintenance/System Change dimension includes the subscales Order and Organization, Leader Control, and Innovation.

Both of length, the GES is probably most appropriate for high school students; however, the true-false format does add to its ease of administration. One potential use is for co-leaders to each rate the group separately and then compare results to perhaps identify differences in perception or areas in need of intervention.

Assessment of Group Therapeutic Factors

Yalom (1995) suggested that 12 therapeutic factors form the basis for what makes groups effective. The 12 factors are Altruism, Catharsis, Cohesiveness, Existentiality, Family Re-Enactment, Guidance, Hope, Identification, Interpersonal Learning Input (Feedback), Interpersonal Learning Output (New Behavior), Self-Understanding, and Universality. Yalom, Tinklenerg, and Guilula's (1968) study of 20 successful long-term therapy groups indicated that Interpersonal Learning Input, Catharsis, Cohesiveness, Self-Understanding, and Interpersonal Learning Output were rated as the five most important factors. Kivlighan and Holmes's (2004) cluster analysis indicated two clusters, cognitive support groups and cognitive insight groups, that most closely resemble psychoeducational groups, emphasizing the importance of Vicarious Learning, Guidance, Interpersonal Learning, and Self-Understanding. *Cognitive support groups* rated Vicarious Learning and Guidance as highly valued, whereas Self-Understanding was rated much lower. *Cognitive insight groups* rated

Interpersonal Learning, Self-Understanding, and Vicarious Learning as the most valued therapeutic factors. Shechtman et al. (1997) found that for adolescents in psychoeducational groups, Interpersonal Learning, Catharsis, and Socializing Techniques were most valued. Little research has been conducted about the importance of different therapeutic factors in psychoeducational groups. In addition, very little research has been conducted about children's and adolescents' perceptions of therapeutic factors in groups. The literature suggests that children and adolescents need more structure, more variation and modality, and more of a focus on skill building. However, at this time, very little research is available to explain how therapeutic factors work in conjunction with these differences. Thus, it is essential for group leaders to not make assumptions about which therapeutic factors are important in psychoeducational groups, but rather to assess them systematically to better understand what happens in effective groups and to plan for the future.

Therapeutic Factors Scale

The Therapeutic Factors Scale (TFS) (Yalom, 1975; Yalom et al., 1968) contains 60 items, five for each therapeutic factor, and can be rated using either a Likert-scale (from 1 = *not helpful at all* to 7 = *extremely helpful*), with higher scores indicating more importance of a factor, or a Q-sort (statements are sorted into categories from *not helpful at all* to *extremely helpful*). Yalom et al. originally found that members of 20 therapy groups using the Q-sort ranked the factors in the following order from most to least important: Interpersonal Learning (Output), Catharsis, Cohesiveness, Self-Understanding, Interpersonal Learning (Input), Existential Factors, Universality, Instillation of Hope, Altruism, Family Reenactment, Guidance, and Identification. Because of the length and the somewhat complex nature of the task, particularly if the Q-sort is used, this measure is probably appropriate only for high school students.

Curative Factors Scale-Revised

Yalom and colleagues (Lieberman et al., 1973) developed the shorter Curative Factors Scale-Revised (CFS-R) (Stone, Lewis, & Beck, 1994) to assess their 12 therapeutic factors in counseling and therapy groups, and, more recently, they adapted it for use in professional training groups. The original CFS contains 14 items: 2 items each for cohesiveness and self-understanding, and 1 item for each of the remaining 10 scales. This measure could be used with most children and adolescents, with some minor adjustments for younger children.

Critical Incidents Questionnaire

The Critical Incidents Questionnaire (CIQ) (Kivlighan & Goldfine, 1991) is probably the best way to assess the impact of specific interventions, activities, and leadership behaviors within a psychoeducational group. It is relatively unobtrusive because it can be used as a verbal activity during the processing part of the group session. Group members can be asked to respond to the following: "Of the events that occurred in this group session today, which one do you feel was the most important to/for you personally? Describe the event—what actually took place, the group members involved, and their reactions. Why was this important to you?"

Integration of group members' responses can be analyzed in terms of what specific interventions, activities, and group leadership behaviors were mentioned. In addition, the responses can be categorized into therapeutic factors to assess which ones appear to present in a particular group session.

Further analysis of the combination of therapeutic factors that appear to be present in a particular group session may provide some indication about group stage based on current research. In addition, Kivlighan and Goldfine (1991) used the CIQ to classify group therapeutic factors into three categories: Affective (Acceptance/Group Cohesion, Catharsis, Instillation of Hope); Behavioral (Altruism, Learning From Interpersonal Actions/Interpersonal Learning, Self-Disclosure); and Cognitive (Guidance, Self-Understanding, Universality, and Vicarious Learning). When examining the relationship between group stage and therapeutic factors, as hypothesized, Hope and Universality predominated the initial stage of group development. Also as hypothesized, Catharsis increased across the stages, reaching its highest level during the working stage and then decreasing in termination. Guidance increased, achieving its highest level during the working stage. The authors concluded that Acceptance is important in all stages of group; members need acceptance not just when exploring personal issues, but also when making an initial commitment to the group. Levels of Self-Understanding, Vicarious Learning, Learning From Interpersonal Actions, Altruism, and Self-Disclosure were not related to stage of group development.

Assessment of In-Session Group Behavior

Some of the oldest instruments used to analyze and assess therapeutic groups are those that rate in-session group leader and member behavior based on videotapes, audiotapes, or a transcript of actual group sessions.

> Interactional analysis attempts to unravel and understand the dialogue of the participants through observational techniques. Basically, the rating systems functioned as coding schemes, assigning behavior to predetermined categories deemed important by the clinician or researcher. . . . Overall patterns can be recognized either within a single session, or over the entire length of the group. Such patterns lend contextual meaning . . . [and] are more likely to capture the dynamic properties of the process. (Fuhriman & Barlow, 1994, p. 192)

Using these rating sessions can be particularly useful for group leaders in training to systematically evaluate their style of leadership, what types of interventions they tend to use, and the impact of specific group leadership behaviors and interventions on group member interactions.

My theory about this process is that group leaders in training need to create cognitive organizers for themselves to use as a foundation for evaluation of group effectiveness and process. The rating systems that follow are particularly helpful as training devices to identify objectively group leadership behaviors and interventions, followed by group members' responses to these interventions. Group leaders can examine objectively their interventions and the intention of the interventions, and then assess whether the intervention achieved the desired group member interaction. One system is not inherently better than another system, because it seems that systematically categorizing and evaluating the effectiveness of interventions is more important than how the interventions are categorized. The Group Sessions Rating Scale seems particularly relevant for psychoeducational groups because of its emphasis on imparting information and practicing skills, but all systems seem useful to evaluate group leadership behaviors from a theoretical perspective. It is useful to videotape a group session and then, as co-leaders, watch the session, categorizing leadership behaviors as they occur and specifying the intent and the outcome. Group leaders may often want to pause the tape to observe something that they had not noticed before or discuss future interventions. It is also a good activity at some point to actually transcribe a tape to be aware of speech patterns as well as interventions. I suggest leaders organize their analysis into six categories:

- Speakers
- Verbalizations (word for word what was being said, including "umm," "you know," "like," etc.)
- Response categories (which type of response based on a rating session)
- Goal of the response
- Whether the response was effective
- Alternative responses/interventions/directions

It is also helpful for group leaders in training to watch group sessions led by other group leaders to learn new strategies and gain a sense of the group dynamics that are inherent in most groups.

Group Sessions Rating Scale

The Group Sessions Rating Scale (GSRS) (Cooney, Kadden, Litt, & Getter, 1991; Getter, Litt, Kadden, & Cooney, 1992) was designed to assess the use of different therapeutic interventions by both group leaders and members of psychoeducational and counseling groups. It was constructed as a process measure to test the differences between two types of groups: coping skills training and short-term interactional group therapy (Kadden, Cooney, Getter, & Litt, 1989). The seven categories consisted of four related to Coping Skills—Education/Skill Training, Problem-Solving, Role Playing, Identifying High-Risk Situations—and three related to Interactional Therapy—Interpersonal Learning, Expression/Exploration of Feelings, and Here-and-Now Focus.

Interaction Process Analysis

The Interaction Process Analysis (IPA) (Bales, 1950) measures task and socioemotional interpersonal behavior using 12 categories that emphasize problem-solving behavior. Bales postulated that episodes of task-oriented activity alternate with episodes of short socioemotional interventions that restore group solidarity. The socioemotional categories consist of Positive Reactions (shows solidarity, shows tension release, and shows agreement) and Negative Reactions (shows disagreement, shows tension, and shows antagonism). The task-oriented categories consist of Attempted Answers (gives suggestions, gives opinion, asks for suggestions) and Questions (asks for information, asks for opinion, asks for suggestions).

Systems for Multiple Level Observation of Groups

Systems for Multiple Level Observation of Groups (SYMLOG) (Bales, Cohen, & Williams, 1979), as a measure of group interaction, focuses on interpersonal behavior and values. The behavior of each group member is rated on 26 items organized into three dimensions: Dominant-Submissive, Unfriendly-Friendly, and Instrumentally Controlled-Emotionally Expressive. Bales et al. suggested that for diagnostic purposes, it is important for raters to rate all possible combinations of the three dimensions, and for group members to receive, as feedback, information regarding their behavior for each of the 26 items. There are also shorter 6-item and 8-item forms that have adequate reliability and correlate strongly with the longer version.

Other Promising Measures

Group Observer Form (GOF). The GOF (Romano, 1998; Romano & Sullivan, 2000) was designed to provide co-facilitators structured and unstructured feedback about the group dynamics and leaders' use of skills observed during the group session. Responses are rated by an independent rater or a supervisor on a 7-point Likert-type scale with anchors from *low* to *high, past* to *present, little* to *much,* and *intellectual* to *feelings,* with high scores indicating more interactive group behavior. Three factors emerged: Group Cohesiveness, Here-and-Now Focus, and Group Conflict.

Individual Group Member Interpersonal Process Scale (IGIPS). The IGIPS (Soldz, Budman, Davis, & Demby, 1993) was designed to "elucidate the therapeutically significant behaviors of individual patients in the group setting, measure change in patient behavior over the course of the group, and illuminate the interactional functioning of the group as a whole" (Soldz et al., 1993, p. 552). The IGIPS was designed to be rated for each statement made by both group leaders and members, with 12 items that identify either the presence/absence of a behavior (e.g., discusses own issues), locational and object designations (to whom the behavior is directed and whether the topic is related to in-group or out-of-group issues), or the intensity or significance of the behavior using a 9-point Likert format. A principal component analysis indicated five factors that accounted for 74% of the variance: Activity, Interpersonal Sensitivity, Comfort with Self, Self-Focus, and Psychological Mindedness. Davis, Budman, and Soldz (2000) provide a more detailed discussion of the use of, and current research related to, the IGIPS.

Summary

In this era of managed care and the focus on prevention, effective psychoeducational groups are critical to the field of counseling and psychotherapy, particularly for children and adolescents. It is crucial that group leaders and group researchers establish the effectiveness of specific group techniques, interventions, leadership behaviors, and activities. Identification of effective group interventions is crucial to the development of the field. In addition, group leaders need to evaluate their groups reliably and validly in order to develop further their group leadership skills and to also plan future effective group interventions. Evaluation should be comprehensive, focusing on both outcome—how group members change behaviorally, cognitively, attitudinally, and affectively as a result of the group—and process—the effective ingredients that promote group member change.

Suggested Training Activities

1. Review of a Group Session

- Observe a live group (with permission), a role-play of a group session, a video-tape of an actual group (with permission), or a commercial training tape.
- Comment on the following:
  - What were the major themes and issues that you saw/heard being discussed?
  - What were major themes and issues that were relevant but not being addressed (by both members and leaders)?
  - Discuss the effectiveness of interventions by the leaders:

    Supporting

    Challenging

    Providing information

    Discussing feelings

    Discussing thought patterns

    Discussing behaviors in and out of the group

    Processing in-group interaction

    Helping members to take what they learned out of the group

    Bringing issues to a deeper level

    Keeping the group on task

  - Give ideas/suggestions that might also have been helpful.
  - In which places could leaders have intervened? How?
  - In which places could leaders have been silent? What might have happened?
  - What did members of the group do to encourage trust? Communication? Disclosure? Examination of feelings and relationships?

2. Systematically Categorize and Evaluate the Effectiveness of Group Leader Interventions

- Create a grid using these five categories of columns:
  - Speakers
  - Verbalizations (word for word what was being said, including "umm," "you know," "like," etc.)
  - Response categories (which type of response based on a rating session)
  - Goal of the response
  - Whether the response was effective
  - Alternative responses/interventions/directions

- Choose a rating system to categorize the response categories.
- Observe a live group (with permission), a role-play of a group session, a videotape of an actual group (yours or someone else's, with permission), or a commercial training tape.
- Complete the grid for a group session.
- Assess which types of interventions achieved the desired result.
- Assess which interventions were not particularly effective.
- Discuss what kinds of interventions might be useful in future sessions.

3. Group Member Assessment of the Effectiveness of an Intervention and Perceptions of Therapeutic Factors

- Choose an activity or series of activities to use in a middle-stage group session.
- Create a Group Planning Sheet for this group session in Appendix D.
- Enlist the help of six people to role-play, and give them a brief history of what the group has been working on and which activities have been done so far.
- Choose an outcome assessment measure specifically related to the goal of the activity to be role-played as a pretest/posttest to assess change as a result of the group session.
- Choose a measure designed to assess group climate.
- Just prior to the role-play, ask group members to complete the pretest of the outcome measure.
- Role-play a 30- to 40-minute group session complete with an opening, working, processing, and ending.
- After the session, ask group members to complete the following:
  - Posttest of the outcome measure
  - Assessment of group climate
  - Critical Incident Questionnaire

- Then, ask them to discuss the following:
  - How did you feel during this session?
  - What were you thinking?
  - What did the leaders do that made you feel comfortable? Be specific.
  - What did the leaders do that helped you to learn something about yourself? Be specific.

- What did the leaders do that helped you learn something about others in the group? Be specific.
- What did the leaders do that helped you learn something about how groups work? Be specific.
- What did the leaders do that maybe wasn't helpful?
- What else could they have talked about that would have been helpful?

CHAPTER 11

Considerations

Much of what has been suggested about psychoeducational groups for children and adolescents can be applied to a variety of different settings, populations, and age groups. Multicultural considerations must also be taken into account in all groups, but in groups where there is considerable diversity, it must be addressed directly and then used to facilitate effective communication and problem-solving strategies. This chapter will discuss two adaptations of psychoeducational groups: classroom guidance activities and group counseling for older adolescents. Because of the importance of and impact on group work, multicultural considerations will also be discussed.

Classroom Guidance

Because the focus of psychoeducational groups for children and adolescents is preventive and targets the development of new skills and ways of thinking, there is an easy transition from planning for psychoeducational groups to classroom guidance. Self-esteem, communication skills, healthy families, conflict resolution, friendship skills, and bullying prevention are all topics that school counselors are often asked to present as a classroom activity. Activity should be conceptualized in the same stages (initial, working, termination) and the same parts of a session (opening, working, processing, closing) as a psychoeducational group, but in a much shorter time span.

In a classroom guidance activity, an initial-stage activity might be as short as 10 minutes. Basic ground rules must be discussed, such as one person talks at a time, everyone should be respectful, and people will be asked but not required to share. An exercise can be used to reinforce the goals of self-disclosure and self-awareness, and highlight the goals of the classroom guidance activity. For example, in a classroom guidance activity focused on making friends, students might be asked to select an animal that would act most similarly to them in a new situation, and then share with the group what the animal was and how that animal explores new situations. The group leader could then highlight the differences in how animals (and people) react in new situations, and how these differences can be used in further activities to brainstorm and problem solve new ways of behaving in different situations.

Dyads, triads, and small groups are useful in classroom guidance to promote interaction on a manageable and relatively nonthreatening level for working activities. Processing and termination questions may also be discussed in these smaller groups to facilitate more discussion and disclosure. Closing activities might be conducted as a large group to summarize learning, but in a nonthreatening way: "When I do this activity with other classes, what should I emphasize? What do they need to know? What activities should I use with them? How will the activities be helpful to them?"

Preplanning for classroom guidance can be an abbreviated version of what is conducted for psychoeducational groups. Deciding on goals will lead to the selection of activities and processing questions to emphasize the major points and facilitate identification and application of learning.

Group Counseling With Older Adolescents

Group counseling may be needed for older adolescents to help them address personal and interpersonal problems of living and promote personal and interpersonal growth and development. However, although the focus may be similar to adult groups, the techniques still need to be adapted to adolescents. Much of what has been described in this book in terms of how to connect and how to motivate participation is relevant because of the developmental issues of children and adolescents. The need for structure and the use of creative and innovative activities to keep adolescents motivated, wanting to come, and interested but on task are necessary.

Because of the emphasis in counseling groups on interpersonal dynamics and how they unfold as a key focus in interventions to help group members identify their adaptive and maladaptive coping and interpersonal strategies, the specificity of the structure of the psychoeducational groups described in this book would interfere with the natural unfolding of these interpersonal dynamics. Thus, it is recommended to keep the format of group with an opening, working, processing, and closing to provide a structure that helps group members organize and predict what will happen throughout the session to promote safety. However, the content of the working part of the group session will be determined by what group members present in the opening as what they want to talk about and work on during that session. Processing and closing will be focused on the application of learning and planning for future sessions based on what occurs in the working part of the session. Some structure with adolescents is necessary, however, to help them focus and identify what they need to talk about and work on. To aid in this process, it is helpful for group leaders to use a brief activity, 10 to 15 minutes at the most, that helps generate some insight into their personal issues and perhaps introduce a framework within which to work on personal issues. Group leaders might choose the activity based on what was said during the closing of the previous session with regard to homework or future topics to work on. Or, as part of the initial stage, group members may decide on the topics that they would like to discuss in group sessions. The group leaders then choose an activity that will introduce that topic and help group members focus on it. For instance, in an eating disorders group, group members may first trace themselves onto large pieces of paper and then identify parts of their body that they like. Processing may then lead into what it is like to look at your body, how you identify what you like (and don't like), and the concepts of body image and self-esteem. In some groups, once group members have internalized the norms, the members choose the introductory activity themselves by taking turns or by group consensus. Another way is that once the group has chosen a topic for the next session, a group member brings in a poem or a song for the group to listen to as a beginning for the session.

Multicultural Considerations

> Is it not true that we all want to claim our specialness resulting in a composite of affiliations and group memberships? All of us have multidimensional identities. . . . All counseling needs to be reframed as multicultural counseling. (Arredondo, 1994, p. 309)

Diversity and multicultural issues groups are inherent in groups and essential to consider. Group leader competence is critical, specifically multicultural group counseling skills. In addition, knowledge of other cultural worldviews and values and how these may inhibit or increase a potential group member's willingness to participate and his or her behavior in group is essential. Acculturation is noted as an important variable in predicting the behavior of potential group members. Effective groups must help members to understand themselves and others as individuals within the context of their culture and choose interventions and methods of change based on the interplay between the individuals and their worldviews.

Several important points should be made when thinking about effective multicultural group work:

- Each group member must conceptualize his or her problem within his or her own personal and cultural constructs so that a plan of action can be implemented that fits with his or her beliefs.
- All events and behaviors must be approached from a functional perspective. Does it work for this individual?
- Groups must help members make sense of new behaviors, feelings, and beliefs within a cultural context.

Thus, problem-solving, brainstorming, decision-making, conflict-resolution, and effective communication strategies, all of which are so inherent in psychoeducational groups, must be conceptualized within the context of each group member's individual and unique cultural context. It is often helpful to ask group members to think about their values related to communication, feelings, and community (along with many other important topics; DeLucia-Waack & Donigian, 2004, include a table of issues to discuss from different perspectives). For example, group members might be asked to think about their values with a series of questions.

- What are your individual values?
- What were your family values growing up?
- What are your nuclear family values?
- What are your extended family values?
- What are your peers' values?
- What are the values of the community around you?
- What are the values of different ethnic groups around you?

Now do the same for communication style. Group processing might include the following questions:

- What did you learn about yourself?
- What was it like to think about your own values in comparison to others with whom you affiliate?
- Would anyone be willing to share some of this?
- What do you notice in terms of similarities and differences?
- How do your values influence how you interact in group?
- What did you learn about other group members based on this discussion?

DeLucia-Waack and Donigian (2004) asked a series of questions of multicultural group work experts to understand their approaches to groups. They suggest that group leaders write their own cultural autobiography to identify how their cultural values affect their approach to group work.

1. Describe who you are in terms of age, race, any physical disability, sexual orientation, ethnicity and culture, family patterns, gender, socioeconomic status, and intellectual ability (educational background).

2. How do you see yourself as a unique individual based on your ethnic, cultural, and family background?

3. How does your background contribute to your view of how groups work?

4. What strengths do you bring to groups based on your cultural background and beliefs? What limitations do you bring as well?

Summary

Guidelines for psychoeducational groups have applications for other types of group work as well. Much of the structure and planning of a psychoeducational group can be modified for classroom guidance activities on a variety of topics. In addition, although the focus for counseling groups for adolescents may be more interpersonal and remedial, there is still a need for structure to help group members focus on and identify what they want to work on and discuss. The structure of psychoeducational group sessions as well as the use of activities facilitates this process for adolescents.

Each person brings his or her cultural context and heritage to his or her relationships, values, and worldview. It is important to take these into consideration when planning and processing activities, and suggesting solutions to group members. There is a need

> for counselors to transcend their own ethnocentric thinking about the content and process of group counseling as they strive to more respectfully and ethically address the needs and perspectives of persons who come from cultural-racial backgrounds different from their own. (D'Andrea, 2004, p. 265)

Suggested Training Activities

1. Write Your Cultural Autobiography as a Group Leader

- Describe who you are in terms of age, race, any physical disability, sexual orientation, ethnicity and culture, family patterns, gender, socioeconomic status, and intellectual ability (educational background).
- How do you see yourself as a unique individual based on your ethnic, cultural, and family background?
- How does your background contribute to your view of how groups work?
- What strengths do you bring to groups based on your cultural background and beliefs? What limitations do you bring as well?

2. Choose and Use Activities to Introduce a Topic in a Counseling Group for Adolescents

- Choose a focus for a counseling group for adolescents.
- Choose a topic for a particular session.
- Select an evaluation measure that assesses progress toward the specific goals of the group.
- Complete the Group Planning Sheet in Appendix D.
- Implement the session as a role-play, videotaping the session. Give your group members some information about goals, interventions, and focus of past sessions.
- After the session is over, ask your members to talk about the following:
  - What was helpful in getting them focused?
  - Interacting with other members?
  - Establishing a goal to work on for this session?
  - Working on that goal?

- Administer the evaluation measures.
- Evaluate the session using the tape, feedback from members, and one or more of the group leadership assessment forms discussed in Chapter 4.
- Complete the Group Processing Sheet for this session in Appendix E.

- Meet with your co-leader using the model of Reporting, Reflection, Integration, Planning, and Evaluation (DeLucia-Waack, 2001) and the CLIN-ICKING section of the Co-Facilitating Inventory (Pfeiffer & Jones, 1975).
- Complete the Group Planning Sheet for the next session in Appendix D.

3. Create a Classroom Guidance Activity

- Choose a specific focus and a population for a classroom guidance activity.
- Choose goals for the session.
- Select an evaluation measure that assesses progress toward the specific goals.
- Complete the Group Planning Sheet, including an opening, working, processing, and closing, in Appendix D.
- Implement the session as a role-play, videotaping the session.
- After the session is over, ask your members to talk about the following:
  - What was helpful in making them feel comfortable?
  - Interacting with other members?
  - Establishing a goal?
  - Working on the goal?

- Administer the evaluation measures.
- Evaluate the session using the tape, feedback from members, Greenberg's (2002) Checklist for Classroom Guidance, and one or more of the group leadership assessment forms discussed in Chapter 4.
- Complete the Group Processing Sheet for this session in Appendix E.

CHAPTER 12

Conclusions

Psychoeducational groups with children and adolescents are exciting and fun. But they can also be trying and discouraging. They are not simply counseling groups for adults in words appropriate for younger group members. The structure, activities used, and emphasis are very different. This book is an effort to provide a framework for how to lead effective psychoeducational groups for children and adolescents. Preplanning is key so that group sessions are sequenced and timed properly, and fit the needs of group members. Specific attention has been paid to providing suggestions for resources related to activities, materials, and assessment in an effort to help group leaders organize and facilitate their groups effectively.

Groups with children and adolescents need to include interventions to help group members discuss feelings, connect with others, and identify potential solutions for their concerns (Smead, 1995). Children often respond better to nonverbal techniques than to verbal exercises because of their limited vocabularies and disposition to display feelings through play (Gladding, 1998). Drawing, singing, dancing, using puppets, conducting role-plays, and writing plays are all ways to identify and express feelings and to brainstorm and practice new behaviors and coping skills. Psychoeducational interventions assist in sharing and developing coping skills and behaviors to deal with new or difficult situations.

The structure and length of groups for children and adolescents are also very different from those for adult groups. Structure is essential to providing safety and continuity to group members. Structure is also necessary to manage time efficiently and focus on relevant issues (DeLucia-Waack, 1997; Gladding, 1998). Opening, working, processing, and closing should be part of each group session. Activities need to be processed to help group members focus on what they have learned and how they will apply it to their lives outside of group. Group leader behavior must be intentional to create community and safety, and promote learning and growth.

Appendices

APPENDIX A

Association for Specialists in Group Work Professional Standards for the Training of Group Workers

Revision Approved by the Executive Board, January 22, 2000

Prepared by F. Robert Wilson and Lynn S. Rapin, Co-Chairs, and Lynn Haley-Banez, Member, ASGW Standards Committee

Consultants: Robert K. Conyne and Donald E. Ward

Preamble

For nearly two decades, the Association for Specialists in Group Work (herein referred to as ASGW or as the Association) has promulgated professional standards for the training group workers. In the early 1980s, the Association published

Author's Note: From the Association for Specialists in Group Work, Professional Standards for the Training of Group Workers. In *Journal for Specialists in Group Work, 25*, pp. 327–342. Reprinted with permission of ASGW.

the ASGW Training Standard for Group Leaders (1983) which established nine knowledge competencies, seventeen competencies, and clock-hour baselines for various aspects of supervised clinical experience in group counseling. The focus on group counseling embodied in these standards mirrored the general conception of the time that whatever counselors did with groups of individuals should properly be referred to as group counseling.

New ground was broken in the 1990 revision of the ASGW Professional Standards for the Training of Group Workers with (a) the articulation of the term, group work, to capture the variety of ways in which counselors work with groups, (b) differentiation of core training, deemed essential for all counselors, from specialization training required of those intending to engage in group work as part of their professional practice, and (c) the differentiation among four distinct group work specializations: task and work group facilitation, group psychoeducational, group counseling, and group psychotherapy. Over the ten years in which these standards have been in force, commentary and criticism has been elicited through discussion groups at various regional and national conferences and through published analyses in the Association's journal, the *Journal for Specialists in Group Work*.

In this Year-2000 revision of the ASGW Professional Standards for the Training of Group Workers, the foundation established by the 1990 training standards has been preserved and refined by application of feedback received through public discussion and scholarly debate. The Year-2000 revision maintains and strengthens the distinction between core and specialization training with requirements for core training and aspirational guidelines for specialization training. Further, the definitions of group work specializations have been expanded and clarified. Evenness of application of training standards across the specialization has been assured by creating a single set of guidelines for all four specializations with specialization specific detail being supplied where necessary. Consistent with both the pattern for training standards established by the Council for Accreditation of Counseling and Related Educational Program accreditation standards and past editions of the ASGW training standard, the Year-2000 revision addresses both content and clinical instruction. Content instruction is described in terms of both course work requirements and knowledged object while clinical instruction is articulated in experiential requirements and skill objectives. This revision of the training standards was informed by and profits from the seminal ASGW Best Practice Guidelines (1998) and the ASGW Principles for Diversity-Competent Group Workers (1999). Although each of these documents have their own form of organization, all address the group work elements of planning, performing, and processing and the ethical and diversity competent treatment of participants in group activities.

Purpose

The purpose of the Professional Standards for the Training of Group Workers is to provide guidance to counselor training programs in the construction of their curricula for graduate programs in counseling (e.g., masters, specialist, and doctoral degrees and other forms of advanced graduate study). Specifically, core standards express the Association's view on the minimum training in group work all programs in counseling should provide for all graduates of their entry level, master's degree programs in counseling, and specialization standards provide a framework for documenting the training philosophy, objectives, curriculum, and outcomes for each declared specialization program.

Core Training in Group Work. All counselors should possess a set of core competencies in general group work. The Association for Specialists in Group Work advocates for the incorporation of core group work competencies as part of required entry level training in all counselor preparation programs. The Association's standards for core training are consistent with and provide further elaboration of the standards for accreditation of entry level counseling programs identified by the Council for Accreditation of Counseling and Related Educational Programs (CACREP, 1994). Mastery of the core competencies detailed in the ASGW training standards will prepare the counselor to understand group process phenomena and to function more effectively in groups in which the counselor is a member. Mastery of basic knowledge and skill in group work provides a foundation which specialty training can extend but does not qualify one to independently practice any group work specialty.

Specialist Training in Group Work. The independent practice of group work requires training beyond core competencies. ASGW advocates that independent practitioners of group work must possess advanced competencies relevant to the particular kind of group work practice in which the group work student wants to specialize (e.g., facilitation of task groups, group psychoeducational, group counseling, or group psychotherapy). To encourage program creativity in development of specialization training, the specialization guidelines do not prescribe minimum trainee competencies. Rather, the guidelines establish a framework within which programs can develop unique training experiences utilizing scientific foundations and best practices to achieve their training objectives. In providing these guidelines for specialized training, ASGW makes no presumption that a graduate program in counseling must provide training in a group work specialization nor that adequate training in a specialization can be accomplished solely within a well-rounded master's degree program in counseling. To provide adequate specialization training, completion of post-master's options such as certificates of post-master's study or doctoral degrees may be required. Further, there is no presumption that an individual who may have received adequate training in a given declared specialization will be prepared to function effectively with all group situations in which the graduate may want to or be required to work. It is recognized that the characteristics of specific client populations and employment settings vary widely. Additional training beyond that which was acquired in a specific graduate program may be necessary for optimal, diversity-competent, group work practice with a given population in a given setting.

Definitions

Group Work: is a broad professional practice involving the application of knowledge and skill in group facilitation to assist an interdependent collection of people to reach their mutual goals which may be intrapersonal, interpersonal, or work-related. The goals of the group may include the accomplishment of tasks related to work, education, personal development, personal and interpersonal problem solving, or remediation of mental and emotional disorders.

Core Training in Group Work: includes knowledge, skills, and experiences deemed necessary for general competency for all master's degree prepared counselors. ASGW advocates for all counselor preparation programs to provide core training in group work regardless of whether the program intends to prepare trainees for independent practice in a group work specialization. Core training in group work is considered a necessary prerequisite for advanced practice in group work.

Specialization Training in Group Work: includes knowledge, skills, and experiences deemed necessary for counselors to engage in independent practice of group work. Four areas of advanced practice, referred to as specializations, are identified: Task Group Facilitation, Group Psychoeducational, Group Counseling, and Group Psychotherapy. This list is not presumed to be exhaustive and while there may be no sharp boundaries between the specializations, each has recognizable characteristics that have professional utility. The definitions for these group work specializations have been built upon the American Counseling Association's model definition of counseling (adopted by the ACA Governing Council in 1997), describing the methods typical of the working stage of the group being defined and the typical purposes to which those methods are put and the typical populations served by those methods. Specialized training presumes mastery of prerequisite core knowledge, skills, and experiences.

Specialization in Task and Work Group Facilitation:

- The application of principles of normal human development and functioning
- through group based educational, developmental, and systemic strategies
- applied in the context of here-and-now interaction
- that promote efficient and effective accomplishment of group tasks
- among people who are gathered to accomplish group task goals.

Specialization in Psychoeducational Group Leadership:

- The application of principles of normal human development and functioning
- through group based educational and developmental strategies
- applied in the context of here-and-now interaction
- that promote personal and interpersonal growth and development and the prevention of future difficulties
- among people who may be at risk for the development of personal or interpersonal problems or who seek enhancement of personal qualities and abilities.

Specialization in Group Counseling:

- The application of principles of normal human development and functioning
- through group based cognitive, affective, behavioral, or systemic intervention strategies

- applied in the context of here-and-now interaction
- that address personal and interpersonal problems of living and promote personal and interpersonal growth and development
- among people who may be experiencing transitory maladjustment, who are at risk for the development of personal or interpersonal problems, or who seek enhancement of personal qualities and abilities.

Specialization in Group Psychotherapy:

- The application of principles of normal and abnormal human development and functioning
- through group based cognitive, affective, behavioral, or systemic intervention strategies
- applied in the context of negative emotional arousal
- that address personal and interpersonal problems of living, remediate perceptual and cognitive distortions or repetitive patterns of dysfunctional behavior, and promote personal and interpersonal growth and development
- among people who may be experiencing severe and/or chronic maladjustment.

Core Training Standards

I. Coursework and Experiential Requirements

A. Coursework Requirements. Core training shall include at least one graduate course in group work that addresses but is not limited to scope of practice, types of group work, group development, group process and dynamics, group leadership, and standards of training and practice for group workers.

B. Experiential Requirements. Core training shall include a minimum of 10 clock hours (20 clock hours recommended) observation of and participation in a group experience as a group member and/or as a group leader.

II. Knowledge and Skill Objectives

A. Nature and Scope of Practice

1. *Knowledge Objectives.* Identify and describe:
   a. the nature of group work and the various specializations within group work
   b. theories of group work including commonalities and distinguishing characteristics among the various specializations within group work
   c. research literature pertinent to group work and its specializations

2. *Skill Objectives.* Demonstrate skill in:
   a. preparing a professional disclosure statement for practice in a chosen area of specialization
   b. and applying theoretical concepts and scientific findings to the design of a group and the interpretation of personal experiences in a group

B. Assessment of Group Members and the Social Systems in Which They Live and Work

1. *Knowledge Objectives.* Identify and describe:
   a. principles of assessment of group functioning in group work
   b. use of personal contextual factors (e.g., family-of-origin, neighborhood-of-residence, organizational membership, cultural membership) in interpreting behavior of members in a group

2. *Skill Objectives.* Demonstrate skill in:
   a. observing and identifying group process,
   b. observing the personal characteristics of individual members in a group,
   c. developing hypotheses about the behavior of group members,
   d. employing contextual factors (e.g., family of origin, neighborhood of residence, organizational membership, cultural membership) in interpretation of individual and group data

Planning Group Interventions

1. *Knowledge Objectives.* Identify and describe:
   a. environmental contexts, which affect planning for group interventions
   b. the impact of group member diversity (e.g., gender, culture, learning style, group climate preference) on group member behavior and group process and dynamics in group work
   c. principles of planning for group work

2. *Skill Objectives.* Demonstrate skill in:
   a. collaborative consultation with targeted populations to enhance ecological validity of planned group interventions
   b. planning for a group work activity including such aspects as developing overarching purpose, establishing goals and objectives, detailing methods to be used in achieving goals and objectives, determining methods for outcome assessment, and verifying ecological validity of plan

Implementation of Group Interventions

1. *Knowledge Objectives.* Identify and describe:
   a. principles of group formation including recruiting, screening, and selecting group members
   b. principles for effective performance of group leadership functions
   c. therapeutic factors within group work and when group work approaches are indicated and contraindicated
   d. principles of group dynamics including group process components, developmental stage theories, group member roles, group member behaviors

2. *Skill Objectives.* Demonstrate skill in:
   a. encouraging participation of group members
   b. attending to, describing, acknowledging, confronting, understanding, and responding empathetically to group member behavior
   c. attending to, acknowledging, clarifying, summarizing, confronting, and responding empathetically to group member statements
   d. attending to, acknowledging, clarifying, summarizing, confronting, and responding empathetically to group themes
   e. eliciting information from and imparting information to group members
   f. providing appropriate self-disclosure
   g. maintaining group focus; keeping a group on task
   h. giving and receiving feedback in a group setting

Leadership and Co-Leadership

1. *Knowledge Objectives.* Identify and describe:
   a. group leadership styles and approaches
   b. group work methods including group worker orientations and specialized group leadership behaviors
   c. principles of collaborative group processing

2. *Skill Objectives.* To the extent opportunities for leadership or co-leadership are provided, demonstrate skill in:
   a. engaging in reflective evaluation of one's personal leadership style and approach
   b. working cooperatively with a co-leader and/or group members
   c. engaging in collaborative group processing

Evaluation

1. *Knowledge Objectives.* Identify and describe:
   a. methods for evaluating group process in group work
   b. methods for evaluating outcomes in group work

2. *Skill Objectives.* Demonstrate skill in:
   a. contributing to evaluation activities during group participation
   b. engaging in self-evaluation of personally selected performance goals

Ethical Practice, Best Practice, Diversity-Competent Practice

1. *Knowledge Objectives.* Identify and describe:
   a. ethical considerations unique to group work
   b. best practices in group work
   c. diversity competent group work

2. *Skill Objectives.* Demonstrate skill in:
   a. evidencing ethical practice in planning, observing, and participating in group activities;
   b. evidencing best practice in planning, observing, and participating in group activities;
   c. evidencing diversity-competent practice in planning, observing, and participating in group activities

Specialization Guidelines

I. Overarching Program Characteristics

A. The program has a clearly specified philosophy of training for the preparation of specialists for independent practice of group work in one of the forms of group work recognized by the Association (i.e., task and work group facilitation, group psychoeducational, group counseling, or group psychotherapy).

1. The program states an explicit intent to train group workers in one or more of the group work specializations.

2. The program states an explicit philosophy of training, based on the science of group work, by which it intends to prepare students for independent practice in the declared specialization(s).

B. For each declared specialization, the program specified education and training objectives in terms of the competencies expected of students completing the specializations training. These competencies are consistent with:

1. the program's philosophy and training model,

2. the substantive area(s) relevant for best practice of the declared specialization area, and

3. standards for competent, ethical, and diversity sensitive practice of group work.

C. For each declared specialization, the program specifies a sequential, cumulative curriculum, expanding in breadth and depth, and designed to prepare students for independent practice of the specialization and relevant credentialing.

D. For each declared specialization, the program documents achievement of training objectives in terms of student competencies.

II. Recommended Coursework and Experience

A. *Coursework.* Specialization training may include coursework which provides the student with a broad foundation in the group work domain in which the student seeks specialized training.

1. Task/Work Group Facilitation: coursework includes but is not limited to organizational development, management, and consultation, theory and practice of task/work group facilitation.

2. Group Psychoeducational: coursework includes but is not limited to organizational development, school and community counseling/psychology, health promotion, marketing, program development and evaluation, organizational consultation, theory and practice of group psychoeducational.

3. Group Counseling: coursework includes but is not limited to normal human development, health promotion, theory and practice of group counseling.

4. Group Psychotherapy: coursework includes but is not limited to normal and abnormal human development, assessment and diagnosis of mental and emotional disorders, treatment of psychopathology, theory and practice of group psychotherapy.

B. *Experience.* Specialization training includes:

1. Task/Work Group Facilitation: a minimum of 30 clock hours (45 clock hours recommended) supervised practice facilitating or conducting an intervention with a task or work group appropriate to the age and clientele of the group leader's specialty area (e.g., school counseling, student development counseling, community counseling, mental health counseling).

2. Group Psychoeducational: a minimum of 30 clock hours (45 clock hours recommended) supervised practice conducting a psychoeducational group appropriate to the age and clientele of the group leader's specialty area (e.g., school counseling, student development counseling, community counseling, mental health counseling).

3. Group Counseling: a minimum of 45 clock hours (60 clock hours recommended) supervised practice conducting a counseling group appropriate to the age and clientele of the group leader's specialty area (e.g., school counseling, student development counseling, community counseling, mental health counseling).

4. Group Psychotherapy: a minimum of 45 clock hours (60 clock hours recommended) supervised practice conducting a psychotherapy group appropriate to the age and clientele of the group leader's specialty area (e.g., mental health counseling).

III. Knowledge and Skill Elements

In achieving its objectives, the program has and implements a clear and coherent curriculum plan that provides the means whereby all students can acquire and demonstrate substantial understanding of and competence in the following areas:

A. *Nature and Scope of Practice.* The program states a clear expectation that its students will limit their independent practice of group work to those specialization areas for which they have been appropriately trained and supervised.

B. *Assessment of Group Members and the Social Systems in Which They Live and Work.* All graduates of specialization training will understand and demonstrate competence in the use of assessment instruments and methodologies for assessing individual group member characteristics and group development, group dynamics, and process phenomena relevant for the program's declared specialization area(s). Studies should include but are not limited to:

1. methods of screening and assessment of populations, groups, and individual members who are or may be targeted for intervention;

2. methods for observation of group member behavior during group interventions;

3. methods of assessment of group development, process, and outcomes.

C. *Planning Group Interventions.* All graduates of specialization training will understand and demonstrate competence in planning group interventions consistent with the program's declared specialization area(s). Studies should include but are not limited to:

1. establishing the overarching purpose for the intervention;

2. identifying goals and objectives for the intervention;

3. detailing methods to be employed in achieving goals and objectives during the intervention;

4. selecting methods for examining group process during group meetings, between group sessions, and at the completion of the group intervention;

5. preparing methods for helping members derive meaning from their within-group experiences and transfer within-group learning to real-world circumstances;

6. determining methods for measuring outcomes during and following the intervention;

7. verifying ecological validity of plans for the intervention.

D. *Implementation of Group Intervention.* All graduates of specialization training will understand and demonstrate competence implementing group interventions consistent with the program's declared specialization area(s). Studies should include but are not limited to:

1. principles of group formation including recruiting, screening, selection, and orientation of group members;

2. standard methods and procedures for group facilitation;

3. selection and use of referral sources appropriate to the declared specialization;

4. identifying and responding constructively to extra-group factors which may influence the success of interventions;

5. applying the major strategies, techniques, and procedures;

6. adjusting group pacing relative to the stage of group development;

7. identifying and responding constructively to critical incidents;

8. identifying and responding constructively to disruptive members;

9. helping group members attribute meaning to and integrate and apply learning;

10. responding constructively to psychological emergencies;

11. involving group members in within group session processing and on-going planning.

E. *Leadership and Co-Leadership.* All graduates of specialization training will understand and demonstrate competence in pursuing personal competence as a leader and in selecting and managing the interpersonal relationship with a co-leader for group interventions consistent with the program's declared specialization area(s). Studies should include but are not limited to:

1. characteristics and skills of effective leaders,

2. relationship skills required of effective co-leaders,

3. processing skills required of effective co-leaders.

F. *Evaluation.* All graduates of specialization training will understand and demonstrate competence in evaluating group interventions consistent with the program's declared specialization area(s). Studies should include but are not limited to methods for evaluating participant outcomes and participant satisfaction.

G. *Ethical Practice, Best Practice, Diversity-Competent Practice.* All graduates of specialization training will understand and demonstrate consistent effort to comply with principles of ethical, best practice, and diversity-competent practice of group work consistent with the program's declared specialization area(s). Studies should include but are not limited to:

1. ethical considerations unique to the program's declared specialization area,

2. best practices for group work within the program's declared specialization area,

3. diversity issues unique to the program's declared specialization area.

Implementation Guidelines

Implementation of the Professional Standards for the Training of Group Workers requires a commitment by a program's faculty and a dedication of program resources to achieve excellence in preparing all counselors at core competency level and in preparing counselors for independent practice of group work. To facilitate implementation of the training standards, the Association offers the following guidelines.

Core Training in Group Work

Core training in group work can be provided through a single, basic course in group theory and process. This course should include the elements of content instruction detailed below and may also include the required clinical instruction component.

Content Instruction

Consistent with accreditation standards (CACREP, 1994; Standard II.J.4), study in the area of group work should provide an understanding of the types of group work (e.g., facilitation of task groups, psychoeducational groups, counseling groups, psychotherapy groups); group development, group dynamics, and group leadership styles; and group leadership methods and skills. More explicitly, studies should include, but not be limited to the following:

- principles of group dynamics including group process components, developmental stage theories, and group members' roles and behaviors;
- group leadership styles and approaches including characteristics of various types of group leaders and leadership styles;
- theories of group counseling including commonalities, distinguishing characteristics, and pertinent research and literature;
- group work methods including group leader orientations and behaviors, ethical standards, appropriate selection criteria and methods, and methods of evaluating effectiveness;
- approaches used for other types of group work, including task groups, prevention groups, support groups, and therapy groups; and
- skills in observing member behavior and group process, empathic responding, confronting, self-disclosing, focusing, protecting, recruiting and selecting members, opening and closing sessions, managing, explicit and implicit teaching, modeling, giving and receiving feedback.

Clinical Instruction

Core group work training requires a minimum of 10 clock hours of supervised practice (20 clock hours of supervised practice is recommended). Consistent with

CACREP standards for accreditation, the supervised experience provides the student with direct experiences as a participant in a small group, and may be met either in the basic course in group theory and practice or in a specially conducted small group designed for the purpose of meeting this standard (CACREP, 1994; Standard II.D). In arranging for and conducting this group experience, care must be taken by program faculty to assure that the ACA ethical standard for dual relationships and ASGW standards for best practice are observed.

Specialist Training in Group Work

Though ASGW advocates that all counselor training programs provide all counseling students with core group work training, specialization training is elective. If a counselor training program chooses to offer specialization training (e.g., task group facilitation, group psychoeducational, group counseling, group psychotherapy), ASGW urges institutions to develop their curricula consistent with the ASGW standards for that specialization.

Content Instruction

Each area of specialization has its literature. In addition to basic coursework in group theory and process, each specialization requires additional coursework providing specialized knowledge necessary for professional application of the specialization:

- *Task Group Facilitation:* coursework in such areas as organization development, consultation, management, or sociology so students gain a basic understanding of organizations and how task groups function within them.
- *Group Psychoeducational:* coursework in community psychology, consultation, health promotion, marketing, curriculum design to prepare students to conduct structured consciousness raising and skill training groups in such areas as stress management, wellness, anger control and assertiveness training, problem solving.
- *Group Counseling:* coursework in normal human development, family development and family counseling, assessment and problem identification of problems in living, individual counseling, and group counseling, including training experiences in personal growth or counseling group.
- *Group Psychotherapy:* coursework in abnormal human development, family pathology and family therapy, assessment and diagnosis of mental and emotional disorders, individual therapy, and group therapy, including training experiences in a therapy group.

Clinical Instruction

For Task Group Facilitation and Group Psychoeducational, group specialization training recommends a minimum of 30 clock hours of supervised practice

(45 clock hours of supervised practice is strongly suggested). Because of the additional difficulties presented by Group Counseling and Group Psychotherapy, a minimum of 45 clock hours of supervised practice is recommended (60 clock hours of supervised practice is strongly suggested). Consistent with CACREP standards for accreditation, supervised experience should provide an opportunity for the student to perform under supervision a variety of activities that a professional counselor would perform in conducting group work consistent with a given specialization (i.e., assessment of group members and the social systems in which they live and work, planning group interventions, implementing group interventions, leadership and co-leadership, and within-group, between-group, and end-of-group processing and evaluation).

In addition to courses offering content and experience related to a given specialization, supervised clinical experience should be obtained in practical and internship experience. Following the model provided by CACREP for master's practical, we recommend that one quarter of all required supervised clinical experience be devoted to group work:

- *Master's Practicum:* At least 10 clock hours of the required 40 clock hours of direct service should be spent in supervised leadership or co-leadership experience in group work, typically in Task Group Facilitation, Group Psychoeducational, or Group Counseling (at the master's practicum level, experience in Group Psychotherapy would be unusual) (CACREP, 1994; Standard III.H.1).
- *Master's Internship:* At least 60 clock hours of the required 240 clock hours of direct services should be spent in supervised leadership or co-leadership in group work consistent with the program's specialization offering(s) (i.e., in Task Group Facilitation, Group Psychoeducational, Group Counseling, or Group Psychotherapy).
- *Doctoral Internship:* At least 150 clock hours of the required 600 clock hours of direct service should be spent in supervised leadership or co-leadership in group work consistent with the program's specialization offering(s) (i.e., in Task Group Facilitation, Group Psychoeducational, Group Counseling, or Group Psychotherapy).

References

Association for Specialists in Group Work. (1983). *ASGW Professional Standards for Group Counseling.* Alexandria, VA: Author.

Association for Specialists in Group Work. (1990). *Professional Standards for the Training of Group Workers.* Alexandria, VA: Author.

Association for Specialists in Group Work. (1998). ASGW Best Practice Guidelines. *Journal for Specialists in Group Work, 23,* 237–244.

Association for Specialists in Group Work. (1999). ASGW Principles for Diversity-Competent Group Workers. *Journal for Specialists in Group Work, 24,* 7–14.

Council for Accreditation of Counseling and Related Educational Programs (CACREP). (1994). *CACREP accreditation standards and procedures manual.* Alexandria, VA: Author.

APPENDIX B

Association for Specialists in Group Work Best Practice Guidelines

Approved by the Executive Board, March 29, 1998

Prepared by Lynn S. Rapin and Linda Keel, ASGW Ethics Committee Co-Chairs

Preamble

The Association for Specialists in Group Work (ASGW) is a division of the American Counseling Association whose members are interested in and specialize in group work. We value the creation of community; service to our members, clients, and the profession; and value leadership as a process to facilitate the growth and development of individuals and groups.

The Association for Specialists in Group Work recognizes the commitment of its members to the Code of Ethics and Standards of Practice (as revised in 1995) of its parent organization, the American Counseling Association, and nothing in this document shall be construed to supplant that code. These Best Practice Guidelines are intended to clarify the application of the ACA Code of Ethics and Standards of Practice to the field of group work by defining Group Workers' responsibility and scope of practice involving those activities, strategies, and interventions that are consistent and current with effective and appropriate professional ethical and

Author's Note: From the Association for Specialists in Group Work, Professional Standards for the Training of Group Workers. In *Journal for Specialists in Group Work, 24,* pp. 7–14. Reprinted with permission from ASGW.

community standards. ASGW views ethical process as being integral to group work and views Group Workers as ethical agents. Group Workers, by their very nature in being responsible and responsive to their group members, necessarily embrace a certain potential for ethical vulnerability. It is incumbent upon Group Workers to give considerable attention to the intent and context of their actions because the attempts of Group Workers to influence human behavior through group work always have ethical implications. These Best Practice Guidelines address Group Workers' responsibilities in planning, performing and processing groups.

Section A: Best Practice in Planning

A.1. Professional Context and Regulatory Requirements

Group Workers actively know, understand and apply the ACA Code of Ethics and Standards of Best Practice, the ASGW Professional Standards for the Training of Group Workers, these ASGW Best Practice Guidelines, the ASGW diversity competencies, the ACA Multicultural Guidelines, relevant state laws, accreditation requirements, relevant National Board for Certified Counselors Codes and Standards, their organization's standards, and insurance requirements impacting the practice of group work.

A.2. Scope of Practice and Conceptual Framework

Group Workers define the scope of practice related to the core and specialization competencies defined in the ASGW Training Standards. Group Workers are aware of personal strengths and weaknesses in leading groups. Group Workers develop and are able to articulate a general conceptual framework to guide practice and a rationale for use of techniques that are to be used. Group Workers limit their practice to those areas for which they meet the training criteria established by the ASGW Training Standards.

A.3. Assessment

a. Assessment of self. Group Workers actively assess their knowledge and skills related to the specific group(s) offered. Group Workers assess their values, beliefs and theoretical orientation and how these impact upon the group, particularly when working with a diverse and multicultural population.

b. Ecological assessment. Group Workers assess community needs, agency or organization resources, sponsoring organization mission, staff competency, attitudes regarding group work, professional training levels of potential group leaders regarding group work, client attitudes regarding group work, and multicultural and diversity considerations. Group Workers use this information as the basis for making decisions related to their group practice, or to the implementation of groups for which they have supervisory, evaluation, or oversight responsibilities.

A.4. Program Development and Evaluation

a. Group Workers identify the type(s) of group(s) to be offered and how they relate to community needs.

b. Group Workers concisely state in writing the purpose and goals of the group. Group Workers also identify the role of the group members in influencing or determining the group goals.

c. Group Workers set fees consistent with the organization's fee schedule, taking into consideration the financial status and locality of prospective group members.

d. Group Workers choose techniques and a leadership style appropriate to the type(s) of group(s) being offered.

e. Group Workers have an evaluation plan consistent with regulatory, organization and insurance requirements, where appropriate.

f. Group Workers take into consideration current professional guidelines when using technology, including but not limited to Internet communication.

A.5. Resources

Group Workers coordinate resources related to the kind of group(s) and group activities to be provided, such as: adequate funding; the appropriateness and availability of a trained co leader; space and privacy requirements for the type(s) of group(s) being offered; marketing and recruiting; and appropriate collaboration with other community agencies and organizations.

A.6. Professional Disclosure Statement

Group Workers have a professional disclosure statement which includes information on confidentiality and exceptions to confidentiality, theoretical orientation, information on the nature, purpose(s) and goals of the group, the group services that can be provided, the role and responsibility of group members and leaders, Group Workers' qualifications to conduct the specific group(s), specific licenses, certifications and professional affiliations, and address of licensing/credentialing body.

A.7. Group and Member Preparation

a. *Group Workers screen prospective group members if appropriate to the type of group being offered.* When selection of group members is appropriate, Group Workers identify group members whose needs and goals are compatible with the goals of the group.

b. *Group Workers facilitate informed consent.* Group Workers provide in oral and written form to prospective members (when appropriate to group type): the professional disclosure statement; group purpose and goals; group participation expectations including voluntary and involuntary membership; role expectations of members and leader(s); policies related to entering and exiting the group; policies governing substance use; policies and procedures governing mandated groups (where relevant); documentation requirements; disclosure of information to others; implications of out-of-group contact or involvement among members; procedures for consultation between group leader(s) and group member(s); fees and time parameters; and potential impacts of group participation.

c. *Group Workers obtain the appropriate consent forms for work with minors and other dependent group members.*

d. *Group Workers define confidentiality and its limits (for example, legal and ethical exceptions and expectations; waivers implicit with treatment plans, documentation and insurance usage).* Group Workers have the responsibility to inform all group participants of the need for confidentiality, potential consequences of breaching confidentiality and that legal privilege does not apply to group discussions (unless provided by state statute).

A.8. Professional Development

Group Workers recognize that professional growth is a continuous, ongoing, developmental process throughout their career.

a. Group Workers remain current and increase knowledge and skill competencies through activities such as continuing education, professional supervision, and participation in personal and professional development activities.

b. Group Workers seek consultation and/or supervision regarding ethical concerns that interfere with effective functioning as a group leader. Supervisors have the responsibility to keep abreast of consultation, group theory, process, and adhere to related ethical guidelines.

c. Group Workers seek appropriate professional assistance for their own personal problems or conflicts that are likely to impair their professional judgment or work performance.

d. Group Workers seek consultation and supervision to ensure appropriate practice whenever working with a group for which all knowledge and skill competencies have not been achieved.

e. Group Workers keep abreast of group research and development.

A.9. Trends and Technological Changes

Group Workers are aware of and responsive to technological changes as they affect society and the profession. These include but are not limited to changes in mental health delivery systems; legislative and insurance industry reforms; shifting population demographics and client needs; and technological advances in Internet and other communication and delivery systems. Group Workers adhere to ethical guidelines related to the use of developing technologies.

Section B: Best Practice in Performing

B.1. Self Knowledge

Group Workers are aware of and monitor their strengths and weaknesses and the effects these have on group members.

B.2. Group Competencies

Group Workers have a basic knowledge of groups and the principles of group dynamics, and are able to perform the core group competencies, as described in the ASGW Professional Standards for the Training of Group Workers. Additionally, Group Workers have adequate understanding and skill in any group specialty area chosen for practice (psychotherapy, counseling, task, psychoeducational, as described in the ASGW Training Standards).

B.3. Group Plan Adaptation

a. Group Workers apply and modify knowledge, skills and techniques appropriate to group type and stage, and to the unique needs of various cultural and ethnic groups.

b. Group Workers monitor the group's progress toward the group goals and plan.

c. Group Workers clearly define and maintain ethical, professional, and social relationship boundaries with group members as appropriate to their role in the organization and the type of group being offered.

B.4. Therapeutic Conditions and Dynamics

Group Workers understand and are able to implement appropriate models of group development, process observation and therapeutic conditions.

B.5. Meaning

Group Workers assist members in generating meaning from the group experience.

B.6. Collaboration

Group Workers assist members in developing individual goals and respect group members as co-equal partners in the group experience.

B.7. Evaluation

Group Workers include evaluation (both formal and informal) between sessions and at the conclusion of the group.

B.8. Diversity

Group Workers practice with broad sensitivity to client differences including but not limited to ethnic, gender, religious, sexual, psychological maturity, economic class, family history, physical characteristics or limitations, and geographic location. Group Workers continuously seek information regarding the cultural issues of the diverse population with whom they are working both by interaction with participants and from using outside resources.

B.9. Ethical Surveillance

Group Workers employ an appropriate ethical decision making model in responding to ethical challenges and issues and in determining courses of action and behavior for self and group members. In addition, Group Workers employ applicable standards as promulgated by ACA, ASGW, or other appropriate professional organizations.

Section C: Best Practice in Group Process

C.1. Processing Schedule

Group Workers process the workings of the group with themselves, group members, supervisors or other colleagues, as appropriate. This may include assessing progress on group and member goals, leader behaviors and techniques, group dynamics and interventions; developing understanding and acceptance of meaning. Processing may occur both within sessions and before and after each session, at time of termination, and later follow up, as appropriate.

C.2. Reflective Practice

Group Workers attend to opportunities to synthesize theory and practice and to incorporate learning outcomes into ongoing groups. Group Workers attend to session dynamics of members and their interactions and also attend to the relationship between session dynamics and leader values, cognition and affect.

C.3. Evaluation and Follow-Up

a. *Group Workers evaluate process and outcomes.* Results are used for ongoing program planning, improvement and revisions of current group and/or to contribute to professional research literature. Group Workers follow all applicable policies and standards in using group material for research and reports.

b. *Group Workers conduct follow-up contact with group members, as appropriate, to assess outcomes or when requested by a group member(s).*

C.4. Consultation and Training With Other Organizations

Group Workers provide consultation and training to organizations in and out of their setting, when appropriate. Group Workers seek out consultation as needed with competent professional persons knowledgeable about group work.

APPENDIX C

Association for Specialists in Group Work Principles for Diversity-Competent Group Workers

Approved by the Executive Board, August 1, 1998

Prepared by Lynn Haley-Banez, Sherlon Brown, and Bogusia Molina

Consultants: Michael D'Andrea, Patricia Arredondo, Niloufer Merchant, and Sandra Wathen

Preamble

The Association for Specialists in Group Work (ASGW) is committed to understanding how issues of diversity affect all aspects of group work. This includes but is not limited to: training diversity-competent group workers; conducting research that will add to the literature on group work with diverse populations; understanding how diversity affects group process and dynamics; and assisting group facilitators in various settings to increase their awareness, knowledge, and skills as they relate to facilitating groups with diverse memberships.

As an organization, ASGW has endorsed this document with the recognition that issues of diversity affect group process and dynamics, group facilitation,

Author's Note: From the Association for Specialists in Group Work, Professional Standards for the Training of Group Workers. In *Journal for Specialists in Group Work, 25*, pp. 327–342. Reprinted with permission from ASGW.

training, and research. As an organization, we recognize that racism, classism, sexism, heterosexism, ableism, and so forth, affect everyone. As individual members of this organization, it is our personal responsibility to address these issues through awareness, knowledge, and skills. As members of ASGW, we need to increase our awareness of our own biases, values, and beliefs and how they impact the groups we run. We need to increase our awareness of our group members' biases, values, and beliefs and how they also impact and influence group process and dynamics. Finally, we need to increase our knowledge in facilitating, with confidence, competence, and integrity, groups that are diverse on many dimensions.

A. Definitions

For the purposes of this document, it is important that the language used is understood. Terms such as "dominant," "nondominant," and "target" persons and/or populations are used to define a person or groups of persons who historically, in the United States, do not have equal access to power, money, certain privileges (such as access to mental health services because of financial constraints, or the legal right to marry, in the case of a gay or lesbian couple), and/or the ability to influence or initiate social policy because of unequal representation in government and politics. These terms are not used to denote a lack of numbers in terms of representation in the overall U.S. population. Nor are these terms used to continue to perpetuate the very biases and forms of oppression, both overt and covert, that this document attempts to address.

For the purposes of this document, the term "disabilities" refers to differences in physical, mental, emotional, and learning abilities and styles among people. It is not meant as a term to define a person, such as a learning disabled person, but rather in the context of a person with a learning disability.

Given the history and current cultural, social, and political context in which this document is written, the authors of this document are limited to the language of this era. With this in mind, we have attempted to construct a "living document" that can and will change as the sociopolitical and cultural context changes.

The Principles

I. Awareness of Self

A. Attitudes and Beliefs

1. Diversity-competent group workers demonstrate movement from being unaware to being increasingly aware and sensitive to their own race, ethnic and cultural heritage, socioeconomic status (SES), sexual orientation, abilities, and religion and spiritual beliefs, and to valuing and respecting differences.

2. Diversity-competent group workers demonstrate increased awareness of how their own race, ethnicity, culture, gender, SES, sexual orientation, abilities, and religion and spiritual beliefs are impacted by their own experiences and histories, which in turn influence group process and dynamics.

3. Diversity-competent group workers can recognize the limits of their competencies and expertise with regard to working with group members who are different from them in terms of race, ethnicity, culture (including language), SES, gender, sexual orientation, abilities, religion, and spirituality and their beliefs, values, and biases. (For further clarification on limitations, expertise, and type of group work, refer to the training standards and best practice guidelines, Association for Specialists in Group Work, 1998; and the ethical guidelines, American Counseling Association, 1995.)

4. Diversity-competent group workers demonstrate comfort, tolerance, and sensitivity with differences that exist between themselves and group members in terms of race, ethnicity, culture, SES, gender, sexual orientation, abilities, religion, and spirituality and their beliefs, values, and biases.

B. Knowledge

1. Diversity-competent group workers can identify specific knowledge about their own race, ethnicity, SES, gender, sexual orientation, abilities, religion, and spirituality, and how they personally and professionally affect their definitions of "normality" and the group process.

2. Diversity-skilled group workers demonstrate knowledge and understanding regarding how oppression in any form—such as racism, classism, sexism, heterosexism, ableism, discrimination, and stereotyping—affects them personally and professionally.

3. Diversity-skilled group workers demonstrate knowledge about their social impact on others. They are knowledgeable about communication style differences, how their style may inhibit or foster the group process with members who are different from themselves along the different dimensions of diversity, and how to anticipate the impact they may have on others.

C. Skills

1. Diversity-competent group workers seek out educational, consultative, and training experiences to improve their understanding and effectiveness in working with group members who self-identify as Indigenous Peoples, African Americans, Asian Americans, Hispanics, Latinos/Latinas, gays, lesbians, bisexuals, or transgendered persons and persons with physical, mental/emotional, and/or learning disabilities, particularly with regard to race and ethnicity. Within this context, group workers are able to recognize the limits of their competencies and: (a) seek consultation, (b) seek further training or education, (c) refer members to more qualified group workers, or (d) engage in a combination of these.

2. Group workers who exhibit diversity competence are constantly seeking to understand themselves within their multiple identities (apparent and unapparent differences), for example, gay, Latina, Christian, working-class, and female, and are constantly and actively striving to unlearn the various behaviors and processes they covertly and overtly communicate that perpetuate oppression, particularly racism.

II. Group Worker's Awareness of Group Member's Worldview

A. Attitudes and Beliefs

1. Diversity-skilled group workers exhibit awareness of any possible negative emotional reactions toward Indigenous Peoples, African Americans, Asian Americans, Hispanics, Latinos/Latinas, gays, lesbians, bisexuals, or transgendered persons and persons with physical, mental/emotional, and/or learning disabilities that they may hold. They are willing to contrast in a nonjudgmental manner their own beliefs and attitudes with those of Indigenous Peoples, African Americans, Asian Americans, Hispanics, Latinos/Latinas, gays, lesbians, bisexuals, or transgendered persons and persons with physical, mental/emotional, and/or learning disabilities who are group members.

2. Diversity-competent group workers demonstrate awareness of their stereotypes and preconceived notions that they may hold toward Indigenous Peoples, African Americans, Asian Americans, Hispanics, Latinos/Latinas, gays, lesbians, bisexuals, or transgendered persons and persons with physical, mental/emotional, and/or learning disabilities.

B. Knowledge

1. Diversity-skilled group workers possess specific knowledge and information about Indigenous Peoples, African Americans, Asian Americans, Hispanics, Latinos/Latinas, gays, lesbians, bisexuals, and transgendered people and group members who have mental/emotional, physical, and/or learning disabilities with whom they are working. They are aware of the life experiences, cultural heritage, and sociopolitical background of Indigenous Peoples, African Americans, Asian Americans, Hispanics, Latinos/Latinas, gays, lesbians, bisexuals, or transgendered persons and group members with physical, mental/emotional, and/or learning disabilities. This particular knowledge-based competency is strongly linked to the various racial/minority and sexual identity development models available in the literature (Atkinson, Morten, & Sue, 1993; Cass, 1979; Cross, 1995; D'Augelli & Patterson, 1995; Helms, 1992).

2. Diversity-competent group workers exhibit an understanding of how race, ethnicity, culture, gender, sexual identity, different abilities, SES, and other immutable personal characteristics may affect personality formation, vocational choices, manifestation of psychological disorders, physical "dis-ease" or somatic symptoms, help-seeking behavior(s), and the appropriateness or inappropriateness of the various types of and theoretical approaches to group work.

3. Group workers who demonstrate competency in diversity in groups understand and have the knowledge about sociopolitical influences that impinge upon the lives of Indigenous Peoples, African Americans, Asian Americans, Hispanics, Latinos/Latinas, gays, lesbians, bisexuals, or transgendered persons and persons with physical, mental/emotional, and/or learning disabilities.

Immigration issues, poverty, racism, oppression, stereotyping, and/or power-lessness adversely impacts many of these individuals and therefore impacts group process or dynamics.

C. Skills

1. Diversity-skilled group workers familiarize themselves with relevant research and the latest findings regarding mental health issues of Indigenous Peoples, African Americans, Asian Americans, Hispanics, Latinos/Latinas, gays, lesbians, bisexuals, or transgendered persons and persons with physical, mental/emotional, and/or learning disabilities. They actively seek out educational experiences that foster their knowledge and understanding of skills for facilitating groups across differences.

2. Diversity-competent group workers become actively involved with Indigenous Peoples, African Americans, Asian Americans, Hispanics, Latinos/Latinas, gays, lesbians, bisexuals, or transgendered persons and persons with physical, mental/emotional, and/or learning disabilities outside of their group work/counseling setting (community events, social and political functions, celebrations, friendships, neighborhood groups, etc.) so that their perspective of minorities is more than academic or experienced through a third party.

III. Diversity-Appropriate Intervention Strategies

A. Attitudes and Beliefs

1. Diversity-competent group workers respect clients' religious and/or spiritual beliefs and values, because they affect worldview, psychosocial functioning, and expressions of distress.

2. Diversity-competent group workers respect indigenous helping practices and respect Indigenous Peoples, African Americans, Asian Americans, Hispanics, Latinos/Latinas, gays, lesbians, bisexuals, or transgendered persons and persons with physical, mental/emotional, and/or learning disabilities and can identify and utilize community intrinsic help-giving networks.

3. Diversity-competent group workers value bilingualism and sign language and do not view another language as an impediment to group work.

B. Knowledge

1. Diversity-competent group workers demonstrate a clear and explicit knowledge and understanding of generic characteristics of group work and theory and how they may clash with the beliefs, values, and traditions of Indigenous Peoples, African Americans, Asian Americans, Hispanics, Latinos/Latinas, gays, lesbians, bisexuals, or transgendered persons and persons with physical, mental/emotional, and/or learning disabilities.

2. Diversity-competent group workers exhibit an awareness of institutional barriers that prevent Indigenous Peoples, African Americans, Asian Americans, Hispanics, Latinos/Latinas, gays, lesbians, bisexuals, or transgendered members and members with physical, mental/emotional, and/or learning disabilities from actively participating in or using various types of groups, that is, task groups, psychoeducational groups, counseling groups, and psychotherapy groups or the settings in which the services are offered.

3. Diversity-competent group workers demonstrate knowledge of the potential bias in assessment instruments and use procedures and interpret findings, or actively participate in various types of evaluations of group outcome or success, keeping in mind the linguistic, cultural, and other self-identified characteristics of the group member.

4. Diversity-competent group workers exhibit knowledge of the family structures, hierarchies, values, and beliefs of Indigenous Peoples, African Americans, Asian Americans, Hispanics, Latinos/Latinas, gays, lesbians, bisexuals, or transgendered persons and persons with physical, mental/ emotional, and/or learning disabilities. They are knowledgeable about the community characteristics and the resources in the community as well as about the family.

5. Diversity-competent group workers demonstrate an awareness of relevant discriminatory practices at the social and community level that may be affecting the psychological welfare of persons and access to services of the population being served.

C. Skills

1. Diversity-competent group workers are able to engage in a variety of verbal and nonverbal group-facilitating functions, dependent upon the type of group (task, counseling, psychoeducational, psychotherapy), and the multiple, self-identified status of various group members (such as Indigenous Peoples, African Americans, Asian Americans, Hispanics, Latinos/Latinas, gays, lesbians, bisexuals, or transgendered persons and persons with physical, mental/emotional, and/or learning disabilities). They demonstrate the ability to send and receive both verbal and nonverbal messages accurately, appropriately, and across/between the differences represented in the group. They are not tied down to one method or approach to group facilitation and recognize that helping styles and approaches may be culture-bound. When they sense that their group facilitation style is limited and potentially inappropriate, they can anticipate and ameliorate its negative impact by drawing upon other culturally relevant skill sets.

2. Diversity-competent group workers have the ability to exercise institutional intervention skills on behalf of their group members. They can help a member determine whether a "problem" with the institution stems from the oppression of Indigenous Peoples, African Americans, Asian Americans,

Hispanics, Latinos/Latinas, gays, lesbians, bisexuals, or transgendered persons and persons with physical, mental/emotional, and/or learning disabilities, such as in the case of developing or having a "healthy" paranoia, so that group members do not inappropriately personalize problems.

3. Diversity-competent group workers do not exhibit a reluctance to seek consultation with traditional healers and religious and spiritual healers and practitioners in the treatment of members who are self-identified Indigenous Peoples, African Americans, Asian Americans, Hispanics, Latinos/Latinas, gays, lesbians, bisexuals, and transgendered persons and/or group members with mental/emotional, physical, and/or learning disabilities when appropriate.

4. Diversity-competent group workers take responsibility for interacting in the language requested by the group member(s) and, if not feasible, make an appropriate referral. A serious problem arises when the linguistic skills of a group worker and a group member or members, including sign language, do not match. The same problem occurs when the linguistic skills of one member or several members do not match. This being the case, the group worker, should (a) seek a translator with cultural knowledge and appropriate professional background, and (b) refer to a knowledgeable, competent bilingual group worker or a group worker competent or certified in sign language. In some cases, it may be necessary to have a group for group members of similar languages or to refer the group member for individual counseling.

5. Diversity-competent group workers are trained and have expertise in the use of traditional assessment and testing instruments related to group work, such as in screening potential members, and they also are aware of the cultural bias/limitations of these tools and processes. This allows them to use the tools for the welfare of diverse group members following culturally appropriate procedures.

6. Diversity-competent group workers attend to as well as work to eliminate biases, prejudices, oppression, and discriminatory practices. They are cognizant of how sociopolitical contexts may affect evaluation and provision of group work and should develop sensitivity to issues of oppression, racism, sexism, heterosexism, classism, and so forth.

7. Diversity-competent group workers take responsibility in educating their group members to the processes of group work, such as goals, expectations, legal rights, sound ethical practice, and the group worker's theoretical orientation with regard to facilitating groups with diverse membership.

Conclusion

This document is the "starting point" for group workers as we become increasingly aware, knowledgeable, and skillful in facilitating groups whose memberships represent the diversity of our society. It is not intended to be a "how to" document. It is written as a call to action and/or a guideline and represents ASGW's commitment to moving forward with an agenda for addressing and understanding the needs of the populations we serve. As a "living document," the Association for Specialists in Group Work acknowledges the changing world in which we live and work and therefore recognizes that this is the first step in working with diverse group members with competence, compassion, respect, and integrity. As our awareness, knowledge, and skills develop, so too will this document evolve. As our knowledge as a profession grows in this area and as the sociopolitical context in which this document was written changes, new editions of these Principles for Diversity-Competent Group Workers will arise. The operationalization of this document (article in process) will begin to define appropriate group leadership skills and interventions as well as make recommendations for research in understanding how diversity in group membership affects group process and dynamics.

References

American Counseling Association. (1995). *Code of ethics and standards.* Alexandria, VA: Author.

Association for Multicultural Counseling and Development. (1996). *Multicultural competencies.* Alexandria, VA: American Counseling Association.

Association for Specialists in Group Work. (1991). Professional standards for training of group workers. *Together, 20,* 9–14.

Association for Specialists in Group Work. (1998). Best practice guidelines. *Journal for Specialists in Group Work, 23,* 237–244.

Atkinson, D. R., Morten, G., & Sue, D. W. (Eds.). (1993). *Counseling American minorities* (4th ed.). Madison, WI: Brown & Benchmark.

Cass, V. C. (1979). Homosexual identity formation: A theoretical model. *Journal of Homosexuality, 4,* 219–236.

Cross, W. E. (1995). The psychology of Nigrescence: Revising the cross model. In J. G. Ponterotto, J. M. Casas, L. A. Suzuki, & C. M. Alexander (Eds.), *Handbook of multicultural counseling* (pp. 93–122). Thousand Oaks, CA: Sage.

D'Augelli, A. R., & Patterson, C. J. (Eds.). (1995). *Lesbian, gay and bisexual identities over the lifespan.* New York: Oxford University Press.

Helms, J. E. (1992). *A race is a nice thing to have.* Topeka, KS: Context Communications.

APPENDIX D

Group Planning Sheet*

Date: _____   Session #: _____

Group Leaders: _____

Members already excused: _____

_____

_____

_____

Check in With:

Members who need to be checked in with who didn't finish working on an issue
last week: _____

Members who were given an assignment or were going to report back this week:

_____

Other members who might need to be checked in with and about what:

_____

*Group Topics or Issues That Need to
Be Finished and/or Revisited:*

Related to individual member or group goals: _____

_____

Related to group process: _____

_____

Group Topics or Issues to Be Addressed for the 1st Time:

Content issues that need to be addressed for the 1st time:

_____

Process issues that need to be addressed for the 1st time:

_____

Specific Interventions:

Opening: _____

_____

Processing: _____

_____

The Closing: _____

_____

Other Issues/Topics to Be Addressed: _____

_____

_____

Issues to Be Discussed in Supervision:

_____

_____

_____

*From DeLucia-Waack (2002c).

APPENDIX E

Group Processing Sheet*

Group Process Notes

Date: _____   Session #: _____

Group Leaders: _____

Members Present: _____

Members Excused: _____

Members Not Excused: _____

Themes for the Group:

Content:

Process:

Notes for the Group:

Opening:

Working:

Ending:

Notes About Each Group Member:

Member A:

Member B:

Member C:

Member D:

Member E:

Member F:

(This ends what should be included in a group notes file and/or a client file.) (For a client file, include all the notes up to this point and then just the notes in the last section for that particular group member.)

Processing of the Group Session

Comments About the Group:

Content:

Process:

Specific Members:

To Be Discussed in Supervision:

Evaluation of Intervention Strategies:

Executive Functions:

What worked?:

What didn't (and what could you do differently next time)?:

Meaning Attribution:

What worked?:

What didn't (and what could you do differently next time)?:

Caring:

What worked?:

What didn't (and what could you do differently next time)?:

Emotional Stimulation:

What worked:

What didn't (and what could you do differently next time)?:

Critical Incidents Related to Therapeutic Factors: (Instillation of Hope, Universality, Imparting of Information, Altruism, The Corrective Recapitulation of the Primary Family Group, Interpersonal Learning–Input, Interpersonal Learning–Output, Cohesiveness, Catharsis, Existential Factors, Identification, Self-Understanding).

Briefly describe the 3 most critical incidents that happened this week in group and how each illustrates a therapeutic factor.

1.

2.

3.

Now name the critical incident for each group member and what therapeutic factor it illustrates.

Member A:

Member B:

Member C:

Member D:

Member E:

Member F:

Member G:

Member H:

Countertransference:

Towards Specific Members: Briefly describe the feeling towards the member, who the person reminds you of (if any), and how you behave towards the member based on this. Is your reaction based on something that a person is doing in group or based on assumptions you are making about the person based on relationships with others? What could you do in the future to respond to this person as they are in the group and not as if they were someone else?

1.

2.

Towards Specific Incidents or Group Topics: Briefly describe the event, the feeling(s) elicited from you as a result of the event, what other situation this reminds you of, what behavior it is based on, what your personal reactions and issues are related to this event, and what you can do differently in future interactions.

1.

2.

---

*From DeLucia-Waack (2002c).

Examples of Group Planning and Processing Session Notes for a Psychoeducational Children-of-Divorce Group

Group Planning Sheet for a 10-Session Children-of-Divorce Group

Date: 10/12   Session #: 8   Group Leaders: J

Members already excused:

Sandra (told us last week that she has a doctor's appt.)

Check in with:

Members who need to be checked in with who didn't finish working on an issue last week:

Tommy still didn't think he could tell his Dad to stop asking him to relay messages to his Mom

Members who were given an assignment or were going to report back this week:

Kristin was going to talk to her older sister about her feelings about the divorce

Other members who might need to be checked in with and about what:

Justin was very quiet last session

*Group Topics or Issues That Need
to Be Finished and/or Revisited:*

Related to individual member or group goals:

Check-in on how members expressed their feelings during the week

Related to group process:

How to let each person have some time to talk

*Group Topics or Issues to Be
Addressed for the 1st Time:*

Content issues that need to be addressed for the 1st time:

How to deal with parents' new relationships

Process issues that need to be addressed for the 1st time:

Members being quiet for a whole session

Specific Interventions:

Session: I Tried to Get My Mom and Dad Back Together Again*

Materials:

Banner with group name and ground rules hanging on the wall

"If You Believe in You" tape (specifically the "I Tried" song)

A large notepad with markers

Group Session:

Review and Check-In (7 minutes)

1. Play the "I Tried" song (3 minutes).

2. What's the song about? Emphasize how hard it is to meet the new boyfriends and girlfriends when parents start dating and how most children of divorce want their parents to get back together again (4 minutes).

Working Activities (30 minutes)

3. "Getting My Parents Back Together" (5 minutes). Today we are going to talk about the idea that just about everyone wants his or her parents to get back together. Let's start by talking about why this is so. Why do children want both of their parents to live in the same house?

4. "When My Parents Lived Together" (10 minutes). Now let's try to remember what it was like when both parents did live in the same house. (If some of the children don't remember, ask them to think about what it is like when their parents spend time together now). Let's make a list of the good things and the not-so-good things about parents being together. Use the large notepad to record two columns: Good Things and Not-So-Good Things. (Leave room between the columns so that you can add two more columns later.)

5. "How Would It Be Different?" (5 minutes). Now let's work on both of those lists one at a time. Let's first talk about the Not-So-Good Things list. How would those be different if your parents got back together now? Do you think they would change? Emphasize that parents would probably still fight and argue about the same things because they are still different people.

6. "Good Things and How to Make Them Happen" (10 minutes). Now let's work on the list of the Good Things. Let's add another column called How to Make the Good Things Happen Now. How can this happen now? Let's brainstorm ways to make this happen. Let's also identify things that can't happen and maybe suggest other things that can take their place (e.g., Sunday dinner with Mom and Dad both being replaced with Sunday dinner with Mom and her family).

Processing (5 minutes)

7. When families change, some good things happen and some bad things happen. Let's everyone go around and finish the sentence: *One good thing that can still happen in my family is XXX.*

Closing (3 minutes)

8. Let's listen to "I Tried" again. Feel free to sing along. Let's listen to the end to the message. . . . I let go and stopped trying to get my parents back together again.

Other Issues/Topics to Be Addressed:

This is our last session to talk about new issues and strategies; termination sessions begin next week.

Issues to Be Discussed With Supervisor:

How to introduce termination without taking too much time but to get the children to start to think about what they have learned and what they can do outside of group.

Group Processing Sheet for 10-Session Children-of-Divorce Group

Group Process Notes:

Date: 10/13   **Session #:** 8   **Group Leaders:** J & T

Members Present: Tommy, Justin, Kristin, Susan, Andy

Members Excused: Sandy

Members Not Excused:

Themes for the Group:

Content: How kids try to get their parents back together again

Sadness over the divorce

Good things that happen now that parents are divorced

Process: It's hard to talk about feelings

Notes for the Group:

Opening: Listened to "I Tried." Talked about how Kelly and Cory didn't like their parents' new boyfriends and girlfriends.

Working: Came up with several reasons why children want their parents in the same house: to see both of them, to be a family, to get love from both of them. Made lists of Good Things and Not-So-Good Things about parents being together. Then talked about how things from the Not-So-Good Things list would/would not change if their parents got back together. Tommy and Justin started by saying that things would be different and their parents wouldn't fight anymore. But then Susan pointed out that her parents still fight when they are living apart, so she didn't think it would change if they lived together again. Shifted the discussion about How to Make the Good Things Happen Now. Susan suggested that her parents could both still come to her soccer game, but they didn't need to sit with each other. Tommy said he could have a special dinner with Mom once a week, just she and him, like they used to. Others talked about how they could ask to do things with their father that they had stopped doing because they didn't live together, like helping with homework, washing the car, or taking walks.

Ending: Everyone took a turn and stated "One good thing that can still happen in my family is . . ." Answers focused on spending time with both parents. Sang "I Tried."

Notes About Each Group Member:

Andy: Really wanted to believe that his parents wouldn't fight anymore and could get back together again.

Justin: Still quiet but did talk and had some good ideas about good stuff that he could do with his family right now, particularly his Dad.

Kristin: Wants her parents back together but not if they will fight.

Sandy: Excused.

Susan: Seems to have accepted that her parents are divorced; doesn't like that they still argue now. Was going to talk to her Mom about things they could do together.

Tommy: Was quiet at the beginning when talking about parents' boyfriends or girlfriends; laughed really hard about spilling wine on her dress. Says Mom doesn't date now.

(This ends what should be included in a group notes file and/or a client file.) (For a client file, include all the notes up to this point and then just the notes in the last section for that particular group member.)

Processing of the Group Session

Comments About the Group:

Content: Lots of talk about what was bad when parents were together but hard to make suggestions to make it good now

Process: Laughed a lot about not liking parents' new boyfriends and girlfriends. Had a hard time at first coming up with good things that happened after the divorce but then were able to

Specific Members: Justin talked more this session

To Be Discussed in Supervision: How to get them all to talk more about their feelings

Evaluation of Intervention Strategies:

Executive Functions:

What worked: Starting on time

What didn't (and what could you do differently next time): Trying to nonverbally get Tommy to stop tapping his pencil (sit next to him)

Meaning Attribution:

What worked: Asking them what was different now so that their parents wouldn't fight anymore if they got back together

What didn't (and what could you do differently next time): Asking them if they had similar feelings to Kelly and Cory about their parents' boyfriends and girlfriends (ask them how Kelly and Cory might act out their feelings)

Caring:

What worked: Saying yes, this is tough to talk about sometimes and then asking for a group hug

What didn't (and what could you do differently next time): Asking them to say what is tough at the end

Emotional Stimulation:

What worked: I don't think I did anything to do this, this time

What didn't (and what could you do differently next time):

Critical Incidents Related to Therapeutic Factors: (Instillation of Hope, Universality, Imparting of Information, Altruism, The Corrective Recapitulation of the Primary Family Group, Interpersonal Learning–Input, Interpersonal Learning–Output, Cohesiveness, Catharsis, Existential Factors, Identification, Self-Understanding). Briefly describe the 3 most critical incidents that happened this week in group and how each illustrates a therapeutic factor.

1. Instillation of hope when Susan said that she had hoped for a long time that her parents would stop fighting and it didn't happen, but she focuses on how much each of them loves her and that makes her feel better.

2. Universality when all of the members said that sometimes they wished their parents would get back together again.

3. Imparting of information when I said that it is normal to want your parents back together, most children do, and they are sad when it doesn't happen.

Countertransference:

Towards Specific Members: Briefly describe the feeling towards the member, who the person reminds you of (if any), and how you behave based on this towards the member. Is your reaction based on something that a person is doing in group or based on assumptions you are making about the person based on relationships with others? What could you do in the future to respond to this person as they are in the group and not as if they were someone else?

1. I don't feel very connected to Justin because it is so hard to know what he is thinking because he is so quiet and doesn't display many nonverbals. I am trying to engage him more to see what he does think and who he is like as a person.

2. Susan reminds me of myself when I was young—wanting very much for everything to be OK and to connect with all members of her family. I probably support her more than others because of this so I need to watch and make sure that I don't smooth things over to make them OK for her, but do support her efforts to connect with others.

Towards Specific Incidents or Group Topics: Briefly describe the event, the feeling(s) elicited from you as a result of the event, what other situation this reminds you of, what behavior it is based on, what your personal reactions and issues are related to this event, and what you can do differently in future interactions.

1. It is hard to listen to the children say that they want their parents back together when I know rationally that it was probably a pretty uncomfortable situation for a lot of them. I want to fix it for them and may rush in too soon. I need to step back, help them discuss and process feelings, and come to their own conclusions.

---

*From Delucia-Waack (2001).

APPENDIX G

Resource Guide for Group Interventions by Topic, Including Books, Games, and Videos

For Parents

General Resources

Barkley, R. A. (2000). *Taking charge of ADHD: The complete, authoritative guide for parents* (rev. ed.). New York: Guilford.

Copeland, E., & Love, V. (1991). *Attention, please! A comprehensive guide for successfully parenting children with attention disorders and hyperactivity.* Atlanta, GA: SPI.

Dendy Zeigler, C. A. (1995). *Teenagers with ADD: A parents' guide.* Bethesda, MD: Woodbine House.

Fowler, M. (1990). *Maybe you know my kid: A parent's guide to identifying, understanding, and helping your child with ADHD.* New York: Birch Lane Press.

Monastra, V. J. (2004). *Parenting children with ADHD: 10 lessons that medicine cannot teach.* Washington, DC: American Psychological Association.

Morris, J. (1998). *Facing AD/HD: A survival guide for parents of children with attention deficit/hyperactivity disorder.* Champaign, IL: Research Press.

Munden, A., & Arcelus, J. (1999). *The ADHD handbook: A guide for parents and professionals.* Philadelphia: Jessica Kingsley.

Rief, S. F. (2002). *The ADD/ADHD checklist.* San Francisco: Jossey-Bass.

Taylor, J. F. (2001). *Helping your ADD child: Hundreds of practical solutions for parents and teachers of ADD children and teens (with or without hyperactivity)* (3rd ed.). Three Rivers, MI: Three Rivers Press.

Umansky, W., & Steinberg Smalley, B. (2003). *AD/HD: Helping your child: A comprehensive program to treat attention deficit/hyperactivity disorders at home and in school* (rev. ed.). New York: Warner Books.

Weiss, L. (1996). *Give your ADD teen a chance: A guide for parents of teenagers with attention deficit disorder.* Colorado Springs, CO: Pinon Press.

Videos and Audio Tapes

Kevin Dawkins Production. (Producer). (1993). *ADHD—What can we do?* [Video]. New York: Guilford.

The Parents Resource Network's Lecture Library. (Producer). (1996). *An evening with Dr. Russell Barkley: New thoughts on ADHD* [Video]. New York: Guilford.

Rief, S. F. (n.d.). *How to help your child succeed in school: Strategies and guidance for parents of children with ADHD and/or learning disabilities* [Video]. Port Chester, NY: National Professional Resources.

Wagonseller, B. R. (n.d.). *What every parent should know about ADD* [Video]. Champaign, IL: Research Press.

For Counselors
General Resources

Asher, M. J., & Gordon, S. B. (1998). *The AD/HD forms book: Identification, measurement, and intervention.* Champaign, IL: Research Press.

Barkley, R. A. (1998). *Attention-deficit hyperactivity disorder: A handbook for diagnosis and treatment* (2nd ed.). New York: Guilford.

DuPaul, G. J., & Stoner, G. (2004). *ADHD in the schools: Assessment and intervention strategies* (2nd ed.). New York: Guilford.

Lovecky, D. V. (2004). *Different minds: Gifted children with AD/HD, Asperger Syndrome, and other learning deficits.* Philadelphia: Jessica Kingsley.

Nadeau, K. G., Littman, E., & Quinn, P. O. (2000). *Understanding girls with AD/HD.* Longwood, FL: Advantage Books.

Rief, S. F. (2003). *The ADHD book of lists: A practical guide for helping children and teens with attention deficit disorders.* San Francisco: Jossey-Bass.

Robin, A. L. (1999). *ADHD in adolescents: Diagnosis and treatment.* New York: Guilford.

Ryser, G., & McConnell, K. (2002). *Scales for diagnosing attention-deficit/hyperactivity disorder.* Austin, TX: Pro-Ed.

Videos and Audio Tapes

American Psychological Association. (Producer). (2004). *Treating adolescents with ADHD* [Video]. New York: Insight Media.

Campbell & Co. (Producer). (2001). *Attention deficit disorder in the 21st century.* [Video].

DuPaul, G. J., & Stoner, G. (Producer). (1998). *Assessing ADHD in the schools* [Video]. New York: Guilford.

DuPaul, G. J., & Stoner, G. (Producer). (1998). *Classroom interventions for ADHD* [Video]. New York: Guilford.

Rief, S. F. (2004). *ADHD & LD: Powerful teaching strategies and accommodations (K-8)* [Video]. Port Chester, NY: National Professional Resources.

For Use in Group

General Resources

Carpenter, P., & Ford, M. (2000). *Sparky's excellent misadventures: My A.D.D. journal.* Washington, DC: Magination Press.

Galvin, M. (1998). *Otto learns about his medicine: A story about medication for children with ADHD* (3rd ed.). Washington, DC: Magination Press.

Gordon, M. (1991). *Jumpin' Johnny, get back to work! A child's guide to ADHD/hyperactivity.* DeWitt, NY: GSI Publications.

Quinn, P. O. (1995). *Adolescents and ADD: Gaining the advantage.* Washington, DC: Magination Press.

Rogers, B. T., Montgomery, T. R., Lock, T. M., & Accardo, P. J. (2001). *Attention deficit hyperactivity disorder: The clinical spectrum.* Austin, TX: Pro-Ed.

Walker, B. (2004). *The girls' guide to AD/HD: Don't lose this book!* Bethesda, MD: Woodbine House.

Videos and Audio Tapes

American Psychological Asssociation. (Producer). (2004). *Treating adolescents with ADHD* [Video]. New York: Insight Media.

Group Activities

Flick, G. L. (2002). *ADD/ADHD behavior-change resource kit: Ready-to-use strategies and activities for helping children with attention deficit disorder.* San Francisco: Jossey-Bass.

McConnell, K., & Ryser, G. R. (2005). *Practical ideas that really work for students with ADHD* (2nd ed.). Austin, TX: Pro-Ed.

Nadeau, K. G., & Dixon, E. B. (1997). *Learning to slow down and pay attention: A book for kids about ADD.* Washington, DC: Magination Press.

Power, T. J., Karustis, J. L., & Habboushe, D. F. (2001). *Homework success for children with ADHD: A family-school intervention program.* New York: Guilford.

Quinn, P. O., & Stern, J. M. (2000). *The best of brakes: An activity book for kids with ADD.* Washington, DC: Magination Press.

Quinn, P. O., Stern, J. M., & Russell, N. (1993). *The "putting on the brakes" activity book for young people with ADHD.* Washington, DC: Magination Press.

Rief, S. F. (1993). *How to reach and teach ADD/ADHD children: Practical techniques, strategies, and interventions for helping children with attention problems and hyperactivity.* San Francisco: Jossey-Bass.

Anger Management/Aggression

For Parents

General Resources

Bloomquist, M. L. (1996). *Skills training for children with behavior disorders: A parent and therapist guidebook.* New York: Guilford.

Kellner, M. H. (2003). *Staying in control: Anger management skills for parents of young adolescents.* Champaign, IL: Research Press.

Moles, K. (2003). *Strategies for anger management: Reproducible worksheets for teens and adults.* Plainsview, NY: Wellness Reproductions & Publishing.

For Counselors

General Resources

Beck, R., & Fernandez, E. (1998). Cognitive-behavioral therapy in the treatment of anger: A meta-analysis. *Cognitive Therapy and Research, 22,* 63–74.

Bloomquist, M. L., & Schnell, S. V. (2002). *Helping children with aggression and conduct problems: Best practices for interventions.* New York: Guilford.

Charlesworth, J. (2004). Helping students manage anger. In B. T. Erford (Ed.), *Professional school counseling: A handbook of theories, programs, and practices* (pp. 805–811). Austin, TX: CAPS Press.

Fryxel, D., & Smith, D. C. (2000). Personal, social, and family characteristics of angry students. *Professional School Counseling, 4,* 86–97.

Goldstein, A., Nensen, R., Daleflod, B., & Kalt, M. (Eds.). (2004). *New perspectives on aggression replacement training: Practice, research, and application.* Indianapolis, IN: Wiley.

Goldstein, A. P. (1999). *Low-level aggression: First steps on the ladder to violence.* Champaign, IL: Research Press.

Kassinove, H., & Tafrate, R. C. (2002). *Anger management: The complete treatment guide for practitioners.* Atascadero, CA: Impact.

Larson, J., & Lochman, J. E. (2002). *Helping school children cope with anger: A cognitive-behavioral intervention.* New York: Guilford.

Simmons, R. (2001). *Odd girl out: The hidden culture of aggression in girls.* Orlando, FL: Harcourt.

Videos and Audio Tapes

Amendola, M., Feindler, E. L., McGinnis, E., & Oliver, R. (Producer). *Aggression replacement training video: A comprehensive intervention for aggressive youth.* [Video]. Champaign, IL: Research Press.

Anger. (1995). [Video]. New York: Insight Media.

Anger management. (2001). [Video]. New York: Insight Media.

Coping with anger. (1994). [Video]. New York: Insight Media.

Understanding anger. (2002). [Video]. New York: Insight Media.

For Use in Group

General Resources

Carr, T. (2001). *131 creative strategies for reaching children with anger problems.* Minneapolis, MN: Educational Media Corporation.

Clark, L. (1998). *SOS! Help for emotions: Managing anxiety, anger, and depression.* Berkeley, CA: Parents' Press.

Cummings, A. L., Hoffman, S., & Leschied, A. W. (2004). A psychoeducational group for aggressive girls. *Journal for Specialists in Group Work, 29,* 285–299.

Ditta-Donahue, G. (2003). *Josh's smiley faces: A story about anger.* Washington, DC: Magination Press.

Dwivedi, K., & Gupta, A. (2000). Keeping cool: Anger management through group work. *Support for Learning, 15,* 76–81.

Kooser, D. (2000). *Potter pig in control.* Warminster, PA: Marco Products.

Larson, J. (2003). Group counseling with aggressive adolescents in the school setting: A cognitive-behavioral perspective. In C. T. Dollarhide & K. A. Saginak (Eds.), *School counseling in the secondary schools: A comprehensive process and program* (pp. 342–352). Boston: Pearson.

Sharry, J., & Owens, C. (2000). "The rules of engagement": A case study of a group with "angry" adolescents. *Clinical Child Psychology and Psychiatry, 5,* 53–62.

Shechtman, Z. (2001). Prevention groups for angry and aggressive children. *Journal for Specialists in Group Work, 26,* 228–236.

Shechtman, Z., & Nachshol, R. (1996). A school-based intervention to reduce aggressive behavior in maladjusted adolescents. *Journal of Applied Developmental Psychology, 17,* 535–553.

Simmons, R. (2004). *Odd girl speaks out.* Orlando, FL: Harcourt.

Snyder, K. V., Kymissis, P., & Kessler, K. (1999). Anger management for adolescents: Efficacy of brief group therapy. *Journal of the American Academy of Child and Adolescent Psychiatry, 38,* 1409–1416.

Verdick, E., & Lisovskis, M. (2003). *How to take the grrr out of anger.* Minneapolis, MN: Free Spirit.

Videos and Audio Tapes

Aggression replacement training: A comprehensive intervention for aggressive youth. (2003). [Video]. New York: Insight Media.

Anger: Who's to blame? (2003). [Video]. Hawthorne, NY: Sunburst Visual Media.

Cage the rage: Handling your anger. (1997). [Video]. Plainview, NY: The Bureau for At-RiskYouth.

Hammond, W. R., & Gipson, V. (n.d.). *Dealing with anger: A violence prevention program for African American youth* [Video]. Champaign, IL: Research Press.

Institute for Mental Health Initiatives. (Producer). (n.d.). *Learning to manage anger: The RETHINK workout for teens* [Video]. Champaign, IL: Research Press.

Youth life skills series: Anger management. (n.d.). [Video]. Plainview, NY: The Bureau for At- RiskYouth.

Group Activities

Akin, T. (2000). *Learning the skills of anger management.* Carson, CA: Jalmar.

Bohensky, A. (2001). *Anger management workbook for kids and teens.* New York: Growth Publishing.

Carrell, S. (2000). Living with emotionality. In S. Carrell (Ed.), *Group exercises for adolescents: A manual for therapists* (pp. 121–140). Thousand Oaks, CA: Sage.

Currie, M. (2004). Doing anger differently: A group percussion therapy for angry adolescent boys. *International Journal of Group Psychotherapy, 54,* 275–319.

Davidson, P. (1997). The mad game. In H. G. Kaduson & C. E. Schaefer (Eds.), *101 favorite play therapy techniques* (pp. 224–225). Northvale, NJ: Aronson.

Driscoll, N. A. (2002). *Anger bingo for teens* [Board game]. Modesto, CA: Nasco.

From rage to reason. (2000). [Board game]. Plainview, NY: The Bureau for At-Risk Youth.

Goldstein, A. P. (1999). *The prepare curriculum* (2nd ed.). Champaign, IL: Research Press.

Goldstein, A. P., Glick, B., & Gibbs, J. C. (1998). *Aggression replacement training: A comprehensive intervention for aggressive youth.* Champaign, IL: Research Press.

Hanna, F. J., & Hunt, W. P. (1999). Techniques for psychotherapy with defiant, aggressive adolescents. *Psychotherapy, 36,* 56–68.

Jewett, J. (2000). Aggression and cooperation: Helping young children develop constructive strategies. *Elementary and Early Childhood Education, 7,* 23–28.

Kellner, M. H. (2001). *In control: A skill-building program for teaching young adolescents to manage anger.* Champaign, IL: Research Press.

Madrid, L. (2001). *Activities and songs for healing and support.* Carson, CA: Jalmar.

Modrcin-McCarthy, M. A., Barnes, A. F., & Alpert, J. (1998). Childhood anger: So common, yet so misunderstood. *Journal of Child and Adolescent Psychiatric Nursing, 11,* 69–79.

Morganett, R. S. (1990). Better ways of getting mad: Anger management skills. In R. S. Morganett, *Skills for living: Group counseling activities for young adolescents* (pp. 129–151). Champaign, IL: Research Press.

Phillips-Hershey, E., & Kanagy, B. (1996). Teaching students to manage personal anger constructively. *Elementary School Guidance and Counseling, 30,* 229–234.

Rose, S. D., & Martsch, M. D. (1998). Group strategies for reducing anger and aggression. In S. D. Rose, *Group therapy with troubled youth: A cognitive behavioral interactive approach* (pp. 433–460). Thousand Oaks, CA: Sage.

Simmonds, J. (2003). *Seeing red: An anger management and peacemaking curriculum for kids.* Gabriola Island, British Columbia, Canada: New Society Publishers.

Smead, R. (2000). Agree to disagree: Learning to manage anger. In R. Smead, *Skills for living: Group counseling activities for young adolescents* (pp. 203–231). Champaign, IL: Research Press.

Stewart, J. (2004). *Learning about anger.* Alameda, CA: Hunter House.

Wilde, J. (2001). Interventions for children with anger problems. *Journal of Rational Emotive and Cognitive-Behavior Therapy, 19,* 191–197.

Antisocial Behavior/Defiance

For Parents

General Resources

Barkely, R. A., & Benton, C. M. (1998). *Your defiant child: Eight steps to better behavior.* New York: Guilford.

Dishion, T. J., & Kavanagh, K. (2003). *Intervening in adolescent problem behavior: A family-centered approach.* New York: Guilford.

Videos and Audio Tapes

Counseling and parenting difficult teens. (1995). [Video]. New York: Insight Media.

Kevin Dawkins Production. (Producer). (1997). *Managing the defiant child: A guide to parent training* [Video]. New York: Guilford.

Managing the defiant child. (1997). [Video]. New York: Insight Media.

For Counselors

General Resources

Barkley, R. A., Edwards, G. H., & Robin, A. L. (1999). *Defiant teens: A clinician's manual for assessment and family intervention.* New York: Guilford.

Conner, D. F. (2002). *Aggression and antisocial behavior in children and adolescents: Research and treatment.* New York: Guilford.

Hall, R. V., & Hall, M. L. (Eds.). (1998). *How to manage behavior series.* Austin, TX: Pro-Ed.

Holmes-Robinson, J. (2004). Helping at-risk students. In B. T. Erford (Ed.), *Professional school counseling: A handbook of theories, programs, and practices* (pp. 735–744). Austin, TX: CAPS.

McMahon, R. J., & Forehand, R. L. (2003). *Helping the noncompliant child: Family-based treatment for oppositional behavior* (2nd ed.). New York: Guilford.

Reid, J. B., Patterson, G., & Snyder, J. J. (Eds.). (2002). *Antisocial behavior in children and adolescents: A developmental analysis and model for intervention.* Washington, DC: American Psychological Association.

Sells, S. P. (1998). *Treating the tough adolescent: A family-based, step-by-step guide.* New York: Guilford.

Wachtel, E. F. (1994). *Treating troubled children and their families.* New York: Guilford.

Wagner, C. L., & Heflin, L. J. (1994). *Managing behaviors: A therapist's guide.* San Antonio, TX: Communication Skill Builders.

Videos and Audio Tapes

Barkley, R. (Presenter). (1997). *Understanding the defiant child* [Video]. New York: Guilford.

Kevin Dawkins Production. (Producer). (1997). *Understanding the defiant child* [Video]. New York: Guilford.

Managing oppositional youth. (1997). [Video]. New York: Insight Media.

Working with hostile and resistant teens. (1992). [Video]. New York: Insight Media.

For Use in Group

General Resources

Dennison, S. T. (1997). *Creating positive support groups for at-risk children: Ten complete curriculums for the most common problems among elementary students, grades 1–8.* Carson, CA: Jalmar.

McConnell, K., Ryser, G., & Patton, J. R. (2002). *Practical ideas that really work for students with disruptive, defiant, or difficult behaviors.* Austin, TX: Pro-Ed.

O'Dell, F. L., Rak, C. F., Chermonte, J. P., & Hamlin, A. (1994). The boost club: A program for at-risk third- and fourth-grade students. *Journal for Specialists in Group Work, 19,* 227–231.

Wilson, F. R., & Owens, P. C. (2001). Group-based prevention programs for at-risk adolescents and adults. *Journal for Specialists in Group Work, 26,* 246–255.

Group Activities

Bloomquist, M. L. (1996). *Skills training for children with behavior disorders: A parent and therapist guidebook.* New York: Guilford.

Body Image/Eating Disorders

For Parents

General Resources

Hollis, J. (1996). *Fat is a family affair.* Cedar City, MN: Hazelden.

For Counselors

General Resources

Baumann, J. (1992). Reflections on group psychotherapy with eating disorder patients. *Group Psychotherapy for Eating Disorders, 16,* 95–100.

Berg, F. (2001). *Children and teens afraid to eat: Helping youth in today's weight-obsessed world.* Hettinger, ND: Healthy Weight Network.

Bilker, L. (1993). Male or female therapists for eating-disordered adolescents: Guidelines suggested by research and practice. *Adolescence, 28,* 393–422.

Brooks, U., & Tepper, I. (1997). High school students' attitudes and knowledge of food consumption and body image: Implications for school based education. *Patient Education and Counseling, 28,* 155–164.

DeLucia-Waack, J. L. (1999). Supervision for counselors working with eating disordered groups: Countertransference issues related to body image, food, and weight. *Journal of Counseling & Development, 77,* 379–888.

Hamburg, P., & Herzog, D. (1990). Supervising the therapy of patients with eating disorders. *American Journal of Psychotherapy, 44,* 369–380.

Johnson, N. G., Roberts, M. C., & Worell, J. (Eds.). (2001). *Beyond appearance: A new look at adolescent girls.* Washington, DC: American Psychological Association.

Kalodner, C. R., & DeLucia-Waack, J. L. (2003). Theory and research on eating disorders and disturbances in women: Suggestions for practice. In M. Kopala & M. Keitel (Eds.), *Handbook of counseling and women* (pp. 506–532). Thousand Oaks, CA: Sage.

Lask, B. (2000). Eating disorders in childhood and adolescents. *Current Pediatrics, 10,* 254–258.

Lock, J., Le Grange, D., Agras, W. S., & Dare, C. (2002). *Treatment manual for anorexia nervosa: A family-based approach.* New York: Guilford.

Lynch, M., Myers, B. J., Kliewer, W., & Kilmartin, C. (2001). Adolescent self-esteem and gender: Exploring relations to sexual harassment, body image, media influences, and emotional expression. *Journal of Youth and Adolescence, 30,* 225–243.

Mussell, M. P., Binford, R. B., & Fulkerson, J. A. (2000). Eating disorders: Summary of risk factors, prevention programming, and prevention research. *The Counseling Psychologist, 28,* 764–796.

Thompson, J. K., Heinberg, L. J., Altabe, M., & Tantleff-Dunn, S. (1999). *Exacting beauty: Theory, assessment, and treatment of body image disturbance.* Washington, DC: American Psychological Association.

Thompson, J. K., & Smolak, L. (Eds.). (2001). *Body image, eating disorders, and obesity in youth: Assessment, prevention, and treatment.* Washington, DC: American Psychological Association.

Videos and Audio Tapes

Eating disorders. (1996). [Video]. Princeton, NJ: Films for the Humanities and Sciences.

Understanding eating disorders. (2002). [Video]. New York: Insight Media.

For Use in Group

General Resources

Bardick, A. D., Bernes, K. B., McCulloch, A. R. M., Witko, K. D., Spriddle, J. W., & Roest, A. R. (2004). Eating disorder intervention, prevention, and treatment: Recommendations for school counselors. *Professional School Counseling, 8,* 168–175.

Brisman, J., & Siegel, M. (1985). The bulimia workshop: A unique integration of group treatment approaches. *International Journal of Group Psychotherapy, 35,* 585–601.

Cash, T. (1995). *What do you see when you look in the mirror? Helping yourself to a positive body image.* New York: Bantam.

Dokter, D. (Ed.). (1994). *Art therapies and clients with eating disorders.* Philadelphia: Jessica Kingsley.

Fettes, P. A., & Peters, J. M. (1992). A meta-analysis of group treatment for bulimia nervosa. *International Journal of Eating Disorders, 11,* 97–110.

Harvey, K. H., & Powers, P. S. (1998). The "Free to Be Me" psychoeducational group: A conceptual model for coping with being overweight. *Journal for Specialists in Group Work, 23,* 312–325.

Jensen-Scott, R. L., & DeLucia-Waack, J. L. (1993). Developing guidance programming in junior and senior high schools: Eating disorders and weight management units. *The School Counselor, 41,* 109–117.

Kalodner, C. R., & Coughlin, J. (2004). Psychoeducational and counseling groups to prevent and treat eating disorders and disturbances. In J. L. DeLucia-Waack, D. A. Gerrity, C. R. Kalodner, & M. T. Riva (Eds.), *Handbook of group counseling and psychotherapy* (pp. 481–496). Thousand Oaks, CA: Sage.

Levitt, D. H. (2004). Helping students with eating disorders. In B. T. Erford (Ed.), *Professional school counseling: A handbook of theories, programs, and practices* (pp. 503–514). Austin, TX: CAPS.

O'Dea, J. (2000). School-based interventions to prevent eating problems: First do no harm. *Eating Disorders, 8,* 123–130.

O'Dea, J. A., & Abraham, S. (2000). Improving body image, eating attitudes, and behaviors of young male and female adolescents: A new educational approach that focuses on self-esteem. *International Journal of Eating Disorders, 28,* 43–57.

Paxton, S. (1993). A prevention program for disturbed eating and body dissatisfaction in adolescent girls: A one-year follow-up. *Health Education Research: Theory & Practice, 8,* 43–50.

Phelps, L., Dempsey, M., Sapia, J., & Nelson, L. (1999). The efficacy of an eating disorder school-based prevention program: Building physical self-esteem and personal competence. In N. Piran, M. Levine, & C. Steiner-Adair (Eds.), *Preventing eating disorders: A handbook of interventions and special challenges.* Philadelphia: Brunner/Mazel.

Phelps, L., Sapia, J., Nathanson, D., & Nelson, L. (2000). An empirically supported eating disorder prevention program. *Psychology in the Schools, 37,* 443–452.

Rhyne-Winkler, M. C., & Hubbard, G. T. (1994). Eating attitudes and behavior: A school counseling program. *The School Counselor, 41,* 195–198.

Videos and Audio Tapes

Angel, C. (Producer), Weber, A. (Producer), & Friedman, G. (Producer). (2000). *Eating disorders: The inner voice* [Video]. Monmouth Junction, NJ: Cambridge Educational.

Cambridge Educational Production. (Producer). (2002). *Body image for boys* [Video]. Princeton, NJ: Films for the Humanities and Sciences.

Picture perfect: Chasing an impossible goal. (2000). [Video]. Princeton, NJ: Films for the Humanities and Sciences.

The thin line: Eating disorders and teens. (2004). [Video]. Plainview, NY: The Bureau for At-Risk Youth.

Wasting away: Anorexia nervosa. (2000). [Video]. Princeton, NJ: Films for the Humanities and Sciences.

When food is the enemy: Eating disorders. (1996). [Video]. Princeton, NJ: Films for the Humanities and Sciences.

Group Activities

Cash, T. F. (1997). *The body image workbook: An 8-step program for learning to like your looks.* Oakland, CA: New Harbinger.

Daigneault, S. D. (2000). Body talk: A school based intervention for working with disordered eating behaviors. *Journal for Specialists in Group Work, 25,* 191–213.

Goodman, L., & Villapiano, M. (2001). *Eating disorders: Journal to recovery workbook.* New York: Brunner-Routledge.

Goodman, L., & Villapiano, M. (2001). *Eating disorders: A time for change: Plans, strategies, and worksheets.* New York: Brunner-Routledge.

Migliore, M. A., with Ross, P. (1998). *The hunger within: A twelve-week guided journey from compulsive eating to recovery.* New York: Main Street.

Piran, N., Levine, M. P., & Steiner-Adair, C. (1999). *Preventing eating disorders: A handbook of interventions and special challenges.* New York: Brunner-Routledge.

Russell, S., & Ryder, S. (2001a). BRIDGE (Building the relationship between body image and disordered eating graph and explanation): A tool for parents and professionals. *Eating Disorders: The Journal of Treatment and Prevention, 9,* 1–14.

Russell, S., & Ryder, S. (2001b). BRIDGE 2 (Building the relationship between body image and disordered eating graph and explanation): Interventions and transitions. *Eating Disorders: The Journal of Treatment and Prevention, 9,* 15–27.

Russell, S., Ryder, S., & Marcoux, G. (2001). *BRIDGE: A resource collection for promoting healthy body image, grades 7–9, grades 10–12.* Available from Alberta Mental Health Board, http://www.amhb.ab.ca.

Sacker, I. M., & Zimmer, M. A. (1987). *Dying to be thin: Understanding and defeating anorexia nervosa and bulimia: A practical, lifesaving guide.* New York: Warner.

Stout, E. J., & Frame, M. W. (2004). Body image disorder in adolescent males: Strategies for school counselors. *Professional School Counselor, 8,* 176–181.

Van Lone, J. S., Kalodner, C. R., & Coughlin, J. W. (2002). Using short stories to address eating disturbances in group. *Journal for Specialists in Group Work, 27,* 59–77.

Weiss, L., Katzman, M., & Wolchick, S. (1985). *Treating bulimia: A psychoeducational approach.* New York: Pergamon.

Bullying Prevention

For Parents

General Resources

Coloroso, B. (2004). *The bully, the bullied, and the bystander: From preschool to high school, how parents and teachers can help break the cycle of violence.* New York: Harper Resource.

Freedman, J. S. (2002). *Easing the teasing: Helping your child cope with name-calling, ridicule, and verbal bullying.* Columbus, OH: McGraw-Hill.

Fried, S., & Fried, P. (1996). *Bullies and victims: Helping your child survive the schoolyard battlefield.* New York: M. Evans.

For Counselors

General Resources

Bierman, K. L. (2003). *Peer rejection: Developmental processes and intervention strategies.* New York: Guilford.

Bortner, L. (2004). Resolving conflicts, providing skills. *ASCA School Counselor, 42,* 14–15.

Cowen, D. (1992). *Teaching the skills of conflict resolution.* Torrance, CA: Innerchoice.

Frenzen, A. (2004). Sugar and spice and everything nice? *ASCA School Counselor, 42,* 20–24.

Guerra, N. G., Tolan, P. H., & Hammond, R. W. (1994). Prevention and treament of adolescent violence. In L. D. Eron, J. H. Gentry, & P. Schlegel (Eds.), *A reason to hope: A psychosocial perspective on violence and youth* (pp. 383–403). Washington, DC: American Psychological Association.

Hoover, J. H., & Oliver, R. (1993). *The bullying prevention handbook: A guide for principals, teachers and counselors.* Amherst, MA: National Educational Service.

Juvonen, J., & Graham, S. (2001). *Peer harassment in school: The plight of the vulnerable and victimized.* New York: Guilford.

Renshaw, D. C. (2001). Bullies. *The Family Journal, 9,* 341–342.

Ross, D. M. (2003). *Childhood bullying, teasing, and violence: What school personnel, other professionals, and parents can do* (2nd ed.). Alexandria, VA: American Counseling Association.

Saufler, C. (2004). A promising approach. *ASCA School Counselor, 42,* 14–18.

Stephens, R. D. (2004). Gangs in schools. *ASCA School Counselor, 42,* 10–13.

Underwood, M. K. (2003). *Social aggression among girls.* New York: Guilford.

Weinhold, B. K. (2002). Uncovering the hidden causes of bullying and school violence. In J. Carlson & J. Lewis (Eds.), *Counseling the adolescent: Individual, family, and school interventions* (4th ed., pp. 181–213). Denver, CO: Love Publishing.

Videos and Audio Tapes

Managing school violence: Before, during, and after. (2000). [Video]. New York: Insight Media.

Shore, K. (2004). *The ABC's of bullying prevention* [Video]. Port Chester, NY: National Professional Resources.

For Use in Group

General Resources

Brinson, J. A., Kottler, J. A., & Fisher, T. A. (2004). Cross-cultural conflict resolution in the schools: Some practical intervention strategies for counselors. *Journal of Counseling and Development, 82,* 294–301.

Crothers, L. M., & Levinson, E. M. (2004). Assessment of bullying: A review of methods and instruments. *Journal of Counseling and Development, 82,* 496–503.

DePino, C. (2004). *Blue cheese breath and stinky feet: How to deal with bullies.* Washington, DC: Magination Press.

Kaufman, G., Raphael, L., & Espeland, P. (1999). *Stick up for yourself! Every kid's guide to personal power and positive self-esteem.* Minneapolis, MN: Free Spirit.

Moss, P. (2004). *Say something.* Gardiner, ME: Tilbury House.

Palomares, S., & Schilling, D. (2001). *How to handle a bully.* Torrance, CA: Innerchoice.

Taylor, J. (2004). Middle grade madness—Debunking the myth of the queen bee. *ASCA School Counselor, 42,* 24–26.

Weinhold, B. (Ed.). (1996). *Spreading kindness: A program guide for reducing youth violence in the schools.* Colorado Springs, CO: Kindness Campaign.

Videos and Audio Tapes

Beane, A. L. (1999). *The bully free classroom* [CD-ROM]. Minneapolis, MN: Free Spirit.

Bullying: You don't have to take it anymore (grade level: 7–12). (2002). [Video]. Port Chester, NY: National Professional Resources.

Elkind and Sweet Communication. (Producer). (1995). *Prevent violence with Groark (grades K-3)* [Video]. San Francisco: Live Wire Media.

Fisher, R. (Producer). (1995). *Conflict resolution: Elementary grades* [Video]. Pleasantville, NY: Sunburst Communications.

Group Activities

The assignment: Girls, cliques, and cruelty. (2003). [DVD]. Plainview, NY: The Bureau for At-Risk Youth.

Beane, A. L. (1999). *The bully free classroom.* Minneapolis, MN: Free Spirit.

Boulden, J., & Boulden, J. (1994). *Push & shove: The bully and victim activity book.* Weaverville, CA: Boulden Publishing.

Boulden, J., & Boulden, J. (1995). *Give and take: A conflict resolution activity book.* Weaverville, CA: Boulden Publishing.

Huerta, J. P. (1991). Refusal skills: Middle school, high school. In G. Brigman & B. Earley (Eds.), *Group counseling for school counselors: A practical guide* (pp. 120–130). Portland, ME: J. Weston Walch.

Newman-Carlson, D., & Horne, A. M. (2004). Bully busters: A psychoeducational intervention for reducing bullying behavior in middle school students. *Journal of Counseling and Development, 82,* 259–267.

Perlstein, R., & Thrall, G. (1998). *Ready-to-use conflict resolution activities for secondary students.* Indianapolis, IN: Wiley.

Pittman, S. (1991). Handling conflict: Stand up to bullies. In G. Brigman & B. Earley (Eds.), *Group counseling for school counselors: A practical guide* (pp. 131–142). Portland, ME: J. Weston Walch.

Romain, T. (2000). *Bullies are a pain in the brain.* New York: Scholastic.

Romain, T. (2001). *Cliques, phonies, and other baloney.* Minneapolis, MN: Free Spirit.

Sheridan, S. M. (1998). *Why don't they like me?* Longmount, CO: Sopris West.

Teolis, B. (1998). *Ready-to-use conflict resolution activities for elementary students.* Indianapolis, IN: Wiley.

Children of Divorce

For Parents

General Resources

Beyer, R., & Winchester, K. (2001). *Speaking of divorce: How to talk with your kids and help them cope.* Minneapolis, MN: Free Spirit.

Duncan, T. R., & Duncan, D. (1979). *You're divorced, but your children aren't.* Englewood Cliffs, NJ: Prentice Hall.

Gardner, R. (1991). *The parents' book about divorce.* New York: Bantam.

Kalter, N. (1990). *Growing up with divorce: Helping your child avoid immediate and later emotional problems.* New York: Free Press.

Sommers-Flanagan, R., Elander, C., & Sommers-Flanagan, J. (2000). *Don't divorce us! Kids' advice to divorcing parents.* Alexandria, VA: American Counseling Association.

Stahl, P. M. (2000). *Parenting after divorce: A guide to resolve conflicts and meeting your children's needs.* Atascadero, CA: Impact.

Wallerstein, J. S., & Kelly, J. B. (1980). *Surviving the break-up: How children and parents cope with divorce.* New York: Basic Books.

For Counselors

General Resources

Alpert-Gillis, L. J., Pedro-Carroll, J. L., & Cowen, E. L. L. (1989). Children of Divorce Intervention program: Development, implementation, and evaluation of a program for young urban children. *Journal of Consulting and Clinical Psychology, 57,* 538–587.

Bernstein, J. (1990). *Books to help children cope with separation and loss* (2nd ed.). New York: Bowker.

Berry, J. (1990). *Good answers to tough questions about divorce.* San Francisco: Children's Press.

Freeman, K. A., Adams, C. D., & Drabman, R. S. (1998). Divorcing parents: Guidelines for promoting children's adjustment. *Child & Family Behavior Therapy, 20,* 1–26.

Hodges, W. (1986). *Interventions for children of divorce: Custody, access and psychotherapy.* New York: Wiley.

Lesowitz, M., Kalter, N., Pickar, J., Chethik, M., & Schaefer, M. (1987). School-based developmental facilitation groups for children of divorce: Issues of group process. *Psychotherapy, 24,* 90–95.

Lockhart, E. J. (2004). Helping students from changing families. In B. T. Erford (Ed.), *Professional school counseling: A handbook of theories, programs, and practices* (pp. 719–733). Austin, TX: CAPS.

Oppawsky, J. (1991). Utilizing children's drawings in working with children following divorce. *Journal of Divorce and Remarriage, 15,* 125–141.

Wilcoxon, S. A., & Magnusom, S. (1999). Considerations for school counselors serving non-custodial parents: Premises and suggestions. *Professional School Counseling, 2,* 275–279.

Videos and Audio Tapes

Stepfamilies: A coming together. (1984). [Video]. New York: Insight Media.

Working with stepfamilies. (2004). [Video]. New York: Insight Media.

For Use in Group

Books

Berger, F. (1983). *Nuisance.* New York: Morrow.

Beyer, R., & Winchester, K. (2001). *What in the world do you do when your parents divorce? A survival guide for kids.* Minneapolis, MN: Free Spirit.

Blume, J. (1972). *It's not the end of the world.* New York: Bradbury.

Boekman, C. (1980). *Surviving your parents' divorce.* Danbury, CT: Franklin Watts.

Boelts, M. (1992). *With my Mom, with my Dad.* New York: Pacific Press.

Brown, L. K., & Brown, M. (1986). *Dinosaurs' divorce.* Boston: Little, Brown.

Cain, B., & Benedek, E. (1976). *What would you do? A child's book about divorce.* Washington, DC: American Psychiatric Press.

Cantor, D. W., & Drake, E. A. (1983). *Divorced parents and their children.* New York: Springer.

Field, M., & Shore, H. (1994). *My life turned upside down, but I turned it rightside up: A self-esteem book about dealing with shared custody.* New York: Center for Applied Psychology.

Heegaard, M. (1991). *When Mom and Dad separate: Children can learn to cope with grief about divorce.* Minneapolis, MN: Woodland.

Hoffman, E. (1995). *Kids can cope with divorce.* Warminster, PA: Marco Products.

Lash, M. (1990). *My kind of family: A book for kids in single-parent homes.* Burlington, VT: Waterfront.

MacGregor, C. (2001). *The divorce helpbook for kids.* Atascadero, CA: Impact.

MacGregor, C. (2004). *The divorce helpbook for teens.* Atascadero, CA: Impact.

Mayle, P. (1988). *Why are we getting a divorce?* New York: Harmony.

Rogers, F. (1996). *Let's talk about it: Stepfamilies.* New York: Putnam.

Rogers, F. (1997). *Let's talk about it: Divorce.* New York: Putnam.

Swan-Jackson, A. (1998). *When your parents split up . . . How to keep yourself together.* New York: Penguin Putnam.

Videos and Audio Tapes

Cambridge Educational Media. (Producer). (2002). *Divorce: A survival guide for kids* [Video]. Princeton, NJ: Films for the Humanities and Sciences.

Cooper, J., & Martenz, A. (1993). *Divorce I.* Warminster, PA: Marco Products.

Cooper, J., & Martenz, A. (1993). *Stepfamilies I.* Warminster, PA: Marco Products.

Kids Rights. (1995). *No fault kids: A focus on kids with divorced parents* [Video]. Charlotte, NC: Author.

Kids Rights. (1995). *When Mom and Dad break up* [Video]. Charlotte, NC: Author.

Sunburst Communications. (1997). *If your parents break up . . .* [Video]. Pleasantview, NY: Author.

Yours, mine, and ours. (1988). [Video]. New York: Insight Media.

Group Activities

Banks, A. (1990). *When your parents get a divorce: A kid's journal.* New York: Viking.

Beyer, R. (2002). *The Mom and Dad pad: A divorce communication tool.* Minneapolis, MN: Free Spirit.

Deaton, W. (1994). *A separation in my family: A child's workbook about parental separation and divorce.* New York: Hunter House.

DeLucia-Waack, J. L. (1996). Children of divorce group work in the schools. In S. T. Gladding (Ed.), *Group process and group counseling* (pp. 27–28). Greensboro, NC: ERIC/CASS.

DeLucia-Waack, J. L. (2001). Effective children of divorce groups for elementary school children. *The Family Journal, 9,* 273–284.

DeLucia-Waack, J. L. (2001). *Using music in children of divorce groups: A session-by-session manual for counselors.* Alexandria, VA: American Counseling Association.

Earley, B. (1991). Family group—Divorce. In G. Brigman & B. Earley (Eds.), *Group counseling for school counselors: A practical guide* (pp. 145–164). Portland, ME: J. Weston Walch.

Epstein, Y. M., & Borduin, C. M. (1985). Could this happen? A game for children of divorce. *Psychotherapy, 22,* 770–773.

Games, T. (1997). *The divorce game.* Pleasantville, NY: Sunburst Communications.

Garigan, E., & Urbanski, M. (1991). *Living with divorce—Primary grades: Activities to help children cope with difficult situations.* New York: Good Apple.

Hage, S. M., & Nosanow, M. (2000). Becoming stronger at broken places: A model for group work with young adolescents from divorced families. *Journal for Specialists in Group Work, 25,* 50–66.

Hayes, R. L., & Hayes, B. A. (2002). Remarried families: Counseling parents and their children. In J. Carlson & J. Lewis (Eds.), *Counseling the adolescent: Individual, family, and school interventions* (4th ed., pp. 303–315). Denver, CO: Love Publishing.

Ives, S. (1985). *The divorce workbook: A guide for kids and families.* New York: Waterfront.

Ives, S., Fassler, D., & Lash, M. (1985). *The divorce workbook.* Burlington, VT: Waterfront.

Margolin, S. (1996). Changes activity. In *Complete group counseling program for children of divorce* (pp. 46–50). West Nyack, NY: The Center for Applied Research in Education.

Margolin, S. (1996). *Complete group counseling program for children of divorce: Ready-to-use plans and materials for small and large divorce groups, 1–6.* Indianapolis, IN: Wiley.

Morganett, R. S. (1990). Dealing with a divorce in the family. In R. S. Morganett, *Skills for living: Group counseling activities for young adolescents* (pp. 13–30). Champaign, IL: Research Press.

Muro, J. J., & Kottman, T. (1995). Counseling specific populations: Children of divorce. In J. J. Muro & T. Kottman, *Guidance and counseling in the elementary and middle schools: A practical approach* (pp. 217–250). Madison, WI: Brown & Benchmark.

Pedro-Carroll, J. L. (1985). *The Children of Divorce Intervention program: A procedures manual for facilitating a divorce support group for 4th-6th grade children.* Rochester, NY: University of Rochester Center for Community Study.

Pedro-Carroll, J. L., & Cowen E. L. (1987). The Children of Divorce Intervention program: Implementation and evaluation of a time-limited group approach. In J. P. Vincent (Ed.), *Advances in family intervention, assessment and theory* (Vol. 4, pp. 281–307). Greenwich, CT: JAI.

Prokop, M. (1986). *Divorce happens to the nicest kids: A self-help book for kids and adults.* Warren, OH: Alegra House.

Rose, S. R. (1998). Applications of group work: Parental divorce. In S. R. Rose, *Group work with children and adolescents: Prevention and intervention in school and community systems* (pp. 87–105). Thousand Oaks, CA: Sage.

Worthen, T. (Ed.). (2001). *Broken hearts . . . healing: Young poets speak out on divorce.* Logan, UT: Poet Tree Press.

For a complete list see: DeLucia-Waack (2001).

Children of Parents Who Have Cancer

For Parents

General Resources

American Cancer Society. (1986). *Helping children understand: A guide for a parent with cancer* [Pamphlet]. Atlanta, GA: Author.

Heiney, S. P., Hermann, J. F., Bruss, K. V., & Fincannon, J. L. (2001). *Cancer in the family: Helping children cope with a parent's illness.* Atlanta, GA: American Cancer Society.

Kroll, L., Barnes, J., Jones, A. L., & Stein, A. (1998). Cancer in parents: Telling children. *British Medical Journal, 316,* 880–881.

McCue, K. (1994). *How to help children through a parent's serious illness.* New York: St. Martin's.

Russell, N. (2001). *Can I still kiss you? Answering your children's questions about cancer.* Deerfield Beach, FL: Health Communications Inc.

Texas Medical Center, Methodist Hospital Cancer Program. (1997). *How to talk to a child when you have cancer.* Houston, TX: Author.

For Counselors

General Resources

Call, D. A. (1990). School-based groups: A valuable support for children of cancer patients. *Journal of Psychosocial Oncology, 8,* 97–118.

Compas, B. E., Ey, S., Worsham, N. L., & Howell, D. C. (1996). When Mom or Dad has cancer: II. Coping, cognitive appraisals, and psychological distress in children of cancer patients. *Health Psychology, 15,* 167–175.

Stanko, C. A., & Taub, D. J. (2002). A counseling group for children of cancer patients. *Journal for Specialists in Group Work, 27,* 43–58.

Taylor-Brown, J., Acheson, A., & Farber, J. M. (1993). Kids can cope: A group for children whose parents have cancer. *Journal of Psychosocial Oncology, 11,* 41–53.

For Use in Group

General Resources

Ackermann, A., & Ackermann, A. (2001). *Our Mom has cancer.* Atlanta, GA: American Cancer Society.

Bedway, A. J., & Smith, L. H. (1996). "For Kids Only": Development of a program for children from families with a cancer patient. *Journal of Psychosocial Oncology, 14,* 19–28.

Carney, K. L. (2001). *What is cancer anyway? Explaining cancer to children of all ages.* Wethersfield, CT: Dragonfly.

Kohlenberg, S. (1994). *Sammy's mommy has cancer.* Milwaukee, WI: Gareth Stevens.

Lansdale, M. T., Jr. (2000). *Cancer books for children.* Health Information Resources. Michigan Electronic Library. Available: http://mel.lib.mi.us/health/cancerbooks

Lewandowski, L. A. (1996). A parent has cancer: Needs and responses of children. *Pediatric Nursing, 22,* 518–523.

Numeroff, L., & Schlessel Harpham, W. (2001). *The hope tree: Kids talk about breast cancer.* New York: Simon & Schuster.

Speltz, A. (2002). *The year my mother was bald.* Washington, DC: Magination Press.

Group Activities

American Cancer Society. (2002). *Because someone I love has cancer: Kids' activity book.* Atlanta, GA: Author.

Bedway, A. J., & Smith, L. H. (1996). "For Kids Only": Development of a program for children from families with a cancer patient. *Journal of Psychosocial Oncology, 14,* 19–28.

Greening, K. (1992). The "Bear Essentials" program: Helping young children and their families cope when a parent has cancer. *Journal of Psychosocial Oncology, 10,* 47–61.

Harpham, W. (1997). *When a parent has cancer: A guide to caring for your children/ Becky and the worry cup: A children's book about a parent's cancer* (2-book package). New York: HarperCollins.

National Cancer Institute and National Institutes of Health. (2001). *When someone in your family has cancer.* Available: http://rex.nci.nih.gov/NCI_Pub_Interface/guide_for_kids/kidscontents.html

Taylor-Brown, J., Acheson, A., & Farber, J. M. (1993). Kids can cope: A group for children whose parents have cancer. *Journal of Psychosocial Oncology, 11,* 41–53.

Communication Skills

For Parents

Videos and Audio Tapes

Communication in single-parent and other family forms. (1997). [Video]. New York: Insight Media.

Communication rules and family secrets. (1997). [Video]. New York: Insight Media.

Teaching families new skills. (1996). [Video]. New York: Insight Media.

For Counselors

General Resources

Clark, M. A. (2005). Building connections, communication and character in classrooms. *ASCA School Counselor, 42,* 8–13.

Corder, B. F. (1994). *Structured adolescent psychotherapy groups.* Sarasota, FL: Professional Resource Exchange.

For Use in Group

General Resources

McGann, W., & Werven, G. (1999). *Social communication skills for children: A workbook for principle centered communication.* Austin, TX: Pro-Ed.

Nims, D. R. (1998). Searching for self: A theoretical model for applying family systems to adolescent group work. *Journal for Specialists in Group Work, 23*(2), 133–144.

Palomares, S., Schuster, S., & Watkins, C. (1992). *The sharing circle handbook: Topics for teaching self-awareness, communication, and social skills.* Torrance: CA: Innerchoice.

Robin, A. L., & Foster, S. L. (2002). *Negotiating parent-adolescent conflict: A behavioral-family systems approach.* New York: Guilford.

Videos and Audio Tapes

Communication. (2004). [Video]. New York: Insight Media.

Communication. (n.d.). [Youth Life Skills Series Video]. Plainview, NY: The Bureau for At-Risk Youth.

Group Activities

Gettinger, M., Doll, B., & Salmon, D. (1994). Effects of social problem solving, goal setting, and parent training on children's peer relations. *Journal of Applied Developmental Psychology, 15,* 141–163.

Hargrave, G. E., & Hargrave, M. C. (1979). A peer group socialization therapy program in the school: An outcome investigation. *Psychology in the Schools, 16,* 546–550.

Hess, L. J. (1993). *FACE to FACE: Facilitating adolescent communication experiences.* San Antonio, TX: Communication Skill Builders/Therapy Skill Builders.

Hightower, E., & Riley, B. (2002). *Our family meeting book: Fun and easy ways to manage time, build communication, and share responsibility.* Minneapolis, MN: Free Spirit.

Jones, A. E. (1998). *104 activities that build: Self-esteem, teamwork, communication, anger management, self-discovery, and coping skills.* Richland, WA: Rec. Room.

Kelly, A. (2001). *Talkabout: A social communication skills package.* Oxfordshire, UK: Speechmark.

Kelly, A. (2003). *Talkabout activities: Developing social communication skills.* Oxfordshire, UK: Speechmark.

Mood swings flipchart. (n.d.). [Activity]. Minneapolis, MN: Free Spirit.

Walker, H. M., Todis, B., Holmes, D., & Horton, G. (1987). *The ACCESS program: Adolescent curriculum for communication and effective social skills.* Austin, TX: Pro-Ed.

Depression

For Parents

General Resources

Fassler, D. G., & Dumas, L. S. (1998). *"Help me, I'm sad": Recognizing, treating, and preventing childhood and adolescent depression.* East Rutherford, NJ: Penguin.

Fristad, M. A., & Goldberg, J. S. (2003). *Raising a moody child: How to cope with depression and bipolar disorder.* New York: Guilford.

Kaufman, M. (2001). *Overcoming teen depression: A guide for parents (issues in parenting).* Toronto, Ontario: Firefly.

Miller, J. A. (1999). *The childhood depression sourcebook.* New York: McGraw-Hill.

Mondimore, F. M. (2002). *Adolescent depression: A guide for parents.* Baltimore, MD: Johns Hopkins University Press.

Oster, G. D., & Montgomery, S. S. (1994). *Helping your depressed teenager: A guide for parents and caregivers.* Indianapolis, IN: Wiley.

Wilens, T. E. (2001). *Straight talk about psychiatric medications for kids* (rev. ed). New York: Guilford.

For Counselors

General Resources

Asarnow, J. R., Jaycox, L. H., & Tompson, M. C. (2001). Depression in youth: Psychosocial interventions. *Journal of Clinical & Child Psychology, 30,* 33–47.

Cash, R. E. (2001). *Depression in children and adolescents.* Bethesda, MD: The Guidance Channel and the National Association of School Psychologists.

Clarke, G., Lewinsohn, P., & Hops, H. (1990). *Coping with adolescent depression course: Leader's manual for adolescent groups.* Eugene, OR: Castalia.

Cytryn, L., & McKnew, D. H. (1998). *Growing up sad: Childhood depression and its treatment.* New York: Norton.

Empfield, M., & Bakalar, N. (2001). *Understanding teenage depression: A guide to diagnosis, treatment, and management.* New York: Owl Books.

Hazler, R. J., & Mellin, E. A. (2004). The developmental origins and treatment needs of female adolescents with depression. *Journal of Counseling and Development, 82,* 18–24.

Herman-Stahl, M., & Peterson, A. (1996). The protective role of coping social resources for depressive symptoms among young adolescents. *Journal of Youth and Adolescence, 25,* 733–753.

Kaslow, N. J., & Thompson, M. P. (1998). Applying the criteria for empirically supported treatments to studies of psychosocial interventions for child and adolescent depression. *Journal of Clinical Child Psychology, 27,* 146–155.

Kazdin, A. E. (1987). Assessment of childhood depression: Current issues and strategies. *Behavioral Assessment, 9,* 291–319.

Koplewicz, H. S. (2003). *More than moody: Recognizing and treating adolescent depression.* Available: http://www.AboutOurKids.org

Lewinsohn, P. M., Pettit, J. W., Joiner, T. E., Jr., & Seeley, J. R. (2003). The symptomatic expression of major depressive disorder in adolescents and young adults. *Journal of Abnormal Psychology, 112,* 244–252.

Maag, J. W., & Forness, S. R. (2002). Depression in children and adolescents. In J. Carlson & J. Lewis (Eds.), *Counseling the adolescent: Individual, family, and school interventions* (4th ed., pp. 135–165). Denver, CO: Love Publishing.

Merrell, K. W. (2001). *Helping students overcome depression and anxiety: A practical guide.* New York: Guilford.

Mufson, L., Dorta, K. P., Moreau, D., & Weissman, M. M. (Eds.). (2004). *Interpersonal psychotherapy for depressed adolescents* (2nd ed.). New York: Guilford.

Newcomer, P. L., Barenbaum, E. M., & Bryant, B. R. (1994). *Depression and Anxiety in Youth Scale.* Austin, TX: Pro-Ed.

Newsome, D. (2004). Helping students with depression. In B. T. Erford (Ed.), *Professional school counseling: A handbook of theories, programs, and practices* (pp. 515–531). Austin, TX: CAPS.

Possell, P. D., Horn, A. B., Groen, G., & Hautzinger, M. (2004). School-based prevention of depression symptoms in adolescence: A six-month follow-up. *Journal of the American Academy of Child and Adolescent Psychiatry, 43,* 1003–1010.

Pozanski, E. O., & Mokros, H. B. (1996). *Children's Depression Rating Scale—Revised edition.* Austin, TX: Pro-Ed.

Reynolds, W. M. (1990). Depression in children and adolescents: Nature, diagnosis, assessment, and treatment. *School Psychology Review, 19,* 158–174.

Rice, A. (1995). Structured groups for the treatment of depression. In K. R. MacKensie (Ed.), *Effective use of group therapy in managed care* (pp. 61–96). Washington, DC: Psychiatric Press.

Shocket, I. M., Dadds, M. R., Holland, D., Whitefield, K., Hartnet, P. H., & Osgarby, S. (2001). The efficacy of a universal school-based program to prevent adolescent depression. *Journal of Clinical Child Psychology, 30,* 303–315.

Spence, S. H., Sheffield, J. K., & Donovan, C. L. (2003). Preventing adolescent depression: An evaluation of the problem solving for life program. *Journal of Consulting and Clinical Psychology, 71,* 3–13.

Stark, K. D. (1990). *Childhood depression: School-based intervention.* New York: Guilford.

Stark, K. D., & Kendall, P. C. (1996). *Treating depressed children: Therapist's manual for ACTION.* Ardmore, PA: Workbook Publishing.

Vandervoort, D. J., & Fuhriman, A. (1991). The efficacy of group therapy for depression: A review of the literature. *Small Group Research, 22,* 320–338.

Wilkes, T. C. R., Belsher, G., Rush, A. J., & Frank, E. (1994). *Cognitive therapy for depressed adolescents.* New York: Guilford.

Videos and Audio Tapes

CBT for depressed adolescents. (1998). [Video]. New York: Insight Media.

Distance Learning Network. (Producer). (1998). *Treatment and assessment of childhood depression and anxiety* [Video]. New York: Insight Media.

For Use in Group

General Resources

Burak-Maholik, S. (1993). Psychoeducational strategies for depressed students. *Journal of Emotional and Behavioral Problems, 2,* 45–47.

Cobain, R. N. (1998). *When nothing matters anymore: A survival guide for depressed teens.* Minneapolis, MN: Free Spirit.

Frank, K., & Smith-Rex, J. (1996). *Getting over the blues: A kid's guide to understanding and coping with unpleasant feelings and depression.* Minneapolis, MN: Educational Media.

Garland, E. J. (1997). *Depression is the pits, but I'm getting better: A guide for adolescents.* Washington, DC: Magination Press.

Rice, A. H. (2004). Group treatment of depression. In J. L. DeLucia-Waack, D. A. Gerrity, C. R. Kalodner, & M. T. Riva (Eds.), *Handbook of group counseling and psychotherapy* (pp. 532–546). Thousand Oaks, CA: Sage.

Videos and Audio Tapes

Dartmouth-Hitchcock Medical Center. (Producer). (2000). *Childhood depression* [Video]. Princeton, NJ: Films for the Humanities and Sciences.

Depression: A teenager's guide. (1999). [Video]. Princeton, NJ: Films for the Humanities and Sciences.

Group Activities

Copeland, M. E., & Copans, S. (2002). *Recovering from depression: A workbook for teens* (rev. ed.). Baltimore, MD: Paul H. Brookes.

Hendricks, B. C., Robinson, B., Bradley, L. J., & Davis, K. (1999). Using music techniques to treat adolescent depression. *Journal of Humanistic Counseling, Education and Development, 38,* 39–46.

Sommers-Flanagan, R., Barrett-Hakanson, T., Clarke, C., & Sommers-Flanagan, J. (2000). A psychoeducational school-based coping and social skills group for depressed students. *Journal for Specialists in Group Work, 25,* 170–190.

Stark, K. D., Simmons Brookman, C., & Frazier, R. (1990). A comprehensive school-based treatment program for depressed children. *School Psychologists Quarterly, 5,* 111–140.

Friendship Skills

For Parents

General Resources

Frankel, F., & Wetmore, B. (1996). *Good friends are hard to find: Helping your child find, make, and keep friends.* London: Perspective.

For Counselors

General Resources

Brown, L. M., Way, N., & Duff, J. L. (1999). The others in my I: Adolescent girls' friendships and peer relations. In N. G. Johnson, M. C. Roberts, & J. Worell (Eds.), *Beyond appearance: A new look at adolescent girls* (pp. 205–226). Washington, DC: American Psychological Association.

Grunnebaum, H., & Solomon, L. (1991). Peer relationships, self-esteem and self. *International Journal of Group Psychotherapy, 37,* 475–506.

Kupersmidt, J. B., & Dodge, K. A. (2004). *Children's peer relations: From development to intervention.* Washington, DC: American Psychological Association.

Schwartz, L. (1988). *Feelings about friends: Grades 3–6.* New York: Learning Works.

Sharabany, R. (1994). Continuities in the development of intimate friendships: Object relations, interpersonal and attachment perspectives. In R. Guilmour & R. Erber (Eds.), *Theoretical frameworks for personal relationships* (pp. 157–178). Hillsdale, NJ: Lawrence Erlbaum.

For Use in Group

General Resources

Herron, R., & Peter, V. J. (1998). *A good friend: How to make one, how to be one.* Boys Town, NE: Boys Town Press.

Packer, A. J. (2004). *The How Rude!™ handbook of friendship and dating manners for teens.* Minneapolis, MN: Free Spirit.

Rose, S. R. (1998). Applications of group work: Peer relationships and social competence. In S. R. Rose, *Group work with children and adolescents: Prevention and intervention in school and community systems* (pp. 106–122). Thousand Oaks, CA: Sage.

Shechtman, Z. (1996). Group psychotherapy and close friendships. In S. T. Gladding (Ed.), *Group process and group counseling* (pp. 77–79). Greensboro, NC: ERIC/CASS.

Shechtman, Z., Freidman, Y., Kashti, Y., & Sharabany, R. (2002). Group counseling to enhance adolescents' close friendships. *International Journal of Group Psychotherapy, 52,* 537–553.

Silverstein, S. (1981). *The missing piece meets the big O.* New York: HarperCollins.

Smead, R. (2000). Girlfriends: Understanding and managing friendships. In R. Smead, *Skills for living: Group counseling activities for young adolescents* (pp. 29–54). Champaign, IL: Research Press.

Group Activities

Brigman, G. (1991). Friendship: Middle school. In G. Brigman & B. Earley (Eds.), *Group counseling for school counselors: A practical guide* (pp. 69–84). Portland, ME: J. Weston Walch.

Cheatham, G. B. (1991). Friendship: Upper elementary. In G. Brigman & B. Earley (Eds.), *Group counseling for school counselors: A practical guide* (pp. 59–68). Portland, ME: J. Weston Walch.

Morganett, R. S. (1990). Meeting, making, and keeping friends. In R. S. Morganett, *Skills for living: Group counseling activities for young adolescents* (pp. 31–55). Champaign, IL: Research Press.

Schmidt, J. J. (2002). *Making and keeping friends: Ready-to-use lessons, stories, and activities for building relationships.* San Francisco: Jossey-Bass.

Tips for making and keeping friends [Poster]. Minneapolis, MN: Free Spirit.

Grief

For Parents

General Resources

The Dougy Center. (1999). *What about the kids? Understanding their needs in funeral planning and services.* Minneapolis, MN: Free Spirit.

Grollman, E. (1990). *Talking about death: A dialogue between parent and child.* Boston: Beacon.

Kroen, W. C., & Espeland, P. (1996). *Helping children cope with the loss of a loved one: A guide for grownups.* Minneapolis, MN: Free Spirit.

Tedeschi, R. G., & Calhoun, L. G. (2003). *Helping bereaved parents: A clinician's guide.* New York: Brunner-Routledge.

For Counselors

General Resources

Akin, T., Cowan, D., Palomares, S., & Schilling, D. (2000). *Helping kids manage grief, fear, and anger.* Torrance, CA: Innerchoice.

Aspinall, S. Y. (1996). Educating children to cope with death: A preventative model. *Psychology in the Schools, 33,* 341–349.

Bernstein, J. (1990). *Books to help children cope with separation and loss* (2nd ed.). New York: Bowker.

The Dougy Center. (1998). *Helping children cope with death.* Minneapolis, MN: Free Spirit.

The Dougy Center. (1999). *Helping teens cope with death.* Minneapolis, MN: Free Spirit.

The Dougy Center. (1999). *35 ways to help a grieving child.* Minneapolis, MN: Free Spirit.

Freudenberger, H. J., & Gallagher, K. M. (1995). Emotional consequences of loss for our adolescents. *Psychotherapy, 32*(5), 150–153.

Glass, J. C. (1991). Death, loss, and grief among middle school children: Implications for the school counselor. *Elementary School Guidance and Counseling, 26,* 139–148.

Goldman, L. (1999). *Life and loss: A guide to helping grieving children.* Philadelphia: Brunner-Routledge.

Haasl, B., & Marnocha, J. (1999). *Bereavement support group program for children: Leader manual and participant workbook.* Philadelphia: Accelerated Development.

Heegaard, M. (1991). *When something terrible happens: Children can learn to cope with grief.* Minneapolis, MN: Woodland.

Heegaard, M. (1992). *Drawing out feelings: Facilitator's guide for leading grief support groups.* Minneapolis, MN: Woodland.

Klicker, R. L. (2000*). A student dies, a school mourns: Dealing with death and loss in the school community.* Philadelphia: Taylor & Francis.

Perschy, M. K. (2004). *Helping teens work through grief* (2nd ed.). New York: Brunner-Routledge.

Seager, K. M., & Spencer, S. C. (1996). Meeting the bereavement needs of kids in patient/ families—Not just playing around. *Hospice Journal, 11,* 41–66.

Stroebe, M. S., Hansson, R. O., Stroebe, W., & Schut, H. (Eds.). (2001). *Handbook of bereavement research: Consequences, coping, and care.* Washington, DC: American Psychological Association.

Webb, N. B. (1993). Assessment of the bereaved child. In N. B. Webb (Ed.), *Helping bereaved children: A handbook for practitioners* (pp. 19–42). New York: Guilford.

Webb, N. B. (2002). *Helping bereaved children: A handbook for practitioners* (2nd ed.). New York: Guilford.

Worden, J. W. (2001). *Children and grief: When a parent dies.* New York: Guilford.

Videos and Audio Tapes

Grieving for children. (2000). [Video]. New York: Insight Media.

A look at children's grief. (2001). [Video]. New York: Insight Media.

For Use in Group

General Resources

Baulkwill, J., & Wood, C. (1995). Sharing experiences—The value of groups for bereaved children. In S. C. Smith & M. Pennells (Eds.), *Interventions with bereaved children* (pp. 160–171). London: Jessica Kingsley.

Beckman, R. (1999). *Children who grieve: A manual for conducting support groups.* Holmes Beach, FL: Learning Publications.

Buscaglia, L. (1982). *The fall of Freddie the leaf.* Thorofare, NJ: Slack.

Cunningham, A. (2001). *A child's simple guide through grief.* Carson, CA: Jalmar.

Cunningham, A. (2001). *A teen's simple guide through grief.* Carson, CA: Jalmar.

Desetta, A., & Wolin, S. (2000). *The struggle to be strong: True stories by teens about overcoming tough times.* Minneapolis, MN: Free Spirit.

Finn, C. A. (2003). Helping students cope with loss: Incorporating art into group counseling. *Journal for Specialists in Group Work, 28,* 155–165.

Goldberg, F. R. (1998). Left and left out: Teaching children to grieve through a rehabilitation curriculum. *Professional School Counseling, 2,* 123–127.

Granot, T. (2004). *Without you: Children and young people growing up with loss and its effects.* Philadelphia: Jessica Kingsley.

Healy-Romanello, M. A. (1993). The invisible griever: Support groups for bereaved children. *Special Services in the Schools, 8,* 67–89.

Heegaard, M. E. (1988). *Facilitator's guide: For when someone very special dies.* Minneapolis, MN: Woodland.

Hetzel, S., Winn, V., & Tolstoshev, H. (1991). Loss and change: New directions in death education for adolescents. *Journal of Adolescence, 14*(4), 323–334.

Huss, S. N., & Ritchie, M. (1999). Effectiveness of a group for parentally bereaved children. *Journal for Specialists in Group Work, 24,* 186–196.

Keitel, M. A., Kopala, M., & Robin, L. (1998). Loss and grief groups. In K. C. Stoiber & T. R. Kratochwill (Eds.), *Handbook of group intervention for children and families* (pp. 159–171). Boston: Allyn & Bacon.

Mallon, B. (1998). *Helping children to manage loss: Positive strategies for renewal and growth.* Philadelphia: Jessica Kingsley.

Mills, J. C. (2003). *Gentle willow: A story for children about dying* (2nd ed.). Washington, DC: Magination Press.

Palmer, P. (1994). *"I wish I could hold your hand . . .": A child's guide to grief and loss.* Atascadero, CA: Impact.

Peterson, J. (1995). *Talk with teens about feelings, family, relationships, and the future: 50 guided discussions for school and counseling groups.* Minneapolis, MN: Free Spirit.

Rofes, E. (1985). *The kids' book about death and dying.* Boston: Little, Brown.

Romain, T., & Verdick, E. (1999). *What on earth do you do when someone dies?* Minneapolis, MN: Free Spirit.

Salloum, A. (2004). *Group work with adolescents after violent death: A manual for practitioners.* New York: Brunner-Routledge.

Samide, L. L., & Stockton, R. (2002). Letting go of grief: Bereavement group for children in the school setting. *Journal for Specialists in Group Work, 27,* 192–204.

Schoeman, L. H., & Kreitzman, R. (1997). Death of a parent: Group intervention with bereaved children and their caregivers. *Psychoanalysis and Psychotherapy, 14,* 221–245.

Tait, D. C., & Depta, J. L. (1993). Play therapy group for bereaved children. In N. B. Webb (Ed.), *Helping bereaved children: A handbook for practitioners* (pp. 169–188). New York: Guilford.

Turner, M. (2004). *Someone very important has just died: Immediate help for people caring for children of all ages at the time of a close bereavement.* Philadelphia: Jessica Kingsley.

Videos and Audio Tapes

Teens dealing with death. (2004). [Video]. Princeton, NJ: Films for the Humanities and Sciences.

Group Activities

Blair, S. J. (2001). *Group activities for kids who hurt.* Torrance, CA: Innerchoice.

Brigman, G., & Earley, B. (1991). Loss group: All levels. In G. Brigman & B. Earley (Eds.), *Group counseling for school counselors: A practical guide* (pp. 165–174). Portland, ME: J. Weston Walch.

Brown, L. K., & Brown, M. T. (1996). *When dinosaurs die: A guide to understanding death.* Boston: Little, Brown.

Buscaglia, L. (1982). *The fall of Freddie the leaf: A story of life for all ages.* New York: C. B. Slack.

Desetta, A., Wolin, S., & Hefner, K. (2000). *The leader's guide to the struggle to be strong: How to foster resilience in teens.* Minneapolis, MN: Free Spirit.

The Dougy Center. (2001). *After a suicide: A workbook for grieving kids.* Minneapolis, MN: Free Spirit.

The Dougy Center. (2002). *After a murder: A workbook for grieving kids.* Minneapolis, MN: Free Spirit.

Dower, L. (2001). *I will remember you: What to do when someone you love dies: A guidebook through grief for teens.* New York: Scholastic.

Engel, G. L. (1980). A group dynamics approach to teaching and learning about grief. *Omega: Journal of Death and Dying, 11,* 45–49.

Morganett, R. S. (1990). Coping with grief and loss. In R. S. Morganett, *Skills for living: Group counseling activities for young adolescents* (pp. 181–200). Champaign, IL: Research Press.

Murthy, R., & Smith, L. L. (2005). *Grieving, sharing, and healing: A guide for facilitating early adolescent bereavement groups.* Champaign, IL: Research Press.

Smith, S. C., & Pennells, M. (1995). *Interventions with bereaved children.* Philadelphia: Jessica Kingsley.

When a loved one dies. (n.d.). Plainview, NY: The Bureau for At-Risk Youth.

Zalaznik, P. W. (1986). *Dimensions of loss and death education: A resource and curriculum guide.* Minneapolis, MN: EDU-PAC.

Relationship Skills

For Parents

General Resources

Miron, A. G., & Miron, C. D. (2002). *How to talk with teens about love, relationships, and s-e-x.* Minneapolis, MN: Free Spirit.

Videos and Audio Tapes

American Psychological Association. (Producer). (2004). *Parenting young children* [Video]. New York: Insight Media.

Family togetherness. (2004). [Video]. New York: Insight Media.

For Counselors

General Resources

Burnett, P. C. (1994). Self-concept and self-esteem in elementary school. *Psychology in the Schools, 31,* 164–171.

Davies, D. (1999). *Child development: A practitioner's guide.* New York: Guilford.

Hamilton, S. F., & Hamilton, M. A. (Eds.). (2004). *The youth development handbook: Coming of age in American communities.* Thousand Oaks, CA: Sage.

Kupersmidt, J. B., & Dodge, K. A. (2004). *Children's peer relations: From development to intervention.* Washington, DC: American Psychological Association.

Patterson, J., Pryor, J., & Field, J. (1995). Adolescent attachment to parents and friends in relation to aspects of self-esteem. *Journal of Youth and Adolescence, 24,* 365–376.

Siegel, D. J. (2001). *The developing mind: How relationships and the brain interact to shape who we are.* New York: Guilford.

For Use in Group

General Resources

Abrahams, G., & Ahlbrand, S. (2002). *Boy vs. girl: How gender shapes who we are, what we want, and how we get along.* Minneapolis, MN: Free Spirit.

Akos, P. (2000). Building empathic skills in elementary school children through group work. *Journal for Specialists in Group Work, 25,* 214–223.

Fox, A. (2000). *Can you relate? Real-world advice for teens on guys, girls, growing up, and getting along.* Minneapolis, MN: Free Spirit.

Packer, A. J. (2004). *The How Rude!™ handbook of friendship and dating manners for teens.* Minneapolis, MN: Free Spirit.

Smead, R. (2000). Dating and relating: Male/female relationship issues. In R. Smead, *Skills for living: Group counseling activities for young adolescents* (pp. 83–118). Champaign, IL: Research Press.

Smead, R. (2000). Give a little, take a little: Relationships at home. In R. Smead, *Skills for living: Group counseling activities for young adolescents* (pp. 147–172). Champaign, IL: Research Press.

Videos and Audio Tapes

Cambridge Educational Production. (Producer). (2000). *Healthy relationships* [Video]. Princeton, NJ: Films for the Humanities and Sciences.

Group Activities

Carrell, S. (2000). Living with sexuality. In S. Carrell, *Group exercises for adolescents: A manual for therapists* (pp. 111–119). Thousand Oaks, CA: Sage.

Espeland, P. (2001). *Knowing you, knowing me: The 1-sight way to understand yourself and others.* Minneapolis, MN: Free Spirit.

Kaufman, G., Raphael, L., & Epseland, P. (1999). *Stick up for yourself! Every kid's guide to personal power and positive self-esteem.* Minneapolis, MN: Free Spirit.

Kaufman, G., Raphael, L., & Epseland, P. (1999). *Stick up for yourself! In a jar.* Minneapolis, MN: Free Spirit.

Peterson, J. S. (1995). *Talk with teens about feelings, family, relationships, and the future.* Minneapolis, MN: Free Spirit.

Self-Harm/Suicide Prevention

For Parents

Videos and Audio Tapes

It's never too late: Stopping teen suicide. (2004). [Video]. New York: Insight Media.

For Counselors

General Resources

Bongar, B. (2001). *The suicidal patient: Clinical and legal standards of care* (2nd ed.). Washington, DC: American Psychological Association.

Fox, C., & Hawton, K. (2004). *Deliberate self-harm in adolescence*. Philadelphia: Jessica Kingsley.

Goldston, D. B. (2003). *Measuring suicidal behavior and risk in children and adolescents*. Washington, DC: American Psychological Association.

Kirk, W. G. (1993). *Adolescent suicide: A school-based approach to assessment and intervention*. Champaign, IL: Research Press.

Klott, J., & Jongsman, A. E. (2004). *The suicide and homicide risk assessment and prevention treatment planner*. Indianapolis, IN: Wiley.

McBrian, R. (1983). Are you thinking of killing yourself? Confronting suicidal thoughts. *School Counselor, 31,* 75–82.

Nelson, R., & Crawford, B. (1990). Suicide among elementary school-age children. *Elementary School Guidance and Counseling, 25,* 123–128.

Rittner, B., & Smyth, N. (1999). Time-limited cognitive-behavioral interventions with suicidal adolescents. *Social Work with Groups, 22*(3), 55–75.

Sattem, L. (1991). Suicide prevention in elementary schools. In A. Leenaars & S. Wenckstern (Eds.), *Suicide prevention in schools* (pp. 71–82). New York: Hemisphere.

Shneidman, E. S. (2001). *Comprehending suicide: Landmarks in 20th-century suicidology*. Washington, DC: American Psychological Association.

Smaby, M., Peterson, T., Bergmann, P., Bacig, K., & Swearingen, S. (1990). School-based community intervention: The school counselor as lead consultant for suicide prevention and intervention programs. *School Counselor, 37,* 370–377.

Stefanowski-Harding, S. (1990). Child suicide: A review of the literature and implications for school counselors. *School Counselor, 37,* 328–336.

Videos and Audio Tapes

Assessing suicide risk. (1997). [Video]. New York: Insight Media.

Cambridge Educational Production. (Producer). (2000). *Skin deep: Understanding self-injury* [Video]. Princeton, NJ: Films for the Humanities and Sciences.

Depression and suicidal behavior in adolescents. (1996). [Video]. New York: Insight Media.

Helping students in crisis. (2001). [Video]. New York: Insight Media.

Suicide: A guide for prevention. (2000). [Video]. New York: Insight Media.

Teenage suicide: The silent threat. (1999). [Video]. New York: Insight Media.

For Use in Group

General Resources

Muro, J. J., & Kottman, T. (1995). Crisis intervention: Working with suicidal children. In J. J. Muro & T. Kottman, *Guidance and counseling in the elementary and middle schools: A practical approach* (pp. 320–328). Madison, WI: Brown & Benchmark.

Nelson, R. E., & Galas, J. C. (1994). *The power to prevent suicide: A guide for teens helping teens*. Minneapolis, MN: Free Spirit.

Robertson, D., & Mathews, B. (1989). Preventing adolescent suicide with group counseling. *Journal for Specialists in Group Work, 14,* 34–39.

Schmidt, U., & Davidson, K. (2004). *Life after self-harm: A guide to the future.* New York: Brunner-Routledge.

Tierney, R., Ramsay, R., Tanney, B., & Long, W. (1991). Comprehensive school suicide prevention programs. In A. Leenaars & S. Wenckstern (Eds.), *Suicide prevention in schools* (pp. 83–96). New York: Hemisphere.

Vidal, J. A. (1986). Establishing a suicide prevention program. *National Association of Secondary School Principals Bulletin, 70,* 68–71.

White Kress, V. E., Gibson, D. M., & Reynolds, C. A. (2004). Adolescents who self-injure: Implications and strategies for school counselors. *Professional School Counselor, 7,* 195–201.

Videos and Audio Tapes

Cambridge Educational Production. (Producer). (2000). *Skin deep: Understanding self-injury* [Video]. Princeton, NJ: Films for the Humanities and Sciences.

Self-Esteem

For Parents

General Resources

Huebner, E. S. (1995). Best practices in assessment and intervention with children with low self-esteem. In A. Thomas & J. Grimes (Eds.), *Best practices in school psychology-III* (pp. 831–840). Washington, DC: National Association of School Psychologists.

Johnston, P. J. (2001). Help your child develop self-esteem. *Brown University Child and Adolescent Behavior Letter, 17,* 1–3.

Roehlkepartain, J. L. (2001). *Raising healthy children day by day: 366 readings for parents, teachers, and caregivers (birth to age 5).* Minneapolis, MN: Free Spirit.

For Counselors

General Resources

Akin, T. (1990). *The best self-esteem activities for the elementary grades.* Torrance, CA: Innerchoice.

Arnold, E., Estreicher, D., & Arnold, L. E. (1985). *Parent-child group therapy: Building self-esteem in a cognitive behavioral group.* Lanham, MD: Lexington Books.

Dunne, G. (1990). *IMPACT!: A self-esteem based skill-development program for secondary students.* Torrance, CA: Innerchoice.

Elbaum, B., & Vaughn, S. (2001). School-based interventions to enhance the self-concept of students with learning disabilities: A meta-analysis. *Elementary School Journal, 101,* 303–329.

Khalsa, S. S. (1996). *Group exercises for enhancing social skills & self-esteem.* Sarasota, FL: Professional Resource Press.

Social Skills

For Parents

General Resources

Borba, M. (2003). *No more misbehavin': 38 difficult behaviors and how to stop them.* San Francisco: Jossey-Bass.

Borba, M. (2004). *Don't give me that attitude: 24 rude, selfish, insensitive things kids do and how to stop them.* Indianapolis, IN: Wiley.

Christophersen, E. R., & Mortweet, S. L. (2003). *Parenting that works: Building skills that last a lifetime.* Washington, DC: American Psychological Association.

Vernon, A., & Al-Mabuk, R. H. (1995). *What growing up is all about: A parent's guide to child and adolescent development.* Champaign, IL: Research Press.

Videos and Audio Tapes

Teaching social competence video. (n.d.). [Video]. Champaign, IL: Research Press.

For Counselors

General Resources

Bear, G. T., Minke, K. M., Griffin, S. M., & Deemer, S. A. (2000). Self-concept. In G. T. Bear, K. M. Minke, & A. Thomas (Eds.), *Children's needs II: Development, problems and alternatives* (pp. 257–269). Bethesda, MD: National Association of School Psychologists.

Bursuk, W. D., & Asher, S. R. (1986). The relationship between social competence and achievement in elementary school children. *Journal of Child Clinical Psychology, 15,* 41–49.

Cartledge, G., & Milburn, J. F. (1996). *Cultural diversity and social skills instruction: Understanding ethnic and gender differences.* Champaign, IL: Research Press.

Elliot, S. N., & Gresham, F. M. (1993). Social skills interventions for children. *Behavior Modification, 17,* 287–313.

Gresham, F. M. (2002). Best practices in social skills training. In A. Thomas & J. Grimes (Eds.), *Best practices in school psychology IV* (pp. 1007–1028). Bethesda, MD: National Association of School Psychologists.

Husson, A. (2005). Character counts in elementary school. *ASCA School Counselor, 42,* 25.

Kennedy, J. H. (1990). Determinants of peer social status: Contributions of physical appearance, reputation, and behavior. *Journal of Youths and Adolescents, 19,* 233–244.

Luxmoore, N. (2000). *Listening to young people in school, youth work and counseling.* Philadelphia: Jessica Kingsley.

Mehaffey, J. I., & Sandberg, S. K. (1992). Conducting social skills training groups with elementary school children. *School Counselor, 40,* 61–67.

Ramsey, P. G. (1991). *Making friends in school: Promoting peer relationships in early childhood.* New York: Teachers College Press.

Shechtman, Z., & Bar-El, O. (1994). Group guidance and group counseling to foster social acceptability and self-esteem in adolescence. *Journal for Specialists in Group Work, 19,* 188–196.

Videos and Audio Tapes

Explosions: Biosocial development during adolescence. (2003). [Video]. New York: Insight Media.

For Use in Group

General Resources

Akos, P. (2000). Building empathic skills in elementary school children through group work. *Journal for Specialists in Group Work, 25*(2), 214–223.

Cain, B. (2001). *Double-dip feelings: Stories to help children understand emotions* (2nd ed.). Washington, DC: Magination Press.

Campbell, C. A., & Brigman, G. (2005). Closing the achievement gap: A structured approach to group counseling. *Journal for Specialists in Group Work, 30,* 67–82.

Foster, C. (1995). *Teenagers preparing for the real world.* Conyers, GA: Chad Foster.

Hanken, D., & Kennedy, J. (2000). *Getting to know you! A social skills curriculum.* Minneapolis, MN: Educational Media.

Herron, R. (1996). *Getting along with others: An activity book.* Boys Town, NE: Boys Town Press.

Katz, L. G., McClellan, D. E., Fuller, J. O., & Walz, G. R. (1995). *Building social competence in children: A practical handbook for counselors, psychologists, and teachers.* Austin, TX: Pro-Ed.

Mannix, D. (2002). *Social skills activities for secondary students with special needs.* Austin, TX: Pro-Ed.

Packer, A. J. (1997). *How rude! The teenagers' guide to good manners, proper behavior, and not grossing people out.* Minneapolis, MN: Free Spirit.

Palmer, P., & Froehner, M. A. (2000). *Teen esteem: A self-direction manual for young adults* (2nd ed.). Atascadero, CA: Impact.

Pearson, M. (2004). *Emotional healing and self-esteem: Inner-life skills of relaxation, visualization and mediation for children and adolescents.* Philadelphia: Jessica Kingsley.

Plummer, D. (2001). *Helping children to build self-esteem: A photocopiable activities book.* Philadelphia: Jessica Kingsley.

Plummer, D. (2004). *Helping adolescents and adults to build self-esteem: A photocopiable resource book.* Philadelphia: Jessica Kingsley.

Stallard, P. (2002). *Think good, feel good: A cognitive behavioral therapy workbook for children and young people.* Indianapolis, IN: Wiley.

Videos and Audio Tapes

Teens: That's another story. (2000). [Video]. Princeton, NJ: Films for the Humanities and Sciences.

Group Activities

Altman, H., & Firnesz, K. (1973). A role playing approach to influencing behavioral change and self-esteem. *Elementary School Guidance and Counseling, 7,* 276–281.

Baker, S. B. (2001). Coping-skills training for adolescents: Applying cognitive behavioral principles to psychoeducational groups. *Journal for Specialists in Group Work, 26,* 219–227.

Barrett, P. M., Webster, H. M., & Wallis, J. R. (1999). Adolescent self-esteem and cognitive skills training: A school-based intervention. *Journal of Child and Family Studies, 8,* 217–227.

Begun, R. (1996). *Ready-to-use social skills lessons and activities: For grades 4–6.* New York: Center for Applied Research in Education.

Begun, R. (2002). *Ready-to-use social skills lessons and activities: For grades 1–3.* New York: Center for Applied Research in Education.

Begun, R. (2002). *Ready-to-use social skills lessons and activities: For grades PreK-K.* New York: Center for Applied Research in Education.

Borba, M. (1996). *Esteem builders program: Complete kit.* Carson, CA: Jalmar.

Brigman, G., & Earley, B. (1991). Understanding yourself and others: Upper elementary, middle school. In G. Brigman & B. Earley (Eds.), *Group counseling for school counselors: A practical guide* (pp. 37–58). Portland, ME: J. Weston Walch.

Canfield, J., & Wells, H. (1994). *100 ways to enhance self-concept in the classroom* (2nd ed.). Boston: Allyn & Bacon.

Coombs-Richardson, R., & Evans, E. T. (1997). *Connecting with others: Lessons for teaching social and emotional competence (Grades 6–8).* Champaign, IL: Research Press.

Coombs-Richardson, R., & Meisgeier, C. H. (2001). *Connecting with others: Lessons for teaching social and emotional competence (Grades 9–12).* Champaign, IL: Research Press.

Curtis, K., & Whitman, W. (n.d.). *Hidden treasure of assets™: For children and adolescents* [Board Game]. Champaign, IL: Research Press.

Fox, R. G. (1990). Social skills training: Teaching troubled youths to be socially competent. In M. A. Krueger & N. W. Powell (Eds.), *Choices in caring: Contemporary approaches to child and youth care work* (pp. 39–64). Washington, DC: Child Welfare League of America.

Hazel, J. S., Schumaker, J. B., Sherman, J. A., & Sheldon, J. (n.d.). *ASSET: A social skills program for adolescents.* Champaign, IL: Research Press.

Hildreth, A. (1991). Self-concept: Elementary 4–5. In G. Brigman & B. Earley (Eds.), *Group counseling for school counselors: A practical guide* (pp. 93–106). Portland, ME: J. Weston Walch.

Khalsa, S. S. (1996). *Group exercises for enhancing social skills & self-esteem.* Sarasota, FL: Professional Resource Press.

Leber, N. (2002). *Easy activities for building social skills.* New York: Scholastic.

LeCroy, C. W. (1987). Teaching children social skills: A game format. *Social Work, 32,* 440–442.

McGinnis, E., & Goldstein, A. P. (1997). *Skillstreaming the elementary school child: New strategies and perspectives for teaching prosocial skills* (rev. ed.). Champaign, IL: Research Press.

Muldoon, J. A. (1998). *Helping teens cope: When personal problems become school problems.* Champaign, IL: Research Press.

O'Dell, F. L., Rak, C. F., Chermonte, J. P., & Hamlin, A. (1994). The boost club: A program for at-risk third and fourth grade students. *Journal for Specialists in Group Work, 19*(4), 227–231.

Schilling, D., & Dunne, G. (1992). *Understanding me: Activity sheets for building life skills and self-esteem in secondary students.* Torrance, CA: Innerchoice.

Schilling, D., & Palomares, S. (1997). *Social skills activities for the elementary grades.* Torrance, CA: Innerchoice.

Sheridan, S. M. (1995). *The tough kid social skills book.* Longmont, CO: Sopris West.

Snider, M., & Crate, P. (1991). Celebrating self: Middle school. In G. Brigman & B. Earley (Eds.), *Group counseling for school counselors: A practical guide* (pp. 107–119). Portland, ME: J. Weston Walch.

Stahler, S. (1991). Self-concept: Elementary K-1. In G. Brigman & B. Earley (Eds.), *Group counseling for school counselors: A practical guide* (pp.84–92). Portland, ME: J. Weston Walch.

Stickel, S. A. (1990). Using a multimodal social-skills group with kindergarten children. *Elementary School Guidance & Counseling, 24,* 281–288.

Vernon, A. (1998). *The PASSPORT program: A journey through emotional, social, cognitive, and self-development.* Champaign, IL: Research Press.

Waksman, S. (1988). *The Waksman social skills curriculum for adolescents* (3rd ed.). Austin, TX: Pro-Ed.

Walker, H. M., McConnell, S., Holmes, D., Todis, B., Walker, J., & Golden, N. (1988). *The ACCEPTS PROGRAM: A curriculum for children's effective peer and teacher skills.* Austin, TX: Pro-ed.

Substance Abuse

For Parents

General Resources

Ketcham, K., & Pace, N. A. (2003). *Teens under the influence: The truth about kids, alcohol, and other drugs—How to recognize the problem and what to do about it.* New York: Ballantine.

For Counselors

General Resources

American Academy of Pediatrics. (1995). Alcohol use and abuse: A pediatric concern. *American Academy of Pediatrics, 95,* 439–442.

Biglan, A., Brennan, P. A., Foster, S. L., Holder, H. D., & Associates. (2004). *Helping adolescents at risk: Prevention of multiple problem behaviors.* New York: Guilford.

Bleuer, J. (2005). *Counseling young students at risk.* Austin, TX: Pro-Ed.

Bukstein, O. (1996). Aggression, violence, and substance abuse in adolescents. *Adolescent Substance Abuse and Dual Disorders, 5,* 93–109.

Carrell, S. (2000). *Group exercises for adolescents: A manual for therapists* (2nd ed.). Thousand Oaks, CA: Sage.

Goldberg, R. (1997). *Drugs across the spectrum.* Englewood, CO: Morton.

Kulic, K. R., Horne, A. M., & Dagley, J. C. (2004). A comprehensive review of prevention groups for children and adolescents. *Group Dynamics, 8,* 139–151.

Leccese, M., & Waldron, H. (1994). Assessing adolescent substance use: A critique of current measurement instruments. *Journal of Substance Abuse Treatment, 11,* 553–563.

Martino, S., Grilo, C., & Fehon, D. (2000). Development of the drug abuse screen test for adolescents (DAST-A). *Addictive Behaviors, 25*(1), 57–70.

Monti, P. M., Colby, S. M., & O'Leary, T. A. (Eds.). (2001). *Adolescents, alcohol, and substance abuse: Reaching teens through brief interventions.* New York: Guilford.

Perkinson, R. R. (2004). *Treating alcoholism: Helping your clients find the road to recovery.* Indianapolis, IN: Wiley.

Sales, A. (Ed.). (2000). *Substance abuse and counseling.* Austin, TX: CAPS.

Sales, A. (2004). *Preventing substance abuse: A guide for school counselors.* Austin, TX: CAPS.

Segal, B., & Stewart, J. (1996). Substance use and abuse in adolescence: An overview. *Child Psychiatry and Human Development, 26*(4), 193–210.

Tapert, S., & Brown, S. (1999). Neuropsychological correlates of adolescent substance abuse: Four-year outcomes. *Journal of International Neuropsychological Society, 5,* 481–493.

Van Doren, D. (2003). The role of the secondary school counselor in substance abuse prevention. In C. T. Dollarhide & K. A. Saginak (Eds.*), School counseling in the secondary schools: A comprehensive process and program* (pp. 373–379). Boston: Pearson.

Walton, S. C. (2001). *Get the dope on dope: First Response guide to street drugs.* Calgary, Alberta, Canada: Burnand.

White, H., Brick, J., & Hansell, S. (1993). A longitudinal investigation of alcohol use and aggression in adolescence. *Journal of Studies on Alcohol, 11*(Suppl.), 62–77.

Videos and Audio Tapes

Alcohol and drug counseling skills. (2002). [Video]. New York: Insight Media.

For Use in Group

General Resources

Juhnke, G. A. (2004). Helping students with alcohol and other drug (AOD) problems: Cognitive-behavioral interventions for school counselors. In B. T. Erford (Ed.), *Professional school counseling: A handbook of theories, programs, and practices* (pp. 495–501). Austin, TX: CAPS.

Robinson-Kurpius, S. E. (2002). Prevention of substance abuse among teenagers. In J. Carlson & J. Lewis (Eds.), *Counseling the adolescent: Individual, family, and school interventions* (4th ed., pp. 121–134). Denver, CO: Love Publishing.

Wodarski, J. S., & Smyth, N. J. (1994). Adolescent substance abuse: A comprehensive approach to prevention and intervention. *Journal of Child and Adolescent Substance Abuse, 2,* 22–58.

Videos and Audio Tapes

Alternative to substance abuse. (2002). [Video]. New York: Insight Media.

Breaking the cycle of addiction and abuse: Donna's story. (2001). [Video]. Princeton, NJ: Films for the Humanities and Science.

Elgin, S. H. (1980). *The gentle art of saying no: Principles of assertiveness* [Filmstrip kit]. Pleasantville, NY: Sunburst Communications.

Martin, G. (Producer). (2001). *Meeting at the crossroads: Straight talk from real teens about substance abuse* [Video]. Champaign, IL: Research Press.

Social skills. (2002). [Video]. New York: Insight Media.

Straight talk: Alcohol and other drugs: Voices of addiction, voices of recovery. (1992). [Video]. Plainview, NY: The Bureau for At-Risk Youth.

Group Activities

Carrell, S. (2000). Living with chemicals. In S. Carrell, *Group exercises for adolescents: A manual for therapists* (pp. 171–180). Thousand Oaks, CA: Sage.

Dunne, G., Palomares, S., & Schuster, S. (1991). *Prime time: A comprehensive drug education program.* Torrance, CA: Innerchoice.

Drug prevention bingo. (n.d.). [Board Game]. Plainview, NY: The Bureau for At-Risk Youth.

Wagner, E., Brown, S., Monti, P., Myers, M., & Waldron, H. (1999). Innovations in adolescent substance abuse intervention. *Alcoholism, Clinical and Experimental Research, 23,* 236–249.

Teen Pregnancy/Parenting Skills

For Parents

General Resources

Gulley, B. (1982). *Parent education.* Carbondale: University of Illinois, Division of Human Development.

Schooler, J. E., & Baer, K. (2004). *Mom, Dad . . . I'm pregnant: When your daughter or son faces an unplanned pregnancy.* Colorado Springs, CO: Navpress.

For Counselors

General Resources

Bradley, L. J., Jarcow, E., & Robinson, B. (1999). *All about sex: The school counselor's guide to handling tough adolescent problems.* Thousand Oaks, CA: Corwin.

Furstenberg, F. F. (1976). *Unplanned parenthood: The social consequences of teenage child-bearing.* New York: Free Press.

Hardy, J. B., & Zabin, L. S. (1991). *Adolescent pregnancy in an urban environment: Issues, programs, and evaluations.* Washington, DC: Urban Institute Press.

Jones, D. J., & Battle, S. F. (1990). *Teenage pregnancy: Developing strategies for change in the twenty-first century.* New Brunswick, NJ: Transaction Books.

Kiselica, M .S., & Pfaller, J. (1993). Helping teenage parents: The independent and collaborative roles of counselor educators and school counselors. *Journal of Counseling and Development, 72,* 42–48.

Mathes, P. G. (1993). *Teen pregnancy and parenting handbook: Discussion guide.* Champaign, IL: Research Press.

Musick, J. S. (1993). *Young, poor, and pregnant: The psychology of teenage motherhood.* New Haven, CT: Yale University Press.

Romer, D. (Ed.). (2003). *Reducing adolescent risk: Toward an integrated approach.* Thousand Oaks, CA: Sage.

For Use in Group

General Resources

Arther, S., & Bergman, P. (1996). *Surviving teen pregnancy: Your choices, dreams, and decisions* (rev. ed.). Buena Park, CA: Morning Glory Press.

Barnes, N. D., & Harrod, S. E. (1993). Teen pregnancy prevention: A rural model using school and community collaboration. *School Counselor, 41,* 137–140.

Basso, M. J. (2003). *The underground guide to teenage sexuality: An essential handbook for today's teens and parents* (2nd ed.). Minneapolis, MN: Fairview Press.

Bell, R. (1998). *Changing bodies, changing lives: A book for teens on sex and relationships* (3rd ed.). New York: Three Rivers Press.

Carrera, M. A. (1992). Involving adolescent males in pregnancy and STD prevention programs. *Adolescent Medicine: State of the Art Reviews, 3,* 1–13.

Davis, D. (2004). *You look too young to be a mom: Teen mothers speak out on love, learning, and success.* East Rutherford, NJ: Perigee.

Kiselica, M. S., Rotzien, A., & Doms, J. (1994). Preparing teenage fathers for parenthood: A group psychoeducational approach. *Journal for Specialists in Group Work, 19,* 83–94.

Lindsay, J. W. (1998). *Your baby's first year: A guide for teenage parents* (teens parenting series) (rev. ed.). Buena Park, CA: Morning Glory Press.

Lindsay, J. W., & Brunelli, J. (2004). *Your pregnancy and newborn journey: A guide for pregnant teens* (teen pregnancy and parenting series) (3rd ed.). Buena Park, CA: Morning Glory Press.

Mathes, P. G., & Irby, B. J. (1994). *Teen pregnancy and parenting handbook.* Champaign, IL: Research Press.

Williams-Wheeler, D. (2004). *The unplanned pregnancy book for teens and college students.* Virginia Beach, VA: Sparkledoll Productions.

Videos and Audio Tapes

Baby talk: The video guide for new parents. (2000). [Video]. Poly Health Media.

Baby to be: The video guide to pregnancy. (2002). [Video]. Poly Health Media.

Discipline from birth to three series. (2001). [Video]. Buena Park, CA: Morning Glory Press.

Planned Parenthood Association of Cincinnati. (Producer). (1987). *Fathers too soon?* [Motion picture]. Cincinnati: Producer.

Teen files: The truth about sex. (1999). [Motion picture]. Plainview, NY: The Bureau for At-Risk Youth.

Wagonseller, B. R. (Producer). (n.d.). *The practical parenting series: Teenage pregnancy.* [Motion picture]. Champaign, IL: Research Press.

Your baby's first year series. (n.d.). [Motion picture]. Buena Park, CA: Morning Glory Press.

Group Activities

Grimes, M. B. (1991). Pregnancy education/support group: Middle school, high school. In G. Brigman & B. Earley (Eds.), *Group counseling for school counselors: A practical guide* (pp. 231–244). Portland, ME: J. Weston Walch.

Lindsay, J. W., & Enright, S. G. (1997). *Books, babies and school-age parents: How to teach pregnant and parenting teens to succeed.* Buena Park, CA: Morning Glory Press.

Smallwood, D. (2000). *Two-in-one pregnancy bingo* [Board Game]. Buena Park, CA: Morning Glory Press.

APPENDIX H

Example of Group Interest Survey Form

P lace a check next to any and all topics for group meetings in which you and/or other students might be interested.

	Career exploration		Multicultural issues
	Career decision making		Sexual harassment
	Computer resources related to careers		Career or job surveys
	Making friends		Scholarships
	Study and test-taking skills		College selection
	Social skills		SAT interpretation
	Just to talk		Jobs & job skills
	Death of someone at school		Eating disorders
	Death (friend, relative)		Bullying
	Transition to middle/high school		Divorce
	Friend problems		Relaxation skills
	Felt sad/down		Getting along with teachers

	Conflict resolution		Anger management
	Transition/adjustment to new school		Worried about a friend
	Dating, relationships, and sex		Self-esteem
	Alcohol/drugs/cigarettes		Family violence/abuse
	Family problems		Body image
	Stress management		Anger management skills
	Learning to make better decisions		Assertiveness
	Other, please specify:		

Now tell us, *How likely are you* to attend these groups? How likely is it that *other students* will attend these groups? And finally, give *reasons* why you might or might not want to meet on these topics. (For example, you might want to meet for a topic but don't think others will, or you might not be interested but you think your best friend needs a group on this topic.)

1 = No way!

2 = Maybe or somewhat likely

3 = Set it up and I am there

Topic	Me	Others	Reasons
Example: Relationships	*1*	*2*	*My friend needs more friends but is shy.*

Example of an Informational Sheet for Parents About Psychoeducational Groups

Purpose of the Group

This section should be tailored to the specific type of psychoeducational group being led. Include a brief paragraph on the problem or focus of the group (e.g., self-esteem, social skills, body image) and then another brief paragraph on how this group is typically helpful for children and adolescents.

The following two paragraphs are examples of what appears in an informational sheet for parents about children-of-divorce groups.

Divorce has long-term implications for children as well as their parents. The National Center for Health estimates that one million divorces are granted each year in the United States. One million children experience the divorce of their parents each year. Parental divorce is the issue of most concern for elementary school children. Children of divorce need a place to receive support, talk about their experiences of the divorce, and realize that they are not alone in these experiences or feelings. This group will be a psychoeducational group that focuses on supporting children as they experience a divorce as well as promoting new skills to cope with the feelings and experiences related to the divorce.

We have formed this group for a couple of reasons. The first is that people, particularly children, are often uncomfortable talking about family stresses. This group will encourage them to talk about it and give them a safe place to do so. Second, children tend to talk to each other better than they do to adults, and so this will be a place for your child to express some of his or her thoughts and feelings about the divorce with other children who are having similar experiences. Hopefully, your child will find others that he or she can talk with long after the group ends. Because all children who are experiencing a divorce are encouraged to join, the groups are not designed just for those who are having problems.

What Is a Psychoeducational Group?

Psychoeducational groups emphasize the usefulness of a group setting to help children to not feel isolated, to connect with and learn from others, and to normalize some of their experiences. Psychoeducational groups, in contrast to counseling and therapy groups, focus specifically on the teaching of skills that may be helpful in difficult situations, such as communication skills, assertiveness, anger management, and expression of feeling. Problem solving, communication skills, role-playing, and conflict resolution will be emphasized.

The Group Leaders

The group leaders are responsible for using their knowledge of group dynamics to promote and facilitate individual and group growth. They are also responsible for creating an atmosphere of trust and support through specific ground rules, discussions of confidentiality, and their direction of each session. The group leaders are trained counselors who have a good understanding of the issues that children and adolescents may be dealing with and a series of interventions that may be helpful to these children.

Example of a Group Screening Interview Outline

Hello _____. I'm _____, a counselor here at _____. What I'd like to do today is share some basic information related to the group, so that you can get a sense of what the group is about and so that you can begin to think about a goal for the group.

The group that we are running is a psychoeducational group. This means that many of the activities are designed to teach participants skills or behaviors that they can use in their lives. This is not a counseling group, so the focus will not be big problems and/or deep personality change. This is an important distinction. Do you have any questions about that?

The goals of this group are: 1. _____, 2. _____, 3. _____. Groups can be beneficial in this process. They allow people to learn ideas from others, meet others who have similar concerns, and practice new behaviors.

Now let's go over some administrative issues.

- _____ and I will be the co-leaders of this group. _____ is a counselor at _____.
- There will be 6 to 8 participants in the group as well.
- Our group will meet for _____ sessions. Each session will last for _____ minutes.

I'd like to go over some of the ground rules for our group.

- In order for the group to operate effectively, we must be able to share personal things, but you may choose what you share. You won't be forced to share something you consider private.
- It is important to participate in all activities.
- Another important ground rule is that there is no fighting or hurting other members, either physically or emotionally. This is so that everyone will feel safe in the group.
- Also, each group member is responsible for creating and working toward his or her own goal or goals. This includes practicing skills learned in group in other places.
- Confidentiality is a very important aspect of any group. Nothing said or done in group is talked about outside the group. Other group members will also have this expectation. It is important to note, though, that there are limits to confidentiality. These relate to situations involving injury to self or others, abuse, or when required by the courts. Under these circumstances, information could be shared.
- You will be asked to share reactions to activities that we do.
- One last important note. Everyone needs to be on time for the group. Otherwise, the activities will become disrupted.

Questions to Ask to Assess Appropriateness for Group

1. Do you have any questions about what I've already told you? Is there anything else that you'd like to know about the group or the leaders?

2. Can you tell me some examples of _____?

3. Tell me some times when you have been able to _____. What happened then?

4. Are you willing to talk about some of these things with other students who might be having the same kinds of problems?

5. Here's an important question. What would you most like to work on in group? What would you change right now if you could? In other words, what goals are you most interested in fulfilling?

6. Are you willing to work on making progress toward your goals?

7. Do you think the group will help you meet your goals?

8. How do you work with others?

9. What would you bring to the group?

10. Can you keep what others say confidential? Can you follow the other rules of the group?

11. Do you have any other questions or concerns relating to anything we've said or to the questionnaires you've completed?

APPENDIX K

Example of a Preparation Session Outline

1. Introduce (or reintroduce) yourself as the group leader

Explain that the preparation session occurs after students have been selected to participate in the group, but prior to the first session. It allows potential group members to gain a better understanding of how the group will work, as well as gives them an opportunity to practice some of the behaviors that will be expected. Some may elect not to participate in group after the preparation session. It also allows group leaders to assess members' participation and interactions in group, and with each other. Preparation sessions are often used to give potential group members a preview of how groups work and to make sure that this group would be a good fit for them.

People learn differently, so a preparation session has been designed that includes three different kinds of learning. Hopefully, at least one will match your style of learning: cognitive, vicarious, and experiential. The cognitive part consists of a handout that describes how groups typically work and how to get the most out of it. Please take about 5 minutes and read the handout. You'll have a chance to ask questions after you have read.

Note: If there are two or more group members participating in the preparation session, ask them to introduce themselves with first names only. Suggest that it will be a little more comfortable if we at least know each other's first names. Remind them, however, that confidentiality is essential and that even if you decide not to join the group, please don't disclose who attended this session.

2. Cognitive Component (typically 10 minutes)

a. Pass out Handout #1, "What Are Psychoeducational Groups?" Say: "The goal of this session is to provide a chance to gain information about how groups work as well as to observe and practice behaviors that will be used in group." Ask each group member to read the handout. Ask if there are any questions.

This handout covers a wide range of topics such as the value and goals of psychoeducational groups, the role of the group leader(s), typical things that happen in group, common stumbling blocks, and how to get the most out of their group experience.

Handout 1   What Are Psychoeducational Groups?

Psychoeducational groups provide individuals with the opportunity to learn about themselves and how they relate to others. They allow members to learn effective communication, interpersonal skills, and problem-solving strategies. A psychoeducational group is a special type of group experience in which members learn skills that will enable them to better handle life situations while sharing feelings and thoughts with other members. It provides them with meaningful interactions and a sense of belonging. It also gives members an opportunity to share, cooperate, learn, and practice new skills.

Goals of All Psychoeducational Groups

- Teach and practice new skills.
- Practice and apply skills in and outside of group.
- Use effective communication skills, such as assertiveness, honest sharing of feelings and thoughts, and empathic listening.
- Use problem-solving skills, such as listing potential solutions, advantages and disadvantages of these, and requesting feedback from other members.
- Share emotions, including positive and negative feelings.
- Give feedback to other members when requested.
- Request feedback about thoughts, behaviors, and situations when needed for problem solving and to develop coping strategies and plans for change.
- Gain support and show support for others in similar situations.

The Value of Psychoeducational Groups

In everyday life, it is difficult to get useful and accurate information about how we present ourselves and what impressions others form about us. People rarely take time to observe others carefully, and there seems to be a social taboo against giving others honest feedback. Groups allow individuals to observe and share impressions in honest, genuine, and caring ways. Such feedback helps group members to increase their self-knowledge.

Groups also help reduce feelings of alienation and loneliness. Members quickly discover that others have similar problems and concerns. One's own motivation for growth and improvement is enhanced by seeing others struggle with and solve their problems. The many strengths of each individual group member serve as a model for other group members.

Groups provide an arena for learning. Members brainstorm ideas and use problem-solving techniques when tough issues arise. They learn new behaviors and are able to try them out within the safety of the group through role-plays. Other members provide support and constructive feedback, so success with these new behaviors outside the group becomes more likely.

(Continued)

(Continued)

The Group Leaders

The group leaders are responsible for using their knowledge of individual and group dynamics to promote and facilitate individual and group growth. Their activities include helping the group understand what is happening in the group, making sure each member has the opportunity to be heard, protecting members from attack, establishing ground rules and norms, facilitating expression of honest feelings and thoughts, and clarifying communications within the group. The group leaders are also responsible for creating an atmosphere of trust, support, and challenge within the group.

Expectations for Group Members

The way to gain the maximum benefit from the group experience is to be honest and direct about your immediate feelings, thoughts, and opinions, especially toward the other members and leaders. As the group develops trust, hopefully you will feel more confident about revealing personal aspects of yourself. You will not be forced to reveal until you are ready and willing. Groups do, however, provide a setting and the opportunity for risk taking and experimenting with new behaviors. Members are also encouraged and expected to practice new behaviors in their everyday lives in order to facilitate maximum transfer and generalization of these behaviors in the outside world.

When entering a group, members are typically asked to identify specific changes they would like to work on during the group experience. Sharing of these goals with the other group members will help them provide feedback on your progress and actively support your efforts to change.

Much like the group leaders, members are expected to support, challenge, and encourage each other; accept and develop respect for each other's uniqueness; listen empathically; provide honest feedback; and, in general, create a safe atmosphere for growth and positive change in the group.

In summary, the amount of benefit you receive from this experience will depend on the extent to which you actively participate.

Typical Group Leader and Member Behaviors and Interventions*

Self-Disclosure: Sharing personal feelings, beliefs, and behaviors that are not usually shared with others. The member may fear being evaluated negatively by others, being embarrassed, or feeling vulnerable. Self-disclosure helps group members get to know each other better and feel connected to each other.

Example: "I'm here in this group because I want to learn how to make and keep friends."

Example: "I am feeling really sad right now because of the things that others have shared."

Example: "When I am in a social situation, I feel scared that everyone is judging me because I am overweight."

Example: "Often when I start to think about how my family used to be, I get very sad and lonely. I feel like nobody understands me."

Example: "I get so angry at my parents when they stick me in the middle. Sometimes, I just want to break something to let the anger out."

Example: "When I have a fight with my boyfriend, he sometimes calls me really awful names or pushes me around."

Example: "When I start getting close to someone, I'm frightened by my feelings that they will leave me or will embarrass me."

Giving Feedback: Relating how one member of the group comes across to another member, offering a point of view or an opinion about what was said, or sharing a feeling in response to the discussion.

Example: "I don't like it when you say that you're stupid."

Example: "I am proud of you for telling your parents that you don't want to be a messenger for them. You really did a good job of using your assertive communication skills."

Example: "I feel very close to you now that you've opened up and shown me a different side of you."

Example: "You seem to be afraid that you won't be able to be assertive to your boyfriend if he pressures you to have sex."

Example: "You seemed angry at me when I said that you should forget about getting your parents back together."

Challenging: Inviting a member to examine what he or she is saying or doing in relation to others in the group, or to explore a discrepancy between words and actions—a caring challenge.

Example: "You are complimenting me, but your body language seems like you are angry at me."

Example: "You say when your dad left it made you angry, but you're laughing about it."

Example: "You keep saying that you want to try out new behaviors, but everything that the group suggests, you say no to."

Example: "Let's all think for a minute about what has been happening today and one thing you want to do differently to make things so we can work together more effectively."

Example: "As homework, I would like each of you to notice and identify one obstacle that prevents you from honestly expressing your feelings to your friends."

Role-Playing: Using hypothetical situations within the safety of the group experience to practice new skills and allow for constructive feedback.

Example: "Now that we have just finished learning about I statements, I want Mary to tell her parents how she feels when they make her the messenger. John and Sally will act as Mary's parents."

Example: "Let's practice some of the skills we just displayed. Who wants to share a situation? Who wants to model a new strategy?

Using I-Statements: Expressing one's feelings or beliefs in such a way as to emphasize the role of the self rather than other, "owning" the feelings rather than blaming the other person (in contrast to "you make me feel sad or you make me so angry").

Example: "I feel defensive when I get feedback from other members."

Example: "I'm feeling really sad after hearing that story."

(Continued)

(Continued)

Brainstorming:

Example: The leader will say, "Let's brainstorm ways to help Lisa reach her goal of feeling more comfortable talking to new people."

Here and Now: Talking about feelings and thoughts related to current group interaction and experiences among members (as opposed to discussing events and people outside the group).

Example: "It seems that everyone is having a hard time participating today. What's going on?"

Example: "We seem to keep avoiding this topic of how to manage conflict. Every time we start to discuss it, we go off on a tangent. What makes it so hard to talk about it? What might happen if we do?"

Example: "The group did a great job today of working together, taking risks, and giving each other feedback. How did we do it? What made it work?"

Example: "I am very upset by what you just said, John. My feelings are really hurt. Can we talk about it?"

How to Get the Most From a Group Experience

1. Examine and decide on your level of commitment. If you are not willing to invest yourself, you probably will not gain much from the experience. Decide for yourself what your goals are and how you can best accomplish them.

2. Clarify your personal goals. Most members come to the group with general and abstract goals. Clarify your goals within concrete terms. Consider making a specific contract—a clear statement concerning the behavior you want to change and the steps you are willing to take to bring about this change. For example, an abstract goal is, "I want to feel better about myself." A concrete goal is, "I would like to practice more assertive behavior when I'm with people I don't know well."

3. Use the group to practice new behaviors. The group can be a means to help you make changes you desire in your everyday life. Allow the other members to help you practice social and problem-solving skills.

4. Become actively involved. You'll get far more out of the group if you take the initiative rather than remain a passive observer. Don't postpone the risk taking involved in letting others know you. Decide for yourself what you will share with others. In making that decision, however, remember that the others in your group can help you and care for you only when they know who you are.

5. Realize your contribution is vital in creating trust in the group. You don't have to reveal your innermost feelings or some personally sensitive experience. Being open means that you reveal to the group persistent feelings that you have while participating. It is important that everyone participate for trust to develop.

6. Be willing to discover positive as well as negative sides of yourself. If you keep yourself hidden for fear that others will see your weaknesses, you also keep others from seeing your strengths, talents, wit, and compassion. See the group as a vehicle for growth.

7. Keep in mind that change takes time and effort. If you expect to see instant changes as a result of your participation in the group, you are not being realistic. Change is often slow and subtle and is a never-ending process. Concentrate on the process of change rather than striving for a "finished product."

8. Think of ways of applying what you are learning in the group to your everyday life. The group can provide you with new insights and opportunities for practice, but the ultimate test of the value of the experience is the degree to which your work applies to your life outside of the group.

---

*Group leaders may choose to emphasize three or four of these listed behaviors for consistency across the preparation session: in the handout, in the discussion of the video, and in the experiential practice role-plays. Group leaders may also want to choose two or three examples under a behavior, or adapt some of the examples to be specific to the psychoeducational group they are leading.

Note: Keep the questions focused on the information in the handout. Questions about specifics on ground rules such as confidentiality will be discussed in more detail when the group begins, in the first session.

3. Vicarious Component (typically 15 minutes)

a. Show a 10-minute clip of a group session (e.g., Corey & Corey, 1999; Smead, 1996) that includes the working and processing stages.

b. Tell the group: "Some people learn vicariously—by watching—so we have a videotape of a simulated group, one where the group members have gotten to know and trust each other, and they are taking some risks to learn new information about themselves. Groups typically follow a developmental sequence. This group has just moved into the working stage, which is characterized by increased member self-disclosure, the expression of both positive and negative feelings, active listening, resistance to deeper self-exploration, and caring confrontation. The leader's role at this stage of the group development is that of a facilitator, encouraging members to relate to each other honestly and directly and to share responsibility for leadership.

As you watch the video, look for examples of these and other group dynamics. There will be a brief discussion afterward to identify key behaviors and interventions."

c. Show the video.

d. Process reactions to the video:

- How was this group session similar to what you expected a group session to be like? How was it different?
- Ask specific questions about what they saw in the video related to the behaviors they will be practicing (i.e., behaviors discussed in the handout and vignettes).
  a. What examples of *self-disclosure* did you observe? What were the group members' reactions?
  b. What examples of *challenging* did you observe? What were the group members' reactions?
  c. What examples of giving and receiving *positive* and *negative feedback* did you see?

  POSITIVE FEEDBACK:

  _____

  _____

  NEGATIVE FEEDBACK:

  _____

  _____

  What were the members' reactions?

  TO POSITIVE FEEDBACK:

  _____

  _____

  TO NEGATIVE FEEDBACK:

  _____

  _____

  d. What examples of role-playing did you observe? What were the members' reactions?
  e. What did the *group leader* do that facilitated these behaviors?

4. Experiential Behavioral Practice

a. Tell the group: "This is the part where you get to practice and experience some of what happens in groups. In the next 10 to 15 minutes, you will be practicing a series of group skills to assist you in becoming more familiar with and comfortable using self-disclosure, challenging, and giving and receiving positive feedback (and other behaviors that have been described in the handout or identified in the video). For each behavior, one dyad will model it, all of you will have a chance to role-play the behavior, and then your partner will have a chance to respond."

b. Distribute the exercises (Handout #2)

Handout 2   Practice Role-Play of Behaviors and Skills in Psychoeducational Groups*

Group members should work in dyads for this activity. They should decide prior to starting who is Person #1 and who is Person #2. They stay Person #1 and Person #2 throughout each vignette so that they get a chance to practice each new behavior and also a chance to respond to each new behavior.

Vignette #1: Self-Disclosure

A. *Person #1:* You have just finished the opening activity at the first group session. You are feeling nervous and are not sure of how to react to the group. The group leader asks every member to share what he or she was thinking and feeling during the opening activity. Every member has shared and now it is your turn. (Use "I" statements.)

Person #2: Respond to Person #1's disclosure.

B. *Person #2:* You have just finished drawing a picture of your family as it really is, and a picture of how you would like your family to be. The leader has asked each individual to briefly share his or her picture. The leader then asks how you felt when your parents got divorced, and how you feel now. (Hint: Use "I" statements.)

Person #1: Respond to Person #2's disclosure.

Vignette #2: Reluctance

A. *Person #1:* When individuals are in an uncomfortable situation, they will often resist sharing their thoughts and feelings. Many people resist sharing because their thoughts and feelings are painful. What would you do if you felt that you were beginning to resist sharing in group? Role-play how you would resist (i.e., behaviors, comments, body language).

Person #2: Reflect what behaviors Person #1 was showing.

B. *Person #2:* Every week, when the leader encourages the group members to practice their new skills outside of group, Person #2 rolls her eyes. Also, she never shares when others talk about how they applied what they had learned the week before through their homework.

Person #1: Respond to Person #2's behavior.

Other Options for Reluctance

C. *Person #2:* A typical resistant behavior in groups is giving advice—telling others what they should or should not do or feel. A group member has just disclosed that her parents' fighting makes her scared, and she does not think that she could tell them how she feels. Person #2 has just told the member that if her parents were fighting, she would not hide out in her bedroom, she would "give them a piece of (her) mind," and that the member has to stop being so scared and just stand up to her parents.

Person #1: Respond to Person #2's advice giving.

D. *Person #1:* Every week, when the leader encourages the group members to practice their new skills outside of group, Person #1 rolls her eyes. Also, she never shares when others talk about how they applied what they had learned the week before through their homework.

Person #2: Respond to Person #1's behavior.

(Continued)

(Continued)

Vignette #3: Challenging

A. *Person #1:* A group member has been relatively quiet and has opted to pass when the others were sharing drawings of their "real" and "ideal" families. Although she hasn't spoken, she has been listening attentively and appears interested in the discussion. You are curious how she is feeling about her participation and if she wants to become involved. Challenge her.

Person #2: Respond to Person #1's challenge.

B. *Person #2:* Another member of the group has been saying since the beginning of group that her relationship with her parents is great and she does not need to learn any communication skills. She has not shared anything personal since group began, but you often observe her looking distracted, disgusted, and angry, and she usually sits with her chair slightly outside the circle, distancing herself from others. You have just observed her displaying another disgusted look in reaction to something you shared in the group. You want to know what she is thinking/feeling. Confront her. (Hint: Identify specific behaviors and use "I" statements.)

Person #1: Respond to Person #2's confrontation.

Vignette #4: Feedback

A. *Person #1:* You have now been interacting with Person #2 for several minutes. Please share with Person #2 your first impressions of him or her.

Person #2: Respond to Person #1's feedback about you.

B. *Person #2:* Give Person #1 an example of a positive communication skill you have noticed him or her use and an example of a negative one.

Person #1: Respond to Person #2's feedback about you.

Vignette #5: Brainstorming

A. *Person #1:* The leader has asked group members to brainstorm ways to feel better about themselves. Think of three things that make you feel good (e.g., go outside, listen to music) and share them.

Person #2: Respond to this sharing.

Vignette #6: Using I-Statements

A. *Person #1:* You are sitting in group and listening. You notice your friend has a rubber band in his hand and is stretching it back and pointing it around the room. The leaders do not notice. Tell your friend what you think about his action. (Hint: Tell your friend why this is not a good idea, and tell him what you want him to do. Use "I" statements.)

Person #2: Respond to Person #1's comment to you.

B. *Person #2:* Your friend is not following one of the group rules you helped create. Tell your friend what rule he broke, and what he could do instead. (Hint: Use "I" statements, and tell him why his behavior was against the rules.)

Person #1: Respond to Person #2's feedback.

Vignette #7: Respectful Participation

A. *Person #1:* You want to say what is on your mind, but your friend is talking. Join the discussion without interrupting your friend.

   Person #2: Respond to your friend's attempt to join in the discussion.

B. *Person #2:* Your friend interrupted you while you were talking to the group. Tell your friend a more appropriate way to join in the discussion.

   Person #1: Respond to your friend.

Vignette #8: Cooperation

A. *Person #1:* You are doing a teamwork activity in group. You want your friend to do part of the activity for your team. Try to get him to do it.

   Person #2: Respond to Person #1.

B. *Person #2:* Your friend asked you to do something for a teamwork activity that you do not wish to do. Let him know.

   Person #1: Let your friend know how you felt when he refused.

---

*Group leaders may choose to emphasize three or four of the behaviors listed for consistency across the preparation session: in the handout, in the discussion of the video, and in the experiential practice role-plays. Group leaders may also want to adapt the vignettes to be specific to the psychoeducational group they are leading.

c. Pair up group members. If there is an odd number of members, use one triad or one group leader can role-play with one group member (choose that member carefully to facilitate cohesion and/or trust). Have the group members count off as 1 or 2 and remind them that if they are Person #1, they are always Person #1 and if they are Person #2, they are always Person #2. This allows them to practice new skills and also how to respond to someone using that skill.

d. Ask one dyad to take a risk and be first to model the behaviors in **Vignette 1A.** One dyad will read and then role-play a vignette for each of the four behaviors highlighted, so really, everyone will have a chance to model skills for the group. Or, you and your co-leader could model the first one if that seems to work better.

e. Critique the exchange. If the member performs the skill correctly, provide positive reinforcement about the member's accurate delivery and note the (hopefully) appropriate response it generated from the receiver.

   If the person does not portray the skill accurately, encourage him or her for the effort, explain why he or she did not perform the skill appropriately, demonstrate the accurate portrayal of the skill, then have the member repeat the effort until the skill is mastered. Also note the reaction of the receiver to the appropriate and inappropriate demonstrations of the skill.

If you and your co-leader perform the role-play, ask the group members to give you feedback, both positive and constructive, related to what you did.

f. Have remaining dyads practice Vignette 1A.

g. After about 3 minutes, with group leaders circulating and giving feedback (positive and corrective where needed), ask all pairs to practice Vignette 1B. Remind them that Person #1 is still Person #1 and Person #2 is still Person #2, so this time Person #2 gets to practice self-disclosing.

h. Ask another dyad to model for the group the next skill in Vignette 2A.

i. Critique the exchange.

j. Have remaining dyads practice Vignette 2A.

k. After about 2 minutes, with group leaders circulating and giving feedback (positive and corrective where needed), ask the pairs to practice Vignette 2B. Remind them that Person #1 is still Person #1 and Person #2 is still Person #2, so this time Person #2 gets to practice the new skill.

Continue until all skills have been practiced by both partners.

At the end, thank all group members for coming and remind them of the status of participation. (If they are planning on being in the group, they should come at this time; if they are not sure or do not want to participate, they should schedule a meeting with you, etc. Be specific.)

Example of a Parent and Group Member Consent Form for Psychoeducational Groups

This is to certify that I, _____, agree to allow my child, _____, to participate in a psychoeducational group titled _____, under the leadership of _____.

I understand that my child will attend a small group experience with the goals of*:
1. _____, 2. _____, 3. _____.
Topics will include self-esteem, communication skills, problem solving, _____, _____, and _____.**

I understand that any information that I and my child provide will remain confidential except as discussed below.

I understand that if my child discloses that a minor is being abused or neglected in any way, the group facilitator and/or principal investigators are required by law to report this information to Child Protective Services and/or law enforcement agencies, even without my permission to do so.

I have been given the opportunity to ask any questions that I have. I am aware that if I have any more questions, I may contact _____ at _____.

_____

Parent's Signature   Date

_____

Parent's Signature   Date

_____

Group Member's Signature   Date

_____

* Add group goals.
** Add specific topics related to group goals.

APPENDIX M

Group-Related Measures

Readiness for Group Assessment

Date: _____   Name: _____

Directions: Check one of the five statements in each of the following categories that best described the behavior of the group member and the focus of the group leader.

I. AMOUNT OF COMMUNICATION (Participation)

_____ 0. None, silence, total withdrawal.

_____ 1. Minimum "yes" and "no" answers, pays some attention.

_____ 2. Somewhat more talkative.

_____ 3. Usually has something to say, readily responsive.

_____ 4. Always talking.

II. QUALITY OF RELATEDNESS AND COMMUNICATION

_____ 0. Not listening to group leader.

_____ 1. Listening, but not always hearing what leader is saying.

_____ 2. Reacts to group leaders, not always on topic.

_____ 3. Initiates topics, mostly relevant to group goals.

_____ 4. Expresses self well, very perceptive, able to relate both interpersonally and intrapersonally.

Author's Note: From Kivlighan & Goldfine (1991). Critical Incidents in Group Work. *Journal of Counseling Psychology.* Reprinted with permission.

III. CAPACITY FOR CHANGE

_____ 0. Passive, no involvement, more disturbed, participation mostly defensive.

_____ 1. No indication of apparent change, guarded talk, resistive, poor motivation for change.

_____ 2. Some slight improvement, interested in discussions, beginning to reach out to others.

_____ 3. Seems to be changing, grasps ideas, more interest in transferential involvement.

_____ 4. Making good use of therapy, gaining some insight, apparent desire to change.

IV. AMOUNT OF INTERVIEWER VERBAL ACTIVITY

_____ 0. Talking most of the time.

_____ 1. Talks more than client, but client expresses him/herself.

_____ 2. Equal participation by client/interviewer.

_____ 3. Interviewer speaks less than client.

_____ 4. Interviewer mostly listening, almost never speaks.

V. GROUP MEMBER WILLINGNESS TO DISCUSS PROBLEMS OPENLY

_____ 0. States has no problems to work on.

_____ 1. States has few problems with people; doesn't need help with them.

_____ 2. States has some problems to work on but expresses major concern about discussing them in group.

_____ 3. States has some problems to work on but expresses some concern about discussing them in group.

_____ 4. States has some problems to work on but expresses little or no concern about discussing them in group.

VI. GROUP MEMBER STATED COMMITMENT TO CHANGE

_____ 0. Not willing to make changes.

_____ 1. Hesitant to change.

_____ 2. Willing to examine behavior but some hesitation.

_____ 3. Some commitment to change.

_____ 4. A great deal of commitment to change.

VII. GROUP MEMBER IDENTIFICATION OF GOALS

_____ 0. Not willing to identify a goal.

_____ 1. Hesitant to identify a goal.

_____ 2. With some help was able to identify a goal.

_____ 3. Identified a goal; with some help, made it very realistic, interpersonal, and/or here-and-now focused.

_____ 4. Clearly identified a goal that was realistic, interpersonal, and/or here-and-now focused.

VIII. SPECIFICITY OF GOALS

_____ 0. No goals.

_____ 1. One vague goal.

_____ 2. Several goals but vague.

_____ 3. One goal that was realistic, interpersonal, and/or here-and-now focused.

_____ 4. Two or more goals that were realistic, interpersonal, and/or here-and-now focused.

IX. POTENTIAL FOR CONNECTION WITH OTHER GROUP MEMBERS

_____ 0. No one in the group with whom he or she would connect.

_____ 1. Possibly one member.

_____ 2. At least one or two members.

_____ 3. Probably three or four members.

_____ 4. Most or all group members.

Names: _____

X. ABILITY TO SERVE AS A ROLE MODEL FOR OTHERS

_____ 0. No one in the group for whom he or she could serve as a role model.

_____ 1. Possibly one member for whom he or she could serve as a role model.

_____ 2. At least one or two members for whom he or she could serve as a role model.

_____ 3. Probably three or four members for whom he or she could serve as a role model.

_____ 4. Most or all group members for whom he or she could serve as a role model.

Names: _____

XI. INTERVIEWER CONNECTION WITH POTENTIAL GROUP MEMBER

_____ 0. No connection at all.

_____ 1. Very little connection.

_____ 2. A little to some connection.

_____ 3. Moderate connection.

_____ 4. Strong rapport and respect for group member.

XII. EXPECTATION THAT GROUP WILL BE BENEFICIAL

_____ 0. Expressed no benefit in group participation.

_____ 1. Expressed a great deal of hesitation that group would be helpful.

_____ 2. Expressed some hesitation but some belief that group would be helpful.

_____ 3. Expressed that group would probably be helpful.

_____ 4. Expressed strong belief that group would be helpful.

CRITICAL INCIDENTS IN GROUP WORK

Of the events that occurred in this group session today, which one do you feel was the most important to/for you personally? Describe the event: what actually took place, the group members involved, and their reactions.

Why was this important to you?

What did you learn from this event? (Kivlighan & Goldfine, 1991)

Evaluation at the End of Group by Members (for Grades K-12)

Name: _____   Date: _____

Group Member: _____

I think the group can help kids:	Yes	No	I don't know
1. Feel better about themselves			
2. Get their feelings out			
3. Learn new things that will help them deal with friends, family, and teachers			
4. Overall the group was helpful.			
5. The group leader did a good job.			
6. Something I learned in group was:			
	Yes	No	Maybe
7. I would tell friends to join a group.			
8. Ideas I have for making group better are:			

References

American Counseling Association. (1997). *Code of ethics and standards of practice.* Alexandria, VA: Author.

Anderson, A. (1994). Stories I'd tell my patients: Pulling weeds and planting flowers. *Eating Disorders: The Journal of Treatment and Prevention, 2,* 184–185.

Antonuccio, D. O., Davis, C., Lewinson, P. M., & Breckenridge, J. S. (1987). Therapist variables related to cohesiveness in a group treatment for depression. *Small Group Behavior, 18,* 557–564.

Arredondo, P. (1994). MTC theory and Latina(o)-American population. In D. W. Sue, A. E. Ivey, & P. B. Pedersen (Eds.), *A theory of multicultural counseling and therapy* (pp. 217–235). Pacific Grove, CA: Brooks/Cole.

Ashida, S. (2000). The effects of reminiscence music therapy sessions on changes in depressive symptoms in elderly persons with dementia. *Journal of Music Therapy, 37,* 170–182.

Asner-Self, K. K. (2002a). Country of origin fairy tales. In J. L. DeLucia-Waack, K. H. Bridbord, & J. S. Kleiner (Eds.), *Group work experts share their favorite activities: A guide to choosing, planning, conducting, and processing* (pp. 60–62). Alexandria, VA: Association for Specialists in Group Work.

Asner-Self, K. K. (2002b). No question about it ice-breaker. In J. L. DeLucia-Waack, K. H. Bridbord, & J. S. Kleiner (Eds.), *Group work experts share their favorite activities: A guide to choosing, planning, conducting, and processing* (pp. 24–25). Alexandria, VA: Association for Specialists in Group Work.

Association for Specialists in Group Work. (1998). Association for Specialists in Group Work best practice guidelines. *Journal for Specialists in Group Work, 23,* 237–244.

Association for Specialists in Group Work. (1999). Association for Specialists in Group Work principles for diversity-competent group workers. *Journal for Specialists in Group Work, 24,* 7–14.

Association for Specialists in Group Work. (2000). Association for Specialists in Group Work professional standards for the training of group workers. *Journal for Specialists in Group Work, 25,* 327–342.

Bales, R. F. (1950). *Interaction process analysis: A method for the study of small groups.* Reading, MA: Addison-Wesley.

Bales, R. F., Cohen, S. P., & Williams, S. A. (1979). *SYMLOG: A system for the multiple level observation of groups.* New York: Free Press.

Barkham, M., Hardy, G. E., & Startup, J. (1996). Inventory of interpersonal problems. *British Journal of Clinical Psychology, 35,* 21–35.

Beck, A. (1967). *Depression: Clinical, experimental, and theoretical aspects.* New York: Harper & Row.

Beck, A. T., Rush, J. A., Shaw, B. G., & Emery, G. (1979). *The cognitive therapy of depression.* New York: Guilford.

Bednar, R. L., & Kaul, T. J. (1994). Experiential group research: Can the cannon fire? In A. E. Bergin & S. L. Garfield (Eds.), *Handbook of psychotherapy and behavior change* (4th ed., pp. 631–663). Oxford, UK: Wiley.

Beech Acres Airing Institute. (1993). *The boys and girls of group: Divorce and stepfamilies* (4th ed.). Cincinnati, OH: Author.

Bernard, H. S., Drob, S. L., & Lifshutz, H. (1987). Compatibility between co-therapists: An empirical report. *Psychotherapy, 24,* 96–104.

Bolman, L. (1971). Some effects of trainers on their T-groups. *Journal of Applied Behavioral Science, 7,* 309–325.

Bowman, V., & DeLucia, J. L. (1993). Preparation for group therapy: The effects of preparer and modality on group process and individual functioning. *Journal for Specialists in Group Work, 18,* 67–79.

Bowman, V., & DeLucia-Waack, J. L. (1996). Preparation for counseling revisited: New applications to meet the goals of brief counseling. *Crisis Interventions and Time-Limited Treatment, 2,* 255–266.

Brand, A. C. (1979). The uses of writing in psychotherapy. *Journal of Humanistic Psychology, 19,* 53–72.

Bridbord, K. H. (2002). Autobiography. In J. L. DeLucia-Waack, K. H. Bridbord, & J. S. Kleiner (Eds.), *Group work experts share their favorite activities: A guide to choosing, planning, conducting, and processing* (pp. 26–27) Alexandria, VA: Association for Specialists in Group Work.

Bridbord, K. H., DeLucia-Waack, J. L., & Gerrity, D. (2006). *Predicting group co-leadership relationship satisfaction from personality and leadership style variables.* Manuscript submitted for publication.

Brigman, G., & Earley, B. (1990). *Peer helping: A training manual.* Portland, ME: J. Weston Walch.

Brigman, G., & Earley, B. (1991). *Group counseling for school counselors: A practical guide.* Portland, ME: J. Weston Walch.

Broday, S. F., Gieda, M. J., Mullison, D. D., & Sedlacek, W. E. (1989). Factor analysis and reliability of the Group Therapy Survey. *Educational and Psychological Measurement, 49,* 457–459.

Brooks-Harris, J. E., Heesacker, M., & Mejia-Millan, C. (1996). Changing men's male gender role attitudes by applying the Elaboration Likelihood Model of attitude change. *Sex Roles, 35,* 563–580.

Brown, B. M. (2002). Looking at process. In J. L. DeLucia-Waack, K. H. Bridbord, & J. S. Kleiner (Eds.), *Group work experts share their favorite activities: A guide to choosing, planning, conducting, and processing* (pp. 28–30). Alexandria, VA: Association for Specialists in Group Work.

Brown, N. W. (2002). A group image. In J. L. DeLucia-Waack, K. H. Bridbord, & J. S. Kleiner (Eds.), *Group work experts share their favorite activities: A guide to choosing, planning, conducting, and processing* (pp. 63–64). Alexandria, VA: Association for Specialists in Group Work.

Burlingame, G. M., & Fuhriman, A. (1994). Epilogue. In A. Fuhriman & G. M. Burlingame (Eds.), *Handbook of group psychotherapy: An empirical and clinical synthesis* (pp. 559–562). New York: Wiley.

Burlingame, G. M., Fuhriman, A., & Johnson, J. E. (2001). Cohesion in group psychotherapy. *Psychotherapy, 38,* 373–379.

Burns, D. D. (1980). *Feeling good: The new mood therapy.* New York: Signet.

Campbell, C. A., & Brigman, G. (2005). Closing the achievement gap: A structured approach to group counseling. *Journal for Specialists in Group Work, 30,* 67–82.

Carlson, J. M. (1999). Cooperative games: A pathway to improving health. *Professional School Counseling, 2,* 230–236.

Carrell, S. (2000). *Group exercises for adolescents: A manual for therapists* (2nd ed.). Thousand Oaks, CA: Sage.

Carroll, M. (1985). *Group work: Leading in the here and now* [Video]. Alexandria, VA: Association for Counseling and Development.

Carroll, M. (2001, Fall). Leading in the here and now. *ASGW Together Newsletter,* pp. 10–11.

Carter, E. F., Mitchell, S. L., & Krautheim, M. D. (2001). Understanding and addressing clients' resistance to group counseling. *Journal for Specialists in Group Work, 26,* 66–80.

Cassity, M. D. (1976). The influence of music therapy activity upon peer acceptance, group cohesiveness, and interpersonal relationships of adult psychiatric patients. *Journal of Music Therapy, 13,* 66–76.

Comstock, D. (2002). "Learning from the margin" power line. In J. L. DeLucia-Waack, K. H. Bridbord, & J. S. Kleiner (Eds.), *Group work experts share their favorite activities: A guide to choosing, planning, conducting, and processing* (pp. 107–110). Alexandria, VA: Association for Specialists in Group Work.

Conley, D. (1994). *If you believe in you* [Cassette]. New York: Treehouse Music.

Conroy, K. (2002). Getting to know you—Now and then. In J. L. DeLucia-Waack, K. H. Bridbord, & J. S. Kleiner (Eds.), *Group work experts share their favorite activities: A guide to choosing, planning, conducting, and processing* (pp. 31–34). Thousand Oaks, CA: Sage.

Conyne, R. K. (1997). Group work ideas I have made aphoristic (for me). *Journal for Specialists in Group Work, 22,* 149–156.

Conyne, R. K. (1999). *Failures in group work: How we can learn from our mistakes.* Thousand Oaks, CA: Sage.

Conyne, R. K. (2002). Agenda setting for a team. In J. L. DeLucia-Waack, K. H. Bridbord, & J. S. Kleiner (Eds.), *Group work experts share their favorite activities: A guide to choosing, planning, conducting, and processing* (pp. 174–176). Alexandria, VA: Association for Specialists in Group Work.

Conyne, R. K. (2003). Best practice in leading prevention groups. *Group Work Practice Ideas: Association for Specialists in Group Work, 32,* 9–12.

Cooney, N. L., Kadden, R. M., Litt, M. D., & Getter, H. (1991). Matching alcoholics to coping skills or interactional therapies: Two-year follow-up results. *Journal of Consulting & Clinical Psychology, 59,* 598–601.

Corey, M. S., & Corey, G. (1987). *Groups: Process and practice* (2nd ed.). Belmont, CA: Brooks/Cole.

Corey, M. S., & Corey, G. (2002). *Groups: Process and practice* (6th ed.). Belmont, CA: Brooks/Cole.

Corey, M. S., Corey, G., & Haynes, R. (1999). *Evolution of a group* [Video]. New York: Wadsworth.

Costa, P. T., & McCrae, R. R. (1992). *Professional manual: Revised NEO Personality Inventory (NEO PI-R) and NEO Five-Factor Inventory (NEO-FFI).* Odessa, FL: Psychological Assessment Resource.

Couch, R. D. (1995). Four steps for conducting pregroup screening interview. *Journal for Specialists in Group Work, 20,* 18–25.

Cummins, P. N. (1996). Preparing clients with eating disorders for group counseling: A multimedia approach. *Journal for Specialists in Group Work, 21,* 4–10.

Curtis, K., & Whitman, W. (n.d.). *Hidden treasure of assets: For children and adolescents* [Board Game]. Champaign, IL: Research Press Publishing.

Dagley, J. C., Gazda, G. M., Eppinger, S. J., & Stewart, E. A. (1994). Group psychotherapy research with children, preadolescents, and adolescents. In A. Fuhriman & G. M. Burlingame (Eds.), *Handbook of group psychotherapy: An empirical and clinical synthesis* (pp. 340–369). New York: Wiley.

D'Andrea, M. (2004). The impact of racial-cultural identity of group leaders and members: Theory and recommendations. In J. L. DeLucia-Waack, D. Gerrity, C. R. Kalodner, & M. T. Riva (Eds.), *Handbook of group counseling and psychotherapy* (pp. 265–282). Thousand Oaks, CA: Sage.

Darst, K. V., & Drury, A. (2002). M&M game. In J. L. DeLucia-Waack, K. H. Bridbord, & J. S. Kleiner (Eds.), *Group work experts share their favorite activities: A guide to choosing, planning, conducting, and processing* (pp. 35–36). Alexandria, VA: Association for Specialists in Group Work.

Davis, M., Budman, S., & Soldz, S. (2000). The Individual Group Member Interpersonal Process Scale. In A. P. Beck & C. M. Lewis (Eds.), *The process of group psychotherapy: Systems for analyzing change.* Washington, DC: American Psychological Association.

de l'Etoile, S. K. (2002). The effectiveness of music therapy in group psychotherapy for adults with mental illness. *The Arts in Psychotherapy, 29,* 69–78.

DeLucia, J. L., & Bowman, V. E. (1991). Internal consistency and factor structure of the Group Counselor Behavior Rating Form. *Journal for Specialists in Group Work, 16,* 109–114.

DeLucia-Waack, J. L. (1997). Measuring the effectiveness of group work: A review and analysis of process and outcome measures. *Journal for Specialists in Group Work, 22,* 277–293.

DeLucia-Waack, J. L. (1999). Supervision for counselors working with eating disordered groups: Countertransference issues related to body image, food, and weight. *Journal for Specialists in Group Work, 77,* 379–388.

DeLucia-Waack, J. L. (2001). *Using music in children of divorce groups: A session-by-session manual for counselors.* Alexandria, VA: American Counseling Association.

DeLucia-Waack, J. L. (2002a). Closing: Thanking others. In J. L. DeLucia-Waack, K. H. Bridbord, & J. S. Kleiner (Eds.), *Group work experts share their favorite activities: A guide to choosing, planning, conducting, and processing* (pp. 159–161). Alexandria, VA: Association for Specialists in Group Work.

DeLucia-Waack, J. L. (2002b). Closing: What have we learned about ourselves? In J. L. DeLucia-Waack, K. H. Bridbord, & J. S. Kleiner (Eds.), *Group work experts share their favorite activities: A guide to choosing, planning, conducting, and processing* (pp. 156–158). Alexandria, VA: Association for Specialists in Group Work.

DeLucia-Waack, J. L. (2002c). A written guide for planning and processing group sessions in anticipation of supervision. *Journal for Specialists in Group Work, 27,* 341–357.

DeLucia-Waack, J. L. (2006). *Assessing readiness for group.* Manuscript in preparation.

DeLucia-Waack, J. L., & Bridbord, K. H. (2004). Measures of group process, dynamics, climate, leadership behaviors, and therapeutic factors: A review. In J. L. DeLucia-Waack, D. Gerrity, C. R. Kalodner, & M. T. Riva (Eds.), *Handbook of group counseling and psychotherapy* (pp. 120–135). Thousand Oaks, CA: Sage.

DeLucia-Waack, J. L., Bridbord, K. H., & Kleiner, J. S. (Eds.). (2002). *Group work experts share their favorite activities: A guide to choosing, planning, conducting, and processing.* Alexandria, VA: Association for Specialists in Group Work.

DeLucia-Waack, J. L., & Donigian, J. (2004). *The practice of multicultural group work: Visions and perspectives from the field.* Pacific Grove, CA: Wadsworth.

DeLucia-Waack, J. L., Gerrity, D., Kalodner, C., & Riva, M. (Eds.). (2004). *Handbook of group counseling and psychotherapy.* Thousand Oaks, CA: Sage.

Dies, R. R. (1994). Therapist variables in group psychology research. In A. Fuhriman & G. M. Burlingame (Eds.), *Handbook of group psychotherapy: An empirical and clinical synthesis* (pp. 113–154). New York: Wiley.

Donigian, J., & Hulse-Killacky, D. (1999). *Critical incidents in group therapy* (2nd ed.). Pacific Grove, CA: Brooks/Cole.

Donigian, J., & Malnuti, R. (1997). *Systemic group therapy: A triadic model.* Pacific Grove, CA: Brooks/Cole.

Dossick, J., & Shea, E. (1990). *Creative therapy II: 52 more exercises for groups.* Sarasota, FL: Professional Resource Exchange.

Doughty, L. (2002). Guess who? In J. L. DeLucia-Waack, K. H. Bridbord, & J. S. Kleiner (Eds.), *Group work experts share their favorite activities: A guide to choosing, planning, conducting, and processing* (pp. 37–38). Alexandria, VA: Association of Specialists in Group Work.

Downing, T. K. E., Smaby, M. H., & Maddux, C. D. (2001). A study of the transfer of group counseling skills from training to practice. *Journal for Specialists in Group Work, 26,* 155–167.

Driscoll, N. A. (2002). *Anger bingo for teens* [Board Game]. Plainview, NY: The Bureau for At-Risk Youth.

Drug prevention bingo. (n.d.). [Board Game]. Plainview, NY: The Bureau for At-Risk Youth.

Dugo, J. M., & Beck, A. P. (1997). Significance and complexity of early phases in the development of the co-therapy relationship. *Group Dynamics: Theory, Research, and Practice, 1,* 294–305.

Dye, H. A. (2002). Previewing. In J. L. DeLucia-Waack, K. H. Bridbord, & J. S. Kleiner (Eds.), *Group work experts share their favorite activities: A guide to choosing, planning, conducting, and processing* (pp. 177–180). Alexandria, VA: Association of Specialists in Group Work.

Egan, G. (1986). *The skilled helper* (3rd ed.). Pacific Grove, CA: Brooks/Cole.

Ellis, A. (1962). *Reason and emotion in psychotherapy.* New York: Stuart.

Ernst, J. M., & Heesacker, M. (1993). Application of the Elaboration Likelihood Model of attitude change to assertion training. *Journal of Counseling Psychology, 40,* 37–45.

Flowers, J. V. (1979). Behavioral analysis of group therapy and a model for behavioral group therapy. In D. Upper & S. M. Ross (Eds.), *Behavioral group therapy, 1979: An annual review* (pp. 5–37). Champaign, IL: Research Press.

Flowers, J. V., & Schwartz, B. (1980). Behavioral group therapy with clients with heterogeneous problems. In D. Upper & S. M. Ross (Eds.), *Handbook of behavioral group therapy* (pp. 145–170). New York: Plenum.

Freeman, S. J. (1991). Group facilitation of the grieving process with those bereaved by suicide. *Journal of Counseling and Development, 69,* 328–331.

From rage to reason game. (n.d.). [Board Game]. Plainview, NY: The Bureau for At-Risk Youth.

Fuhriman, A., & Barlow, S. H. (1994). Interaction analysis: Instrumentation and issues. In A. Fuhriman & G. M. Burlingame (Eds.), *Handbook of group psychotherapy: An empirical and clinical synthesis* (pp. 191–222). New York: Wiley.

Fuhriman, A., & Burlingame, G. M. (Eds.). (1990). *Handbook of group psychotherapy: An empirical and clinical synthesis.* New York: Wiley.

Furr, S. R. (2000). Structuring the group experience: A format for designing psychoeducational groups. *Journal for Specialists in Group Work, 25,* 29–49.

Gazda, G. (1989). *Group counseling: A developmental approach* (4th ed.). Boston: Allyn & Bacon.

Gazda, G. M., Ginter, E. J., & Horne, A. M. (2001). *Group counseling and psychotherapy.* Boston: Allyn & Bacon.

Gerrity, D. A. (2002). Our two faces. In J. L. DeLucia-Waack, K. H. Bridbord, & J. S. Kleiner (Eds.), *Group work experts share their favorite activities: A guide to choosing, planning, conducting, and processing* (pp. 123–124). Alexandria, VA: Association for Specialists in Group Work.

Getter, H., Litt, M. D., Kadden, R. M., & Cooney, N. L. (1992). Measuring treatment process in coping skills and interactional group therapies for alcoholism. *International Journal of Group Psychotherapy, 42,* 419–430.

Gilbert, B. J., Heesacker, M., & Gannon, L. J. (1991). Changing the sexual aggression-supportive attitudes of men: A psychoeducational intervention. *Journal of Counseling Psychology, 38,* 197–203.

Gillam, S. L. (2002). What a character! In J. L. DeLucia-Waack, K. H. Bridbord, & J. S. Kleiner (Eds.), *Group work experts share their favorite activities: A guide to choosing, planning, conducting, and processing* (pp. 39–41). Alexandria, VA: Association of Specialists in Group Work.

Gladding, S. T. (1991). *Counseling as an art: The creative arts in counseling.* Alexandria, VA: American Counseling Association.

Gladding, S. T. (1995). *Group work: A counseling specialty* (2nd ed.). Englewood Cliffs, NJ: Merrill.

Gladding, S. T. (1998). *Counseling as an art: The creative arts in counseling* (2nd ed.). Alexandria, VA: American Counseling Association.

Gladding, S. T. (2000, Fall). The use of creative arts in groups. *The Group Worker, 28,* 7–9.

Gladding, S. T. (2002). Lines of feelings. In J. L. DeLucia-Waack, K. H. Bridbord, & J. S. Kleiner (Eds.), *Group work experts share their favorite activities: A guide to choosing, planning, conducting, and processing* (pp. 181–182). Alexandria, VA: Association of Specialists in Group Work.

Gladding, S. T. (2003). *Group work: A counseling specialty* (4th ed.). Upper Saddle River, NJ: Merrill Prentice Hall.

Glass, J. S., & Benshoff, J. M. (1999). PARS: A processing model for beginning group leaders. *Journal for Specialists in Group Work, 24,* 15–26.

Goldstein, A. P., & McGinnis, E. (1997). *Skillstreaming the adolescent: New strategies and perspectives for teaching prosocial skills.* Champaign, IL: Research Press.

Greenberg, K. R. (2002). *Group counseling in K-12 schools: A handbook for school counselors.* Boston: Allyn & Bacon.

Guth, L. J. (2002) Getting to know each other. In J. L. DeLucia-Waack, K. H. Bridbord, & J. S. Kleiner (Eds.), *Group work experts share their favorite activities: A guide to choosing, planning, conducting, and processing* (pp. 42–44). Alexandria, VA: Association of Specialists in Group Work.

Halbur, D. (2002). Ball in play. In J. L. DeLucia-Waack, K. H. Bridbord, & J. S. Kleiner (Eds.), *Group work experts share their favorite activities: A guide to choosing, planning, conducting, and processing* (pp. 45–46). Alexandria, VA: Association of Specialists in Group Work.

Halbur, D., & Nowparvar, J. (2002). Set my life to music. In J. L. DeLucia-Waack, K. H. Bridbord, & J. S. Kleiner (Eds.), *Group work experts share their favorite activities: A guide to choosing, planning, conducting, and processing* (pp. 125–127). Alexandria, VA: Association of Specialists in Group Work.

Hammell, H. (1986). How to design a debriefing session. *Journal of Experiential Education, 9,* 20–26.

Harter, S. (1982). The Perceived Competence Scale for Children. *Child Development, 53,* 87–97.

Hayes, B. (2002). More or less. In J. L. DeLucia-Waack, K. Bridbord, & J. Kleiner (Eds.), *Group work experts share their favorite activities: A guide to choosing, plannng, conducting, and processing* (pp. 47–48). Alexandria, VA: Association for Specialists in Group Work.

Hayes, R. L. (2002). Why are we meeting like this? In J. L. DeLucia-Waack, K. H. Bridbord, & J. S. Kleiner (Eds.), *Group work experts share their favorite activities: A guide to choosing, planning, conducting, and processing* (pp. 49–51). Alexandria, VA: Association of Specialists in Group Work.

Heesacker, M., Conner, K. M., & Prichard, S. (1995). Individual counseling and psychotherapy: Applications from the social psychology of attitude change. *The Counseling Psychologist, 23*, 611–632.

Henderson, S. M. (1983). Effects of a music therapy program upon awareness of mood in music, group cohesion, and self-esteem among hospitalized adolescent patients. *Journal of Music Therapy, 20*, 14–20.

Hiebert, B., Uhlemann, M. R., Marshall, A., & Lee, D. Y. (1998). The relationship between self-talk, anxiety, and counseling skill. *Canadian Journal of Counseling, 32*, 163–171.

Hilliard, R. E. (2001). The effects of music therapy-based bereavement groups on mood and behavior of grieving children: A plot study. *Journal of Music Therapy, 38*, 291–306.

Hines, P. L., & Fields, T. H. (2002). Pregroup screening issues for school counselors. *Journal for Specialists in Group Work, 27*, 358–376.

Hines, P. L., Stockton, R., & Morran, D. K. (1995). Self-talk of group therapists. *Journal of Counseling Psychology, 42*, 242–248.

Hoag, M. J., & Burlingame, G. M. (1997). Evaluating the effectiveness of child and adolescent group treatment: A meta-analytic review. *Journal of Clinical Psychology, 26*, 234–246.

Horne, A. (2002). Fiddler on the roof. In J. L. DeLucia-Waack, K. H. Bridbord, & J. S. Kleiner (Eds.), *Group work experts share their favorite activities: A guide to choosing, planning, conducting, and processing* (pp. 128–129). Alexandria, VA: Association of Specialists in Group Work.

Horne, A., & Campbell, L. (1997). Round pegs for square holes: Working with difficult clients in group therapy. In H. Forester-Miller & J. Kottler (Eds.), *Advanced methods of group work* (pp. 57-80). Denver, CO: Love Publishing.

Horrocks, S., & DeLucia-Waack, J. L. (2006). *An examination of the therapeutic factors of a year-long group for alternative middle school students.* Manuscript in preparation.

Hulse-Killacky, D. (1996). Using the classroom as a group to integrate knowledge, skills, and supervised practice. *Journal for Specialists in Group Work, 21*, 163–168.

Hulse-Killacky, D. (2002). The names activity. In J. L. DeLucia-Waack, K. H. Bridbord, & J. S. Kleiner (Eds.), *Group work experts share their favorite activities: A guide to choosing, planning, conducting, and processing* (pp. 52–53). Alexandria, VA: Association of Specialists in Group Work.

Huss, S. N., & Ritchie, M. (1999). Effectiveness of a group for parentally bereaved children. *Journal for Specialists in Group Work, 24*, 186–196.

Hutchins, A. M. (2002). A what? In J. L. DeLucia-Waack, K. H. Bridbord, & J. S. Kleiner (Eds.), *Group work experts share their favorite activities: A guide to choosing, planning, conducting, and processing* (pp. 78–83). Alexandria, VA: Association of Specialists in Group Work.

Jacobs, E. (2002). Your personal board of directors. In J. L. DeLucia-Waack, K. H. Bridbord, & J. S. Kleiner (Eds.), *Group work experts share their favorite activities: A guide to choosing, planning, conducting, and processing* (pp. 134–135). Alexandria, VA: Association of Specialists in Group Work.

Jacobs, E. F., Harvill, R. L., & Masson, R. L. (1988). *Group counseling: Strategies and skills.* Pacific Grove, CA: Brooks/Cole.

Jensen, K. L. (2001). The effects of selected classical music on self-disclosure. *Journal of Music Therapy, 38,* 2–27.

Johnson, V. A. (2002). Where in the world can I be? In J. L. DeLucia-Waack, K. H. Bridbord, & J. S. Kleiner (Eds.), *Group work experts share their favorite activities: A guide to choosing, planning, conducting, and processing* (pp. 162–163). Alexandria, VA: Association of Specialists in Group Work.

Jones, A., & Crandall, R. (1985). Preparing newcomers to enhance assimilation into groups: A group therapy example. *Small Group Behavior, 16,* 31–57.

Jones, K. D., & Robinson, E. H. III. (2000). Psychoeducational groups: A model for choosing topics and exercises appropriate to group stage. *Journal for Specialists in Group Work, 25,* 343–355.

Kadden, R. D., Cooney, N. L., Getter, H., & Litt, M. D. (1989). Matching alcoholics to coping skills or interactional therapies: Post treatment results. *Journal of Consulting and Clinical Psychology, 57,* 698–704.

Kalodner, C. A. (1995). *Group work for eating disorders and food issues* [Video]. Alexandria, VA: Association for Specialists in Group Work.

Kalter, N. (1998). Group interventions for children of divorce. In K. C. Stoiber & T. R. Kratochwill (Eds.), *Handbook of group intervention for children and families* (pp. 120–140). Boston: Allyn & Bacon.

Karp, C. L., Butler, T. L., & Bergstrom, S. C. (1998). *Activity manual for adolescents.* Thousand Oaks, CA: Sage.

Kees, N. L., & Jacobs, E. (1990). Conducting more effective groups: How to select and process group exercises. *Journal for Specialists in Group Work, 15,* 21–29.

Kew, C. E. (1975). A pilot study of an evaluation scale for group-psychotherapy patients. *ETS Test Collection (Set A).* Princeton, NJ: Educational Testing Services. (Tests in Microfiche No. 004944).

Kim, U. (1988). *Acculturation of Korean immigrants to Canada: Psychological, demographic, and behavioral profiles of emigrating Koreans, non-emigrating Koreans, and Korean Canadians.* Unpublished doctoral dissertation, Queens University, Kingston, Ontario, Canada.

Kivlighan, D. M., Jr., & Goldfine, D. C. (1991). Endorsement of therapeutic factors as a function of stage of group development and participant interpersonal attitudes. *Journal of Counseling Psychology, 38,* 150–158.

Kivlighan, D. M., Jr., & Holmes, S. E. (2004). The importance of therapeutic factors: A typology of therapeutic factor studies. In J. L. DeLucia-Waack, D. A. Gerrity, C. R. Kalodner, & M. Riva (Eds.), *Handbook of group counseling and psychotherapy* (pp. 23–36). Alexandria, VA: Association of Specialists in Group Work.

Kivlighan, D. M., Jr., Jauquet, C. A., Hardie, A. W., Francis, A. M., & Hershberger, B. (1993). Training group members to set session agendas: Effects on in-session behavior and member outcome. *Journal of Counseling Psychology, 40,* 182–187.

Kivlighan, D. M., Jr., & Lilly, R. L. (1997). Developmental changes in group climate as they relate to therapeutic gain. *Group Dynamics: Theory, Research, and Practice, 1,* 208–221.

Kivlighan, D. M., Jr., & Quigley, S. T. (1991). Dimensions used by experienced and novice group therapists to conceptualize group process. *Journal of Counseling Psychology, 38,* 415–423.

Kivlighan, D. M., Jr., Schuetz, S. A., & Kardash, C. A. (1998). Counselor trainee achievement goal orientation and the acquisition of time-limited dynamic psychotherapy skills. *Journal of Counseling Psychology, 45,* 189–195.

Kivlighan, D. M., Jr., & Shaughnessey, P. (1993). *Dimensions of group leader behavior.* Unpublished manuscript, University of Missouri, Columbia.

Klauser, H. A. (1997). *Write it down, make it happen.* New York: Scribner.

Kottler, J. (1995). *Encouraging risk taking in groups* [Video]. Alexandria, VA: Association for Specialists in Group Work.

Kovacs, M. (1981). Rating scales to assess depression in school-aged children. *Acta Paedopsychiatrica, 46,* 305–315.

Kovacs, M. (1992). *The Children's Depression Inventory manual.* North Tonawanda, NY: Multi Health Systems.

Kulic, K. R., Horne, A. M., & Dagley, J. C. (2004). A comprehensive review of prevention groups for children and adolescents. *Group Dynamics: Theory, Research, and Practice, 8,* 139–151.

Kurdek, L., & Berg, B. (1987). Children's Beliefs About Parental Divorce Scale: Psychometric characteristics and concurrent validity. *Journal of Consulting and Clinical Psychology, 55,* 712–718.

Larson, L. M., Suzuki, L. A., Gillespie, K. N., Potenz, M. T., Bechtel, M. A., & Toulouse, A. L. (1992). Development and validation of the Counseling Self-Estimate Inventory. *Journal of Counseling Psychology, 39,* 105–120.

Law, M. B. (2004). Set the stage. *ASCA School Counselor, 41,* 14–19.

LeGrand, K. (2002). The kids' grief kit. In J. L. DeLucia-Waack, K. H. Bridbord, & J. S. Kleiner (Eds.), *Group work experts share their favorite activities: A guide to choosing, planning, conducting, and processing* (pp. 136–137). Alexandria, VA: Association of Specialists in Group Work.

Leong, F. T. L., Wagner, N. S., & Kim, H. H. (1995). Group counseling expectations among Asian American students: The role of culture-specific factors. *Journal of Counseling Psychology, 42,* 217–222.

Lerner, H. (1985). *The dance of anger: A woman's guide to changing the patterns of intimate relationships.* New York: Harper & Row.

Leszcz, M., & Murphy, L. (1994). Supervision of group psychotherapy. In S. E. Greben & R. Ruskin (Eds.), *Clinical perspectives on psychotherapy supervision* (pp. 99–120). Washington, DC: American Psychiatric Press.

Lieberman, M. A., Yalom, I. D., & Miles, M. B. (1973). *Encounter groups: First facts.* New York: Basic Books.

Littlepage, G. E., Cowart, L., & Kerr, B. (1989). Relationships between group environment scales and group performance and cohesion. *Small Group Behavior, 20,* 50–61.

Locke, E. A., & Latham, G. P. (1990). *A theory of goal setting and task performance.* Englewood Cliffs, NJ: Prentice Hall.

Lugris, V., & Bridbord, K. (2002, May). *Co-leading effective groups.* Paper presented at the New York Association for Group Work Conference, Buffalo.

Lynn, G. L. (1994). The GAF: The Group Assessment Form: A screening instrument for adolescent group therapy. *Journal of Child and Adolescent Group Therapy, 4,* 135–146.

MacKenzie, K. R. (1983). The clinical application of group climate measure. In R. R. Dies & K. MacKenzie (Eds.), *Advances in group psychotherapy: Integrating research and practice* (pp. 159–170). New York: International Universities Press.

MacKenzie, K. R. (1990). *Introduction to time-limited group therapy.* Washington, DC: American Psychiatric Press.

MacKenzie, K. R., Dies, R. R., Coche, E., Rutan, J. S., & Stone, W. N. (1987). An analysis of AGPA Institute groups. *International Journal of Group Psychotherapy, 37,* 55–74.

Makuch, L. (1997). *Measuring dimensions of counseling and therapeutic group leadership style: Development of a Leadership Characteristics Inventory.* Unpublished doctoral dissertation, Indiana University, Bloomington.

Martin, V. (2002). Masks of shyness. In J. L. DeLucia-Waack, K. H. Bridbord, & J. S. Kleiner (Eds.), *Group work experts share their favorite activities: A guide to choosing, planning, conducting, and processing* (pp. 84–86). Alexandria, VA: Association of Specialists in Group Work.

Marziali, E., Munroe-Blum, L., & McCleary, L. (1997). The contribution of group cohesion and group alliance to the outcome of group psychotherapy. *International Journal of Group Psychotherapy, 47,* 475–497.

Mathis, R. D., & Tanner, Z. (2000). Structured group activities with family-of-origin themes. *Journal for Specialists in Group Work, 25,* 89–96.

Merrill, K. W. (2001). *Helping students overcome depression and anxiety: A practical guide.* New York: Guilford.

Moore, J., & Herlihy, B. (1993). Grief groups for students who have had a parent die. *School Counselor, 41,* 54–59.

Moos, R. H. (1986). *Group Environment Scale manual.* Palo Alto, CA: Consulting Psychologists Press.

Morgan, R. D. (2004). Groups with offenders and mandated clients. In J. L. DeLucia-Waack, D. A. Gerrity, C. R. Kalodner, & M. T. Riva (Eds.), *Handbook of group counseling and psychotherapy* (pp. 388–400). Thousand Oaks, CA: Sage.

Morganett, R. S. (1990). *Skills for living: Group counseling for young adolescents.* Champaign, IL: Research Press.

Morganett, R. S. (1994). *Skills for living: Group counseling for elementary school students.* Champaign, IL: Research Press.

Morran, D. K., Robison, R. F., & Stockton, R. (1985). Feedback exchange in counseling groups: An analysis of message content and receiver acceptance as a function of leader versus member delivery, session and valence. *Journal of Counseling Psychology, 32,* 57–67.

Morran, D. K., Stockton, R., Cline, R. J., & Teed, C. (1998). Facilitating feedback exchange in groups: Leader interventions. *Journal for Specialists in Group Work, 23,* 257–268.

Morran, D. K., Stockton, R., & Harris, M. (1991). Analysis of group leader and member feedback messages. *Journal of Group Psychotherapy, Psychodrama, and Sociometry, 44,* 126–135.

Morran, D. K., Stockton, R., & Whittingham, M. H. (2004). Effective leader interventions for counseling and psychotherapy groups. In J. L. DeLucia-Waack, D. A. Gerrity, C. R. Kalodner, & M. T. Riva (Eds.), *Handbook of group counseling and psychotherapy* (pp. 91–103). Thousand Oaks, CA: Sage.

Nakkula, M. J., & Watts, C. L. (1997). The particulars of pair supervision. In R. L. Selman, C. L. Watts, & L. H. Schultz (Eds.), *Fostering friendship: Pair therapy for treatment and prevention: Modern applications of social work* (pp. 145–164). New York: Aldine de Gruyter.

Nutt-Williams, E., & Hill, C. E. (1996). The relationship between self-talk and therapy process. *Journal of Counseling Psychology, 43,* 170–178.

O'Leary-Kelly, A. M., Martocchio, J. J., & Frink, D. D. (1994). A review of the influence of group goals on group performance. *Academy of Management Journal, 37,* 1285–1301.

Pack-Brown, S. P. (2002). Drumming. In J. L. DeLucia-Waack, K. H. Bridbord, & J. S. Kleiner (Eds.), *Group work experts share their favorite activities: A guide to choosing, planning, conducting, and processing* (pp. 183–186). Alexandria, VA: Association of Specialists in Group Work.

Page, B. J., & Hulse-Killacky, D. (1999). Development and validation of the Corrective Feedback Self-Efficacy Instrument. *Journal for Specialists in Group Work, 24,* 37–54.

Page, B. J., Pietrzak, D. R., & Lewis, T. F. (2001). Development of the Group Leader Self-Efficacy Instrument. *Journal for Specialists in Group Work, 26,* 168–184.

Paisley, P. (2002). Paper quilt. In J. L. DeLucia-Waack, K. H. Bridbord, & J. S. Kleiner (Eds.), *Group work experts share their favorite activities: A guide to choosing, planning, conducting, and processing* (pp. 164–165). Alexandria, VA: Association of Specialists in Group Work.

Pederson, P. (2002). Nested emotions. In J. L. DeLucia-Waack, K. Bridbord, & J. Kleiner (Eds.), *Group work experts share their favorite activities: A guide to choosing, plannng, conducting, and processing* (pp. 140–141). Alexandria, VA: Association for Specialists in Group Work.

Petty, R. E., & Cacioppo, J. T. (1986). *Communication and persuasion: Central and peripheral routes to attitude change.* New York: Springer-Verlag.

Petty, R. E., Heesacker, M., & Hughes, J. N. (1997). The Elaboration Likelihood Model: Implications for the practice of school psychology. *Journal of School Psychology, 35,* 107–136.

Pfeffer, C. R., Jiang, H., Kakuma, T., Hwang, J., & Metsch, M. (2002). Group intervention for children bereaved by the suicide of a relative. *Journal of the American Academy of Child and Adolescent Psychiatry, 41,* 505–513.

Pfeiffer, J. W., & Jones, J. E. (1975). Co-facilitating. In J. W. Pfeiffer & J. E. Jones (Eds.), *The 1975 annual handbook for group facilitators* (pp. 219–225). Iowa City, IA: University Associates.

Phillips, L. B., & Zastowny, T. R. (1988). Leadership behavior, group climate and outcome in group psychotherapy: A study of outpatient psychotherapy groups. *Group, 12,* 157–171.

Piper, W. E., & McCallum, M. (1994). Selection of patients for group interventions. In H. S. Bernard & K. R. MacKenzie (Eds.), *Basics of group psychotherapy* (pp. 1–34). New York: Guilford.

Possel, P. D., Horn, A. B., Groen, G., & Hautzinger, M. (2004). School-based prevention of depressive symptoms in adolescence: A 6-month follow-up. *Journal of the American Academy of Child and Adolescent Psychiatry, 43,* 1003–1010.

Prout, S. M., & Prout, H. (1998). A meta-analysis of school-based studies of psychotherapy. *Journal of School Psychology, 36,* 121–136.

Provost, J. A. (2002). Group exploration of a member's dream. In J. L. DeLucia-Waack, K. H. Bridbord, & J. S. Kleiner (Eds.), *Group work experts share their favorite activities: A guide to choosing, planning, conducting, and processing* (pp. 142–146). Alexandria, VA: Association of Specialists in Group Work.

Rapin, L. (2002). What is my relationship with the group? In J. L. DeLucia-Waack, K. Bridbord, & J. Kleiner (Eds.), *Group work experts share their favorite activities: A guide to choosing, plannng, conducting, and processing* (pp. 87–88). Alexandria, VA: Association for Specialists in Group Work.

Reynolds, C. R., & Richmond, B. O. (1985). *Revised Children's Manifest Anxiety Scale.* Los Angeles: Western Psychological Services.

Reynolds, W. M. (1990). Depression in children and adolescents: Nature, diagnosis, assessment, and treatment. *School Psychology Review, 19,* 158–165.

Rhine, B., Schoenfeld, M., & O'Shaben, L. (2002). Your place in the group. In J. L. DeLucia-Waack, K. H. Bridbord, & J. S. Kleiner (Eds.), *Group work experts share their favorite activities: A guide to choosing, planning, conducting, and processing* (pp. 87–88). Alexandria, VA: Association of Specialists in Group Work.

Rice, A. H. (1995). Structured group treatment of depression. In K. R. MacKenzie (Ed.), *Effective use of group in managed care.* Washington, DC: American Psychiatric Press.

Ritchie, M., & Huss, S. N. (2000). Recruitment and screening of minors for group counseling. *Journal for Specialists in Group Work, 25,* 146–156.

Riva, M. T., & Haub, A. (2004). Group counseling in the schools. In J. Delucia-Waack, D. Gerrity, C. Kalodner, & M. Riva (Eds.) *Handbook of group counseling and psychotherapy* (pp. 309–321). Thousand Oaks, CA: Sage Publications.

Riva, M. T., Lippert, L., & Tackett, M. J. (2000). Selection practices of group leaders: A national survey. *Journal for Specialists in Group Work, 25,* 157–169.

Riva, M. T., Wachtel, M., & Lasky, G. B. (2004). Effective leadership in group counseling and psychotherapy: Research and practice. In J. DeLucia-Waack, D. Gerrity, C. Kalodner, & M. Riva (Eds.), *Handbook of group counseling and psychotherapy* (pp. 37–48). Thousand Oaks, CA: Sage.

Romano, J. L. (1998). Simulated group counseling: An experiential training model for group work. *Journal for Specialists in Group Work, 23,* 119–132.

Romano, J. L., & Sullivan, B. A. (2000). Simulated group counseling for group work training: A four-year research study of group development. *Journal for Specialists in Group Work, 25,* 366–375.

Samide, L. L., & Stockton, R. (2002). Letting go of grief: Bereavement groups for children in the school setting. *Journal for Specialists in Group Work, 27,* 192–204.

Sandler, I. N., Ayers, T. S., Wolchik, S. A., Tein, J., Kwok, O., Haine, R. A., Twohey-Jacobs, J., Suter, J., Lin, K., Padgett-Jones, S., Weyer, J. L., Cole, E., Kriege, G., & Griffin, W. A. (2003). The family bereavement program: Efficacy evaluation of a theory-based prevention program for parentally bereaved children and adolescents. *Journal of Consulting and Clinical Psychology, 71,* 587-600.

Scime, M., & Lewis, M. (2004). *Grief group for middle school students.* Unpublished manuscript.

Scott, C. G. (1996). Understanding attitude change in developing effective substance abuse prevention programs for adolescents. *School Counselor, 43,* 187–195.

Shapiro, E. (1999). Cotherapy. In J. R. Price & D. R. Hescheles (Eds.), *A guide to starting psychotherapy groups* (pp. 53–61). San Diego, CA: Academic Press.

Shechtman, Z. (1997). Enhancing classroom climate and social acceptability at the elementary and secondary school levels. *Journal of Educational Research, 91,* 99–107.

Shechtman, Z. (2004). Group counseling and psychotherapy with children and adolescents: Current practice and research. In J. L. DeLucia-Waack, D. A. Gerrity, C. Kalodner, & M. Riva (Eds.) *Handbook of group counseling and psychotherapy* (pp. 429–444). Thousand Oaks, CA: Sage.

Shechtman, Z., Bar-El, O., & Hadar, E. (1997). Therapeutic factors in counseling and psychoeducation groups for adolescents: A comparison. *Journal for Specialists in Group Work, 22,* 203–213.

Shure, M. (1992). *I Can Problem Solve (ICPS): An interpersonal cognitive problem solving program for children.* Champaign, IL: Research Press.

Simon, C. C. (2004, August 1). Adolescents, sunny side up. *The New York Times,* pp. 14, 16–17.

Slayton, T. (1995). *Group work with adolescent children of alcoholics* [Video]. Alexandria, VA: Association for Specialists in Group Work.

Slocum, Y. S. (1987). A survey of expectations about group therapy among clinical and non-clinical populations. *International Journal of Group Psychotherapy, 37,* 39–54.

Smaby, M. H., Maddux, C. D., Torres-Rivera, E., & Zimmick, R. (1999). A study of the effects of a skills-based versus a conventional group counseling training program. *Journal for Specialists in Group Work, 24,* 152–163.

Smallwood, D. (2000). *Two-in-one pregnancy bingo* [Board Game]. Buena Park, CA: Morning Glory Press.

Smead, R. (1995). *Skills and techniques for group work with children and adolescents.* Champaign, IL: Research Press.

Smead, R. (Presenter). (1996). *Skills and techniques for group counseling with youth* [Video]. Champaign, IL: Research Press.

Smead, R. (2000a). *Skills and techniques for group counseling with youth* [Video]. Champaign, IL: Research Press.

Smead, R. (2000b). *Skills for living: Group counseling activities for young adolescents* (Vol. 2). Champaign, IL: Research Press.

Smead, R. (2003). Enhancing groups with youth through the use of props. *The Group Worker, 31,* 11–14.

Soldz, S., Budman, S., Davis, M., & Demby, A. (1993). Beyond the interpersonal circumplex in group psychotherapy: The structure and relationship to outcome of the Individual Group Member Interpersonal Process Scale. *Journal of Clinical Psychology, 49,* 551–563.

Sommers-Flanagan, R., Barrett-Hakanson, T. B., Clark, C., & Sommers-Flanagan, J. (2000). A psychoeducational school-based coping and social skills group for depressed students. *Journal for Specialists in Group Work, 25,* 170–190.

Spence, S. H., Sheffield, J. K., & Donovan, C. L. (2003). Preventing adolescent depression: An evaluation of the Problem-Solving for Life program. *Journal of Consulting and Clinical Psychology, 71,* 13–31.

Spielberger, C. D. (1983). *State-Trait Anxiety Inventory.* Palo Alto, CA: Mind Garden.

Stockton, R. (1992). *Developmental aspects of group counseling* [Video]. Alexandria, VA: Association for Specialists in Group Work.

Stockton, R., Morran, D. K., & Krieger, K. M. (2004). An overview of current research and best practices for training beginning group leaders. In J. L. DeLucia-Waack, D. Gerrity, C. R. Kalodner, & M. Riva (Eds.), *Handbook of group counseling and psychotherapy* (pp. 65–75). Thousand Oaks, CA: Sage.

Stockton, R., Morran, D. K., & Nitza, A. G. (2000). Processing group events: A conceptual map for leaders. *Journal for Specialists in Group Work, 25,* 343–355.

Stockton, R., Rohde, R. I., & Haughey, J. (1992). The effects of structured group exercises on cohesion, engagement, avoidance, and conflict. *Small Group Research, 23,* 1555–1568.

Stockton, R., & Toth, P. (1996). A skill-based approach to teaching group counselor interventions. *Journal for Specialists in Group Work, 21,* 101–109.

Stone, M. H., Lewis, C. M., & Beck, A. P. (1994). The structure of Yalom's Curative Factors Scale. *International Journal of Group Psychotherapy, 44,* 239–245.

Subich, L. M. (1983). Expectancies for counselors as a function of counselor gender specification and subject sex. *Journal of Counseling Psychology, 30,* 421–424.

Thomas, M. C. (2002). My core self: The center of the quilt. In J. L. DeLucia-Waack, K. H. Bridbord, & J. S. Kleiner (Eds.), *Group work experts share their favorite activities: A guide to choosing, planning, conducting, and processing* (pp. 166–168). Alexandria, VA: Association of Specialists in Group Work.

Thompson, C. L., & Rudolph, L. B. (1988). *Counseling children* (2nd ed.). Pacific Grove, CA: Brooks/Cole.

Tinsley, H. E., Workman, K. R., & Kass, R. A. (1980). Factor analysis of the domain of client expectancies about counseling. *Journal of Counseling Psychology, 27,* 561–570.

Toth, P. L., Stockton, R., & Erwin, W. J. (1998). Application of a skill-based training model for group counselors. *Journal for Specialists in Group Work, 23,* 33–49.

Trotzer, J. P. (2000). Problem solving procedures in group work. *Group Worker, 29,* 9–12.

Trotzer, J. P. (2002). Boxed in: An activity for overcoming resistance and obstacles to problem solving in groups. In J. L. DeLucia-Waack, K. H. Bridbord, & J. S. Kleiner (Eds.), *Group work experts share their favorite activities: A guide to choosing, planning, conducting, and processing* (pp. 95–100). Alexandria, VA: Association of Specialists in Group Work.

Trotzer, J. P. (2004). Conducting a group: Guidelines for choosing and using activities. In J. Delucia-Waack, D. Gerrity, C. Kalodner, & M. Riva (Eds.) *Handbook of group counseling and psychotherapy* (pp. 76–90). Thousand Oaks, CA: Sage.

Tyson, L. E., Perusse, R., & Whitledge, J. (Eds.). (2004). *Critical incidents in group counseling.* Alexandria, VA: American Counseling Association.

Vera, E. M., & Reese, L. E. (2000). Preventive interventions with school-age youth. In S. D. Brown & R. W. Lent (Eds.), *Handbook of counseling psychology* (pp. 411–434). New York: Wiley.

Vines, G. (2004). Turn on the music. *ASCA School Counselor, 41,* 10–13.

Ward, D., & Litchy, M. (2004). The effective use of processing in groups. In J. DeLucia-Waack, D. Gerrity, C. Kalodner, & M. Riva (Eds.), *Handbook of group counseling and psychotherapy* (pp. 104–119). Thousand Oaks, CA: Sage.

Weiss, L., Katzman, M., & Wolchik, S. (1985). *Treating bulimia: A psychoeducational approach.* New York: Pergamon.

Wenz, K., & McWhirter, J. J. (1990). Enhancing the group experience: Creative writing exercises. *Journal for Specialists in Group Work, 15,* 37–42.

Wheelan, S. (2005). Groups in the workplace. In J. DeLucia-Waack, D. Gerrity, C. Kalodner, & M. Riva (Eds.), *Handbook of group counseling and psychotherapy* (pp. 401–413). Thousand Oaks, CA: Sage.

Wilcoxon, S. A., & Magnuson, S. (1999). Considerations for school counselors serving non-custodial parents: Premises and suggestions. *Professional School Counseling, 2,* 275–279.

Wile, D. B. (1972). Group leadership questionnaire (GTQ-C). In J. W. Pfeiffer & J. E. Jones, *The 1972 annual handbook for group facilitation.* LaJolla, CA: University Associates.

Wilson, F. R. (2002). Feedback as poetry. In J. L. DeLucia-Waack, K. H. Bridbord, & J. S. Kleiner (Eds.), *Group work experts share their favorite activities: A guide to choosing, planning, conducting, and processing* (pp. 166–168). Alexandria, VA: Association of Specialists in Group Work.

Wolfe, D. A., Werkerle, C., Gough, R., Reitzel-Jaffe, D., Grasley, C., Pittman, A., Lefebvre, L., & Stumpf, J. (1996). *The youth relationships manual: A group approach with adolescents for the prevention of woman abuse and the promotion of healthy relationships.* Thousand Oaks, CA: Sage.

Wubbolding, R. (1995). *Reality therapy group work* [Video]. Alexandria, VA: Association for Specialists in Group Work.

Yalom, I. (2000). *Understanding group psychotherapy, Volume 1: Outpatients.* San Francisco: Psychotherapy.net.

Yalom, I. D. (1975). *The theory and practice of group psychotherapy* (2nd ed.). New York: Basic Books.

Yalom, I. D. (1985). *The theory and practice of group psychotherapy* (3rd ed.). New York: Basic Books.

Yalom, I. D. (1995). *The theory and practice of group psychotherapy* (4th ed.). New York: Basic Books.

Yalom, I. D., & Elkin, G. (1991). *Every day gets a little closer: A twice-told therapy.* New York: Basic Books.

Yalom, I. D., Tinklenerg, J., & Guilula, M. (1968). *Curative factors in group psychotherapy.* Unpublished manuscript.

Zakich, R. (1987). *The ungame* [Board Game]. Anaheim, CA: The Ungame Co.

Index